1993

FRIENDSHIP

FRIENDSHIP

A Philosophical Reader

EDITED BY

Neera Kapur Badhwar

Cornell University Press

Ithaca and London

First published 1993 by Cornell University Press.

Material from *The Four Loves,* copyright © 1960 by C. S. Lewis and renewed 1988 by Arthur Owen Barfield, reprinted by permission of Harcourt Brace Jovanovich, Inc., and HarperCollins, Publishers.

International Standard Book Number 0-8014-2854-8 (cloth)
International Standard Book Number 0-8014-8097-3 (paper)
Library of Congress Catalog Card Number 92-56786

Printed in the United States of America
Librarians: Library of Congress cataloging information appears on the last page of the book.
⊗The paper in this book meets the minimum requirements of the American National Standard for Information Sciences—Permanence of Paper for Printed Library Materials, ANSI Z39.48-1984.

TO MY MOTHER AND THE
MEMORY OF MY FATHER

Whosoever is delighted in solitude
is either a wild beast or a god.

—Aristotle, *Politics* 1253a

CONTENTS

PREFACE

After a long eclipse, the years since about 1970 have seen a remarkable resurgence of philosophical interest in friendship. This anthology seeks to make some of the best of this recent work accessible to the reader. It also includes two other selections, one from a literary and one from a psychological work, which contain important insights. The readings have been selected with a view to providing a general idea of the nature and importance of friendship; showing the significance of friendship in the context of different ethical theories; and exploring the connection between friendship and certain social and political themes.

I have excluded historical material from this collection, partly because there are already some historical anthologies in existence, and partly because the historical material is in any case more easily available than the contemporary. To my knowledge, there is no collection devoted entirely to contemporary writings on friendship, and the extant anthologies on personal relations contain few articles on friendship. But friendship is sufficiently different from other personal relations, and important enough in its own right, to merit a separate and more extensive study.

With the exception of Amélie Rorty's "The Historicity of Psychological Attitudes: Love Is Not Love Which Alters Not When It Alteration Finds," Robert Adams's "The Problem of Total Devotion," Peter Railton's "Alienation, Consequentialism, and the Demands of Morality," and Marilyn Friedman's "Feminism and Modern Friendship: Dislocating the Community," none of the articles included here has been collected before. Where I had to choose between two equally desirable articles that fit into the general scheme of the anthology, I chose the one that had not been previously anthologized. Even so, however, I had reluctantly to let go of several excellent articles for lack of space. I have included an index, but no bibliography, since lengthy bibliographies are available elsewhere and my introduction contains extensive references to the relevant literature.

I would like to thank those who have helped in various ways to make this volume possible: David Braybrooke and John Ackerman for first giving me the idea for the project, Geoffrey Sayre-McCord for encouraging me to implement it, and Kathleen Kearns, my editor at Cornell, for bringing this work to fruition. I also thank the four anonymous reviewers for their helpful comments on the table of contents and the introduction, and the University of Oklahoma for its support. I am particularly indebted to Catherine Blaha for her generous and skillful help in various administrative matters, and to Judith Little for putting everything aside to prepare the Index. Last but not least I am grateful to Chris Swoyer for his comments on the introduction, and for being a loving friend and caring about this project.

N. K. B

Norman, Oklahoma

FRIENDSHIP

Introduction: The Nature and Significance of Friendship

Neera Kapur Badhwar

Philosophers have long recognized that friendship plays a central role in a meaningful and happy life. Aristotle declared that no one would choose to live without friends, and it is at least true that what most of us most strongly hope for from others is not "glory," as Hobbes thought, but the shared vision that is the spark of friendship. Through such sharing, friendship serves to confirm our sense of things, of the important and the unimportant, and to fuel our interest in our activities.

Plato wrote an entire dialogue, *Lysis,* in an attempt to define friendship, and Aristotle devoted two of the ten books of his *Nicomachean Ethics* to a discussion of friendship and its role in a good human life. Indeed, Aristotle elevated friendship at its best to an ethical ideal, declaring that only good people could be friends in the fullest sense, and that only with such friendship could the virtues be fully exercised. With the advent of Christianity, however, friendship was replaced by agape—the unconditional love of God and of neighbor—as the chief ethical ideal. When friendship was justified, it was justified by its likeness to agape, or by its usefulness in achieving agape. And with Luther, friendship lost even this secondary ethical status, and came to be seen, like other "natural" loves, as a form of self-love. As Søren Kierkegaard was to declare, friendship and erotic love are purely "natural" phenomena that "contain no ethical task."[1] These "natural" loves are nonethical not only because they are forms of self-love, but also because, as expressions of natural preferences and inclinations, they cannot be willed and so cannot be commanded by God's law. Only agape—

[1] Søren Kierkegaard, *Works of Love* (hereafter *WL*), trans. Howard Hong and Edna Hong (New York: Harper & Row, 1962), p. 64. For a discussion of the tensions between friendship and agape, see Gilbert C. Meilander, *Friendship: A Study in Theological Ethics* (Notre Dame: University of Notre Dame Press, 1981).

unconditional, universal neighbor-love, blind to merit or demerit—
transcends the realm of nature to enter the realm of the will.

Under the influence of post-Lutheran Christian thought, secular
philosophers also ceased to think of friendship as central to ethics,
stressing instead universal benevolence or adherence to the universal
commands of reason, as the fundamental moral concept and virtue.
The two most notable representatives of these still dominant moral
positions, utilitarianism (or, more generally, consequentialism) and deontology, were John Stuart Mill and Immanuel Kant, respectively. Although both discussed friendship, neither regarded friendship as central to ethical theory.[2]

Since about 1970, however, the year in which Elizabeth Telfer's article "Friendship" appeared, there has been a marked revival of philosophical interest in friendship.[3] The implications of friendship for
ethics, Christian belief, politics, action theory, and theories of the self
have all have been explored. This anthology seeks to make some of the
best of this recent work accessible to the reader. It also includes one
excerpt from an earlier literary work and one from a psychological
work that provide important insights into the nature of friendship.
The articles have been selected with a view to providing a general idea
of the nature and importance of friendship, the moral status of friendship in the context of different ethical theories and the challenge it
poses to these theories, and the connection between friendship and
certain social and political issues. The three sections of the anthology
correspond to these three themes. In this Introduction I shall give an
overview of the issues discussed in this volume, relate them to contemporary and historical discussions not included here, and provide a
critical framework for thinking about the salient themes of the book.

The word "friendship" is sometimes used to characterize any kind of
amicable relationship, whether between nations, or among citizens
(civic friendship), or members of an organization (associate friendship),
or acquaintances. It is also occasionally used to characterize agape or
caritas, conceived of as a friendship with God and his creatures.[4] But it is
typically used in a more restricted way, to characterize only personal
relationships of a certain kind. In this restricted sense, a friendship is a

---

[2] Although Mill was, apparently, concerned with marital friendship in political theory.
See Essay 13 by Mary Shanley.

[3] Elizabeth Telfer, "Friendship," *Proceedings of the Aristotelian Society*, supplement
1970–71, pp. 223–41; reprinted in Michael Pakaluk, ed., *Other Selves: Philosophers on
Friendship* (Indianapolis: Hackett, 1991), pp. 250–67. One indication of this revival of
interest in friendship is the inclusion of an article on friendship by John Cooper in the
recently published *Encyclopaedia of Ethics*, ed. Lawrence C. Becker (New York: Garland,
1992), pp. 388–91.

[4] See Thomas Aquinas, *Summa Theologiae* (hereafter *ST*), II-II, qq. 23–46.

practical and emotional relationship of mutual and reciprocal goodwill, trust, respect, and love or affection between people who enjoy spending time together (personal friendship). The difference between personal friendship and other forms of personal love can be seen in the fact that people may love each other as siblings, as parent and child, or as wife and husband, without loving each other as friends.

Personal friendships can also differ among themselves in important ways. Aristotle distinguishes between friendships whose object is the friend himself as the person he is, on the one hand, and friendships whose object is the friend insofar as he is useful or pleasant, on the other.[5] Without committing myself to all the features of Aristotle's analysis, I shall borrow this basic distinction in order to classify personal friendships into *end* and *instrumental* friendships. An instrumental friendship is based on features that are in some sense *tangential* or *accidental* to the friend and is motivated primarily by each friend's independently defined goals. Although there is mutual and reciprocal goodwill, trust, affection, and enjoyment between the friends, these are limited in depth and scope by the requirements of each friend's own goals. These goals may be reputable (such as becoming the southwest's foremost trapeze artiste, or having a readily available companion for witty conversations) or disreputable (such as having help in mastering the art of sophistry and manipulation, or having a readily available companion for backbiting and gossip). The important point about an instrumental friendship is that if either friend ceased to be useful in helping the other reach her goals, she would thereby cease to have the features that ground the friendship. It is in this sense that an instrumental friendship is based on features that are tangential to the friend.

By contrast, an end friendship is a relationship in which one loves and cares for the friend as the person she is, and as an essential part of one's ends, and not wholly, or even primarily, as a means to independently defined ends.[6] The basis of an end friendship is the friend

---

[5] Aristotle, *Nicomachean Ethics* (hereafter *NE*), Bk. 8, 3. Sometimes Aristotle marks this distinction by saying that in the former kind of friendship, friends "wish goods to their friend for the friend's own sake" (1156b10), whereas in the latter kind they do so for their own sake (1156a11ff). But in a well-known paper, John Cooper has argued that, according to Aristotle, loving and wishing goods to the friend for his own sake is essential to *all* friendships ("Aristotle on Friendship," ed. Amélie O. Rorty, *Essays on Aristotle's Ethics* [Berkeley: University of California Press, 1980], pp. 301–40). However, since the locution "for the friend's own sake" is used by many writers included in this anthology to mark an important contrast with instrumental friendships, I shall do the same.

[6] Which is not to say that end friendships have *no* instrumental value: a useless friend is no friend. I discuss end friendship, and its differences from instrumental friendship (as well as from agape) in "Friends as Ends in Themselves," *Philosophy and Phenomenological Research* 48 (September 1987): 1–23; reprinted in *Eros, Agape and Philia*, ed. Alan Soble (New York: Paragon House, 1990).

herself as the particular person she is, that is, as constituted by her
fundamental qualities. These include both her character traits—her
central intellectual, moral, and aesthetic qualities—and her unique
perspective on the world. Such a friendship endures only if both
friends continue to be the particular persons they are. If either one
ceased to be that particular person, her continuing usefulness to the
other would not suffice to sustain an end friendship (although it *could*
lead to an instrumental friendship).[7]

Although none of the writers included here uses the term "end
friendship," the kind of personal friendship they discuss fits my characterization of end friendship. So from now on I shall use the word
"friendship" to mean "end friendship." It is friendship in this sense
that is the exclusive topic of all except three of the essays in this volume. Essay 6 takes neighbor-love as its primary topic, Essay 14 discusses both associate and personal friendship, and Essay 15 discusses
civic friendship.

Friendship: General Discussions

The essays in the first section are concerned with three philosophical
questions that arise naturally in thinking about friendship: How does
friendship differ from other forms of love, especially parental and
romantic (erotic) love? What is the psychological value of friendship?
What kind of continuity or constancy is desirable in friendship?

Friendship and Other Loves

The collection opens with an excerpt from C. S. Lewis's wide-
ranging discussion of friendship in *The Four Loves,* one of the most
notable literary celebrations of friendship in recent times. Lewis offers
a vision of friendship as one of the highest achievements of the individual. The value of friendship, like that of philosophy or art, Lewis
argues, is mostly a "civilization value," enabling us not to live, but to live
well. Affection for others, and especially for one's children and parents, is natural, necessary for survival, and largely unselective in that it
is independent of the fundamental qualities of the objects of our affection. Friendship, on the other hand, is the most spiritual, "the least
natural of loves," unnecessary from the biological point of view, and

---

[7] And if either or both changed in complementary ways, a *new* end friendship could
arise.

highly selective. It begins in shared interests, in companionship, and becomes friendship when the companions discover that they "see the same truth." Friendship is also "the least jealous of loves," shunning the exclusivity of eros. For no one person can bring out all the facets of a person's character: to see my friend (who may or may not also be my lover) in all his complexity, I need to see him through other friends as well.

Despite his paean to friendship, Lewis is alive to its hazards. Every friendship, he tells us, harbors a danger: the danger of degenerating into a mutual admiration society, indifferent or deaf to the views and needs of "outsiders."[8] This danger is not limited to the friendships of the self-absorbed or conceited, but is inherent in the appreciation or admiration that is a necessary feature of all friendships.

This is a provocative idea, for it suggests that there might be similar hazards in other desirable qualities as well: cowardice in gentleness; harshness in frankness; sloth in amiability; and so on. Equally provocative is Lewis's view that the shared vision or common viewpoint that forges a friendship may be inherently bad. For this challenges a view held by a long line of thinkers—Aristotle, Cicero, Aquinas, Montaigne—that a "true" friendship can exist only between good people. I will discuss this issue in the next section, where the question of the virtues and vices of friendship arises again.

Lewis's view of friendship love as the least natural of loves is in stark contrast to the not uncommon view that all loves, including that of friendship, are entirely an expression of natural preferences and inclinations.[9] There is an undeniable truth in this latter claim, a truth that Lewis overlooks, namely, that natural preferences and inclinations play a role in our attractions, even in as "spiritual" a relationship as friendship. On the other hand, the "natural inclination" view overlooks the fact that our attractions are expressive, in part, of our values and past choices, the choices that make us the persons we are. It also overlooks the fact that when values conflict with natural inclinations, the former may ultimately prevail over the latter and extinguish or undermine the attraction. In any case, there is more to friendship than attraction: friendship is a practical and emotional relationship that arises from, and is sustained by, choice.

Choice is one of the three features that Laurence Thomas picks out

[8] And sometimes, Lewis points out, the common vision that sparked a friendship vanishes, leaving it to become a coterie that exists just for the sake of being a coterie. Lewis seems to think that a coterie is just a bad friendship, but it seems more accurate to say that, having lost its basis, it is not a friendship at all.

[9] This view, already encountered in Kierkegaard, is not limited to him. See the discussion of Kant, below.

as salient in "companion friendship" (Essay 2). The other two are absence of authority of one over the other and mutual trust. Together, he
says, these three features distinguish friendship from the parent-child
relationship, and align it with romantic love. It is obvious that we do
not choose our parents or our children. But friendship and romantic
love require choices, choices that express our values. Again, parents
have the obligation and authority to determine their children's good,
and children the obligation to defer to this authority. In a friendship,
on the other hand, neither friend is under the authority of the other.

Thomas is careful to point out that *absence* of authority is different
from *equality* of authority. For equality of authority is compatible with
equal bossiness and *that,* as even a nine-year-old knows, is not compatible with friendship.[10] But he would probably agree that absence of
authority is an important *element* of the equality that Aristotle emphasizes as essential to character friendship (Essay 5), as well as of the
respect that Kant emphasizes as essential to perfect and moral friendships (Essay 7). Absence of authority is also, Thomas notes, a necessary
condition of the third salient feature of friendship: mutual trust. For it
is only when this obtains that people feel free to disclose important
aspects of their selves to each other, and it is only when they disclose
themselves in this way that they achieve that "intimate or privileged
trust" characteristic of friendship. Such self-disclosure, and therefore
such trust, are almost entirely absent in most parent-child relationships, even when the child becomes an adult, because the presumption
of parental authority is never quite overthrown—at least not, Thomas
wryly remarks, by the parent.[11]

Mutual self-disclosure, Thomas concludes, is one of the most important characteristics of friendship, because it is the chief way in which
friends contribute to the development of each other's character. And
this contribution constitutes one of the chief values of friendship.

Friendship: Self-Knowledge and Other Values

The view that friendship involves intimate self-disclosure is, however, challenged by a common belief that friendship rests upon, and

---

[10] "Brian and I don't like each other now as he bosses me about and I boss him, but we
will be friends again soon I hope," nine-year-olds, quoted in *The Oxford Book of Friendship,*
ed. D. J. Enright and David Rawlinson (Oxford: Oxford University Press, 1991), p. 168.

[11] It is important to add, however, that when this is not the case, friendship *can* exist
between parent and adult child, and friendship here is as much a matter of choice as
friendship between unrelated adults.

encourages, a deliberate evasion of one's own faults as well as the faults of one's friends—"Love is blind; friendship closes its eyes."[12] If this is correct, it poses a serious problem to any attempt to argue that friendship is an important value, because knowledge, including self-knowledge, has correctly been regarded as a prerequisite for right action and for moral authenticity. Thinkers from Socrates on have given pride of place in their teachings to the dictum "Know thyself," and seen knowledge of one's own intentions, values, and traits as necessary for being morally good and leading a good human life. Similarly, knowledge of others is necessary for furthering their good and for giving them their due.

Does friendship encourage mutual self-deception between friends? That a particular friendship *may* do so, to *some* extent, is doubtless true. But friendship also has contrary tendencies. For example, it can lead to jealousy or an unhealthy competitiveness, and thus to a desire to exaggerate each other's faults. Or it can lead to dependence, and thus to a desire to magnify one's own faults. Obviously, then, the psychological pitfalls of friendship cannot be read into its essential nature and used to call its value into question. More important, one may argue that a relationship that is beset by blindness, and that would not survive the light of truth, is not a friendship at all. For if the basis and object of friendship is the friend as the person she is, it must be in the nature of friendship that friends see and love one another as they are, and not as creations of their own fantasies. Hence it must be in the nature of friendship to *discourage* mutual self-deception; to the extent that it does not do so, it is deficient as a friendship.

That friends see each other as they are is often recognized as one of the chief values of friendship. Aristotle argues that being seen as the persons we are is necessary for seeing ourselves as we are and this, in turn, is one of our deepest needs, necessary for acting morally and also, to the extent that we like ourselves, a source of deep pleasure (*NE* 9, 9). Friendship is particularly well-suited to fulfill this need, for a friend is "another self," a self that serves as a "mirror of the soul."[13] As a biblical writer puts it, as "Iron sharpeneth iron; so a man sharpeneth the countenance of his friend."[14] To be a mirror of the soul, friends

[12] "L'amour est aveugle; l'amitié ferme les yeux" (Anonymous). William Hazlitt describes true friendship as "a flattering mirror" in which we see "our virtues magnified and our errors softened" ("On the Spirit of Obligations," quoted in *The Oxford Book of Friendship*, p. 153). This criticism cuts deeper than Lewis's, because it purports to identify a necessary, and not just a possible, fault of friendship.

[13] Aristotle, *NE*, 1169b28–1170a4, 1170b1–14; *Magna Moralia*, 1213a10–26. See also Cooper, "Aristotle on Friendship," pp. 317–34, and Sherman, Essay 5.

[14] Proverbs 27:17.

need not share all of each others' traits or values; complementary traits and values can be just as revealing.[15] What matters is that friends not have traits or values that clash and thus interfere with mutual under- standing and harmony.

The privileged role of friendship in self-knowledge invites further examination. Anyone would acknowledge that friendship is not the *only* source of self-knowledge—parental or agapeic love, or art, philos- ophy, psychology, or psychotherapy can also give us insight into our- selves. For instance, an agapeic act by a stranger may show a person her fundamental frailty as a human being in a way that changes her per- spective on her own individual strengths, and parental love may reveal her history to her in a way that illuminates her present. But friendship does seem to have features that make it a privileged source of self- knowledge and even, perhaps, necessary for *adequate* self-knowledge. Both agape qua agape, and parental love qua parental love, are un- selective and unconditional: agape is directed at all humans by virtue of their common humanity, and parental love at the child by virtue of the biological and nurturing bond. Both forms of love are independent of the loved object's fundamental characteristics as the particular per- son she is; neither love is focused on the joys, griefs, needs, and achievements of the individual as defined by her fundamental fea- tures. Hence neither in agape nor in parental love do we see ourselves mirrored in the other as the particular persons we are. Nor do these loves invite the intimate self-disclosure that enables friends to gain better insight into themselves. Moreover, their unconditionality en- sures their constancy and thus deprives them of an important incentive that friendship contains for self-examination, an incentive that comes from the possibility of the demise of friendship.

Art, philosophy, and psychology share some features with friendship that parental and agapeic love lack. A work of fiction or philosophy or psychology can reflect our values and perspectives, thereby allowing us to see ourselves in vivid and unexpected ways. Or it can portray values that complement or challenge our own, thus inviting us to examine ourselves, sometimes in a quite dramatic and unpredictable fashion.[16] But what neither these nor psychotherapy can provide is that continual self-awareness and self-examination that comes from the active com- munication and interaction of people who share a life. This is why, as Bacon notes, the communication of friendship, more than any other,

[15] For a discussion of this idea in Aristotle, see Essay 5.

[16] Francine Hughes tells of her gradual liberation from feelings of worthlessness and fear—feelings induced by years of virtual enslavement to a sadistic husband—as a result of writing weekly school assignments on the Socratic theme "Know thyself." See Faith McNulty, *The Burning Bed* (New York: Avon Books, 1980).

"maketh *daylight* in the *understanding,* out of darkness and confusion of thoughts."[17]

The idea that friendship reveals us to ourselves finds dramatic and concrete confirmation in Nathaniel Branden's account of the nature and importance of "psychological visibility"—of being seen and seeing oneself as the person one is (Essay 3). What Aristotle and other philosophers *argue* for, Branden *shows,* through a narrative of the way he was led to the idea of psychological visibility.

We read, first, of his pleasure at the sight of the glowingly alive rhododendron plant, and his sense of affinity with it as another living entity living well. We read, next, of his pleasure in his mock-ferocious game with his dog, Muttnik, who, unlike the plant, responds to him, and responds with perfect understanding of his playful intentions. We see how Muttnik's behavior makes him feel psychologically *visible,* both to her and to himself—and, indeed, reveals to him a hitherto unknown aspect of his personality. But Muttnik's range of consciousness, and thus her repertoire of responses, are much more limited than a human being's. We see Branden being gradually led to realize that the need for psychological visibility is one of our most profound needs, and that it is satisfied most profoundly in friendship and romantic love. For when we meet someone who shares our values, who responds to the world as we do, and responds to us in consonance with our self-concept, we perceive our selves reflected in that person and achieve a more vivid sense of our selves.

A necessary presupposition of such visibility, Branden states, is that our self-concept be largely accurate: those whose self-concept is seriously distorted can take pleasure neither in being seen, nor in seeing *themselves,* as they are. Perhaps it would be impossible for them even to accept that they are being seen as they are. Hence, if my earlier argument that end friendship requires (largely) veridical perception of one another is sound, then such friendship is not possible for those whose self-concept is seriously distorted.[18]

Branden goes on to claim that the sexual involvement that is a part of romantic love makes romantic love an even greater source of visibility

[17] Francis Bacon, "Of Friendship," *Essays or Counsels Civil and Moral,* excerpts reprinted in Pakaluk, *Other Selves,* pp. 202–7, quoted on p. 205.

[18] We are all, of course, prone to varying degrees of bias in our self-image. The achievement of sufficient objectivity with oneself and thus of self-knowledge is, in part, a matter of experience and maturity, just as is knowledge of others and of the world. Thus the bias in one's self-image might be the result of ignorance, rather than of willful self-deception or rationalization. If the friend is likewise ignorant, she will automatically confirm the bias and thereby encourage it. But although unfortunate, this does not point to a moral failing of friendship: morality requires honesty and authenticity, not perfect knowledge.

than friendship. Is this true? Or is Thomas right in arguing that sexual involvement is just a conventional sign of union, no more or less significant than other conventional signs, such as the exchange of crystal glasses between two friends? There does seem to be a difference of focus between the way people relate as friends and the way they relate as lovers. This difference is well expressed in Lewis's picture of lovers as standing "face to face, absorbed in each other; Friends, side by side, absorbed in some common interest."[19] What this difference of focus implies for mutual visibility and self-disclosure, though, requires a discussion of the psychology of sex and, in particular, of how sexual love ramifies through an individual's psychology. And this is a topic for another anthology.

The articles in this section do not, of course, discuss *all* the ways in which friendship is of value to us. But one of the ways not discussed by any of them is particularly worth noting, namely, the ability of friendship to increase our knowledge of others. Through our identification with another, we can learn to look at things from a different point of view, to understand and feel in new ways, and thus to realize the immense potentiality for different forms of experience.[20] Here again friendship performs a role akin to that of great literature. For one of the chief values of literature is that, as Lewis notes, it satisfies our desire "to see with other eyes, to imagine with other imaginations, to feel with other hearts . . . [to] become these other selves."[21] Indeed, literature offers more opportunities for becoming "other selves" than friendship does but, once again, friendship offers something that literature cannot: friends are not just objects of contemplation or analysis, but other selves who interact with us, responding to us and requiring that we respond to them in appropriate ways.

Friendship: Continuity and Loss

The theme of mutual visibility emerges again in Amélie Rorty's essay, but this time in the context of the issue of the permanence of love (Essay 4). Rorty challenges the dogma that love is love only if it alters not when it alteration finds. She compares such *constant* love to a rigidly designating expression, in that it remains directed at the same individ-

[19] Or is this just a *male* view of friendship? See Louise Bernikow: "They [men] are shoulder to shoulder. Female friends are more often eye to eye," *Among Women* (New York: HarperCollins, 1981), p. 119.

[20] See Telfer, "Friendship," pp. 240–41.

[21] C. S. Lewis, *An Experiment in Criticism* (Cambridge: Cambridge University Press, 1961), pp. 137, 139.

ual through every possible change in her characteristics. We value constant love, she points out, because it protects us in our fragility and vulnerability, but we also value *historically continuous* love, and such love is, in fact, more valuable. Historically continuous love is based on an accurate perception of the friend's central features, tracking changes in those features, as well as expressing changes in one's own features. We need and want such love from a friend because we see ourselves, to some extent, as others see us, and our thriving requires that we not see ourselves falsely. Such love is also "dynamically permeable": permeable in the sense that it changes the lover, dynamic in the sense that "every change generates new changes" in the lover and in the nature of the interactions.

A dynamically permeable love is necessary for thriving, yet it cannot endure through all changes in the friend's characteristics. Rorty does not tell us through which changes a friendship cannot—or should not—endure. But presumably she would accept Aristotle's suggestion that it cannot and should not endure when two people no longer "find the same things enjoyable or painful," either because one has developed and matured while the other has stayed the same, or because one has become "incurably vicious" (*NE* 1165b12–31).[22]

Some of the main themes of this section—the importance of friendship in human life, especially its role in enlarging our self-awareness, and its virtues and vices—are discussed in the next section in the context of different ethical traditions.

Friendship and Ethics

The second section has been arranged to provide a perspective on theories of friendship and ethics as they appear in the history of philosophy. Much of the recent philosophical interest in friendship has been inspired by Aristotle's discussion of the topic (and has, in turn, generated a new interest in Aristotelian ethics as a viable alternative to Kantian and consequentialist theories). However, many philosophers still seek to accommodate friendship within the framework of Kantian or consequentialist theories. There is also a continuing attempt to reconcile friendship with various biblical commandments. I shall start with a general discussion of the connection between friendship and morality, and then turn to the selections on Aristotle, Christian ethics, Kant, and consequentialism.

---

[22] Julius M. E. Moravcsik discusses the issue of continuity and loss and related issues in "The Perils of Friendship and Conceptions of the Self," in Jonathan Dancy, Moravcsik, and Charles C. W. Taylor, eds., *Human Agency: Language, Duty, Value* (Stanford: Stanford University Press, 1988), pp. 133–51.

The Moral Status of Friendship: Three Possibilities

There are three basic possibilities regarding the moral status of end friendship: friendship may be intrinsically moral, that is, friendship may by its very nature involve certain morally good dispositions and acts; friendship may be intrinsically immoral; or friendship may be intrinsically nonmoral. Each of these views has been held by one or another writer on friendship.

The view that the best kind of friendship, the friendship in which people love each other as the persons they are, is intrinsically moral is well expressed by Aristotle when he declares that friendship either *is* a virtue, or *involves* virtue (*NE* 1155a1–2), and apparently endorses the "common belief" that "it is the same people that are good men and are friends" (1155a29–31). Both claims have been repeated by a long line of thinkers, including Cicero, Aquinas, and Montaigne.[23]

As we have seen, however, Lewis implicitly rejects the claim that only good people can be friends of each other for the persons they are when he tells us that a friendship may rest on a bad foundation. Most people, I suspect, would agree with Lewis, for it seems to be a fact that there are vicious people—people who treat most human beings as mere means to their own ends—who are capable of deep friendship.[24] Moreover, this apparent fact can be explained by the common psychological phenomenon of compartmentalization, which makes it possible for people to restrict the scope of their moral (and intellectual) traits, both good and bad. But if generally vicious people can love each other as the persons they are, that is, on the basis of their central features, then they must love and take pleasure in each other on the basis of their bad characters, and their shared activities must involve wrongdoing toward others. And so it might be thought that friendship as such has no intrinsic goodness: its goodness or badness is entirely a function of the moral character of the friends in question.

---

[23] Cicero, *On Friendship*, trans. H. G. Edinger (New York: Bobbs-Merrill, 1967), pp. 18, 20; Aquinas, *ST*, Question 26, Fourth Article; Michel de Montaigne, "Of Friendship," *Essays*, trans. J. M. Cohen (Harmondsworth: Penguin, 1958), p. 98; Gottfried W. Leibniz, *Discourse on Metaphysics*, trans. Peter G. Lucas and Leslie Grint (Manchester: Manchester University Press, 1953), chap. 36, p. 60. Lawrence Blum argues, similarly, that it seems impossible that a "very selfish" person "should care very genuinely and fully for only one person" (Essay 8).

[24] In her book *Do or Die* (New York: HarperCollins, 1991), about the Crips and Bloods, Los Angeles' infamous gangs, Léon Bing describes how the same people who can torture outsiders to death for no worse fault than being outsiders, can also look after wounded and paralyzed fellow gang members "more lovingly" than many families do, and how they try to protect the younger boys from a similar fate. Most strikingly, some gang members, according to Bing, help the younger boys go to school and get out of the gang. See the interview with *Time*'s Janice Castro, March 16, 1992, pp. 12–16.

This, however, would be a mistake: granting that a friendship may be immoral overall is compatible with the thought that friendship has an intrinsic moral goodness. Just as it has been argued that there is a certain morality inherent in cooperation as such, or in law as such,[25] so it can be argued that there is a certain morality, however minimal, inherent in friendship as such, even in the friendship of vicious people.

(1) On many ancient as well as contemporary views of moral goodness, both philosophical and popular, the moral goodness of an act depends on the intended ends as well as on the dispositions or structure of thought and feeling that motivate the act. So, for instance, an act of giving is fully good only if both the end (for example, to bring pleasure rather than to embarrass or harm the recipient), and the thoughts and emotions from which it comes (for example, a sense of joy rather than reluctance or resentment or a desire to show off one's "generosity") are morally good or innocuous. If moral goodness, no matter how limited in scope, is inherent in friendship, then friendship must involve some virtuous acts and, hence, some good ends and dispositions. And an analysis of the shared activities and the mutual and reciprocal goodwill, trust, respect, affection, and pleasure that characterize friendship will show, I believe, that it does involve such ends and dispositions, that to be a friend is, in part, to exercise moral deliberation and virtue.

The mutual goodwill of friends is expressed in an active caring and concern for each other's happiness and success, and their mutual respect expresses their recognition of each other as autonomous individuals with the ability to choose their own ends. This mutual and recognized goodwill and respect form the foundation for their reciprocal trust: friends are, and see each other as being, both trustworthy and trusting. Furthermore, continuing affection and pleasure require a constant effort to perceive, to understand, and to give of one's emotional resources. And being true to the value one places on one's friendship requires (as does any other central value) integrity.

These dispositions of friendship and the acts that issue from them are not, of course, necessarily good, since they may be directed at immoral ends. But they may also be directed at morally innocuous ends like walking, sailing, cooking, eating, or reading. Such ends exist in every friendship, even the friendship of people whose overall pattern of ends is bad. Hence even the friendship of such people includes *some* morally good caring, trust, respect, and so on. Moreover, the very

---

[25] See Plato's remark at *Republic,* 351c-d that even the cooperation of a band of robbers requires justice, and Lon Fuller's argument that even the most unjust law must have a certain internal morality to count as law: Fuller, *The Morality of Law,* rev. ed. (New Haven: Yale University Press, 1969).

mutuality and reciprocity of end friendship requires the virtues of honesty and fairness between friends. For example, mutual and reciprocal trust and understanding are possible only if friends are honest with each other, and mutual and reciprocal caring is possible only if friends are fair in their emotional and practical exchanges. So even if we disagree with Aristotle and Cicero that friendship can exist only between good people, we may agree with them that friendship implies a certain goodness between friends.

(2) It can also be argued that there is a necessary connection between friendship and, to the extent that we are rational, the *recognition* of what morality as such requires. It is often said that the moral point of view is impartial, in the sense that it calls for a recognition of the rightful claims of all to our moral concern and consideration.[26] The mutual concern and respect of friends who love each other as ends involves a mutual acknowledgment that each is a separate individual, with her own ends and powers of decision, and a moral claim to each other's—and other people's—concern and consideration. But if we are rational, this acknowledgment of each other as separate individuals implies the acknowledgment of *others* as likewise separate, and *their* moral claim to our concern and consideration. Furthermore, to the extent that their ends are good, friends must see their friendship and the differential valuing it involves as justified. But then, if we are rational, we must see *others'* friendships and differential valuing as justified as well. (A person who recognizes all this may fail to be *motivated* by the recognition, but that, too, is arguably irrational.[27]) Impartiality—the recognition of the rightful claims of all to our moral concern and consideration—includes the recognition that, insofar as we have a right to our friendships, others do as well.

To summarize this part of the discussion: one may deny that end friendship implies moral goodness *simpliciter,* and still hold that it is an *intrinsically moral phenomenon,* in the sense that (1) friendship necessarily involves *some* moral goodness between friends, and (2) the recognition of the nature of friendship entails, if we are rational, a recognition of what morality in general requires. The thesis of the intrinsic morality of friendship is consistent with recognizing that a given

---

[26] This formulation in terms of the *rightful* claims of all avoids begging the question of whether everyone has an *equal* claim to our concern and consideration, and of whether the moral point of view is independent of our emotional interests. Alternative formulations of the impartial point of view as the impersonal, agent-neutral point of view (consequentialism) or as that which abstracts from all emotional interests (Kantianism) do beg these questions. For the argument that there is a *psychological* connection between caring for one and caring for others see Bernard Williams, *Morality: An Introduction to Ethics* (New York: Harper & Row, 1972), chap. 1.

[27] See Thomas Nagel, *The Possibility of Altruism* (Oxford: Clarendon Press, 1970).

friendship may permit, or even require, that friends do the (irrationally) immoral thing toward nonfriends. What it denies is that friendship is intrinsically, or by its very nature, immoral or nonmoral.

According to the view that friendship *is* intrinsically immoral, friendship necessarily involves a willingness to act wrongly toward others. It is thought to do so because conflicts of interests are endemic to social existence, and because, allegedly, mutual love and concern require that we be willing to lie, cheat, or otherwise act wrongly if our friends' interests so demand.[28] But this view of what mutual love and concern require rests on the assumption that the demands of friendship are unlimited, overriding all other considerations. And this assumption is no more plausible than analogous assumptions about other important values: patriotism, noble causes, love of God, parental love, scientific knowledge, great art, and so on. No credible analysis of friendship can lead to the conclusion that if we allow friendship into our lives, it must take priority over all other values. The prima facie claims of friendship must be considered in the context of competing prima facie claims, and morality consists, in part, of just such a contextual consideration and deliberation. (There may, of course, be irresolvable conflicts among moral claims, but that is a separate point.)

The critic of friendship might now concede that there is nothing in friendship as such that *requires* that we be willing to act wrongly, yet still insist that even in the friendship of generally decent people, the preferential, partial nature of friendship often serves as a *temptation* to wrongdoing. For example, friendship might lead a teacher to give a higher grade to a friend's child than he deserves. Or it might prevent a person from being beneficent toward others, because she would rather spend all her resources on friends.

What should be immediately plain from these examples, however, is that friendship is not the only value that can tempt us to wrongdoing: parental love, scientific curiosity, artistic interest, or devotion to a good cause—all preferential and partial in nature—can also tempt us to violate the impartially determined right act. For example, commitment to the struggle for India's independence seems to have led Mahatma Gandhi to neglect his duties as husband and father. And deliberate, cynical violation of moral and legal norms in the course of scientific

[28] Cicero discusses those who hold this view, *On Friendship*, pp. 36–37. See also Jesse Kalin, "Lies, Secrets, and Love: The Inadequacy of Contemporary Moral Philosophy," *Journal of Value Inquiry* 10, 4 (1976): 253–65. Kalin argues that relations of love require lying, deception, and the sharing of secrets but, instead of concluding that relations of love are immoral, he concludes that lying, etc. are moral in the context of such relations: love, he states, "is a form of trust in which other trusts must be broken, and a form of secrecy in which other secrets must be violated. . . . Love, in a fundamental sense, is a form of mutual honesty that rests on falsehoods" (258).

research are distressingly common. It is safe to conclude, then, that the sources of temptation to wrongdoing are ubiquitous. So if friendship is intrinsically immoral for being such a source, then so are all other preferential and partial values. But this is to condemn the human mode of existence itself as immoral, a condemnation that would surely be implausible even with far stronger arguments than any we have seen so far. The condemnation of friendship and other preferential and partial values as immoral also runs head on into the most commonly held view of morality, namely, that morality is necessarily tied to human good. For on this view, it is these very values that give rise to morality.

The view that friendship necessarily involves (some) moral goodness between friends may be challenged by the claim that friendship is intrinsically nonmoral, i.e., that it can be analyzed independently of ethical categories. As we shall see, the view that morality is a means to the good (as in consequentialist theories) and the view that morality is an end in itself in the sense of being logically independent of human well-being (as in Kantian theories) both imply that friendship is an intrinsically nonmoral good (and its virtues, therefore, intrinsically nonmoral traits). The question for these theories, then, is whether this picture of friendship and its virtues as intrinsically nonmoral is compatible with the nature of end friendship. The importance of friendship in human life suggests that a moral theory that is not so compatible is likely to have other deep-seated problems as well. Compatibility with the nature of end friendship may, therefore, be a good test of a moral theory's adequacy.

The papers in Section II show the distinctive ways in which different ethical theories—Aristotelian, Christian, Kantian, and consequentialist—seek to accommodate friendship as an important value.

Aristotle

According to Aristotle, the best kind of friendship, the friendship of people who are alike in virtue and love each other as the persons they are, is necessary for full virtue and *eudaimonia,* for a truly self-sufficient life. In her book *The Fabric of Character,* Nancy Sherman explains how the intimacy and shared activities of such a friendship—"character friendship"—make it the privileged context in which to know our selves as beings both emotional and rational, and to realize virtue and achieve happiness.[29] In Essay 5, excerpted from that book, Sherman

[29] Nancy Sherman, *The Fabric of Character: Aristotle's Theory of Virtue* (Oxford: Clarendon Press, 1989).

discusses the ways in which Aristotle takes character friendship to provide both the necessary means to virtue and happiness, in the sense in which money or political influence does, and "the very form and mode" of an especially praiseworthy life. For only in a life shared with friends do we have an opportunity for adequate self-knowledge and the continuous moral and intellectual activity that is the major part of happiness. Sherman argues that Aristotle's picture of a friend is not simply the picture of *another self,* but of a *separate self.* Character friends must be alike in having all the virtues, but the "pattern of unified virtues might . . . be different in different persons," and both the similarities and the differences play a role in self-knowledge and moral growth.

Is Aristotle right, however, that friendship is *necessary* for full virtue and happiness? Can't someone who must eschew friendship because it conflicts with her dedication to mathematics or art or medicine—a dedication that has enormous potential for benefiting others—lead a morally praiseworthy and happy life? *That* such conflicts can occur is a commonplace. Lou Andreas-Salomé tells us that in Rilke the "demands of art and of full personal development came increasingly into conflict as his works achieved a degree of reality so great that they excluded everything else."[30] If "everything else" includes friendship, then on Aristotle's view Rilke's life could not have exhibited the full range of virtues and pleasures. But cannot the peak of achievement in a narrow range make up for the loss of breadth? If it can, then Aristotle's claim that friendship is necessary for a praiseworthy and prizeworthy life is too strong. He could still point out, however, that a life that contains *both* the peak of achievement in a narrow range *and* the full range of virtues and pleasures that come with friendship is better than a life with only the former—or, for that matter, with only the latter.

Sherman notes that Aristotle's view of self-sufficiency as relational, as involving friends, marks a decisive break with the ascetic ideal found in Plato's writings, in which happiness is immune to the vagaries of fortune. It also marks a decisive break with Plato's notion of love. In the *Symposium* and the *Lysis* we find a view, revived through the ages in varying guises by other writers, of love as the expression of need or deficiency. Insofar as we are virtuous and wise we are above the contingencies of this world and do not need friends or lovers.[31] Friendship can help us overcome our lacks, but its very success spells its demise. According to this line of thought, our need for friendship bespeaks our moral and psychological deficiencies, not our strengths or virtues.

---

[30] *The Memoirs of Lou Andreas-Salomé* (New York: Paragon House, 1991), quoted in *The New York Times,* May 10, 1991, B5.

[31] Plato, *Lysis* 215a-c, 221e; *Symposium* 203b-c, 210a-212a.

This argument, however, assumes that the self is essentially nonsocial. It is only by virtue of this assumption that friendship can be relegated to the role of a mere *means* to the achievement of self-sufficiency, rather than acknowledged as an essential *constituent* of a self-sufficient life. On Aristotle's view, by contrast, we can realize our selves fully only in friendship, because our selves are essentially social. To be sure, to be capable of the highest kind of friendship we must already have a close to self-sufficient life, for such a friendship is possible only if we already have a good character and, therefore, the major part of happiness.[32] But sharing one's life with another enriches us further in ways that would be impossible for us as isolated beings.

This explanation of the value of friendship, however, might invite the following response: whatever the particular psychological and moral strengths of those who are capable of wanting and sustaining friendships, the human desire for a friend is a clear signal of a *metaphysical* deficiency, a deficiency that reveals a limit in our very *capacity* for self-sufficiency. For, as even Aristotle acknowledges, a perfect being, a god, does not need another to be self-sufficient: a god has perfect self-knowledge with the help of his own powers of perception and thought, and complete pleasure from his awareness of his own life and activities. The human need for a friend, then, is obviously a mark of deficiency.

The problem with this argument, however, is that it measures humans by a metaphysically alien standard of perfection, a standard derived from the nature of divine beings. But measuring humans by a godly standard seems no more sensible than measuring gods by a human standard. By human standards, it is the gods that are sadly deficient, for they lack the ability to love others, and get all their pleasure from contemplating themselves. In human beings, after all, total self-absorption and inability to love are signs of either pathology or bad character. Reflection on the human need for friendship should, properly, reveal its *moral importance,* not our *metaphysical impotence.*

Christian Ethics

Although friendship has sometimes been criticized for resting on or encouraging mutual blindness to shared faults, it has also been criticized for not being blind *enough.* This criticism is grounded in the ideal of universal and unconditional love, whose hallmark is blindness to the loved object's qualities. Hence this criticism is a recurrent theme

[32] We must also be self-sufficient in the more specific sense of being psychologically autonomous or independent. See Stanton Peele (with Archie Brodsky), *Love and Addiction* (New York: Taplinger, 1975).

in Christian ethics. Agape, or "love to one's neighbor," Kierkegaard tells us lyrically, "makes a man blind in the deepest and noblest and holiest sense, so that he blindly loves every man." (*WL* 80). Agape, as the theologian Anders Nygren explains, is directed at saints and sinners alike and is thus indifferent to, and unmotivated by, the value of its object.[33] Only such love is for the other's own sake, rather than for one's own. Friendship, by contrast, is motivated by the (perceived) value of its object, and this is what makes it acquisitive, selfish, and instrumental. For, in Kierkegaard's words, "preference in passion . . . is really another form of self-love" (*WL* 65).

Ironically, however, even agape seems to conflict with an important tenet of Judeo-Christian ethics, the commandment to love God with all one's heart, soul, and mind. Indeed, all earthly loves pose this problem for Judeo-Christian ethics. So even Christian thinkers who believe that end friendship is possible, and who therefore reject the bleak picture of friendship painted by Kierkegaard and Nygren, are faced with the problem of reconciling friendship with the command of total devotion to God. In Essay 6 Robert Adams addresses this problem with specific reference to neighbor-love, but also more generally with reference to love of things and personal love, including friendship.

Adams considers Augustine's "teleological solution" that love of others is a *means* to the love of God and hence not in conflict with the imperative of total devotion to God, but rejects this solution because he believes that a means love is not really love at all. Adams also questions Nygren's solution to the problem of total devotion. Nygren argues that love of neighbor is possible only if we are possessed by God (so that it is really God-in-us who loves the neighbor), and that to be possessed by God is to love God. Hence, he concludes, love of neighbor does not *compete* with love of God but, rather, *expresses* this love. Adams questions this solution because Nygren's understanding of possession by God is a "straightforwardly causal understanding": God causes us to love the neighbor the way a brain surgeon might cause us to love her beloved. But on this causal model, he points out, it is hard to see how neighbor-love (or love of the surgeon's beloved) can be an expression of our love for God (or for the surgeon). (It is also hard to see, Adams might have added, how any of this can be seen as an expression of *our* love for the neighbor.)

Adams's own solution is that neighbor-love is a response *we* make to

[33] Anders Nygren, *Agape and Eros*, trans. Philip S. Watson (Philadelphia: Westminster Press, 1953), pp. 75–80. This view of agape, it should be noted, is not shared by all Christian thinkers. Thus, as Nygren notes disapprovingly, Augustine thinks that agape is directed at the good that remains in the sinner. And Aquinas thinks that those who are greater in goodness ought to be loved more (*ST* q. 26, art. 6).

God's love for the neighbor, so that it is *we* who do the loving, and that such love is a manifestation of our love for God, because he is partly immanent in all his creation. Inspired by God's love for the neighbor for his own sake, we do likewise; in enjoying God's creation, both persons and things, we also enjoy him.

This solution seems to work for neighbor-love. But does it also work for friendship, as Adams seems to suggest? Specifically, can we understand love of friends as inspired by God's love for the neighbor? It is difficult to see how. Since friendship love is *preferential*, its model cannot be God's *nonpreferential* love for his creatures. Since loving a friend for his own sake, as the person he is, is loving him *for the qualities that make him the person he is,* it cannot be likened to God's *unmotivated* love for the neighbor's own sake. Consequently, it also seems unlikely that friendship love can be seen as a manifestation of our love for God himself. Hence there may be no option but to follow Augustine and justify friendship love teleologically, as an *uti* (means), not *frui* (end) love.

The problem of reconciling friendship with total devotion to God has interesting counterparts in the two chief rival theories in contemporary ethics, Kantianism and consequentialism. Each theory in its own way commands total devotion to morality, and each sees friendship as an intrinsically nonethical good in need of justification by the supreme principle of morality. More generally, each sees morality as a system of external constraints on our pursuit of personal, partial, nonmoral goods. Hence, within these traditions, friendship is an intrinsically nonethical good that is *subject* to moral principles, but does not *embody* them.

Kant

Central to Kant's picture of morality is the idea that moral action is the work of "Pure Practical Reason," a reason that is closed off from causal influence by inclination, that is, desire or emotion.[34] Inclinations, including love, are intrinsically nonrational phenomena in the sense that reason plays no role in their constitution, and can neither control them, nor endorse or condemn them. Reason can endorse,

---

[34] Immanuel Kant, *Groundwork of the Metaphysic of Morals* (hereafter *G*), trans. H. J. Paton in *The Moral Law* (London: Hutchinson University Library, 1948). See, in particular, pp. 389–90 on the nature of ethics and its relation to reason, pp. 395–96 on why desire-satisfaction or happiness cannot be the function of reason, pp. 397–98 on the independence of moral motivation from inclination (desire or emotion), and p. 399 on the difference between kindness out of duty and kindness out of love.

condemn, or control only the *choices* we make on the basis of our inclinations. Because morality is a purely rational phenomenon, emotions as such can have no moral status.[35]

This conclusion also follows from another feature of morality and reason, as Kant sees them, a feature that emotion lacks, namely, a certain kind of universality. Morality is concerned with *all* rational beings, but emotions are peculiar to *human* beings. Hence, moral imperatives cannot be grounded in emotional phenomena like love or fellow-feeling (although, of course, they must be applied to them.)

This exclusion of the emotions from morality has led critics to charge that Kant's ethics is cold and inhuman. In Essay 7 H. J. Paton seeks to rebut this charge by examining Kant's discussion of friendship in the *Tugendlehre*,[36] noting both its affinities to and its differences from Aristotle's discussion.

Kant defines friendship in its perfection as "an association of two persons through equal and mutual love and respect," and calls it an "ideal of the emotional and practical concern which each of the friends united through a morally good will takes in the other's welfare" (*T*469). Perfect friendship, like Aristotle's character friendship, is based on a shared moral attitude and is distinguished from friendships based on taste and friendships based on need.[37] To the Aristotelian requirement of equal and mutual love and concern in friendship, Kant adds the requirement of mutual respect to emphasize that, even in the most intimate of relationships, we must, in Paton's words, "show regard for the dignity of every human person as such." The same regard must be shown in everyday social intercourse and by the "friend of man," that is, the person who seeks to live as a citizen of the world, extending his concern to everyone.

Paton's article is valuable for drawing attention to aspects of Kant's thought that are too often overlooked: his psychological acuteness in noting the doubts and tensions that stand in the way of achieving perfect friendship and his sensitivity to the social graces as "the out-

[35] Kant's view of the emotions as intrinsically nonrational phenomena and, hence, inessential to moral agency is shared by many contemporary writers, including those who reject Kant's dualistic metaphysics. The clearest example is David Gauthier, "Reason and Maximization," *Canadian Journal of Philosophy* 4, 3 (March 1975): 411–33 and *Morals by Agreement* (Oxford: Clarendon Press, 1986). But see also Nagel, *The Possibility of Altruism;* and Alan Donagan, *The Theory of Morality* (Chicago: University of Chicago Press, 1977), especially chap. 7. I discuss this view of emotion in the context of friendship in "The Rejection of Ethical Rationalism," *Logos* 10 (1989): 99–131.

[36] Immanuel Kant, *Tugendlehre* (hereafter *T*), trans. as *The Doctrine of Virtue* by Mary J. Gregor (New York: Harper & Row, 1964). Paton's own translation of the discussion of friendship in *T*468–74 is appended as a postscript to his article.

[37] Kant, *Lectures on Ethics* (hereafter *LE*), trans. Louis Infield (New York: Harper & Row, 1963), excerpts reprinted in Pakaluk, *Other Selves*.

works and by-products of virtue." Kant's discussion of personal friendship, of friendship with all human beings, and of casual social intercourse refute, according to Paton, the charge that Kant's ethics is cold
and inhuman.

However, this charge needs to be evaluated in the context of Kant's
general metaphysical and moral framework, especially his view that
love or other emotions cannot be moral motives, and that our duties
must be defined in abstraction from emotion. Paton argues that in
spite of this view of emotion and duty, Kant makes room for emotion
in his ethical system in two important ways: he recognizes the feelings
of love and respect as subjective conditions of our understanding of
the concept of duty and of our susceptibility to it; and he recognizes
that emotions help us to fulfill our duties and regards it a duty to act in
ways likely to induce and develop the emotions.

Both of Paton's claims are, however, problematic in their own ways.
When Kant cites the moral dispositions "on the side of *feeling*" (*T*399)
as subjective conditions of our understanding of and susceptibility to
duty, he means something quite different from ordinary emotional
dispositions such as being in love with or having sympathy for someone. For one thing, unlike the variety of emotional dispositions, the
moral dispositions are limited to moral feeling or respect, love of
neighbor, reverence for self, and conscience (*T*399–403).[38] For another, moral feeling, love, reverence, and conscience are evoked only by
consciousness of rational objects, not by consciousness of empirical
objects. For example, it is consciousness of the imperfect duty of beneficence that elicits love of neighbor, not consciousness of the empirical
circumstances—the weal or woe—of one's fellow human beings. More
generally, as Kant goes to some length to explain, moral feeling or
reverence for the law is a feeling that is "*self-produced* by a rational
concept, and therefore specifically distinct from feelings of the first
kind [emotional], all of which can be reduced to inclination or fear"
(*G*401n16). Again, moral dispositions are *universal* subjective conditions of duty, whereas emotional dispositions are *variable*, differing
from one person to another in their sources and objects. Thus, moral
dispositions differ from emotional dispositions in their provenance,
content, and object, and the love and respect that Paton cites as subjective conditions of moral understanding and motivation are *not*, like
emotions, features of our empirical psychology.

---

[38] Moral feeling is the "subjective aspect" of respect for the law, which "is one and the
same with the consciousness of one's duty" (*T*464). At *G*401n16 Kant calls this "reverence
for the law." See Lewis W. Beck, *A Commentary on Kant's Critique of Practical Reason*
(Chicago: University of Chicago Press, 1960), especially chap. 12, for a discussion of the
moral dispositions.

The difference between emotional and moral dispositions—and, thus, between friendship as an emotional phenomenon and friendship as a moral phenomenon—is tellingly illustrated by Kant's discussion of the difference between *pathological* (emotional) love and *practical* (rational) love (*G*399). Beneficence out of practical love is morally worthy because it is commanded by reason, whereas beneficence out of pathological love is morally neutral because it is prompted by emotion. Moreover, pathological love is *subject* to, but is in no part *defined* in terms of, moral concepts or principles. So the moral dimension of friendship must be divorced from its emotional dimension (*T*471).

It is only in the context of these moral and metaphysical tenets and their implications that we can fully understand the import of Kant's reminders that "the complete moral perfection of heaven must be universal; but friendship is not universal," and that "friendship develops the minor virtues of life" (*LE*206–7, 209). The view of the moral self as the purely rational self implies that the emotional intimacy of friendship can provide no insight into one's *moral* self; consequently, the self-knowledge provided by friendship is highly limited.[39] By the same token, the emotional intimacy of friendship can provide no insight into *others'* moral selves. It is no wonder, then, that Kant finds it necessary to caution us to "so conduct ourselves towards a friend that there is no harm done if he should turn into an enemy. We must give him no handle against us" (*Lectures*, 208).

The second way, according to Paton, that Kant allows the emotions into his ethical system, namely, as aids to the fulfillment of duty, is, strictly speaking, inconsistent with his dualism. For his metaphysics allows of no causal connection between the noumenal world of freedom and duty, and the phenomenal world of necessitation and emotion. How, then, can emotions be an aid—or, for that matter, a hindrance—to duty? And even if this question could be answered satisfactorily, two other questions would remain: Does the view that emotions merely *facilitate* right action do justice to the role of the emotions, especially love, in morality? Can the view that morality is a matter of pure practical reason do justice to friendship?

Two of the next three articles answer these questions in the negative.

In Essay 8 Julia Annas challenges Kantian ethics on the grounds that it has disastrous consequences for a person's life and character, offering as graphic evidence its effects on the characters in Theodor Fontane's *Effi Briest*. Instetten, a major character in the novel, discovers that his wife, Effi, had committed adultery six years before. Although

[39] Sherman, "Aristotle on Friendship and Shared Happiness," *Philosophy and Phenomenological Research* 47 (June 1987): 589–613.

the discovery does not destroy his feelings for her, he decides that these feelings are morally irrelevant and that duty demands that he reject her as a moral offender. In the face of his view of what duty requires, his sympathy with and understanding of Effi become "inert, unable to move him." His conception of morality "amputate[s] not just his capacity for happiness but most sources of moral worth," blinding him "to vital differences between deep and trivial emotions, between commitment to others and self-interest."

But is Instetten's conception of what duty requires truly Kantian? Or has he, in Annas's own words, "confused the sublime moral law with the social conventions of Bismarck's Berlin"? Annas concedes that Instetten's actual decision may not reflect a truly Kantian conception of duty, but insists that the *form* of the thinking that leads him to it does. For Instetten's decision relies crucially on the belief that his love for Effi is irrelevant to the determination of his duty. Annas states that the effect of such thinking on Instetten's moral personality suggests that Kantian ethics is a threat to one's ability to love and lead a meaningful life, which in turn suggests that we should make room in morality for the personal and partial point of view that characterizes relationships of love.

Marcia Baron takes another look at *Effi Briest* (Essay 9) to defend Kant against Annas's objections, and argues forcefully that the disastrous consequences in question result from a narrow-minded, conventional thinking that is *not* Kantian. Instetten's concern, she points out, is not with the moral law, but rather with social rules and his own reputation. Nor is his thinking Kantian when he refuses to let his attachment to Effi provide him with any guidance on the question of what duty requires, because Kant would not have put the commitment and attachment of marriage or friendship on a par with mere inclination. For whereas inclinations are unchosen "raw feels," commitments and attachments involve choice and impose moral duties. We "can and do slowly detach ourselves or deepen an attachment," and agency "plays a central role in commitment." Thus, Instetten chooses to marry Effi, a choice that leads to an emotional attachment to her and creates a marital commitment which imposes certain duties on him.

Whatever the duties imposed by Instetten's marital attachment and commitment, however, we have to keep in mind that they cannot be grounded in the *emotional components* of this attachment or commitment. So his love for Effi can provide neither an *ultimate ground* for his duties, nor a *moral motive* for his dutiful acts. Nor, as Baron herself notes, can it inform his *moral perception*.

As a Kantian agent, Instetten would have to be guided by the thought that only morality and rational nature count as ends in themselves (G427–29). All other values—including what I have called end love—are just means to, or expressions or constituents of, our self-love or happiness.[40] Insofar as our happiness lies in the fulfillment of morally permissible desires, we do have an "indirect duty" to preserve our happiness, because unhappiness can tempt us to transgress our duty (G399). And so, insofar as love is a part of one's (morally permissible) happiness, we also have an indirect duty to act in accordance with the "counsels" of love. But happiness cannot be an end in itself since it is a "natural" rather than rational end (G428–29). Nor, for the same reason, can love. So those who think they love one another as ends in themselves are simply deluded. We can and must *respect* a friend as an end, for the object of respect is her rational nature, but we cannot *love* her as an end, for the object of love is her empirical nature; we have moral duties toward our friends, but love itself is not a moral phenomenon.

Contemporary Responses to Kantian and Christian Themes

The view that emotions are rational or cognitive seems a necessary condition for accepting the possibility that a friend can be loved as an end, and that such love has an intrinsic moral significance.[41] Establishing this view is one of the major concerns of Lawrence Blum's book, *Friendship, Altruism and Morality*. Blum argues that sympathy, compassion, and human concern are cognitive emotions that are intentionally directed at the good of others. Appealing to ordinary moral consciousness, he also argues that these emotions play an essential role in many instances of moral perception, motivation, and action. Hence, he concludes, they are moral emotions and—since friendship is a locus of these emotions—friendship is an intrinsically moral phenomenon.

In Essay 10, Blum argues that, other things being equal, acting out of concern for a friend, for his sake, is morally good and that the "deeper and stronger the concern for the friend . . . the greater the degree of moral worth." He then argues against two familiar conceptions of friendship that imply friendship is without moral significance: friendship as a purely natural phenomenon and friendship as a form of extended self-interest. Blum uses a detailed and realistic example of

[40] Immanuel Kant, *Critique of Practical Reason*, trans. Lewis W. Beck (Indianapolis: Bobbs-Merrill, 1956), p. 20.

[41] In *The Fabric of Character*, Sherman argues that Aristotle holds this view of emotion (pp. 165–71). For contemporary defenses of this view see Ronald de Sousa, *The Rationality of Emotion* (Cambridge: MIT Press, 1987) and Rorty, ed., *Explaining Emotions* (Berkeley: University of California Press, 1980).

a friendship to show that the deep caring it involves is an achievement of thought and effort, not just a natural process, and that the deep caring that gives it moral significance is conditional on the friends' identification with one another, not on self-interest. He also argues that the possibility of genuine conditional altruism in friendship challenges the universalist conception of morality in which caring for another is morally significant only when it is unconditional, that is, directed at another simply as a human being, independent of emotional attachment.[42]

Despite his insightful critique of these Christian and Kantian themes, however, Blum does make a vital concession to them: he relegates justice to the universalist realm, as a virtue that requires a point of view that abstracts from all attachments. Consequently, like most writers on friendship, he excludes justice from the virtues of friendship. Yet in real life justice *is* central to friendship: the commonest complaint of friends when they break up is that they were manipulated, used, misjudged, or wrongly neglected—in short, that they were unjustly treated.[43] The facts of everyday life appear to support Aristotle's observation that "friendship and justice would seem to have the same area of concern and to be found in the same people" (*NE*, 1159b25–6).

The importance of justice in friendship is particularly evident in friends' daily judgments of each other's actions and motives. Judgments of people's merits or demerits, responsibility for undesirable consequences, motives, or character traits, are part of normal human intercourse. The intensity and frequency of interactions among friends increases the frequency of such judgments, and highlights the issue of their justice. Considerations of distributive justice—justice in the distribution of tasks and responsibilities across a whole spectrum of concerns—also play a central role in friendship. It would be a highly deficient friendship in which one friend did all the helping or in which one friend assumed a disproportionate share of the responsibility for

---

[42] This is not, of course, the only sense in which morality can be universalistic: in one everyday sense, a universalistic morality is simply a morality in which *all* human beings have moral standing.

[43] I argue for the constitutive role of justice in friendship in "Friendship, Justice and Supererogation," *American Philosophical Quarterly* 22, 2 (April 1985): 125–31 and also in "The Circumstances of Justice: Pluralism, Community, and Friendship," *Journal of Political Philosophy* 1 (forthcoming 1993). In *What Are Friends For? Essays on Friendship, Personal Relationships, and Moral Theory* (Ithaca: Cornell University Press, forthcoming 1993), Marilyn Friedman argues for "an integration of justice concerns with care concerns." The only other work I am aware of that defends the centrality of justice in friendship is Ferdinand Schoeman's "Adolescent Confidentiality and Family Privacy," *Person to Person,* ed. George Graham and Hugh LaFollette (Philadelphia: Temple University Press, 1989), pp. 213–34.

creating mutual understanding, for initiating joint projects, and for thinking of new ways to enrich their lives together. Such a friendship would fall short of a fair exchange of emotional, moral, and intellectual goods.

It might be objected at this point that there is something awry in this picture of friendship, because justice and rights are inextricably linked to *demands,* and the language of demands is peculiarly ill-suited to friendship. But this picture of rights is far too rigid. For some things to which we have a right are things we *cannot* get in response to a demand—"cannot" in the sense that, if it is only the *demand* that brings the response, what we get is not after all what we had a right to. For example, I have a right to expect that my friend give me more of her time than she gives mere acquaintances, but to get this time as the result of a demand would be self-defeating. For what I really want, and have a right to expect, is not simply that she give me more of her time, but that she do so *because she wants to.* And this is not something I can get simply as the result of a demand. Friendship necessarily involves rights and justice, but rights may be expressed—and pressed—in different ways: sometimes as demands, sometimes even as legal threats, but typically in friendship merely as reminders of legitimate expectations and entitlements.

Aristotle also claims that the demands of justice increase with the closeness of the friendship, so that it is somehow *more* unjust to rob a friend than to rob a fellow-citizen (1160a1–9). This claim may not be true of all acts of injustice, but it does seem true of the situation that Aristotle describes, as well as of some others: for example, to accuse a friend unjustly is usually considered worse than to accuse a stranger unjustly. Yet the idea that everyone has an *equal* right to be treated justly seems equally compelling. How can we have it both ways? One way out of this puzzle—at least with respect to injustice in our judgments of each other—emerges when we note that the ability to judge justly is based on several factors, and that not all of these can be "distributed" equally. To give another person her due in our judgments requires not only the right intention and right standards of justice, but also the right kind of attentiveness to the relevant facts. But such attentiveness requires a complex structure of imagination, sympathy, and identification that we simply do not have enough time or psychic resources to give everyone equally. So although we owe the *right intention* and *standards of justice* to everyone equally, we do not owe—since we cannot give—our *attention* to everyone equally. The closer the relationship, the greater our rightful expectation of each other's time and energy in this regard. For giving of our time and energy is part of the mutual well-wishing and loving of friends. Hence it makes sense to say that the closer the relationship, the greater the injustice of certain acts of injustice.

It is sometimes thought that justice is at odds with the virtues of benevolence (generosity, concern, forgiveness). But whereas there may be certain *psychological* tensions between justice and benevolence, there is no *moral* tension between them—they seem to be mutually supportive character traits. Generosity, concern, and forgiveness require the ability to discriminate between justice and that which goes beyond—or falls short of—justice, both in one's own and in others' actions. Conversely, the disposition to be concerned or generous makes us more perceptive, and hence more able to give others their due. As James Wallace notes, a generous-minded person will see "someone else's merit (technical, moral, etc.) in cases where it is difficult to see because the facts of the case admit of other, not unreasonable interpretations or because the situation is complex and the merit is not immediately apparent."[44] These observations lend support to the idea that there is a certain unity in the virtues.

Consequentialism

Is consequentialism compatible with the idea that a friend can be loved as an end, and that such love has intrinsic moral significance? Consequentialism identifies the moral point of view—the point of view from which the right act (or rule, or motive) is determined—with the impersonal or agent-neutral point of view, and identifies the right act (or rule, or motive) with that which maximizes the overall good. Thus consequentialism is an impersonal, teleological, and maximizing moral theory.[45] A consequentialist agent is required to justify his friendships—as all his other values—as a means to the maximal good. Appar-

[44] James Wallace, *Virtues and Vices* (Ithaca: Cornell University Press, 1978), p. 137. I discuss these issues at greater length in "Friendship, Justice and Supererogation."

[45] See Bernard Williams in J. J. C. Smart and Williams, *Utilitarianism: For and Against* (Cambridge: Cambridge University Press, 1973), pp. 87–89; Samuel Scheffler, *The Rejection of Consequentialism* (Oxford: Clarendon Press, 1982), pp. 1–2; and Derek Parfit, *Reasons and Persons* (Oxford: Oxford University Press, 1984), pp. 24–27. It is impersonality that distinguishes consequentialism from other teleological and maximizing theories, such as contractarianism and egoism. It may be possible to define consequentialism in terms of teleology, impersonality, and *satisfaction* instead of *maximization*. In *Common-Sense Morality and Consequentialism* (London: Routledge & Kegan Paul 1985), Michael Slote discusses a "satisficing" form of consequentialism, which requires the agent merely to do "enough," rather than the best. This is in many ways a more plausible view, but I don't think that it escapes the difficulties that are discussed below, as these stem from the teleological and impersonal features of the theory, rather than from the maximizing features.

ently, then, from the impersonal *moral* point of view he can value his friendships only in instrumental terms, and this suggests that his moral commitments are psychologically incompatible with the attitudes and motivations of end friendship.

The usual consequentialist response to this criticism is that adherence to consequentialism requires only that one accept maximization of the good as a *standard* of rightness and not that one make it the *motive* for all one's actions. Hence the consequentialist agent need only appeal to the maximization standard as a test of the rightness of his actions or—in indirect consequentialism—of the rightness of his rules or motivations.[46] Indeed, consequentialism may demand that an agent cultivate nonconsequentialist motivations if doing so would, all things considered, be the best means to the end of value-maximization.[47] But several philosophers have expressed grave doubts about the psychological possibility of keeping one's motivations separate from one's justifications.[48] Michael Stocker has also criticized the demand for such a separation as a demand for an undesirable moral schizophrenia.[49]

Peter Railton's careful and intricate argument goes a long way toward meeting these objections (Essay 11). Unlike most consequentialists, who try to reconcile nonconsequentialist dispositions with the consequentialist standard of rightness by resorting to indirect consequentialism, Railton tries to effect this reconciliation within the framework of direct or act-consequentialism. He argues that a sophisticated act-consequentialism can (1) regard personal relationships such as friendship as intrinsic (non-instrumental), nonmoral goods, and (2) require that consequentialist agents cultivate the dispositions required for such relationships, subject only to the "counterfactual condition" that if these dispositions were to fail to maximize the good, the consequentialist agent would seek to change them.

Railton's arguments may suffice to show that even an act-consequentialist (AC) can keep his motivations separate from his justifications without schizophrenia or self-deception. But is it plausible to regard friendship as an intrinsic *nonmoral* good? And is the counterfactual

---

[46] *Direct* or *act-consequentialism* judges each act by reference to its overall consequences; *indirect consequentialism* judges each act by its conformity to rules or dispositions which, in turn, are deemed right or wrong according to whether or not they produce the best consequences.

[47] Both direct- and indirect-consequentialists make this argument. See, e.g., Peter Railton (Essay 11) and Smart in Smart and Williams, *Utilitarianism: For and Against*; Richard M. Hare, *Moral Thinking* (New York: Oxford University Press, 1981); and L. Wayne Sumner, *The Moral Foundation of Rights* (Oxford: Clarendon Press, 1987).

[48] Bernard Williams, *Ethics and the Limits of Philosophy* (London: Fontana, 1985), pp. 107–10; Michael Stocker, "The Schizophrenia of Modern Ethical Theories," *Journal of Philosophy* 73 (1976): 453–66.

[49] Stocker, "The Schizophrenia of Modern Ethical Theories," 458.

condition on the dispositions of AC agents *logically* consistent with
loving a friend as an end?[50]

Consider an individual whose friendships detract from the tremen-
dous energy she pours into her genetic research. As an AC agent, she
must renounce her friendships and seek to change her friendly dispositions as morally unjustified. Her own preference for a more balanced
life in which both her work and friendships have a place lacks any *moral*
standing if, when all is said and done, the good is maximized by her
renouncing friendship for the sake of her work. The profound unhappiness and damage to character that might result from such an act also
do not count as *moral* losses if, despite this, greater good is brought
about by renouncing friendship. Nor would any of this change in a
world in which friendship was the *sole* or *highest* nonmoral good; for
even then, any friendship that stood in the way of the maximization of
the good—of maximal friendship—would be potentially sacrificeable
to this good. In short, our friendships, and the personal point of view
from which we value them, have no independent moral force vis-à-vis
the overall good or the impersonal point of view.[51] For friendship and
its virtues, including the mutual honesty and fairness required of
friends, are in themselves just nonmoral goods.

Thus, the idea that friendship is an intrinsically nonmoral good,
justified if and only if it is productive of the greatest good, implies that,
from the *moral* point of view, friendship is only an instrumental good.
And the counterfactual condition on the dispositions of AC agents
requires them to be aware of this. But regarding friendship as a morally instrumental good seems to be logically incompatible with the dispositions of end friendship. For a consequentialist agent is required to
think, "I can be your friend only so long as being your friend is productive of the greatest good. Should this cease to be the case, I will cease to
be your friend—even if you and I remain the persons we are." But in
end friendship one is required to think, "I will be your friend so long as
we remain the persons we are—even if being your friend is not productive of the overall good."[52] And the two thoughts are logically
inconsistent.

[50] For a fuller discussion of these questions than the one below, see my "Why It Is
Wrong to Be Always Guided by the Best: Consequentialism and Friendship," *Ethics* 101
(April 1991): 483–504. There I also reject the occasional attempt to argue that the good
to be maximized is, in part, a *moral* good as either just terminologically confused or, in
the final analysis, inconsistent with a distinction that is basic to consequentialism, namely,
the distinction between rightness and goodness.

[51] For a discussion of the nature of the personal point of view, and the importance of
acknowledging it in moral theory, see Scheffler, *The Rejection of Consequentialism* (Oxford:
Clarendon Press, 1982), especially chap. 3. In "Consequentialism and Partiality" (unpublished), Andrew Moore makes a useful distinction between this objection to consequentialism and the objection that consequentialism is too demanding.

[52] The dispositions of friendship may, however, be compatible with granting a limited,

Does indirect consequentialism (IC) escape this difficulty? According to IC, the principle of maximization justifies those dispositions and principles that best allow our values, including friendship, to flourish. Particular acts are justified if they express our justified pro-friendship dispositions and principles, even if they do not themselves maximize the good.[53] So whereas a sophisticated AC regards all nonmaximizing acts as wrong, an indirect consequentialist (IC) regards nonmaximizing acts that conform to justified dispositions as right. This, however, is the only substantive difference between the sophisticated AC and the IC: their motivational structures must be identical. For the IC's pro-friendship dispositions are also justified only as means to the maximal good, and are subject to the same counterfactual condition as the AC's, namely, that should they cease to maximize the good, the IC agent would seek to change them.[54] Hence the indirect consequentialist must also think, "I can be your friend only so long as being your friend is productive of the greatest good." The indirect consequentialist's motivational structure, no less than the sophisticated act-consequentialist's, seems logically incompatible with the motivational structure required for end friendship. Perhaps only a "self-effacing" consequentialist theory—a theory in which the consequentialist standard of rightness is unknown to, or rejected by, those who nevertheless meet it—can escape this problem.[55]

Stocker's argument in Essay 12 is designed to undercut *all* teleological theories of ethics, moral psychology, and action, that is, all theories that seek to understand or evaluate action entirely in terms of goals. His thesis is that the *telos* of action—that *for the sake of* which an action is done—is not sufficient for identifying, understanding, and assessing many important kinds of acts, including virtuous acts and acts of friendship. Using a concrete example of an act of friendship, Stocker shows that although it involves, it cannot be reduced to, acting for the sake of something, not even *for the sake of* acting out of friendship. The "character structure" of friendship involves "forms of directed attention and sensitivity" that cannot be captured by an analysis in terms of goals or purposes alone ("unless those purposes are already under-

---

secondary, moral status to the principle of value maximization. I discuss this possibility in my article "Why It Is Wrong to Be Always Guided by the Best."

[53] See, e.g., L. W. Sumner, "The Good and the Right," in W. E. Cooper et al., eds., *New Essays on John Stuart Mill and Utilitarianism, Canadian Journal of Philosophy,* supplementary vol. 5 (Guelph: Canadian Association for Publishing in Philosophy, 1979), pp. 111–12.

[54] Note that this fact is not changed by the claim that IC seeks to justify not each individual friendship, but the institution of friendship. For, under unusual circumstances, the institution of friendship in a given society or community can also become counterproductive. Hence the IC agent is required to incorporate this possibility into her motivational structure.

[55] On self-effacing consequentialism see Parfit, *Reasons and Persons,* pp. 40–43.

stood as coming from such forms of attention and sensitivity"). Hence
we need to refer to the *arche* of action—the character traits and other
features we act *from or out of*—in identifying, understanding, and assessing acts of friendship. The same is true of courage and other moral
virtues. Finally, since acts done out of friendship (or out of virtue) are
essential to being a friend (or being virtuous), no adequate theory of
friendship or ethics can be purely teleological.[56]

The papers in this section, taken together, provide an overview of
the ways in which different ethical theories try to make room for end
friendship. In the next section we move on to discussions of friendship
in political philosophy.

Friendship, Society, and Politics

The connection between friendship, on the one hand, and society
and politics, on the other, has been little discussed. This section includes three essays that should stimulate further work in this area. The
first paper discusses John Stuart Mill's view of the legal and social
conditions under which personal friendships flourish; the second discusses the psychological and political importance of personal and "associate" friendships; and the third discusses the idea of a good society
as a society marked by civic friendship, that is, by friendship among
citizens. All three essays also have something to say about liberal individualism and friendship.

In Essay 13 Mary Shanley contends that the usual reading of Mill's
The Subjection of Women as concerned primarily with legal equality for
women overlooks a far more complex and fundamental concern: male-
female equality as a condition of marital friendship. In conceiving of
marriage at its best as a form of the highest kind of friendship, Mill
made a "significant break" with previous writers, who had held that
women were incapable of the highest kind of friendship. Mill believed

---

[56] In "Impartialist Ethics and Personal Relationship" (unpublished), Stephen Darwall
agrees with the critics of deontological and consequentialist theories that these theories,
as traditionally conceived, cannot do justice to the value of personal relationships like
friendship. For, as traditionally conceived, these theories recognize only two points of
view: the impartial (moral), which abstracts from all attachments, and the personal (self-
regarding), which is thought to have no moral value at all. Darwall proposes a modified
deontological theory in which the impartial point of view continues to be *the* moral
standpoint, but in which the value of personal relationships is recognized as an intersub-
jective value from the human standpoint. The virtues of personal relationships—
benevolence, compassion, concern, and so on—may be regarded as intrinsically moral,
he argues, so long as one remembers that they are not essential to moral agency. (It is not
clear if Darwall thinks they are essential to *human* moral agency. But granting this might
be necessary for regarding them as intrinsically moral.)

that marital friendship would create "a school of genuine moral sentiment," liberating *both* men *and* women from their warped consciousness, and that this, in turn, would enhance the quality of public life.
Mill's concerns and arguments, according to Shanley, show that individual rights are not, as often alleged by Marxists and neo-conservatives, a *threat* to friendship and other affective bonds but, rather, a
necessary *means* to them. His essay is also invaluable for suggesting that
a liberal polity ought to strive to promote the conditions that allow
friendship "to take root and flourish."[57]

If the feminist critics of dominant liberal theories are right, however,
this aim is sabotaged by the liberal conception of the atomistic self. On
this conception, according to feminist critics, the individual is a free
and rational chooser of ends, one whose identity is independent of her
social relationships and whose relationships are entirely instrumental
to her ends. Against this overly individualistic view of the self, feminists
have pointed to the constitutive role of social relationships in making
us who we are. "Communitarian" political theorists like Michael Sandel
and Alasdair MacIntyre have also criticized the liberal conception of
the self, arguing that communal ties and norms play a fundamental
role in the constitution of our selves.[58] So a theoretical alliance between
feminists and communitarians might seem both natural and fruitful.

But in Essay 14 Marilyn Friedman warns that "communitarian philosophy as a whole is a perilous ally for feminist theory." For communitarians take family, neighbor, church, and nation as the primary
models of community, oblivious to the fact that these communities have
been "highly oppressive for women." But women, Friedman insists,
need to *choose* the communities that compete for their loyalties and
identities on the basis of the freedom and equality they offer, rather
than just embrace the "communities of place" they find themselves in,
such as family, neighborhood, and church. Arguing that the commu-

---

[57] Can a liberal polity promote the conditions under which friendship flourishes without infringing on people's liberty? Schoeman's "Friendship and Testimonial Privileges"
(*Ethics, Public Policy, and Criminal Justice,* ed. Fredrick Elliston and Norman Bowie [Cam-
bridge: Oelgeschlager, Gunn and Hain, 1982], pp. 257–73) suggests one novel way of
achieving this end. He suggests that the legal privilege of confidential communication,
extended to spouses in criminal cases for the sake of protecting spousal trust and intimacy, should also be extended to intimate friends for the sake of protecting and promoting friendship in society.

[58] Michael Sandel, *Liberalism and the Limits of Justice* (New York: Cambridge University
Press, 1982), pp. 10–11, 150, 175–77, 179; Alasdair MacIntyre, *After Virtue* (Notre
Dame: Notre Dame University Press, 1981), pp. 146, 160–61, 204–5, 213, 215, 219f.
Charles Taylor also charges that modern "society and its institutions are seen as mere
instruments to our private purposes" ("The Nature and Scope of Distributive Justice,"
Philosophy and the Human Sciences: Philosophical Papers, vol. 2 [Cambridge: Cambridge
University Press, 1985], p. 305).

nitarian conception of the communally constituted self is too narrow, Friedman emphasizes the role of chosen urban communities (like professional associations) and of "modern" (personal) friendships in forming—and reforming—our identities. These urban communities and personal friendships, chosen on the basis of shared values, provide social support to those who suffer intolerance from family or neighborhood for their unconventional values or life-styles. In addition, personal and associate friendships also play an important *political* role, that of "dislocating" found communities and, thus, initiating social change.

Friedman's argument provides a refreshingly positive perspective on a feature of friendship that has too often been seen as requiring apology: its exclusiveness and divisiveness. For it is by virtue of this very exclusiveness and divisiveness that friendship is able to provide refuge to those ostracized by family or neighborhood and to challenge the social status quo. Thus, the socially and politically subversive potential of friendship can be an important counterweight to the power of coercive communities and especially to that of the state (which is why dictatorships universally fear and try to suppress friendship).[59] This feature of friendship should make it of particular interest to liberals.

The psychological, moral, and political importance of personal and associate friendships is undeniable. But a society whose citizens felt little or no friendship or sense of community with those outside of their chosen groups would be sadly deficient. A good society, it is commonly thought, is a society united not only by commercial, contractual relations between different groups or individuals, but also by civic friendship. This is the topic of the next and final essay.

In Essay 15 John Cooper explicates Aristotle's notion of civic friendship as a form of advantage-friendship between members of smaller communities—families, households, villages. It is a form of advantage-friendship because it is predicated on the expectation of mutual benefit: the civic community, in which civic friendship is found, has as its goal the common advantage of its members. But civic friendship is a different kind of friendship from personal or associate friendship: like any friendship, civic friendship involves mutual goodwill, trust, and well-wishing, but, unlike personal or associate friendship, it exists among people who may be personally unacquainted with each other.

A society marked by civic friendship differs in important ways from a society based primarily or only on contractual relations. One difference is that, in the latter, citizens are concerned only to *treat* each other justly, whereas, in the former, they are also concerned that their fellow

---

[59] "Every real Friendship," as Lewis points out, "is a sort of secession, even a rebellion" (*An Experiment in Criticism,* p. 75). This is why it is distrusted not only in dictatorships but in every closed society, including boarding school dorms.

citizens *be* just. This interest in the *character* of fellow citizens introduces another difference between the two sorts of societies—a distinctive conception of the common good. In a merely commercial society,
the common good exists simply as the sum total of the good of each
individual, but in a society united by civic friendship, the material and
"spiritual" good accruing to the individual becomes a communal good
in which everyone shares. As Cooper explains, "where each aims in her
cooperative activity at the good of the others, and not just at her own
good, the good attained in the first instance by the others becomes, and
is conceived of by herself as being, also a part of her own good."

Cooper's analysis of Aristotle's conception of civic friendship as a
form of advantage-friendship stands in instructive contrast to MacIntyre's analysis of it as a form of the highest kind of friendship. MacIntyre opposes his conception of Aristotelian civic friendship to the "inferior form of friendship . . . founded on mutual advantage" that,
according to him, prevails in modern liberal society.[60] MacIntyre's dis-
missive attitude toward advantage-friendship seems to be motivated by
the suspicion that advantage-friendship is just mutual commerce by
another name. If Cooper is right, however, there is a real difference
between advantage-friendship and mutual commerce, and the former
exists not only in Aristotle's ideal city-state but also in liberal societies,
despite their official ideology of commercialism. For example, he
points out, the typical American takes pride in the qualities of mind
and character of American writers, workers, or industrialists and feels
injured by news of major wrongdoing by prominent figures in government, industry, or the arts. By contrast, similar qualities in or acts by
prominent figures in foreign countries do not evoke the same personal
reaction.

Another interesting feature of Aristotle's view is the importance he
attaches to justice in civic friendship (as in all friendship). According to
communitarian, certain feminist, and, before them, Marxist critics of
liberalism, the primacy of rights and justice in liberal societies separates one person from another and undermines the possibility of true
friendship. This criticism is based on the assumption that justice is
essentially a remedial virtue, a virtue that remedies our lack of friendship and the virtues of benevolence that friendship brings. But we have
seen that justice plays a constitutive role in friendship and, indeed, that
in many ways it is more important in friendship than elsewhere. According to Aristotle, every community, from the familial to the political, "carries with it," in Cooper's words, "both a specific kind of friendship and a specific set of standards of justice." The critics of liberalism,

[60] MacIntyre, *After Virtue*, p. 147.

it would seem, have an inadequate conception of justice—as well as of friendship.[61]

Conclusion

The essays in this volume provide an overview of the recent philosophical writing about friendship and suggest the unexplored possibilities that friendship offers for philosophical analysis. Although no account of friendship enjoys universal acceptance, there are broad areas of agreement on, for example, the idea that the primary motivation of the best kind of friendship must be non-instrumental, or the idea that an adequate theory of morality must make room for these motivations. These areas of agreement make it possible for friendship to be used as a test—albeit a partial and fallible one—of the adequacy of rival moral and political conceptions. So, for example, we have seen that an adequate analysis of friendship challenges the view that emotions are of only instrumental significance in morality, that justice is a cold, divisive virtue, or that liberalism is inimical to civic friendship. The idea of end friendship as an intrinsically moral phenomenon and as partly constitutive of the friends' well-being challenges the standard view that, if morality is tied to human well-being, it can be only an *instrumental means* to well-being, whereas, if morality is *an end in itself*, it cannot have an essential connection to human well-being. But this challenge, and its implications for moral theory, have yet to be systematically explored.

[61] See my "The Circumstances of Justice: Liberalism, Community, and Friendship."

PART I

FRIENDSHIP:
GENERAL DISCUSSIONS

[1]

Friendship—The Least Necessary Love

C. S. Lewis

When either Affection or Eros is one's theme, one finds a prepared audience. The importance and beauty of both have been stressed and almost exaggerated again and again. Even those who would debunk them are in conscious reaction against this laudatory tradition and, to that extent, influenced by it. But very few modern people think Friendship a love of comparable value or even a love at all. I cannot remember that any poem since *In Memoriam,* or any novel, has celebrated it. Tristan and Isolde, Antony and Cleopatra, Romeo and Juliet, have innumerable counterparts in modern literature: David and Jonathan, Pylades and Orestes, Roland and Oliver, Amis and Amile, have not. To the Ancients, Friendship seemed the happiest and most fully human of all loves; the crown of life and the school of virtue. The modern world, in comparison, ignores it. We admit of course that besides a wife and family a man needs a few "friends." But the very tone of the admission, and the sort of acquaintanceships which those who make it would describe as "friendships," show clearly that what they are talking about has very little to do with that *Philia* which Aristotle classified among the virtues or that *Amicitia* on which Cicero wrote a book. It is something quite marginal; not a main course in life's banquet; a diversion; something that fills up the chinks of one's time. How has this come about?

The first and most obvious answer is that few value it because few experience it. And the possibility of going through life without the experience is rooted in that fact which separates Friendship so sharply from both the other loves. Friendship is—in a sense not at all derogatory to it—the least *natural* of loves; the least instinctive, organic, biological, gregarious and necessary. It has least commerce with our nerves; there is nothing throaty about it; nothing that quickens the pulse or turns you red and pale. It is essentially between individuals; the moment two men are friends they have in some degree drawn apart together from the herd. Without Eros none of us would have been begotten and without Affection none of us would have been reared; but we can live and breed without Friendship. The species, biologically considered, has no need of it. The pack or herd—the community—may even dislike and distrust it. Its leaders very often do. Headmasters and Headmistresses and Heads of religious communities, colonels and ships' captains, can feel uneasy when close and strong friendships arise between little knots of their subjects.

This (so to call it) "non-natural" quality in Friendship goes far to explain why it was exalted in ancient and medieval times and has come to be made light of in our own. The deepest and most permanent thought of those ages was ascetic and world-renouncing. Nature and emotion and the body were feared as dangers to our souls, or despised as degradations of our human status. Inevitably that sort of love was most prized which seemed most independent, or even defiant, of mere nature. Affection and Eros were too obviously connected with our nerves, too obviously shared with the brutes. You could feel these tugging at your guts and fluttering in your diaphragm. But in Friendship—in that luminous, tranquil, rational world of relationships freely chosen—you got away from all that. This alone, of all the loves, seemed to raise you to the level of gods or angels.

But then came Romanticism and "tearful comedy" and the "return to nature" and the exaltation of Sentiment; and in their train all that great wallow of emotion which, though often criticised, has lasted ever since. Finally, the exaltation of instinct, the dark gods in the blood; whose hierophants may be incapable of male friendship. Under this new dispensation all that had once commended this love now began to work against it. It had not tearful smiles and keepsakes and baby-talk enough to please the sentimentalists. There was not blood and guts enough about it to attract the primitivists. It looked thin and etiolated; a sort of vegetarian substitute for the more organic loves.

Other causes have contributed. To those—and they are now the majority—who see human life merely as a development and complication of animal life all forms of behaviour which cannot produce certificates of an animal origin and of survival value are suspect. Friendship's certificates are not very satisfactory. Again, that outlook which values the collective above the individual necessarily disparages Friendship; it is a relation between men at their highest level of individuality. It withdraws men from collective "togetherness" as surely as solitude itself could do; and more dangerously, for it withdraws them by two's and three's. Some forms of democratic sentiment are naturally hostile to it because it is selective and an affair of the few. To say "These are my friends" implies "Those are not." For all these reasons if a man believes (as I do) that the old estimate of Friendship was the correct one, he can hardly write a chapter on it except as a rehabilitation.

. . .

Those who cannot conceive Friendship as a substantive love but only as a disguise or elaboration of eros betray the fact that they have never had a Friend. The rest of us know that though we can have erotic love and friendship for the same person yet in some ways nothing is less like a Friendship than a love-affair. Lovers are always talking to one another about their love; Friends hardly ever about their Friendship. Lovers are normally face to face, absorbed in each other; Friends, side by side, absorbed in some common interest. Above all, Eros (while it lasts) is necessarily between two only. But two, far from being the necessary number for Friendship, is not even the best. And the reason for this is important.

Lamb says somewhere that if, of three friends (A, B, and C), A should die, then B loses not only A but "A's part in C," while C loses not only A but "A's part in B." In each of my friends there is something that only some other friend can fully bring out. By myself I am not large enough to call the whole man into activity; I want other lights than my own to show all his facets. Now that Charles is dead, I shall never again see Ronald's reaction to a specifically Caroline joke. Far from having more of Ronald, having him "to myself" now that Charles is away, I have less of Ronald. Hence true Friendship is the least jealous of loves. Two friends delight to be joined by a third, and three by a fourth, if only the newcomer is qualified to become a real friend. They can then say, as the blessed souls say in Dante, "Here comes one who will augment our loves." For in this love "to divide is not to take away." Of course the scarcity of kindred souls—not to mention practical considerations about the size of rooms and the audibility of voices—set limits to the enlargement of the circle; but within those limits we possess each friend not less but more as the number of those with whom we share him increases. In this, Friendship exhibits a glorious "nearness by resemblance" to Heaven itself where the very multitude of the blessed (which no man can number) increases the fruition which each has of God. For every soul, seeing Him in her own way, doubtless communicates that unique vision to all the rest. That, says an old author, is why the Seraphim in Isaiah's vision are crying "Holy, Holy, Holy" *to one another* (Isaiah VI, 3). The more we thus share the Heavenly Bread between us, the more we shall all have.

. . .

Friendship arises out of mere Companionship when two or more of the companions discover that they have in common some insight or interest or even taste which the others do not share and which, till that moment, each believed to be his own unique treasure (or burden). The typical expression of opening Friendship would be something like, "What? You too? I thought I was the only one." We can imagine that among those early hunters and warriors single individuals—one in a century? one in a thousand years?—saw what others did not; saw that the deer was beautiful as well as edible, that hunting was fun as well as necessary, dreamed that his gods might be not only powerful but holy. But as long as each of these percipient persons dies without finding a kindred soul, nothing (I suspect) will come of it; art or sport or spiritual religion will not be born. It is when two such persons discover one another, when, whether with immense difficulties and semi-articulate fumblings or with what would seem to us amazing and elliptical speed, they share their vision—it is then that Friendship is born. And instantly they stand together in an immense solitude.

Lovers seek for privacy. Friends find this solitude about them, this barrier between them and the herd, whether they want it or not. They would be glad to reduce it. The first two would be glad to find a third.

In our own time Friendship arises in the same way. For us of course the shared activity and therefore the companionship on which Friendship supervenes will not often be a bodily one like hunting or fighting. It may be a common religion, common studies, a common profession, even a common recreation. All who share it will be our companions; but one or two or three who share something more will be our Friends. In this kind of love, as Emerson said, *Do you love me?* means *Do you see the same truth?*—Or at least, "Do you *care about* the same truth?" The man who agrees with us that some question, little regarded by others, is of great importance can be our Friend. He need not agree with us about the answer.

Notice that Friendship thus repeats on a more individual and less socially necessary level the character of the Companionship which was its matrix. The Companionship was between people who were doing something together—hunting, studying, painting or what you will. The Friends will still be doing something together, but something more inward, less widely shared and less easily defined; still hunters, but of some immaterial quarry; still collaborating, but in some work the world does not, or not yet, take account of; still travelling companions, but on a different kind of journey. Hence we picture lovers face to face but Friends side by side; their eyes look ahead.

That is why those pathetic people who simply "want friends" can never make any. The very condition of having Friends is that we should want something else besides Friends. Where the truthful answer to the question *Do you see the same truth?* would be "I see nothing and I don't care about the truth; I only want a Friend," no Friendship can arise—

though Affection of course may. There would be nothing for the Friendship to be *about;* and Friendship must be about something, even if it were only an enthusiasm for dominoes or white mice. Those who have nothing can share nothing; those who are going nowhere can have no fellow-travellers.

When the two people who thus discover that they are on the same secret road are of different sexes, the friendship which arises between them will very easily pass—may pass in the first half-hour—into erotic love. Indeed, unless they are physically repulsive to each other or unless one or both already loves elsewhere, it is almost certain to do so sooner or later. And conversely, erotic love may lead to Friendship between the lovers. But this, so far from obliterating the distinction between the two loves, puts it in a clearer light. If one who was first, in the deep and full sense, your Friend, is then gradually or suddenly revealed as also your lover you will certainly not want to share the Beloved's erotic love with any third. But you will have no jealousy at all about sharing the Friendship. Nothing so enriches an erotic love as the discovery that the Beloved can deeply, truly and spontaneously enter into Friendship with the Friends you already had: to feel that not only are we two united by erotic love but we three or four or five are all travellers on the same quest, have all a common vision.

The co-existence of Friendship and Eros may also help some moderns to realise that Friendship is in reality a love, and even as great a love as Eros. Suppose you are fortunate enough to have "fallen in love with" and married your Friend. And now suppose it possible that you were offered the choice of two futures: "*Either* you two will cease to be lovers but remain forever joint seekers of the same God, the same beauty, the same truth, *or else,* losing all that, you will retain as long as you live the raptures and ardours, all the wonder and the wild desire of Eros. Choose which you please." Which should we choose? Which choice should we not regret after we had made it?

I have stressed the "unnecessary" character of Friendship, and this of course requires more justification than I have yet given it.

It could be argued that Friendships are of practical value to the Community.

· · ·

Others again would say that Friendship is extremely useful, perhaps necessary for survival, to the individual. They could produce plenty of authority: "bare is back without brother behind it" and "there is a friend that sticketh closer than a brother." But when we speak thus we are using *friend* to mean "ally." In ordinary usage *friend* means, or should mean, more than that. A Friend will, to be sure, prove himself to be also an ally when alliance becomes necessary; will lend or give when we are in need, nurse us in sickness, stand up for us among our enemies, do what he can for our widows and orphans. But such good offices are not the stuff of Friendship. The occasions for them are almost interruptions. They are in one way relevant to it, in another not. Relevant, because you would be a false friend if you would not do them when the need arose; irrelevant, because the role of benefactor always remains accidental, even a little alien, to that of Friend. It is almost embarrassing. For Friendship is utterly free from Affection's need to be needed. We are sorry that any gift or loan or night-watching should have been necessary—and now, for heaven's sake, let us forget all about it and go back to the things we really want to do or talk of together. Even gratitude is no enrichment to this love. The stereotyped "Don't mention it" here expresses what we really feel. The mark of perfect Friendship is not that help will be given when the pinch comes (of course it will) but that, having been given, it makes no difference at all. It was a distraction, an anomaly. It was a horrible waste of the time, always too short, that we had together. Perhaps we had only a couple of hours in which to talk and, God bless us, twenty minutes of it has had to be devoted to *affairs!*

For of course we do not want to know our Friend's affairs at all. Friendship, unlike Eros, is uninquisitive. You become a man's Friend without knowing or caring whether he is married or single or how he earns his living. What have all these "unconcerning things, matters of fact" to do with the real question, *Do you see the same truth?* In a circle of true Friends each man is simply what he is: stands for nothing but himself. No one cares twopence about any one else's family, profession, class, income, race, or previous history. Of course you will get to know about most of these in the end. But casually. They will come out bit by bit, to furnish an illustration or an analogy, to serve as pegs for an anecdote; never for their own sake. That is the kingliness of Friendship. We meet like sovereign princes of independent states, abroad, on neutral ground, freed from our contexts. This love (essentially) ignores not only our physical bodies but that whole embodiment which consists of our family, job, past and connections. At home, besides being Peter or Jane, we also bear a general character; husband or wife, brother or sister, chief, colleague or subordinate. Not among our Friends. It is an affair of disentangled, or stripped, minds. Eros will have naked bodies; Friendship naked personalities.

Hence (if you will not misunderstand me) the exquisite arbitrariness and irresponsibility of this love. I have no duty to be anyone's Friend and no man in the world has a duty to be mine. No claims, no shadow of necessity. Friendship is unnecessary, like philosophy, like art, like the universe itself (for God did not need to create). It has no survival value;

rather it is one of those things which give value to survival.

. . .

Three significant facts remain to be taken into account.

The first, already mentioned, is the distrust which Authorities tend to have of close Friendships among their subjects. It may be unjustified; or there may be some basis for it.

Secondly, there is the attitude of the majority towards all circles of close Friends. Every name they give such a circle is more or less derogatory. It is at best a "set"; lucky if not a *coterie,* a "gang," a "little senate," or a "mutual admiration society." Those who in their own lives know only Affection, Companionship and Eros, suspect Friends to be "stuckup prigs who think themselves too good for us." Of course this is the voice of Envy. But Envy always brings the truest charge, or the charge nearest to the truth, that she can think up; it hurts more. This charge, therefore, will have to be considered.

Finally, we must notice that Friendship is very rarely the image under which Scripture represents the love between God and Man. It is not entirely neglected; but far more often, seeking a symbol for the highest love of all, Scripture ignores this seemingly almost angelic relation and plunges into the depth of what is most natural and instinctive. Affection is taken as the image when God is represented as our Father; Eros, when Christ is represented as the Bridegroom of the Church.

Let us begin with the suspicions of those in Authority. I think there is a ground for them and that a consideration of this ground brings something important to light. Friendship, I have said, is born at the moment when one man says to another "What! You too? I thought that no one but myself . . . " But the common taste or vision or point of view which is thus discovered need not always be a nice one. From such a moment art, or philosophy, or an advance in religion or morals might well take their rise; but why not also torture, cannibalism, or human sacrifice? Surely most of us have experienced the ambivalent nature of such moments in our own youth? It was wonderful when we first met someone who cared for our favourite poet. What we had hardly understood before now took clear shape. What we had been half ashamed of we now freely acknowledged. But it was no less delightful when we first met someone who shared with us a secret evil. This too became far more palpable and explicit; of this too, we ceased to be ashamed. Even now, at whatever age, we all know the perilous charm of a shared hatred or grievance. (It is difficult not to hail as a Friend the only other man in College who really sees the faults of the Sub-Warden.)

It is therefore easy to see why Authority frowns on Friendship. Every real Friendship is a sort of secession, even a rebellion. It may be a rebellion of serious thinkers against accepted clap-trap or of faddists against accepted good sense; of real artists against popular ugliness or of charlatans against civilised taste; of good men against the badness of society or of bad men against its goodness. Whichever it is, it will be unwelcome to Top People. In each knot of Friends there is a sectional "public opinion" which fortifies its members against the public opinion of the community in general. Each therefore is a pocket of potential resistance. Men who have real Friends are less easy to manage or "get at"; harder for good Authorities to correct or for bad Authorities to corrupt. Hence if our masters, by force or by propaganda about "Togetherness" or by unobtrusively making privacy and unplanned leisure impossible, ever succeed in producing a world where all are Companions and none are Friends, they will have removed certain dangers, and will also have taken from us what is almost our strongest safeguard against complete servitude.

But the dangers are perfectly real. Friendship (as the ancients saw) can be a school of virtue; but also (as they did not see) a school of vice. It is ambivalent. It makes good men better and bad men worse. It would be a waste of time to elaborate the point. What concerns us is not to expatiate on the badness of bad Friendships but to become aware of the possible danger in good ones. This love, like the other natural loves, has its congenital liability to a particular disease.

It will be obvious that the element of secession, of indifference or deafness (at least on some matters) to the voices of the outer world, is common to all Friendships, whether good, bad, or merely innocuous. Even if the common ground of the Friendship is nothing more momentous than stamp-collecting, the circle rightly and inevitably ignores the views of the millions who think it a silly occupation and of the thousands who have merely dabbled in it. The founders of meteorology rightly and inevitably ignored the views of the millions who still attributed storms to witchcraft. There is no offence in this. As I know that I should be an Outsider to a circle of golfers, mathematicians, or motorists, so I claim the equal right of regarding them as Outsiders to mine. People who bore one another should meet seldom; people who interest one another, often.

The danger is that this partial indifference or deafness to outside opinion, justified and necessary though it is, may lead to a wholesale indifference or deafness.

. . .

From the innocent and necessary act of excluding to the spirit of exclusiveness is an easy step; and thence to the degrading pleasure of exclusiveness. If that is once admitted the downward slope will grow rapidly steeper. We may never perhaps become Titans or plain cads; we might—which is in some ways worse—become "Souls." The common vision which first brought us together may fade quite away. We shall be a *coterie* that exists for the sake of being a *coterie;* a little self-elected (and therefore absurd) aristocracy, basking in the moonshine of our collective self-approval.

. . .

Just because this is the most spiritual of loves the danger which besets it is spiritual too. Friendship is even, if you like, angelic. But man needs to be triply protected by humility if he is to eat the bread of angels without risk.

. . .

Friendship, then, like the other natural loves, is unable to save itself. In reality, because it is spiritual and therefore faces a subtler enemy, it must, even more whole-heartedly than they, invoke the divine protection if it hopes to remain sweet. For consider how narrow its true path is. It must not become what the people call a "mutual admiration society"; yet if it is not full of mutual admiration, of Appreciative love, it is not Friendship at all. For unless our lives are to be miserably impoverished it must be for us in our Friendships as it was for Christiana and her party in *The Pilgrim's Progress:*

> They seemed to be a terror one to the other, for that they could not see that glory each one on herself which they could see in each other. Now therefore they began to esteem each other better than themselves. For you are fairer than I am, said one; and you are more comely than I am, said another.

There is in the long run only one way in which we can taste this illustrious experience with safety. And Bunyan has indicated it in the same passage. It was in the House of the Interpreter, after they had been bathed, sealed and freshly clothed in "White Raiment" that the women saw one another in this light. If we remember the bathing, sealing and robing, we shall be safe. And the higher the common ground of the Friendship is, the more necessary the remembrance. In an explicitly religious Friendship, above all, to forget it would be fatal.

[2]

Friendship and Other Loves

Laurence Thomas

Aristotle observed that a person would not choose to live without friends although he had all other goods (*Nicomachean Ethics* 1156a5). It is clear that Aristotle took friendship to contribute in an enormous way to an individual's flourishing, including his moral flourishing. My aim in this chapter is to offer a systematic account of this rich interpersonal relationship. Although the account offered obviously owes its inspiration to Aristotle, my aim has not been to defend his views as such. There are various species of friendship, such as friendships of pleasure and friendships of convenience. I refer to the species of friendship discussed in this chapter as companion friendship.[1] The account of friendship I offer is both descriptive and normative.

This essay is excerpted from Laurence Thomas, *Living Morally: A Psychology of Moral Character,* copyright © 1990 by Temple University Press, reprinted by permission of Temple University Press.

[1] This taxonomy of friendships is obviously Aristotle's. What I am calling companion friendship is called perfect friendship by some and complete friendship by others. John M. Cooper refers to it as character-friendship. My thinking on Aristotle's account of friendship has been sharpened by John Cooper's discussion of the topic. See, for example, Cooper, "Aristotle on Friendship," in Amélie O. Rorty, ed., *Essays on Aristotle's Ethics* (Los Angeles: University of California Press, 1980.) I have also benefited enormously from the growing contemporary discussions of friendship, including Neera K. Badhwar, "Friendship, Justice, and Supererogation," *American Philosophical Quarterly* 22 (1985): 123–32; Badhwar, "Friends as Ends in Themselves," *Philosophy and Phenomenological Research* 48 (1987): 1–23; Ferdinand Schoeman, "Aristotle on the Good of Friendship," *Australasian Journal of Philosophy* 63 (1985): 269–82; and Nancy Sherman, "Aristotle on Friendship and the Shared Life," *Philosophy and Phenomenologial Research* 47 (1987): 589–613. I have also profited from Marilyn Friedman, "Friendship, Choice and Change" (Bowling Green: Bowling Green State University), photocopy.

The Character of Friendship

Companion friends love each other. But surely this cannot be the distinguishing feature of friendship. For as the parent-child relationship makes abundantly clear, two people can love each other quite deeply and yet not be friends. Indeed, parents and children may not even confide in one another, whereas the idea of deep friends not confiding in one another seems almost unthinkable.

There are three salient features of companion friendships that are not characteristic of the typical parent-child relationship: (1) Companion friendships are a manifestation of a choice on the part of the parties involved. (2) Neither party to the relationship is under the authority of the other. This is not to say that they are equal in the amount of authority they have; nor, in particular, is it to say that neither has influence with the other. (I leave aside job situations when in virtue of rank or responsibilities one has authority over the other.) (3) There is an enormous bond of mutual trust between such friends. This is a bond cemented by equal self-disclosure and, for that very reason, is a sign of the very special regard that each has for the other. I shall discuss these points in turn.

In one sense this first difference requires no explanation. Children do not choose their parents, though they may make lots of other choices in connection with their parents, including sometimes the one with whom they shall live. But is it just as obvious that we do not choose our friends? Well, yes and no. On the one hand, there is clearly something to the idea that friendships are an expression of choice; no one supposes that she or he had no alternative but to be a person's friend. Yet, it is all too obvious that as a rule we do not self-consciously choose our friends in the way that we choose, say, the clothes that we wear. One does not shop for a friend in the way that one shops for an article of clothing. There is a very clear sense in which we grow into friendships; indeed, we can even be surprised that our interaction with someone has given rise to such companion friendship. It might never have occurred to us that so deep a friendship would have developed. Thus, on the other hand, there is a sense in which friendships happen to us. Do we simply have conflicting intuitions about friendship or do they reflect our feelings about different aspects of this kind of interpersonal relationship? It is the latter, so I shall argue.

As I have observed, companion friendship involves love. In fact, it parallels romantic love to a remarkable extent. Now, people are often said to fall in love. I hold that a similar phenomenon can occur with friendship. In the case of romantic love, the conversational implicature[2] is clearly that the person about whom this is said was more or less besieged by feelings of love for so-and-so, as opposed to choosing to have those feelings. Still, no one would say that a person had no choice but to love the individual in question, notwithstanding the fact that initial feelings of love are sometimes experienced as an onslaught. To understand what happens here, some observations about social interaction are in order.

We may think of such interaction as being on a continuum with respect to being structured.[3] At one end we have maximally structured social interaction, where the interaction of the parties in question is highly governed by the social roles they occupy; at the other we have minimally structured social interaction, where how the parties interact is not primarily a function of social roles, and so where matters of propriety and protocol are least apropos, if at all. In the latter instance, morality alone is indispensable to how the parties interact. Most social interaction, of course, falls somewhere between these two extremes.

Interaction between heads of state is generally maximally structured, since it often involves highly ritualized behavior: what one says, the order in which one says it, one's posture while speaking, salutations, and so on are all rather structured. Most interactions between strangers, while not involving highly ritualized behavior, are nonetheless governed by social conventions concerning the roles of the parties involved, as between physicians and their patients, clergy and their parishioners, clerks and customers, and the like. Even behavior between associates is governed considerably by social convention. Associates are people who are not companion friends but who interact from time to time because they occasionally enjoy each other's company. It is a matter of great impropriety for associates to inquire casually about each other's personal life.

While it may be thought that interaction between immediate family members is minimally structured, if any social interaction is, the truth of the matter is that this is rarely the case (except perhaps between siblings). For until very recently social conventions have strongly dictated what the roles and duties of wife and husband should be toward

---

[2] H. P. Grice, "Logic and Conversation," in P. Cole and J. L. Morgan, eds., *Syntax and Semantics,* vol. 3 (New York: Academic Press, 1975), pp. 43–44.

[3] On the topic of social roles, I am much indebted to Erving Goffman, *The Presentation of Self in Everyday Life* (Garden City, N.Y.: Doubleday Anchor, 1959). The notion of a role understood here seems to be generally accepted. Robin R. Vallacher, "An Introduction to Self Theory," in Daniel M. Wegner and Vallacher, eds., *The Self in Social Psychology* (London: Oxford University Press, 1980), writes thus: "A role can be defined as a pattern of behavior that is prescribed (expected or demanded) in a given social relationship" (p. 23).

each other; and, of course, interaction between parents and children is also very much governed by convention.

(Throughout, I shall restrict the use of family to cases in which children are being raised. This restriction would seem to accord with convention; for one can ask a [married] couple whether or when it plans to start a family. If the family is thought of as an institution, this makes sense precisely because it is in the context of having and rearing children that adults would seem to acquire new obligations that cannot be circumvented by agreement. By contrast, a romantically involved couple, whether married or not, could agree to all sorts of arrangements, so long as no moral precepts were violated. Nothing about the wisdom of what is agreed upon is implied.)

As one might surmise, I want to say that companion friendships and romantic loves are characteristically and paradigmatically minimally structured interpersonal relationships. Even matters of etiquette and protocol are often put aside. We would not know quite what to make of two such individuals who, for instance, insisted upon addressing each other formally or holding each other to the minutest detail of etiquette when they were alone together, save that this was a precious form of amusement between the two of them. Deep friendship and romantic love are the only two forms of interpersonal relationships in which the involved parties interact intensely and frequently, but yet, aside from the rules of morality, the nature of that interaction is not defined by this or that set of social rules. If there is a caveat in order here it pertains to the extent to which gender alone is thought to entail a proper conception of behavior. This is a complication that I shall not pursue here. Suffice it to say that gender behavior can and often does make a difference. Females touch and embrace to a far greater degree than males (assuming heterosexual orientation across the board); and if touch is one of the ways in which bonding takes place,[4] then female-

---

[4] Cf. John Bowlby, *The Making and Breaking of Affectional Bonds* (London: Tavistock, 1979), pp. 68–69 and 129 ff. Bowlby cites approvingly the work of Harlow and Mears on rhesus monkeys. See Harry F. Harlow and Clara Mears, *The Human Model: Primate Perspectives* (New York: Wiley, 1979), who observe: "The [monkey] infant differs from the human infant in that the monkey is more mature at birth and grows more rapidly; but the basic responses relating to affection, including nursing, contact, clinging, and even visual auditory exploration, exhibit no fundamental differences in the two species" (p. 103). A few pages later they write as follows of their experiments with monkeys: "We were not surprised to discover that contact comfort was an important basic affectional or love variable, but we did not expect it to overshadow so completely the variable of nursing; indeed, the disparity is so great as to suggest that the primary function of nursing as an affectional variable is that of insuring frequent and intimate body contact of the infant with the mother" (p. 108).

female friendships have an important dimension that male-male
friendships lack.

We are now in a position to give a partial explanation as to why deep
friendships and romantic loves seem to be a matter of choice, on the
one hand, and things that happen to us, on the other. I have claimed
that deep friendships and romantic loves are characteristically and
paradigmatically minimally structured interpersonal relationships.
Needless to say, though, we do not go about our daily activities under
the assumption that we could interact in this way with any person
whom we might come across. Quite the contrary, we have every reason
to believe that there are very few people with whom we could interact
in this way. For minimally structured interaction will be harmonious
only if the parties involved are sufficiently attuned to the way in which
each other views and interacts with the world. Only the most self-
centered of individuals could assume that most people are so attuned
to him or her.

Now, not only do we go about our daily activities under the assumption that we could not have this kind of relationship with most others,
but there is surely no way of knowing that such a relationship with
someone is possible except through interacting with her or him. This is
not to say that we cannot exclude some people outright, but that the
only measure of whether or not it is possible to have such a minimally
structured relationship with someone is to see how one's interaction
with that person proceeds.

Given these considerations, the surprise element of deep friendships
and romantic loves can be put thus: While interacting with a person
under the ubiquitous assumption that most social interaction does not
give rise to minimally structured relationships, we come to have the
feeling that in the instance at hand such a relationship is possible. We
are surprised because we had no more reason to believe that our interaction with this person would have given rise to such feelings than we
had to believe that our interaction with others would have done so,
assuming that all those in question are moral individuals with their
share of foibles. A person may unwittingly generate this feeling in
various ways: by telling a story or revealing a facet of his life that strikes
a rather responsive chord in our hearts, by behaving in a way that we
find particularly moving, and so on. Though we have no control over a
person's doing or saying things that so move us, what we do upon
experiencing such feelings is another matter entirely. That is up to us.

This is where the element of choice in friendships and romantic love
comes into the picture. We can examine our feelings in light of previous ones, if experience permits this. We can more carefully examine
the life of the person whose behavior generated these feelings. In

particular, we can examine our feelings about his behavior in several different contexts to be sure that there was nothing peculiar about the context that initially gave rise to the feeling that we could have a minimally structured relationship with the person. It is one thing to be intrigued, fascinated, and even captivated by a person who can generate this sort of feeling in us. We are rightly or, at any rate, understandably so moved by a person who can cause us to have such feelings. However, it is another thing to lose entirely one's sense of reason and perspective on things. Falling in love undoubtedly sometimes has this effect upon people, but this is not part and parcel of what it means to fall in love or, for that matter, to fall into a deep friendship. Before moving on, I should like to mention that I am well aware of the fact that deep friendships and romantic loves are not alike in all respects. It is generally held that the latter has a sexual element, whereas the former does not. I maintain only that the two are alike with respect to, on the one hand, being an expression of choice and, on the other, being experienced as something that seems to happen to us.

I turn now to the second salient feature of companion friendships, namely, that neither party to the relationship is under the authority of the other, which is not to say that neither is much influenced by the other.[5] (It will be remembered that I leave aside job situations in which in virtue of rank or responsibilities one has authority over the other.) Understandably, friends are quite influential in the lives of one another. We can explain the significance of this feature of friendship by looking briefly at the parent-child relationship in this regard.

Parents are thought to have justified authority over their children. The right of parents to determine the good for their children is regarded as an important part of parental authority. Understandable though this may be—since children rarely have the wherewithal to determine their own good—the fact remains that children initially experience their parents as individuals who are entitled to determine the good for their children, and thus as individuals who are entitled to make authoritative assessments of the behavior in their lives. Hence, there is the presumption that children should defer to their parents' authority. It is this fact that explains why parents and children rarely form companion friendships. Parents generally take this presumption for granted; children spend a lifetime calling it into question.

Even after a child has become an adult and has acquired a defensible vision of his own good, this presumption tends to linger on the part of his parents. Consequently, the bond of trust that is indispensable to

---

[5] On the topic of authority, I am much indebted to Kurt Baier, "The Justification of Governmental Authority," *Journal of Philosophy* 69 (1972): 700–716, especially for his distinction between authority and influence.

deep friendships is rarely formed. For in examining our lives with
another, it is of the utmost importance that neither party feels entitled
to make authoritative assessments of the other's life or feels that she or
he is owed deference. Otherwise self-examination with another is more
like having another sit in judgment upon one rather than the attainment of self-understanding that it is meant to be. The absence of such
authority enhances the willingness of individuals to open the window
of their lives to each other, which in turn cements the bond of trust
between them. These considerations speak to the importance of deep
friendships' being between equals.

While it need not happen as a matter of logic, it often does happen
that when two people are sufficiently unequal with respect to their
stations in life, the one with the higher station is inclined to think that
his utterances have more authority than those of the other. This consideration, in turn, sheds some light on why companion friendships
between the young and the elderly are rather unlikely to flourish in
any society in which the elderly are, in virtue of being such, accorded
special honor and privilege. For the elderly will be inclined to think
that their utterances have more authority than the utterances of those
who are many years younger. Thus, we have an additional factor that
operates against the formation of companion friendships between parents and children, namely, the disparity in age.

We come now to the third salient feature of companion friendships,
which, it will be remembered, is that there is an enormous bond of
mutual trust between such friends and that this bond is cemented by
voluntary self-disclosure and, for that very reason, is a sign of the very
special regard that each has for the other.

There is a great deal of information that anyone can obtain about us
merely by watching what we do and listening to what we say as we go
about performing our various social roles.[6] I shall refer to this information as public information. It constitutes the outline of our lives. It
is information over which we are concerned to exercise little or no
control. Or, to put the matter differently, we are either indifferent or
care very little about those in whose hands the information falls. Then
there is guarded information about our lives, that is, information the
dissemination of which matters considerably to us.[7] This I shall vari-

---

[6] Goffman, *Behavior in Public Places* (Glencoe, Ill.: Free Press, 1963), writes: "Although
an individual can stop talking, he cannot stop communication through body idiom, he
must say either the right thing or the wrong thing. He cannot say nothing. Paradoxically,
the way in which he can give the least amount of information about himself—though still
appreciable—is to fit in and act as persons of his kind are expected to act. (The fact that
information about the self can be held back in this way is one motive for maintaining the
proprieties)" (ch. 3, sec. 3, p. 41).

[7] The importance that I attach to private information is shared by others: cf. Robert S.

ously refer to as private or intimate information. Neither private nor public information is an all-or-nothing matter. Both admit of gradations or degrees. In any event, a person who has enormous public information about our lives will normally not be able to infer much concerning the private information of our lives. One important reason for this is that our motives for doing things constitute a significant aspect of the private information of our lives. And not only are our motives not always transparent, but we can often deny motives attributed to us without incurring much suspicion as to the veracity of our claims. I shall illustrate these points in the next section.

The bond of trust between deep friends is cemented by the equal self-disclosure of intimate information.[8] Why this is so shall become clear in what follows.

The distinction between public and private information can be blurred in one of two ways. We can be public about virtually everything in our lives or we can be exceedingly private. While perhaps both extremes are to be avoided, what is true, surely, is that deep friendships are very nearly impossible in the former instance. This is because the extent to which a person is willing to reveal to us private information is the most significant measure we can have of that person's willingness to trust us, where the trust in question implies considerably more than that the person takes us to be of unquestionable moral character. For we can trust a person in this way and still not have a deep friendship with that person. We can think of our trust that a person has a good or minimally decent moral character as basic trust. The more confident we are of the goodness of a person's moral character, the deeper our basic trust. We have deep basic trust in some neighbors and colleagues with whom we do not have companion friendships. We may think of

Gerstein, "Intimacy and Privacy," *Ethics* 89 (1978): 76–81; Jeffrey Reiman, "Privacy, Intimacy, and Personhood," *Philosophy and Public Affairs* 6 (1976); and Schoeman, "Privacy and Intimate Information," in Schoeman, ed., *Philosophical Dimensions of Privacy* (New York: Cambridge University Press, 1984).

[8] The literature on self-disclosure is voluminous. I am indebted to the following: Richard L. Archer, "Self-Disclosure," in Wegner and Vallacher, *The Self in Social Psychology;* P. C. Cozby, "Self-Disclosure: A Literature Review," *Psychology Bulletin* 79 (1973); Sidney M. Jourard, *The Transparent Self,* 2d ed. (New York: Van Nostrand, 1971); Zick Rubin and Stephen Shenker, "Friendship, Proximity, and Self-Disclosure," *Journal of Personality* 46 (1978); and Lily Schubert Walker and Paul H. Wright, "Self-Disclosure in Friendship," *Perceptual and Motor Skills* 42 (1976). For our purposes, it is particularly important to keep in mind the difference between intimate and nonintimate self-disclosure and that self-disclosure tends to be reciprocal across levels of intimacy. That is, if A conveys to B information of a certain level of intimacy, then B will either respond in kind or attempt to break off the conversation, provided that B is not simply in the business of accumulating facts about A's life. As I hope is clear, the terms *private information* and *public information* as used in the text mark different ends of the intimacy scale with the latter being less intimate than the former.

the trust that is characteristic of companion friendships as intimate or privileged trust.

Now, the point is that if we are public about virtually everything in our lives, then we are left with little that can serve as the basis for intimate trust. We have few, if any, resources left whereby we can convey to another that we regard him as someone in whom we can have intimate trust. And there can be no deep friendship if we cannot convey this. Against this point, it might be said that notwithstanding the fact that we are very public about our lives, we could indicate to another that we regard him as someone in whom we can have privileged trust provided that we only accepted (or solicited) advice about our lives from him. No so, however.

For, if things go as they should, our acceptance of another's advice is contingent upon our believing that he is in the position to give us advice. While various factors determine this, one of the most important is the amount of information the person has about our lives. So, to be very public about our lives is, by the very nature of things, to put ourselves in the position to receive advice from anyone who is frequently within the sound of our voice. Accordingly, we would not have much reason to accept a friend's advice over the advice of anyone else, save that we generally thought that the friend offered sounder advice. But, then, the determining factor in our accepting his advice would not be the friendship, but rather our favorable assessment of the soundness of his advice in comparison to that of others. Consequently, our accepting the friend's advice could hardly serve as an indication of the depth of our regard for him.

This is a good point at which to note the difference between companion friends and therapists, both of whom are good listeners, at least ideally. A therapist-patient relationship is formally unidirectional in that by and large the flow of private information is supposed to be from the patient to the therapist, and not the other way around. For in virtue of her training and experience, the therapist is deemed an expert at helping people to achieve self-understanding by listening to private information about their lives (to put matters rather simply). The psychiatrist's comments, therefore, have the status of authoritative utterances. The client is motivated to reveal private information to the therapist not out of delight in sharing such information with someone whom he loves, but out of a need to achieve self-understanding; and the therapist is regarded by the patient as someone who can facilitate this end.

An upshot of the foregoing considerations is that a marked disparity in the amount of private information that two individuals possess about or self-disclose to each other is an obstacle to the flourishing of a deep friendship because it bespeaks an authority relationship between the two individuals, with the one possessing the greater amount of information being in the superior position. When there is great disparity of this sort, what we have is not a friendship but something akin to a therapist-patient (or counselor-client) relationship.

In a relationship that both parties are interested in maintaining, there is usually reciprocity with respect to self-disclosure. That is, if A self-discloses to B a piece of information of a certain degree of privacy, then B reciprocates by disclosing to A an equally private piece of information. If B fails to reciprocate, then A will usually discontinue self-disclosing information at the level of privacy at which B did not reciprocate. If, however, A should continue self-disclosing to B at a level of privacy at which B will not reciprocate, then either A has a reckless disregard for the amount of private information that he reveals about himself or A finds that he benefits in some way by self-disclosing such information to B. Usually this would be through B's comments and queries on the things told to him by A. In this case, not only is B contributing to the attainment of A's self-understanding, but B's doing so is on the order of the therapist contributing to the client's self-understanding.

It goes without saying that friends are moved to help each other. They are moved to do so out of love; each takes delight in giving to and assisting the other. However, whenever there is a marked and continued difference in the extent to which two people can contribute to each other's good, the more favorably positioned one is likely to be moved out of feelings of pity to help the less favorably positioned one. There are two implicit premises here. One, of course, is that in personal relationships we do not take delight in self-disclosing our private information when self-disclosure at that degree of privacy is not reciprocated. The explanation for this is quite simple. The failure to reciprocate usually indicates one of two things: either the person does not trust us or he does not value our perspectives on his life.

The other implicit premise is that, barring a reckless disregard for revealing private information, only someone in dire need of assistance in getting a perspective on his life would continue self-disclosing private information in the absence of reciprocity. This premise is grounded in the fact that, in the absence of their meeting an important need, we value associating only with those who indicate by their words and deeds that they have a positive regard for us. Those who neither trust us nor value our opinion regarding their lives make it manifestly and painfully clear that they do not have such a regard for us. Thus, self-disclosing private information to someone who does not have a positive regard for us in these ways is belittling and constitutes a form

of self-effacement; hence, we are disposed to reveal private information in such instances only when we find doing so enormously beneficial. And so, like the patient to his therapist, we self-disclose not out of
delight in sharing private information about ourselves with someone
whom we love, but out of the need to obtain a better perspective on our
own lives.

I wish to conclude this section with two comments concerning the
role of self-disclosure in friendship.[9]

First, it is a mistake to suppose that we have reciprocity of self-
disclosure only when the parties in question self-disclose about the
same sorts of things. The emphasis in reciprocity is upon the level of
intimacy as opposed to the type of information. This is as it should be,
since what is deeply revelatory about the lives of individuals may vary.
For some it is their sex life; for others, their struggle to excel; and for
still others, their deep commitment simply to staying alive. It is understandable that during the course of any given conversation reciprocity
of self-disclosure will yield information about the same sorts of things,
since conversations generally have a focus. And sometimes the point of
a conversation can be none other than self-disclosure itself, as when A
reveals something quite intimate to B, and then asks B to reciprocate,
period. If, however, in discussing a personal problem, A discloses certain information to B, it would be very insensitive of B to attempt to
match the intimacy of A's self-disclosure by revealing something related to an entirely different aspect of life. B would do better not to
disclose anything. And it is obvious, I trust, that the idea behind reciprocity of self-disclosure is not that of immediate reciprocity.

The second comment I wish to make is this: It might seem that I
have made so much of the importance of self-disclosure in friendship
that I have lost sight of the other very important aspects of friendship.
After all, so it might be noted, friends—even companion friends—
help one another in quite straightforward ways. This last point is true
enough. I have made much of self-disclosure, however, because I have
assumed that this is the predominant way in which companion friends
can and do contribute to each other's flourishing, where the emphasis
here is upon the improvement of character and personality. Insofar as
individuals can be understood as being self-sufficient in that they have
an adequate livelihood, I have assumed that by and large companion
friends are self-sufficient or, in any case, that the material help each
provides the other is quite ancillary to the friendship. This assumption,

[9] In what follows, I am grateful to Norman Care for helping me to be clearer about
matters.

far from revealing a Western bias, enables us to see more clearly how rich a friendship can be that does not turn upon material offerings.

. . .

Friendship and Romantic Love

A question that naturally arises when reflecting upon both companion friendship and romantic love concerns the nature of the difference between them.[10] The answer that most quickly comes to mind is that complete romantic love includes sexual involvement, whereas the most complete friendship does not require this. I do not believe, however, that this answer is a satisfactory one. For surely the proposal cannot be that the two are alike in all respects save that romantic love involves sexual involvement and friendship does not. To be sure, sexual involvement is significant; it does make a difference. But the issue is whether it makes so profound a difference. Is it that companion friends are all but romantic lovers except for sexual involvement? If so, then what explains why they refrain from taking this further step? Or, to ask the question in a slightly different way, what explains why romantic lovers go on to take this further step?

To resort to biology here would be to make a somewhat tendentious move, since there is no in-principle reason to suppose that romantic love cannot obtain between members of the same gender. Nor is there any in-principle reason to suppose that companion friends must both be of the same gender.

I do not believe that there is a deep formal difference between friendship and romantic love, though I do want to say that any attempt to render the two indistinguishable must make sense of the fact that sexual involvement is generally taken to make the difference between them. It is indisputable that sexual involvement between romantic lovers is taken to signify union. Indeed, it is necessary to consummate a marriage. Surely, though, there is no conceptual reason why, on the one hand, sexual involvement must signify union and why, on the other hand, something else cannot signify it. In the language of convention, it is a deeply and all but universal convention that sexual involvement signifies union, though there is no formal reason why it must signify this.

Now, the fact that there is one widespread and deep convention that signifies union between individuals, namely, sexual involvement, suf-

[10] In writing this section, I am greatly indebted to Andrew Manitsky and Ira Yankwitt for much instructive conversation.

fices to explain why lovers cannot readily designate something else to signify union. Still, there is no conceptual bar to there being something else that signifies union.

By contrast, there is no deep and widespread convention that individuals mark their having become companion friends by engaging in a certain specified behavior. But there is no conceptual reason why this cannot be so. Thus, suppose that the widespread practice was that when two individuals took themselves to have become companion friends, they purchased two very fine glasses of crystal. It is worth noting that the attitude that the friends took toward the crystal would mirror the attitude of fidelity in romantic love. It would certainly be expected by both friends that neither would give his or her crystal glass over to day-to-day use or would allow it to be used by anyone. The expectation, certainly, would be that each would use the crystal glass only on special occasions and, preferably, with each other.

Suppose, now, that a companion friendship of the type described above (i.e., with crystal serving to mark the friendship) between A and B dissolves and A goes on to form a new companion friendship with C. A and C in turn purchase fine crystal. It is very unlikely that A will parade in front of C the crystal glass that belongs to the pair that A and B purchased. As should be obvious, what we have here is a nonsexual analogue to fidelity. Something cannot be widely and generally used and, at the same time, be an indication of something special. The mark of something special is that its use is reserved or restricted in some fashion. More generally, then, it can be said that whenever there is a widespread and deeply entrenched convention according to which a specified behavior is an expression of the fact that two individuals take themselves to have reached a deep level of intimacy, then as a rule the pair will not want either party to engage in that behavior with others. Obviously, there exists such a convention regarding romantic love— namely, sexual involvement—but there is none regarding companion friendship. However, as should now be clear, this difference does not hold as a matter of conceptual truth.

That we have a convention of this sort in connection with romantic love is no doubt due to the importance of the family as a social institution, as well as the high risk of pregnancy (and thus moral and social responsibility) that, until recently, inevitably came with sexual involvement. Technology has significantly minimized the risk that sexual involvement will lead to pregnancy. Consequently, more people have become sexually involved without supposing that their involvement is an indication of romantic love, a fact that strengthens our claim that it is not a matter of conceptual truth that sexual involvement is the mark of romantic love. For, if in a nonromantic context, an evening of sexual involvement need not be any more than that—an evening of sexual involvement—and nonromantic sexual involvement is widespread, then clearly sexual involvement is not seen as something that is reserved for romantic love. And if there is no difficulty in seeing sexual involvement as not being reserved for romantic love, then on that account alone the idea that sexual involvement is not conceptually tied to romantic love achieves greater plausibility.

At best the foregoing considerations suggest that sexual involvement, which is normally characteristic of romantic love, cannot be the distinguishing feature between companion friendship and romantic love. But this truth, assuming it is such, is compatible with there being a profound difference between romantic love and friendship. In what follows I argue in a more general way that companion friendship and romantic love is a distinction without a conceptual difference.

In passing, it was noted that touch is one of the ways in which bonding takes place. I shall assume without argument that however rich a relationship might be, its richness is immeasurably enhanced if touching is an important aspect of it. Touching is not to be understood here simply in terms of sexuality. Much touching is important even though it has absolutely nothing to do with sexuality or, in any case, is not fueled by sexual desire. Touching can be comforting or encouraging. It can be an expression of support or love (not tied to sexual arousal). It can be an expression of togetherness. A hug or caress or affectionate squeeze of the hand can sometimes be more appropriate and effective than a verbal expression of one's love or support. Now, as noted earlier, if females touch and embrace to a far greater degree than males (assuming heterosexual orientation across the board), then female-female friendships have an important dimension that male-male friendships lack. And surely our ordinary observations bear out the truth of the antecedent as a general claim about social interaction. To a far greater extent than men, women can embrace and hold hands without readily having their heterosexual orientation called into question. There is the notion of mothering. Although the idea behind mothering may have its roots in child care, it has come to be more broadly associated with warmth, nurturance, and emotional expressiveness; and touch is central to mothering behavior. I assume, without argument, that the explanation for this difference between men and women is socialization pure and simple. It is not because women have some biological predisposition for touching one another that men happen to lack.

For the sake of convenience, let us refer to touching that is associated with mothering, encouragement, togetherness, and so forth, as nurturing touching. Although as a result of socialization such touching receives greater expression between females than it does between males, it is nonetheless only in romantic love that nurturing touching generally receives its greatest expression. Here, but not in same-gender companion friendships, we have unrestricted nurturing touching, as I shall say. The fantasizing that seems to characterize romantic love and not friendship, while it may surely be sexual, often has nurturing touching as its object: sitting on a beach arm-in-arm, watching the sunset; or walking through a field hand-in-hand on a glorious spring day; or sitting out in the sun with one's lover and caressing her or his forehead as the individual lies in one's lap. While I hardly wish to deny that these activities may escalate into something intensely sexual, the truth remains that these activities are very much enjoyed for their own sake. It seems clear that human beings delight in participating in unrestricted nurturing touching.

But now I take it that there is no compelling explanation for why nurturing touching receives its greatest expression only in romantic love save that this way has been ordained by a conception of social union between two individuals according to which the female-male union represents the very hallmark of a union between any two individuals. That is, I take it that a heterosexual conception of romantic love as this involves the flourishing of two lives together is what accounts for why nurturing touching receives its greatest expression only in romantic love. On this view full nurturing expression, as we might say, between members of the same gender is perverted. There is, however, no more reason to believe that full nurturing expression can occur only between members of the opposite gender than there is to believe that females, but not males, have a biological predisposition for touching one another. And just as there is no reason to believe that touching should be more characteristic of female-female companion friendships than male-male companion friendships (even though it is probably foolish to think that things are likely to change), there is no reason to believe that full nurturing expression should only be between members of the opposite gender (though again, it is probably foolish to think that things are likely to change).

The focus upon nurturing touching has enabled us to identify what must certainly be a deeply and extraordinarily important aspect of romantic love that is not tied to sexual involvement, which, as I have already argued, cannot bear the weight of the supposed distinction between companion friendship and romantic love. Much fantasizing has to do with nurturing touching; and a profound sense of vulnerability may very well come in the wake of this sort of touching between two parties—a sense of vulnerability that is not likely to be had in the absence of nurturing touching. So, the focus upon nurturing touching enables us to account for that "something," not tied to sexual involvement, which seems to be so much a part of romantic love. But as I have tried to show, there is no conceptual reason why the distinction between companion friendship and romantic love should be that the latter is designated the proper and only relationship for full nurturing expression.

A consideration that very much supports this conclusion is that companion friends are given to jealousy in precisely the same way as lovers. Friends make time for each other; and if one fails to do this too often, this becomes a source of concern to the other—which holds, a fortiori, if it turns out too often that it is in order to do something with another person that the other excuses herself or himself. More to the point, a person who appears to be a potential threat to a companion friendship will be a cause of concern and will generally occasion feelings of jealousy. Furthermore, not only is it the case that sometimes a friend is jealous of the other's intended spouse, believing that the friendship will be qualitatively different on account of the marriage, but also there are times when the future spouse, and in some instances the actual spouse, is jealous of the friend, believing that the friend is an obstacle to the flourishing of the marriage in the way that is desired.

Jealousy admits of two senses. One has to do with being especially desirous of an advantage that another has, particularly an advantage that another seems to have preempted one from having. The other has to do with being especially desirous of maintaining the special relationship that one has with another. Companion friends and romantic lovers are jealous in both senses, although in the preceding paragraph I have spoken only about jealousy in the second sense. Yet it is because both are jealous in the second sense that jealousy in the first occurs.

Needless to say, the point here is this: The truth that companion friends and lovers can be jealous of each other in precisely the same way would suggest that, respectively, friends and lovers play a like role in each other's lives—to such an extent that the same emotions are called into play. And if that is so, then it would seem rather arbitrary to suppose that full nurturing expression should be the exclusive domain of romantic love.

This completes our account of companion friendship. Conspicuously absent, no doubt, is a discussion of friendship and autonomy. I have assumed all along that companion friends are autonomous, and the observation that such friends are not sycophants should clearly bring this out. If there is anything particularly interesting to call attention to here, it is that there is no incompatibility between being autonomous and being greatly influenced by another. This is because there is no incompatibility between being autonomous and taking seriously the claims of another—even claims about oneself. For one can have good reasons to do just that, which is not the same thing as uncritically or blindly accepting what another says. Companion friends have especially good reasons to take seriously what each says about the other, since each knows that the other has a commanding perspective of his life and, moreover, that the other cares deeply for him. Indeed, it is precisely because friends have enormous influence with each other that they can play a substantial role in each other's moral flourishing.

[3]

Love and Psychological Visibility

Nathaniel Branden

We shall be dealing here with what I first called the Muttnik Principle and later, more formally, called the Principle of Psychological Visibility. An intense experience of *mutual psychological visibility* is, as we shall see, at the very center of romantic love. Let us see what this means and how and why it is so.

One afternoon in 1960, while sifting alone in the living room of my apartment, I found myself contemplating with pleasure a large philodendron plant standing against a wall. It was a pleasure I had experienced before, but suddenly it occurred to me to wonder: What is the nature of this pleasure? What is its cause?

During that period I would not describe myself as "a nature lover," although I subsequently became one. At the time I was aware of positive feelings that accompanied my contemplation of the philodendron; I was unable to explain them.

The pleasure was not primarily aesthetic. Were I to learn that the plant was artificial, its aesthetic characteristics would remain the same but my response would change radically; the special pleasure I experienced would vanish. It seemed clear that essential to my enjoyment was the knowledge that the plant was heathily and glowingly *alive*. There was a feeling of a bond, almost a kind of kinship, between the plant and me; surrounded by inanimate objects, we were united in the fact of possessing life. I thought of the motive of people who, in the most impoverished conditions plant flowers in boxes on their windowsills— for the pleasure of watching something grow. Apparently, observing successful life is of value to human beings.

Suppose, I thought, I were on a dead planet where I had every material provision to ensure survival but where nothing was alive. I would feel like a metaphysical alien. Then suppose I came upon a living plant. Surely I would greet the sight with eagerness and pleasure. *Why?*

Because, I realized, all life—life by its very nature—entails a struggle, and struggle entails the possibility of defeat; we desire and find pleasure in seeing concrete instances of successful life as confirmation of our knowledge that successful life is possible. It is, in effect, a *metaphysical* experience. We desire the sight, not necessarily as a means of allaying doubts or of reassuring ourselves, but as a means of experiencing and confirming on the perceptual plane, the level of immediate reality, that which we know abstractly, conceptually.

If such is the value a plant can offer to a human being, I mused, then the sight of another being can offer a much more intense form of this experience. The successes and achievements of those around us, in their own persons and in their work, can provide fuel and inspiration for our efforts and strivings. Perhaps this is one of the greatest gifts human beings can offer one another. A greater gift than charity, a greater gift than any explicit teaching or any words of advice—the sight of happiness, achievement, success, fulfillment.

The next crucial step in my thinking occurred on an afternoon, some months later, when I sat on the floor playing with my dog, a wirehaired fox terrier named Muttnik.

We were jabbing at and boxing with each other in mock ferociousness. What I found delightful and fascinating was the extent to which Muttnik appeared to grasp the playfulness of my intention. She was snarling and snapping and striking back while being unfailingly gentle in a manner that projected total, fearless trust. The event was not unusual; it is one with which most dog owners are familiar. But a question suddenly occurred to me, of a kind I had never asked myself before: Why am I having such an enjoyable time? What is the nature and source of my pleasure?

Part of my response, I recognized, was simply the pleasure of watching the healthy self-assertiveness of a living entity. But that was not the essential factor causing my response. That factor pertained to the interaction between the dog and myself, a sense of interacting and communicating with a living consciousness.

If I were to view Muttnik as an automaton without consciousness or awareness and to view her actions and responses as entirely mechanical, then my enjoyment would vanish. The factor of consciousness was of primary importance.

Then I thought once again of being marooned on an uninhabited island. Muttnik's presence there would be of enormous value to me, not because she could make any practical contribution to my physical survival, but because she offered a form of *companionship*. She would be a conscious entity to interact and communicate with—as I was doing now. *But why is that of value?*

The answer to this question, I realized, with a rising sense of excitement, would explain much more than the attachment to a pet. Involved in this issue is the psychological principle that underlies our desire for *human* companionship—the principle that would explain why a conscious entity seeks out and values other conscious entities, *why consciousness is a value to consciousness.*

When I identified the answer I called it the "Muttnik Principle" because of the circumstances under which it was discovered. Let us consider the nature of this principle.

The key to understanding my pleasurable reaction to playing with Muttnik was in the self-awareness that came from the nature of the feedback she was providing. From the moment that I began to "box," she responded in a playful manner; she conveyed no sign of feeling threatened; she projected an attitude of trust and pleasure and pleasurable excitement. Were I to push or jab at an inanimate object, it would react in a purely mechanical way; it would not be responding to *me;* there could be no possibility of its grasping the meaning of my actions, of apprehending my intentions, and of guiding its behavior accordingly. Such communication and response are possible only among conscious entities. The effect of Muttnik's behavior was to make me feel *seen,* to make me feel *psychologically visible* (to a modest extent). Muttnik was responding to me, not as a mechanical object, but as a person.

And, as part of the same process, I was experiencing a greater degree of visibility to *myself;* I was making contact with a playfulness in my personality which, during those years, I generally kept severely contained, so the interaction also contained elements of *self-discovery,* a theme to which I shall return shortly.

What is significant and must be stressed is that Muttnik was responding to me as a person in a way that I regarded as objectively appropriate, that is, in accordance with my view of myself and of what I was conveying to her. Had she responded with fear and an attitude of cowering, I would have experienced myself as being, in effect, misperceived by her and would not have felt pleasure.

While the example of an interaction between a human being and a dog may appear very primitive, I believe that it reflects a pattern that is manifest, potentially, between any two consciousnesses able to respond to each other. All positive interactions between human beings produce the experience of visibility to a degree. The climax of that possibility is achieved in romantic love, as we shall see shortly.

So we must consider the question: Why do we value and find pleasure in the experience of self-awareness and psychological visibility that the appropriate response or feedback from another consciousness can evoke?

Consider the fact that we normally experience ourselves, in effect, as a process—in that consciousness itself is a process, an activity, and the contents of our mind are a shifting flow of perceptions, images, organic sensations, fantasies, thoughts, and emotions. Our mind is not an unmoving entity which we can contemplate objectively—that is, contemplate as a direct object of experience—as we contemplate objects in the external world.

We normally have, of course, a sense of ourselves, of our own identity, but it is experienced more as a feeling than a thought—a feeling which is very diffuse, which is interwoven with all our other feelings, and which is very hard, if not impossible, to isolate and consider by itself. Our "self-concept" is not a single concept, but a cluster of images and abstract perspectives on our various (real or imagined) traits and characteristics, the sum total of which can never be held in focal awareness at any one time; that sum is experienced, but it is not *perceived* as such.

In the course of our life, our values, goals, and ambitions are first conceived in our mind; that is, they exist as data of consciousness, and then—to the extent that our life is successful—are translated into action and objective reality. They became part of the "out there," of the world that we perceive. They achieve expression and reality in material form. This is the proper and necessary pattern of human existence. *To live successfully is to put ourselves into the world, to give expression to our thoughts, values, and goals.* Our life is unlived precisely to the extent that this process fails to occur.

Yet our most important value—our character, soul, psychological self, spiritual being—whatever name one wishes to give it—can never follow this pattern in a literal sense, can never exist apart from our own consciousness. It can never be perceived by us as part of the "out there." But we *desire* a form of objective self-awareness and, in fact, *need* this experience.

Since we are the motor of our own actions, since our concept of who we are, of the person we have evolved, is central to all our motivation, we desire and need the fullest possible experience of the reality and objectivity of that person, of our self.

When we stand before a mirror, we are able to perceive our own face as an object in reality, and we normally find pleasure in doing so, in contemplating the physical entity that is ourself. There is a value in being able to look and think, "That's me." The value lies in the experience of objectivity.

To say it once again: The externalization of the objectification of the internal is of the very nature of successful life. We wish to see our *self* included in this process.

And, in an *indirect* sense, it *is,* every time we act on our judgment, every time we say what we think or feel or mean, every time we honestly express through word and deed our internal reality, our inner being.

But in a *direct* sense? Is there a mirror in which we can perceive our *psychological* self? In which we can, as it were, perceive our own soul? Yes. The mirror is another consciousness.

As individuals alone, we are able to know ourselves conceptually—at least to some extent. What another consciousness can offer is the opportunity for us to experience ourselves perceptually, as concrete objects "out there."

Of course, some people's consciousnesses are so alien to our own that the "mirrors" they provide yield the wildly distorted reflections of an amusement park's chamber of horrors. The experience of significant visibility requires consciousnesses congruent, to some meaningful extent, with our own.

Here is the limitation of Muttnik, or of any lower animal. True enough, in her response I was able to see reflected a small aspect of my own personality. But we can experience optimal self-awareness and visibility only in a relationship with a consciousness possessing an equal range of awareness, that is, another human being.

A word of clarification seems necessary at this point. I do not wish to imply that first we acquire a sense of identity entirely independent of any human relationships, and *then* seek the experience of visibility in interaction with others. Our self-concept is not the creation of others, as some writers have suggested, but obviously our relationships and the responses and feedback we receive contribute to the sense of self we acquire. All of us, to a profoundly important extent, experience who we are in the context of our relationships. When we encounter a new human being our personality contains, among other things, the consequences of many past encounters, many experiences, the internalization of many responses and instances of feedback from others. And we keep growing and evolving *through our encounters.*

In successful romantic love, there is a unique depth of absorption by, and fascination with, the being and personality of the partner. Hence there can be, for each, a uniquely powerful experience of visibility.

Even if this state is not realized optimally, it may still be realized to an unprecedented degree. And this is one of the main sources of the excitement—and nourishment—of romantic love.

But much more needs to be said about the *process* of psychological visibility—how it is engendered and what it entails.

Our basic premises and values, our sense of life, the level of our intelligence, our characteristic manner of processing experience, our basic biological rhythm, and other features commonly referred to as "temperament"—all are made manifest in our personality. "Personality" is the externally perceivable sum of all of the psychological traits and characteristics that distinguish a human being from all other human beings.

Our psychology is expressed through behavior, through the things we say and do, and through the ways we say and do them. It is in this sense that our self is an object of perception to others. When others react to us, to their view of us and of our behavior, their perception is in turn expressed through *their* behavior, by the way they look at us, by the way they speak to us, by the way they respond, and so forth. If their view of us is consonant with our deepest vision of who we are (which may be different from whom we profess to be), and if their view is transmitted by their behavior, we feel perceived, we feel psychologically visible. We experience a sense of the objectivity of our self and of our psychological state of being. We perceive the reflection of our self in their behavior. It is in this sense that others can be a psychological mirror.

More precisely, this is one of the senses in which others can be a psychological mirror. There is another.

When we encounter a person who thinks as we do, who notices what we notice, who values the things we value, who tends to respond to different situations as we do, not only do we experience a strong sense of affinity with such a person but also we can experience our self through our perception of that person. This is another form of the experience of objectivity. This is another manner of perceiving our self in the world, external to consciousness, as it were. And as such, this is another form of experiencing psychological visibility. The pleasure and excitement that we experience in the presence of such a person, with whom we can enjoy this sense of affinity, underscores the importance of the need that is being satisfied.

The experience of visibility, then, is not merely a function of how another individual responds to us. It is also a function of how that individual responds to the world. These considerations apply equally to all instances of visibility, from the most casual encounter to the most intense love affair.

Just as there are many different aspects to our personality and inner life, so we may feel visible in different respects in various human relationships. We may experience a greater or lesser degree of visibility, or a wider or narrower range, of our total personality, depending on the nature of the person with whom we are dealing and on the nature of our interaction.

Sometimes, the aspect in which we feel visible pertains to a basic character trait; sometimes, to the nature of our intention in performing some action; sometimes, to the reasons behind a particular emotional response; sometimes, to an issue involving our sense of life; sometimes, to a matter concerning our work; sometimes, to our sexual psychology; sometimes, to our aesthetic values. The range of possibilities is almost inexhaustible.

All the forms of interaction and communication among people—spiritual, intellectual, emotional, physical—combine to give us the perceptual evidence of our visibility in one respect or another; or, relative to particular people, can produce in us the impression of invisibility. Most of us are largely unaware of the process by which this occurs; we are aware only of the results. We are aware that, in the presence of a particular person, we do or do not feel "at home," do or do not feel a sense of affinity or understanding or emotional attachment.

The mere fact of holding a conversation with another human being entails a marginal experience of visibility, if only the experience of being perceived as a conscious entity. However, in intimate human relationships, with a person we deeply admire and care for, we expect a far more profound visibility, involving highly individual and personal aspects of our inner life.

I shall have more to say about the determinants of visibility in any particular relationship. But it is fairly obvious that a significant mutuality of intellect, of basic premises and values, of fundamental attitude toward life, is the precondition of that projection of mutual visibility which is the essence of authentic friendship, or, above all, of romantic love. A friend, said Aristotle, is another self. This is precisely what lovers experience to the most intense degree. In loving you, I encounter myself. A lover ideally reacts to us as, in effect, we would react to our self in the person of another. Thus, we perceive our self through our lover's reaction. We perceive our own person through its consequences in the consciousness—and, as a result, in the behavior of our partner.

Here, then, we can discern one of the main roots of the human desire for companionship, for friendship and for love: *the desire to perceive our self as an entity in reality, to experience the perspective of objectivity through and by means of the reactions and response of other human beings.*

The principle involved, the Muttnik Principle—let us call it the Principle of Psychological Visibility—may be summarized as follows: *Human beings desire and need the experience of self-awareness that results from perceiving the self as an objective existent, and they are able to achieve this experience through interaction with the consciousness of other living beings.*

[4]

The Historicity of Psychological Attitudes:
Love Is Not Love Which Alters
Not When It Alteration Finds

Amélie O. Rorty

There is a set of psychological attitudes—love, joy, perhaps some sorts of desire—that are individuated by the character of the subject, the character of the object, and the relation between them. Of course, such attitudes can typically be identified without reference to their objects: Mr. Knightly, Raskolnikov, Swann, and Humbert Humbert all love, though Emma, Sonia, Odette, and Lolita are quite different sorts of women. Still, the details of their loves—the dispositions and thoughts that are active in their loving—are radically different in these cases, so much so that each, looking at the others, might wonder whether they really love. When such psychological attitudes are directed to other people, those concerned characteristically want the attitude to be directed to *them*, rather than to this or that trait. "Do you love me for myself alone, or for my yellow hair?" asks one of Yeats's beautiful ladies, and Yeats has a sage reply, truthfully and sadly: "Only God, my dear, could love you for yourself alone, and not for your yellow hair." This concern about the proper object of the attitude is a way of expressing a concern about its constancy or endurance.

The individuation of such psychological attitudes might be a consequence of a general metaphysical fact, that relations are individuated by their subjects and objects. But these relational psychological attitudes are not states identified by the functional relation between the subject and some object: a person, a state of affairs, a propositional content. Although for some purposes it may be convenient to treat such attitudes as states, they arise from, and are shaped by, dynamic interactions between a subject and an object. (As slides of frozen cells

This essay was originally published in *Midwest Studies in Philosophy* 10 (1986):399–412, copyright © by the Regents of the University of Minnesota. Reprinted by permission of Midwest Studies in Philosophy Inc. The author has made slight changes for this volume.

stand to a living, working organism, so do psychological attitudes construed as *states* stand to phenomena of dynamic interaction.) It is this feature of such attitudes—what we might call their *historicity*—that generates a concern about their constancy and that can, as I hope to show, also assuage that concern. (In calling psychological attitudes *activities,* and focusing on interactive attitudes, I do not intend to classify all of them with voluntary or responsible actions. Interactive attitudes are not necessarily caused by intentions or under voluntary control, even though they are certainly intentional, and sometimes voluntary.) These psychological attitudes are identified by the detail of the narrative of the interactions between the subject and the object, interactions that also individuate the persons involved. Relational psychological attitudes of this kind are individuated by their objects, but also the trajectory of the subject's life—the subject's further individuation—is affected by this relational attitude, this activity.

For the moment, I want to set aside the question of whether this characterization defines only a very small class. Because I do not believe passions or emotions form a natural class, as distinct from (say) desires or motives, or some sorts of beliefs and judgments, I shall not even try to determine whether those conditions we now roughly classify as passions or emotions are historical, dynamic, and interactive, and whether their rationality is thereby endangered. I want rather to trace one such interactive attitude through some of its ramifications, to give a sketch of its historicity, showing that far from threatening rationality, it is just this interactivity that shores, though it cannot possibly assure, the sane emendation and corrigibility that is tantamount to rationality. I shall take love, rather than joy, desire, indignation, or fear, as an example. We seem to know more about loving than we do about many other psychological attitudes, not because we are more adept at loving than we are at being joyful or indignant, but because, wanting to be loved, we have given thought to what we want, in wanting to be loved. The characteristics that such an examination uncovers are, as I hope to show, historically specific: they arise in particular social, political, and intellectual contexts. The conditions and criteria set on the identification of love reveal the preoccupations of the era.

Although I shall sketch the place of contemporary conceptions of the conditions of love in its historical context, I want for the moment to set aside the question of whether the contemporary forms provide the central and definitory example of love (if there can be such a thing). Though romantic and erotic love are primary examples, they are by no means the only, or even the clearest, examples of this sort of attitude. The kind of love I have in mind is the love of friendship, and sometimes (though in our culture, rarely) the love of parents and children.

The account I sketch does not assume that such friendship-love is symmetrically reciprocated or even that it is reciprocated at all. Nor does it assume that there is a strict economy of love, such that its expansion to others automatically constitutes a diminution or loss elsewhere. Nevertheless, although such love is by no means exclusive, it cannot include more people than the lover is able to attend closely. If there is an economy involved, it is the economy of focused, interactively forming attention, one that not only wishes but acts to promote the thriving of the friend.

I want to examine some characteristics of dynamic, interactive, historical psychological attitudes: (1) Their proper objects are a person, rather than this or that characteristic of a person.[1] (2) Such attitudes are permeable; that is, the lover is affected, changed not only by loving but by the details of the character of the person loved. (3) Because such attitudes affect the person, they affect the person's actions. Although some lovers do not always reliably act on behalf of the welfare of those whom they love, their not doing so raises a doubt about whether they do truly love. (Parallel: although someone who desires to learn does not necessarily forthwith set about learning, still, not doing so raises a doubt about the desire). (4) These attitudes are identified by a characteristic narrative history. Although there are pangs of love, stabs of fear, twinges of longing, and thrills of joy, these are identifiable as the feeling of love, fear, longing, or joy only within the complex narrative of the living attitude. These psychological attitudes often feature a particular feeling tone that so magnetizes our attention that we tend to confuse it with the dynamic attitude as a whole.[2] But it is the whole history, and not only the focused and highlighted affective aspect, that constitutes the attitude. In the case of love, there is a presumption of some nonaccidental continuity, assured either by the constancy of a particular relation between the lover and the friend or by the character of their interaction.

Let's begin by distinguishing different ways that the continuity of love can be assured, distinguishing its enduring constancy from its

---

[1] This paper originated as a commentary to Robert Kraut's "Love *De Re*" (*Midwest Studies in Philosophy* 10, ed. P. French, T. Uehling, and H. Wettstein [Minneapolis: University of Minnesota Press, 1986]) at a meeting of the Eastern Division of the American Philosophical Association. In that paper, Kraut examined an account of love as a *de re*, rather than a *de dicto* attitude; he also analyzed it on the model of naming, as a rigidly designating relation. In a later paper, he proposed an account of love as defined by a series of specific counterfactuals: if the beloved were to die, the lover would grieve, etc.

[2] The feeling or affective tone of psychological attitudes is, as Michael Stocker has argued, a central feature of their motivating force. Often the effects of psychological attitudes are a consequence of what it feels like to have them. See Stocker, *Plural and Conflicting Values* (Oxford: Clarendon Press, 1990).

interactive historical continuity. When love is constant and enduring, it persists despite changes in the friend's traits, even changes in those traits that first awoke the love and that were its central focus. This kind of constancy is assured only at a very general level: it is directed to the same person, extensionally identified, and the attachment remains at roughly the same level of devotion.[3] If Louis's love for Ella when he is sixty is radically different from his attitude at twenty, has his love been constant? Presumably, constancy can be preserved by defining the object and functional roles of his attitude in a sufficiently general manner. But such generality is unlikely to reassure those who wonder if they still love, when little they desire or do has remained the same.

When Louis and Ella are concerned about the continuity of their loves, they are not only interested in constancy, though perhaps some of their concerns could be rephrased in that way. What might concern Ella is whether it is she who influences or affects the character of Louis's love and whether his delight in her ramifies to affect other things about him. When Ella does not want Louis to love her as Don Juan might have loved Elvira, her concern for his fidelity might be a way of expressing her concern for whether his delight focuses on her rather than on his dazzling gifts as a lover. She wants his speeches, his charming attentions, and his deftly winning ways to be not only directed *at* and *to* her, but to take their tenor and form from his delighted recognition of what is central to her. It is not enough that he gets the color of her eyes right, when he gets to that part of the serenade describing their enchantment. Nor is Ella's worry laid to rest by being assured of his fidelity, assured that Louis is no Don Juan, ranging over variables for his joys as a connoisseur of the subtle and interesting differences between women and their ever so wonderful effects on him. For whatever good such assurance might do her, Ella could be convinced that if she were to die, or if they were to have an irreconcilable falling out, Louis would feel lost, mourn, and only gradually be healed enough to love someone else. But both she and her successor Gloria might be aggrieved that Louis always brings the same love, a love that is contained within *his* biography, to be given as a gift. Presumably Gloria does not want to inherit Louis's love for Ella; she wants Louis to love her in a wholly different way, defined by the two of them. This is a complex and compounded hope: that Louis's love will be formed by his perceiving—his accurately perceiving—the gradual changes in her, and in his responses being appropriately formed by those changes. If

---

[3] The analysis of the constancy of love rests on an account of the criteria for personal identity, as well as the criterion for the identity of psychological attitudes whose functional roles change over time.

Ella and Gloria love Louis, they want the changes they effect in him to be consonant and suitable to him as well as to them, conducing to his flourishing as well as theirs. It is because they want their love to conduce to his flourishing that it is important that they see him accurately and that their interactive responses to him be appropriate.

There is a kind of love—and for some it may be the only kind that qualifies as true love—that is historical precisely because it does not (oh so wonderfully) rigidly designate its object. The details of such love change with every change in the lover and the friend. Such a love might be called *dynamically permeable*. It is permeable in that the lover is changed by loving and changed by truthful perception of the friend. Permeability rejects being obtuse to change as an easy way of assuring constancy. It is dynamic in that every change generates new changes, both in the lover and in interactions with the friend. Having been transformed by loving, the lover perceives the friend in a new way and loves in a new way. Dynamism rejects the regionalization of love as an easy way of assuring constancy: the changes produced by such love tend to ramify through a person's character, without being limited to the areas that first directly were the focus of the lover's attention.

To see how this works out, let's gossip a bit about Ella, Louis, and Gloria. Louis's love for Ella began with his enchantment at her crisp way of playing Scarlatti, the unsentimental lyricism of her interpretation of Schubert, her appreciation of Orwell's journalism. After a while, he found that he was enchanted by traits he'd never noticed or admired in anyone else: the sequence of her moods, the particular way she had of sitting still, head bent when she listened to music. He came to love those traits in her, or her in those traits—he could hardly tell which. He came to appreciate such traits in others because her having them had delighted him. And he changed too, not necessarily in imitation of her, but because of her. An acute observer could discern changes in Louis that had their origins and explanation in his love of Ella, changes that were deeper than those that arose from his desire to please her. Some of these changes might conflict with, and threaten, other long-standing traits. If Louis's interest in Ella brings an interest in medieval music, it brings him into new company as well. The ramified consequences of his new interests are likely to interfere with his Friday night jam sessions with his old friends in the hard rock group. Either his responses to Ella ramify, and he acquires a new taste in companions, or he attempts to regionalize the changes that Ella effects on him. Both alternatives have significant consequences on them, and on him. If his dynamic interactions do not ramify, there will be conflicts between his pre-Ella and his post-Ella self. But if they do ramify, his own psychological continuity is loosened by his being formed and reformed by each new friendship. (Of course, such problems are often solved by Louis and Ella sharing important parts of their lives, partners in common enterprises. Sharing their lives and activities assures their both being formed by a common world as well as by each other.) If Louis and Ella are wise, they are careful to avoid the extremes of both regionalization and ramification. Fortunately, this is not wholly a matter of insight and foresight: a person's previous traits resist transformation. If Louis truly interacts with Ella, he cannot become a person formed by and designed to suit her fantasies.

We shall return to the difficulties of regionalization and ramification, the difficulties of abstract constancy and hypersensitivity. For the moment, let us suppose that in this idyllic fairy tale, Louis came to realize that he would continue to love Ella even if she were to lose those traits that first drew him to her and that were still the focus of his joy in her. Even if someone else played Scarlatti more brilliantly, Schubert more discerningly, and had even more trenchant views on the relation between Orwell and Brecht, he would not transfer his love. This does not mean that he would see or love Ella *de re,* whatever that might mean. Nor does it mean that the character of his devotion would remain unchanged by whatever changes might occur in her. He'd be lunatic to love her at sixty in just exactly the same way as he had at twenty; and he'd be cruel to love her way of playing Scarlatti if her hands had been mangled in an accident. Nor can his love be analyzed by a set of counterfactuals.[4] If she became Rampal's accompanist, he would. . . . If her mother moved next door, he would. . . . If she became paralyzed, he would. . . . If she declared herself impassioned of a punk-rock-schlock electronic guitar player, he would. . . . If Glorious Gloria, the Paragon of his Dreams, invited him to join her in a trip to Acapulco, he would. . . . If this kind of love could be analyzed in a set of counterfactuals, that set would have to be indefinitely large. For there are an indefinite number of changes that will occur and that will affect Louis if he loves Ella.

This explains why even a true historical love might end in dissolution and separation. That it did end would not prove that it had not existed, or that either its permeability or its dynamism were defective. On the contrary, it might be just these that establish—if it is at all sensible to speak of demonstration in this area—that it was indeed Ella that Louis loved, and that he did indeed love rather than swoon. But we have come to a strange outcome. The internal momentum of their interaction—for instance, the consequences of its ramification or its regionalization—might lead to its dissolution. And this might comfort

---

[4] See Kraut, "Love *De Re.*"

them both: if they parted, it was because they had truly affected one another, and not because Louis's love had accidentally lost its rigidity or acquired a new direction, however slowly or grievously. In such cases, what marks theirs as a historical love that could not endure (though it might have remained constant over appropriate counterfactuals) is not that it was a love *de re* that got transferred to another *rem,* or that their resistance to transference or substitution was expressed by a suitable period of mourning. What marked it as historical was that they had both been permanently transformed by having loved just *that* person. In short, such love is not only individuated by its objects; more signifi-cantly, the lovers are individuated by their love. Louis's subsequent history, his new loves, joys, indignations, the details of his continuing individuation—even his love of Gloria—are marked by his having loved Ella. Both the continuity of their love, and its eventual rupture, arose from their interaction.

That dynamic permeability can lead to dissolution should not impel lovers to assure the continuity of their love by preferring constancy assured by rigid nonpermeability. If historical love runs the danger of phasing itself out, constant, rigid, nonpermeable love also has its dan-gers. If Louis's love is fixed only by his own character, its active expres-sion may not respond to Ella's needs, even though he may be, in an abstract way, supportive. When Ella worries about the constancy of Louis's love, she may be expressing her sense of her vulnerability in the world, the ways that she has come to need and to depend on him for her thriving.[5] Besides expressing a fear of being harmed, a desire for constancy can itself sometimes be harmful: Ella's fears about Louis's constancy might betray a self-fulfilling sense of dependency. She may have come to be so dependent on the responsive sensitivity of Louis's attunement to her, as a supporting force in her thriving, that she has diminished herself, perhaps even muted the very things that Louis originally admired in her. And Louis, initially charmed by Ella's need of him, may for his part have colluded in her dependency. On the one hand, constancy assured by dynamic permeability does not always au-tomatically work to the benefit of lovers: insight and foresight (of a sort that is, unfortunately, acquired only through experience, and even then, only rarely) is required to direct and to prune the modifications that dynamic permeability fosters. Without the tempering of sound good sense, dynamic permeability might simply produce a severe case of *folie à deux.* If Ella knows herself to be affected by the ways Louis perceives her, if her sense of herself—and, so, in a way, the self she

[5] See my "Jealousy, Attention, and Loss," chapter 7, *Mind in Action* (Boston: Beacon Press, 1988).

becomes—is in part constituted by the way Louis sees her, she wants more than that Louis's love be historical and dynamically permeable. On the other hand, if she hopes to assure continuity by constant rigidity, she may find Louis's love to be a conserving, conservative prison, binding her to continue as the person Louis originally loved or chooses to see in her. Both those who want the sort of sensitivity assured by dynamic permeability and those who want the sort of security assured by a rather more rigid constancy want their friends to be wise, wiser than either a rock or a sensitive chameleon with a skin of litmus paper can be.[6]

It might be useful to ask why we want all this from our loves. There are two reasons, both obvious, both also sobering. Those who are concerned about the constancy and historicity of love are not necessarily self-important or self-obsessed; they suffer the diseases of the time. It is after all rather remarkable that an attitude and an activity that begins in delight, that carries a desire to share the activities of life, and that brings an active wish for well-being should so quickly move to a concern about continuity. The first reason that contemporary love focuses on constancy is that we sense ourselves fragile, vulnerable in the world. In being aware of our vulnerability, we recognize that among the harms that can befall us are those that endanger or erode just those traits for which we are loved. Because those who delight in us seem to vanquish our sense of vulnerability, we think of them as among our strongest protections in the world. And because lovers characteristically want the flourishing of their friends, they often are actively and objectively central to their thriving. Because the continuity of protective devotion is not automatically assured by the permanent individuating effects of interaction, we want to be loved for ourselves alone rather for our most lovable traits, traits we realize we may lose. Not surprisingly, the idea of individuality and the sense of vulnerability are closely associated. Those who concentrate on the sense of invulnerability that loving delight can sometimes bring, and on the objective protections that devoted lovers often assure, might want constancy and think of nonpermeable rigidity instead of historicity as the best way to achieve it. (The pathological form of this attitude is an attempt to control and to bind the friend.)

The second reason we want continuity is that we are aware of being constituted by the perceptions of others, particularly by the perceptions of those who love or hate us, rejoice in us, fear or admire us. We come to think of ourselves as we perceive they see us. For that reason, it

---

[6] But friends who are not equally wise also have special problems. Perhaps this is why Aristotle thought true friendship could only exist among *phronimoi*.

is important to us that our enemies and lovers—the objects of psychological attitudes—perceive us aright, sensitive to the changes in us. Because we crystallize around what they focus, it is important that they continue to love or hate us for what we are—for what conduces to our thriving—rather than for what we were or what they need us to be. (The pathological form of this attitude is failure of integrity, the readiness to abandon parts of oneself.)

Not all lovers want all this Proustian-Jamesian sensibility from their loves. If Ella is strongly autonomous, so that the details of Louis's love for her do not affect the person she becomes, if his perceptions of her do not further individuate her, she may not care whether Louis's love is historical: appropriate, not-too-rigid constancy may be all she wants, and indeed all she prefers. Ella might be the sort of person who finds an acutely historical love too demanding and time-consuming, preventing her from getting on with other things to which she wants to attend. It is just this sort of difference about preferences for historicity or for mere decent, not-too-rigid general constancy that leads lovers to be baffled by one another's disappointments in what seems to each of them a perfectly adequate fidelity.

A set of observations of prudence seems to follow from this analysis. (1) A friendship between a person who hopes that the constancy of love comes from its historicity and one for whom constancy is a matter of rigidity is likely to lead to deep misunderstanding. But such friends might reach an agreement about asymmetry: one of the friends might want to receive, but be disinclined to give, historical sensitivity; the other might have the appropriate corresponding desire, to give a historical sensitivity but be reassured by a rigid constancy rather than a dynamic permeability. Such a love might be very stable, even though there was considerable asymmetry of understanding between the pair. (2) Although a friendship between two constant, nonhistorical lovers is not likely to lead to misunderstanding, it is also not likely to assure very deep understanding. But both people might prefer to get on with other things in their lives. (3) A friendship between two strongly historical types might phase itself out. It is a difficult empirical question, one that we are not now in any position to answer, whether such differences—differences between a desire for dynamic permeability and a desire for rigidity—are associated with gender or with socioeconomic dependency.

This baroque description of the desire for constancy or continuity of historical psychological attitudes might be thought well replaced by a rather more streamlined Bauhaus approach, a functionalist account of psychological attitudes. They are, we might say, identified by their causal roles, by their etiologies and their effects: that is all that is needed to make sense of the different effects of a preference for rigid constancy or for dynamic permeability. But if we favor Bauhaus functionalism about psychological attitudes, we must accept functionalism everywhere. Not only Louis's love but also his beliefs, his perceptions, hopes, and desires are identified by their functional roles. But the functionalist account will not itself explain why Louis's attitudes play their various typical functional roles. There is, in a way, nothing wrong with functionalism except that it is radically incomplete: it cannot by itself explain why psychological attitudes have their typical—and typically interactive and clustering—roles. (Bauhaus architecture reveals a great deal about how architects solve heating problems; but it does not thereby provide a clear understanding of the needs or even the constitutions of the people who live or work in those buildings.)

Reflecting on why our contemporaries seem to want love to take these forms—why they want their loves to be appropriately interactive and to be enduring—suggests yet another, quite different way that such psychological attitudes are historical. Because the roles that loving friendship play in a person's life vary historically, conceptions of their proper causes and objects and of the behavior that is appropriate to them also change historically. The standard narratives of such attitudes (the usual tales of their dynamic permeability) vary culturally. The story of a dynamic permeable love that I sketched tends to appear quite late and regionally: it arises after Romanticism, after the Industrial Revolution, in a context in which the sense of vulnerability takes quite specific forms. Vulnerable we are, and vulnerable we have always been. But the particular conditions that constitute our sense of our vulnerability varies historically. It takes a particular conception of the course of the life of an isolated individual as something fashioned by that person alone to produce the sense of vulnerability that might seem to make a particular form of love—which after all begins in attentive rejoicing—a protection and a mode of development.

The functional identification of psychological attitudes characterizes their typical causes and effects: to understand why such attitudes as love, indignation, and respect have just those characteristic etiologies and consequences, we need to understand the conceptions of individuality, needs, and vulnerabilities that constitute a typical life. (It is not always needs and concerns that identify the functional roles of psychological attitudes. But because needs and concerns seem to be the primary focus of current theoretical and practical preoccupations, I'll concentrate on them, without being committed to the general view that the functions of psychological attitudes are always defined by needs.) The vicissitudes from which we need protection vary historically: they vary with the sorts of dangers and fortunes that typically arise, with a person's class and condition, with conceptions of individuality.[7] As our conceptions of individuality change, our vulnerabilities change; as our vulnerabilities change, our needs change; as our needs change, our activities take distinctively different forms; as our activities take characteristically different forms, so do our psychological attitudes.

A short and absurdly superficial sketch of the history of changes in the conception of love may help to make this more plausible. Platonic *eros* is a cosmological as well as a psychological force: it has one proper cause and one proper object—the Beautiful Good—that draws us to it. Acting within us as well as on us, it provides the energy and direction of all we do. Although *eros* has nothing to do with individuality or vulnerability—and indeed is meant to transcend particular individuals—it is the principle that assures our real well-being. Aristotle's account of *philia* as a relation among the virtuous, sharing the activities of life together, each actively wishing the other well and seeing his own virtues mirrored in his friend, is hardly recognizable as the ancestor of our notion of loving friendship. The role of loving friendship in that world was radically different from its role for us. Perhaps because family rather than friends provided the primary protections against vulnerability, the philosophical problems concerning *philia* were, for the Greeks, questions about whether friends are primarily like-minded or complementary and whether it is better (more beneficial) to love than to receive love. Christian preoccupations with *eros, philia, caritas,* and *agapē* reflect still different conceptions of individuality. When it is God rather than kin who determines and secures the shape of a life, the primary questions about the fidelity of love are whether it conforms to divine intention, whether it is modeled after Christ's love. Renaissance *amor* brings yet other transformation: it is the descendant of Platonic *eros,* the active energy that moves a person to the realization of excellence. The love of Glory, of the City, of a Lady or Muse are simultaneously passions and the very springs of action. Because the object draws the person toward it, *amor* is classified as a passion, a passive condition. Yet the lover's nature is perfected and fulfilled by *amor* and by the active desires that it engenders. The central question becomes, What is the relation between this one primary motivational force and the many various desires that follow from it and that are its expression? Hobbes transforms *eros* and *amor* into particular desires: the desire for the realization of the Good becomes a desire for the objects and actions that promote self-preservation and self-interest. Following Hobbes, Rousseau makes an individual's self-love the source of all his desires. But self-love has a proper and a corrupt form. *Amour*

[7] See my "Characters, Persons, Selves, Individuals," chapter 4, *Mind in Action.*

de soi is an unselfconscious, noncomparative sense of one's own well-being in healthful activity; by contrast, *amour propre* is comparative and depends on a perception of the estimation of others. (Rousseau would regard the story of Louis and Ellas as a story of the fallen condition, generated by *amour propre* rather than healthful *amour de soi*.) Against this historical background, Freud's account of libidinal *eros* as the basic energetic principle, whose social formation and direction provide the vicissitudes of an individual's psychological history, no longer seems startling.

Now what does all this mean about the rationality of such psychological attitudes?[8] Those who would like to make emotional and psychological attitudes respectable as appropriate sources of action want to assure that their corrigibility and redirection take the same form as the corrigibility of beliefs. To rescue such attitudes from the seething cauldron of the irrational, they attempt to show that psychological attitudes can be rationally reconstructed on the model of the structure of propositional or intellectual attitudes. But this philosophical reconstruction cannot—nor was it ever intended to—assure that the corrigibility of the propositional content of a psychological attitude is sufficient to secure its psychological appropriateness. Presumably we want psychological attitudes to be corrigible because we want them to serve us well, to conduce to our thriving. Certainly psychological attitudes that can be propositionalized are at least in principle capable of being evaluated for their truth value; and certainly such evaluations are essential to intellectual corrigibility. But correcting the cognitive or intentional core of a psychological attitude isn't the only way of making it more appropriate; and truth isn't the only measure of the appropriateness of a psychological attitude. An emphasis on rational corrigibility does not provide an adequate account of the functional appropriateness of psychological attitudes.

It might be helpful to take an indirect approach to the analysis of the connection between the ability of psychological attitudes to be rationalized and their being well formed to conduce to thriving. In principle at any rate, propositional attitudes differ from psychological attitudes in being affected only by changes in a person's relation to evidence and

[8] The first version of this paper was expanded and presented to a colloquium on the emotions sponsored by La Maison des Sciences de l'Homme, 23-25 March 1984. Because organizers of that conference asked participants to address issues concerning the rationality of the emotions, I argued that evaluating psychological attitudes for their rationality is not a particularly perspicuous way of evaluating their appropriateness, their utility, or their soundness. See "Varieties of Rationality, Varieties of Emotions" (*Social Science Information* 24, ed. E. Almasy and A. Rocha-Perazzo [London: Sage, 1985]). But in truth, I think that we should focus on conditions for the functional adaptivity, rather than on those for the narrow rationality, of these attitudes.

other epistemically relevant factors. They are not (or should not be) affected by changes in one's character—by whether, for example, one is depressed or elated, angry or affectionate. But some intellectual or propositional attitudes may be historical and permeable in the same way that hate, fear, and admiration can be, and some psychological attitudes can be intellectualized, functioning as if they were epistemic attitudes, generated and corrigible by true beliefs.

Truth-oriented epistemic attitudes and adaptation-oriented psychological attitudes cannot be sharply and neatly distinguished from one another. Epistemic attitudes whose propositional contents remain unaffected by psychological attitudes do not form a class which is typically distinguishable from the class of dynamically permeable psychological attitudes. There are some people who love constantly and rigidly, nonhistorically. The functional role of their love is intellectualized, assimilable to the functional role of propositional attitudes, in that the intentional object of their attitudes is nonpermeable. But there are also people who believe, doubt, and think in a dynamically permeable way. Their cognitive propositional attitudes are psychologized: their thinking, doubting, believing is affected by their psychology, by their character traits, moods, and desires. Even the propositional contents of their epistemic attitudes are dynamically responsive to the nonepistemic features of their attitudes. Psychological associations (puns, visual associations, memories) connected with the cognitive or propositional content of their attitudes affect their propositional attitudes. They do not stand in the same epistemistic relation to someone they dislike as they stand to those whom they like: they cannot hear what that person says in the same way that they would hear just those words from someone they like. They cannot think about what they fear with the same epistemically sensitive attitude as they take to what does not frighten them. It is more difficult for them to evaluate a core belief about what they fear than it is for them to determine the truth of a belief about what brings them pride, and both are more difficult for them to evaluate than a belief about what does not directly affect them. Not only the system of beliefs, but they themselves are changed by their doubts, distrusts, loves. For such people, thinking is, as one might say, psychological, affected by moods, by likes and dislikes.

One might object that this sort of Proustian differentiation of types of believers and lovers does not affect the basic point, that at least knowledge is not psychologically dynamically permeable. Propositional attitudes that have been formed by idiosyncratic associations rather than by their epistemic relation to their propositional contents are disqualified as knowledge claims. However true or appropriate they may be, beliefs about acquaintances that are formed or affected by

likes and dislikes are not rational. Still, even if the conditions for
knowledge guarantee its immunity to epistemically irrelevant psychological attitudes, the beneficial functioning of such attitudes is not
thereby necessarily best assured by their rational corrigibility. Though
a propositional attitude becomes epistemically suspect when it is
formed by a person's psychological condition (fears, elation, or melancholy), propositionalizing or intellectualizing psychological attitudes
need not be the best way to assure sanity and soundness.

What is it then that we want, when we want psychological attitudes to
be rational? There is often no one whose inferences are more logical,
more formally impeccable, and often there is no one more truthful,
than the local lunatic. It is because his impeccable and exemplary
truth-preserving inferences do not serve him in the right way that the
local lunatic is in trouble. No particular additional truth or inference
can help him. His problem is that his rationality cannot guide or form
what he does because it is not appropriately rooted in his character.
Because we want to avoid the lunatic's troubles, we want more than that
our attitudes be corrigible by considerations of truth and validity. We
also want them to be appropriately formed to serve our thriving.

The direction we take in assuring the correctness and appropriateness of psychological attitudes may vary, as we focus primarily on their
correction or on their formation. If we concentrate on avoiding the
harms of malformation, we emphasize rational corrigibility. We are
then likely to favor propositionalizing the contents of our psychological
attitudes. On the assumption that we at least attempt to free ourselves
of attitudes clustered around false beliefs, we attempt to secure the
appropriateness of psychological attitudes by assimilating them as
closely as we can to propositional attitudes oriented to truth. If, however, we concentrate on developing and forming appropriate psychological attitudes, we emphasize their historicity, attempting to discover
the conditions under which dynamic permeability conduces to flourishing.

Rather than assimilating appropriateness and thriving to rationality,
construed as preserving truth through inferential sequences, we might
construe rationality as itself partially constituted by what serves us well.
If the difference between the lunatic and the wise person is a difference in their rationality, then rationality has acquired a substantive as
well as a formal condition. If rationality is understood to serve thriving, the rationality of a person of practical wisdom is as much a function of her character—her having appropriate habits arising from
well-formed perceptions and desires—as it is from her drawing the
right inferences from the right premises. What makes a person rational is not only the logically impeccable character of her reasoning, but

what she knows and how wisely her knowledge affects the fine attunement of her actions. Rationality serves the wise person by enabling her to do the right thing at the right time in the right way; it is this that keeps her truth-telling and valid inferences from being inconsequential, inappropriate, blind, stubborn, or silly.

How does any of this help Louis and Ella determine what they require from their psychological attitudes, if those attitudes are to conduce to their thriving? Certainly, if their interactions are to be beneficial, they had better perceive one another accurately. To avoid their responses being formed by mere perceptions of the moment, to avoid the *folie à deux* problem, it is also important that their attunement be appropriate. But how is that to be determined? As we saw, what conduces to the continuity of their love might serve neither of them well, and what conduces to Louis's developing and thriving need not serve the interactive harmony between him and Ella. Although the historicity of their attitudes—their attunement—initially seemed to promise the appropriateness of their responses, there can be difficulties in that promise being fulfilled. The beneficial functions of psychological attitudes seem no more assured by their historicity than by their ability to be rationalized.

Standardly, but not necessarily, rationality, appropriateness, and thriving are interwoven. It is the dream of rational social politics that in the long run these converge even if they cannot coincide. Of course these three conditions can vary independently: the lunatic shows that rationality does not assure appropriateness; the dangers of *folie à deux* show that adaptability and attunement do not assure thriving. Still, such counterexamples do not undermine the presumptive interconnections: rationality (as defined by truthfulness supported by validity) is a central guide to appropriateness, and appropriateness a central guide to flourishing. The separation of rationality from appropriateness produces lunacy; the separation of adaptability from appropriateness produces unhappiness.

Still, how have we spoken to Louis and Ella? It would be a mistake to think we've left them in a sound as well as a safe place. Even if they are assured of the connection between rationality, appropriateness, and thriving, they have yet to discover just what these require of them in particular situations. How dynamically permeable should Louis be without endangering his integrity or joining Ella in a case of *folie à deux*? How ramified or regionalized should his responses be? What *does* rationality require? What *would* constitute thriving? How are the thriving of Louis, Ella, Louis-and-Ella to be appropriately weighted when they seem to go in different directions?

We've left them just where they were: in the continuous, delicate, and delicious balancing acts of their lives. But this is just exactly where we should leave them. It is only the details of their particular situation that can determine what would be rational, what would be appropriate, what would constitute (whose?) thriving. No general philosophical conclusion about the presumptive connections between rationality, appropriateness, and thriving can possibly help them determine just what corrections rationality recommends or requires as appropriate to their condition. It can't even help them determine whether their sensitivities are sound or pathological, insufficient or excessive, let alone whether they should ramify or regionalize their responses to one another, to balance integrity with continuity in such a way as to conduce to thriving. The confluence of rationality, appropriateness, and thriving cannot help them to determine the directions in which rationality or appropriateness or even thriving—taken singly or coordinately—lie. And that is as it should be. Our task cannot be to resolve but only to understand the quandaries of Louis and Ella. Since their condition and its problems are historical, that is, particular, their solutions must be particular.

PART II

FRIENDSHIP
AND ETHICS

[5]

Aristotle on the Shared Life

Nancy Sherman

To begin with, we must set down some definitional points. Friendship (*philia*), Aristotle stipulates, is the mutually acknowledged and recipro-cal exchange of goodwill and affection that exists among individuals who share an interest in each other on the basis of virtue, pleasure, or utility (*NE* 8. 2). In addition to voluntary associations of this sort, Aristotle also includes among friendships the non-chosen relations of affection and care that exist among family members and fellow citizens (cf. *NE* 8.9; 8.12, 9.6). The term is thus used quite broadly, though Aristotle's primary focus, and mine as well, is on the paradigmatic case of virtue friendship (or what I shall sometimes call, following Cooper, 'character friendship', in order to remind us that such friendships need not be of *perfectly* virtuous agents).[1] To the degree to which the friendship of parent and child cultivates the capacities for character friendship, it too will be of interest in my account.

This said, let us try to understand the way in which friends figure in Aristotle's general scheme of goods. In *NE* 1. 8 Aristotle argues that virtue, as a good, is alone insufficient for happiness, and requires in addition certain external goods. The argument is roughly this: happi-ness, conceived of as doing well and living well (1098b21), requires not merely ethical (and intellectual) virtues, but activities which manifest these excellences. With regard to ethical virtue, ends of character must be realized and implemented in action (1099a1–6). But for this, the

[1] John Cooper, 'Aristotle on Friendship', in A. O. Rorty (ed.), *Essays on Aristotle's Ethics* (University of California Press, 1980), 307–8; Aristotle himself suggests the term at *NE* 1164a12, 1165b8–9, *EE* 1241a10, 1242b36.

proper resources and opportunities must be at hand. Among these
resources or external goods are friends:

> Yet evidently, as we said, happiness requires in addition external goods;
> for it is impossible or not easy to act finely without resources. For an
> individual performs many actions through the use of instruments,
> through friends, wealth, and political office. And the lack of other goods
> spoils one's happiness, such as fine birth, good children, and beauty. For
> one would hardly be happy if one were thoroughly ugly, or born of low
> birth, or solitary and childless; and perhaps even less so, if one's children
> or friends were thoroughly bad, or if they were good but died. (1099a31–
> b6)

This passage suggests that friends will not only be instrumental to
happiness (as enabling conditions of action), but also intrinsic parts of
it. Aristotle thus seems to have in mind two classes of external goods
(which he recapitulates at 1099b27): those which are instruments of
happiness, i.e. those things which are by nature co-operative and useful as tools (1099b27), and those which are not merely instrumental,
but which are necessary and intrinsic parts of happiness, i.e. 'belong
necessarily' (*huparchein anagkaion*, 1099b27), and the lack of which mars
happiness (1099b2).[2] Friends figure in the lists of both types of external goods. The first class of goods is fairly straight forward. Friends
may be instruments and tools in the sense in which money and political
connection are. They provide us with the means for the promotion of
particular ends. As we have said, we depend upon the aid and support
of friends for accomplishing ends we cannot realize on our own
(1112b11, b28). More broadly, Aristotle says in his initial survey of *ta
endoxa*, we need friends in all circumstances and times of life: in times
of prosperity as beneficiaries, in times of hardship as refuge, in our
youth as tutors, in our old age for care and support, and in our prime
for doing fine actions. Friends thus support our well-being both as co-
partners in our agency and as objects of our virtuous actions. They
provide us with opportunities for virtuous action and sentiment un-
available to the solitary or childless (1155a5–15; cf. 1169b11–15).[3]

The way in which friends figure in the second class of goods, however, is more difficult to grasp. For while friendship has intrinsic worth

[2] My remarks here are indebted to T. H. Irwin's classification of the two types of
external goods in 'Permanent Happiness: Aristotle and Solon' in Julia Annas (ed.), *Oxford
Studies in Ancient Philosophy*, 3 (Oxford University Press, 1985), 89–124.

[3] For a related discussion of the way in which friends figure as external goods, see John
M. Cooper, 'Aristotle on the Goods of Fortune', *Philosophical Review*, 94 (1985), 173–96,
and Martha Nussbaum, *The Fragility of Goodness: Luck and Rational Self-Sufficiency in Greek
Ethical Thought: The Tragic Poets, Plato, and Aristotle* (Cambridge University Press, 1986),
ch. 12.

(certainly Aristotle takes the love parents show towards children to be an end in its own right (*MM* 1211b1–2), and friendship in general 'choice-worthy for its own sake', whatever other benefits it yields (*NE* 1155a29–32, 1159a27)), it does so not in the sense of having some isolated value, like that of an 'adventitious' pleasure (cf. 1169b25–7), which might be added to happiness as one more separate constituent.[4] For there are all sorts of activities in life which we might find intrinsically enjoyable or valuable, but which we would be willing to sacrifice because they play a limited role in our happiness. Thus, I might find backgammon an intrinsically enjoyable activity, but when faced with demands on my time I give it up because I find it insufficiently important or enriching of other activities I value. I can abandon it or replace it without seriously marring my happiness. The intrinsic worth of friendship, in contrast, is of a much more pervasive sort, providing the very form and mode of life within which an agent can best realize her virtue and achieve happiness. To have intimate friends and good children is to have interwoven in one's life, in a ubiquitous way, persons towards whom and with whom one can most fully and continuously express one's goodness. The friendships are not external conditions of those activities, like money or power. Rather, they are the form virtuous activity takes when it is especially fine and praiseworthy (1155a9, 1159a28–31).

We might say living amongst friends is a general, though substantive, way of specifying the formal criterion of happiness as a mode of activity (*energeia*, 1098a8, 1098a16).[5] Just as it would be absurd to call a person happy who slept away his life (1099a1–6), so too it would be absurd to think that the person who lacked friends could be happy (1155a5–6, 1169b8–10, 1169b16–17). These *endoxa* seem to be deeply rooted in our nature, and not unrelated to each other, as Aristotle goes on to argue. For if sustained excellent activity is a basic aspect of our happiness, then a most basic way of sustaining and making more continuous our activity is through a life in companionship with others (1170a5–9; cf. 1177a22). Even when the activity is contemplation, the pursuit is better sustained when it is a co-operative enterprise (1177a34).

In what follows I want to pursue this notion of friendship as structuring the good life and suggest that it is because of this role that Aristotle calls friends the 'greatest' and 'most necessary' of external

---

[4] R. A. Gauthier and J. Y. Jolif imply something like the view I criticize in their account of the second class of external goods: *L' Éthique à Nicomaque*, 2, 1 (Publications Universitaires de Louvain, 1970), 71.

[5] Aristotle also suggests (at 1097b7–12) that it is a substantive way of interpreting the self-sufficiency criterion of *NE* 1.7. I discuss this further below.

goods (*NE* 1169b10, 1154a4), without whom we would not choose to live 'even if we had all other goods' (1155a5–6, cf. 1169b16–17). As suggested, friendship creates a context or arena for the expression of virtue, and ultimately for happiness. More strongly, it extends and redefines the boundaries of the good life in such a way that my happiness or complete good comes to include the happiness of significant others. Happiness or good living is thus ascribable to me, not as an isolated individual, but as a self extended, so to speak, by friends.

Happiness as Including the Happiness of Others

The kernel of this is in Aristotle's remarks in *NE* 1.7 regarding the self-sufficiency of good living. Self-sufficiency is a criterion of the good life entailing that a life is 'lacking in nothing', there being no other good which when added to it would make that life more desirable (1097b15–22). But since friends are among the goods which make a life self-sufficient, self-sufficiency is relational and the good life a life dependent upon and interwoven with others:

> By self-sufficient we do not mean for a solitary individual, for one living a life alone, but for parents, children, and wife, and in general for all friends and fellow citizens since a human being is by nature political and social. (1097b9–11; cf. 1169b18–19)

For human beings, then, the self-sufficient life is a life larger than that of one individual. So, the *Magna Moralia* reminds us, 'we are not investigating the self-sufficiency of a god, but of human beings' (1218a8), and the *Eudemian Ethics* explains, 'for our well-being is relational [*kath' heteron*], whereas in the case of a god, he is himself his own well-being' (1245b18–19).

The historical import of Aristotle's position cannot be underestimated. The ideal of an ascetic life was close at hand in Plato's writings and represented the major alternative conception of the self-sufficient good. In *NE* 10. 7–8, Aristotle himself is of course attracted to this conception, apparently arguing there that a life cannot be perfectly happy if it fully ignores a more divine, contemplative ideal. But Aristotle's claim is not that happiness is to be *identified* with the ascetic life. Rather, it is the more modest claim that happiness must *include* the leisure for contemplation, and that the good person must find time for its incomparable rewards. Contemplative excellence does not supplant the more worldly virtues nor take precedence. It must be conjoined with them in a life which remains essentially political and communal.

This differs considerably from the stark portrait of the *Phaedo*. There needy states which require satisfaction from without—such as appetites and affections—are seen as making happiness vulnerable, for they expose it to conditions outside the agent's control. They are prison houses of the soul from which one must be liberated as best one can, if happiness is to be secured against constant lack and deficiency. Though the *Phaedo* does not single out friendship, it is easy to see how it poses such a threat. Friendships, in so far as they depend upon mutual interests and affections, easily dissolve as these interests and affections shift. To form a friendship is in part to expose oneself to this risk. Even if we try to counteract this vulnerability by making constancy a condition of the best sort of friendship (as Aristotle seems to do in the case of virtue friendship, where the constancy of the friendship derives from the stable interest and disposition of each party towards virtue), still constancy can do little to prevent the permanent dissolution of a friendship through death.[6] If anything, the stability of the friendship leaves us least protected against that contingency. For it is when we have lost a lifelong friend or loved one that we truly feel we have lost a part of ourselves and a substantial part of our happiness. Friendship thus makes us vulnerable, and even if constancy is a feature of that friendship, our self-sufficiency remains at best fragile. (In this regard, although Plato requires in the Diotema passage of the *Symposium* that the ascent to the ideal form of life be accompanied by interaction with others, these relations are essentially to be supplanted by a more secure and self-sufficient good whose beauty and goodness can in no way be diminished.)

That Aristotle chooses friendship as a defining feature of the self-sufficient life reflects not only his break with the ascetic goal but his view of happiness as essentially subject to fortune. The fundamental belief in the sociality of human beings is an *endoxa* which cannot be compromised in the specification of happiness.

In *NE* 9.9 and *EE* 7.12 Aristotle again takes up the relation of friendship to self-sufficiency. In *NE* 9.9 he reports the view held by some that the self-sufficient person does not require friends, 'for the things that are good belong to him, and being self-sufficient, he requires nothing further' (1169b5–7). Aristotle's disagreement (1169b22–8 and *EE* 1244b6 ff.) centres on the interpretation of self-sufficiency

---

[6] Aristotle's worry about these problems structures the very way in which he presents the material on friendship. Within the threefold classification of friendship, into friendship based on pleasure, utility, and good character, the former two are *kata sumbebēkos*, accidental, and inferior primarily because they are more transient and less enduring sorts of friendships than those based on the mutual pursuit of virtue (1156a18–1156b24).

and, correspondingly, the characterization of friendship. The solitary contemplator might have minimal requirements for material goods, and so only minimal need for the sorts of friends that can provide such services. But, Aristotle argues, without friends such an agent could never be self-sufficient with regard to fine activity. The problem with those who claim otherwise is that they fail to conceive of friendship as based on something more than utility or transient pleasures, and self-sufficiency as something correspondingly broader:

> What then does the first party mean, and in what way is it true? Is it that the many identify friends with those who are useful? Of those sorts of friends, indeed the happy person will have no need, since the good things already belong to him; nor will he need friends for pleasure, or only minimally so (for since his life is pleasant, it requires nothing of adventitious pleasure). And having no need for these sorts of friends, he is thought not to need friends. But this is surely not true. (1169b22–8)

The *Eudemian Ethics* amplifies this conclusion: 'This makes it all the clearer that the only real friend is loved not for the sake of utility or benefit, but on account of his virtue' (1244b15).

The upshot of these passages, then, is that while the self-sufficient solitary may not need others as means or instruments for material living (or only minimally so), he will still need others to create jointly a life of virtue. The *Eudemian Ethics* again speaks to this: 'For when we are not in need of something, then we all seek others to share our enjoyment . . . and most of all, we then seek friends who are worthy of living together with us' (1244b18–22). Thus the best sort of friendship provides us with companions with whom we can share goods and interests in a jointly pursued life. This sort of shared happiness constitutes the truly self-sufficient life.

There is considerable further evidence for the claim that friendship entails a weaving of lives together into some shared conception of happiness. Aristotle pursues these issues with some insight in the *Eudemian Ethics*. At 1236b3–6, he argues that the best sort of friendship among relatively virtuous adults (i.e. character friendship) displays not only the acknowledged reciprocation of affection and goodwill, but the acknowledged reciprocation of a choice of one another:

> It is apparent from these things that the primary sort of friendship, that among good persons, requires mutual affection [*antiphilia*] and mutual choice [*antiprohairesis*] with regard to one another . . . This friendship thus only occurs among humans, for they alone are conscious of reasoned choices [*prohaireseis*].

Again, at *EE* 1237a30 ff., he makes a similar point:

If the activity of friendship is a reciprocal choice, accompanied by pleasure, of the acquaintance of one another, it is clear that friendship of the
primary kind is in general a reciprocal choice [*antiprohairesis*] of the things
that are without qualification good and pleasant, because they are good
and pleasant.

The significance of the claim rests on Aristotle's technical term, *prohairesis*. As I have argued elsewhere,[7] a *prohairesis* is a reasoned choice
that is expressive of a character and the overall ends of that character.
The choice of a friend exposes this capacity of practical reason in a
perspicuous way. For in choosing a character friend, we select 'another
self' (*NE* 1170b6–7), who shares a sense of our commitments and ends,
and a sense of what we take to be ultimately 'good and pleasant' in
living. We choose another to be a partner in the joint pursuit of these
ends. In so doing, we choose to arrange our lives around a loyalty to
another, and around a willingness to choose ends and pursuits within
the context of this loyalty.[8] The choice of such a companion, Aristotle
indicates, is not one that is made quickly or easily. It reflects a stable
judgement of another (*to kekrimenon bebaion*, *EE* 1237b11, *krisin orthēn*,
1237b12), and this takes time and trust (1237b13–18). As he says,
'those who become friends without the test of time are not real friends
but only wish to be friends' (1237b17–18).

Indeed, since for Aristotle the real test (*peiran*) of friendship comes
in spending time together (*suzēsai*, 1237b35–7), the specific choices
that are constitutive of the friendship are not so much the initial over-
tures as those that indicate a capacity to share and co-ordinate activities
over an extended period of time. These are the choices that indicate
two lives can be interwoven together into some coherent pattern of
good living.

Significantly, Aristotle does discuss these sorts of choices under the
notion of *homonoia*, literally sameness of mind, or, more idiomatically,
consensus between friends. *Homonoia*, he argues in the *Eudemian Ethics*,
is arriving at the 'same choice' about practical matters (*hē autē prohairesis*), as in the case of civic friendship, where fellow citizens agree
about who should rule and who should be ruled (1241a31–3; cf. *NE*, 9,
6). In the case of intimate friendships, the consensus is not about who
should rule, but about how and what sort of life to live together:

Some have thought friendship to be unanimity of feeling and those who
have such a consensus to be friends. But friendship is not a consensus

---

[7] See 'Character, Planning and Choice in Aristotle', *Review of Metaphysics*, 34 (1985),
83–106 and *The Fabric of Character*, ch. 3.
[8] See *EE* 1214b7 on *prohairesis* as a capacity to arrange life with regard to certain ends.

concerning everything, but a consensus concerning practical matters for the parties involved and concerning those things that contribute to living together [*hosa eis to suzēn suntenei*]. (*EE* 1241a16–18)

The notion of consensus (*homonoia*) can be seen as an extension of Aristotle's notion of reciprocal choice (*antiprohairesis*). In choosing a friend, one chooses to make that person a part of one's life and to arrange one's life with that person's flourishing (as well as one's own) in mind. One takes on, if you like, the project of a shared conception of *eudaimonia*. Through mutual decisions about practical matters, friends continue to affirm that commitment.

Consensus between friends can take various forms. So, for example, two friends come to a mutual decision about how to act fairly and honourably towards another who has wronged them, or about how best to assist a fellow citizen who has come upon hard times. Any happiness or disappointment that follows from these actions belongs to both persons, for the decision so to act was joint and the responsibility is thus shared. This notion of joint deliberation may help us to interpret Aristotle's rather compressed remark that character friends live together, not in the way cattle do, by grazing the same pasture, but 'by sharing in argument and thought' (*koinōnein logōn kai dianoias*, *NE* 1170b11–12).

Equally, consensus may express only a looser agreement about general ends. Two friends may share the conviction that temperance in their personal lives is of the utmost importance, yet each realize that end in a different style and manner. One does it through a scrupulous diet, the other by refusing to take part in frivolous gossip. Their shared commitment is to an end rather than to a specific way of achieving it.

There may nevertheless be a particularly characteristic sort of consensus in friendship. In true friendship, we might say, friends realize shared ends which develop through the friendship and which come to be constitutive of it. Specific common interests are thus a product rather than a precondition of the relationship. Together my friend and I develop a love of Georgian houses, having had no real interest in them earlier. Aristotle's emphasis on developing friendships over time and through a shared history of mutual activity suggests this notion of a common good.[9] But a caveat is in order here. While specific and shared ways of being virtuous will be the product of a friendship, the acquisition of virtuous states of character must, more or less, pre-exist any friendship based on virtue. That is, the agents must choose each other on the basis of a firm and stable character. This is not to deny that through the particular friendship, the commitments of character

[9] I am grateful to Gregory Trianosky for urging me to develop this point.

will deepen and express themselves in ways peculiar to and conditioned by that friendship. So Aristotle insists that the virtuous agent continues to grow, and that friendship itself is the most congenial context for such moral growth (*NE* 1170a11, 1172a10–15, *EE* 1245a15–20; cf. *NE* 1180a1–4); in this way, the notion of a 'firm and stable character' (*NE* 1105a34) does not imply a character that rigidly resists change. Even so, a well-cultivated sense of virtue must be in place from the start, in a way in which the love of Georgian houses need not be.

Friendship may also involve the interweaving of two lives in quite a different way. This can be seen as follows: within a given individual's life, choices (*prohaireseis*) articulate the ends of character in some unified and comprehensive way over time. As we have said, deliberation reflects a sense of planning, and an ability to make choices that best promote not a single end, but a coherent system of ends. Choices of action are made with regard not merely to the parts of good living, but with regard to the whole, and the unity of ends that entails (*NE* 1140a26–8, 1145a1–2).

This model of planning is extended to the shared life of friends. Ends are co-ordinated not merely within lives, but between lives. Thus, just as a particular choice I make is constrained by my wider system of objectives and ends, so too is it constrained by the ends of my friend. So, for example, if a contemplated action of mine precludes a friend from realizing an important goal of hers, then that consideration will figure in my judgement of what is overall best. It may not be an easy matter to determine whose interests should prevail, and as with any decision of the mean, deciding what is right will require giving due consideration to all relevant concerns. But whatever the nature of the solution, the point to be stressed is that what is relevant to the decision goes beyond the *eudaimonia* of a single, isolated individual. The ends of my friend must be taken into account, just as mine must, in the overall assessment of what is to be done. Indeed, the survival of the friendship depends upon our willingness to exhibit loyalty in this way.

These various ways of forming a consensus within friendship fill out Aristotle's more elliptical remarks in the *Eudemian Ethics,* where he says that friends 'wish to share with each other in a joint life [*suzēn*] the end which they are capable of attaining' (1245b8); they pursue together, to the degree to which they can, the best good (*to ariston*) (1245a20–2). This involves not merely sharing space, or even casual discourse (1245a13–15), but sharing activity (*sunergein*, 1245b3) generated through joint study and deliberation. This is the sort of partnership which above all else (*malista*) is included in the final good (1245b4).

We have been focusing on shared happiness as requiring the sharing of general or specific ends, as well as the co-ordination of ends between lives. But there are other nondeliberative aspects of sharing happiness. Simply put, when a friend does well, I feel happy too. Aristotle explains this sort of 'singleness of mind' (*mia psuchē*, *EE* 1240b2, 1240b9–10) through the notions of sympathy and empathy, and argues that these sentiments are heightened the more intimate the friendship. At *NE* 9. 10, he says that the more exclusive the attachment to a friend, the better able I am to minister to that friend's needs and to identify with her joys and sorrows (1171a6 ff.). It may be because of my intimate knowledge of her that I can imagine how *she* feels in a particular situation; or knowing how *I* would feel (or have felt) in that sort of situation, and knowing she is similar to me in certain ways, I can imagine she must feel that way. In the *Eudemian Ethics* Aristotle indicates that friends wish to express not merely sharing of grief (*ou monon sullupeisthai*), but empathy, 'feeling the same pain [*alla kai tēn autēn lupēn*] (for example, when he is thirsty, sharing his thirst), if this were possible, and if not, what is closest to it' (1240a36–9). The qualification suggests that though Hume-like empathy, i.e. coming to feel the same affect may itself be implausible, something like it is none the less desirable, and perhaps the hallmark (or at least, necessary condition) of friendship.[10] That is, in true friendship we want to understand 'from the friend's point of view' what she is going through and how things look to her. Imagining how she must feel ultimately aims at coming to see things from *her* point of view. Thus, it is not that I bypass my imagination, but that it ultimately transports me to her feelings.[11]

There is a related way in which we experience a friend's happiness or sorrow as our own. Accomplishments and failures which are not explicitly our own are none the less, through an extension of self, sources of pride and shame. So Aristotle says in *Rh*. 2. 6: 'And individuals feel shame whenever they have acts or deeds credited to them which bring some disrespect, whether the acts be their own, or those of their ancestors, or those of other persons to whom they bear some close relation' (1385a1–3). Thus, when our children do well, we feel pride in their achievements, and when they do poorly, shame, as if we ourselves had fallen short. It is not that we are responsible for their errors (though as parents we may be), but that through the sense of belonging and attachment we identify with their good. Aristotle thus seems to be suggesting that feelings of shame need not be traced back to actions for which one is oneself responsible: so, for example, I may feel shame for

[10] It was Geoffrey Sayre-McCord who helped me to gain this insight into Aristotle's remarks.

[11] The response to tragedy through pity and fear seems to require something much weaker, namely that we imagine what it would be like for *us*, in our *own* circumstances, to suffer a similar fate (*peri to homoion*). See *Poet*. 1453a4–6, *Rh*. 1385b13–14.

the criminal actions of my sister just in virtue of our relationship, and not because I bear responsibility for her actions or attribute her failings to character traits I share. Whether such feelings of shame are in fact warranted may be a controversial matter, and not one that Aristotle explores carefully.[12]

Friendship and Wider Altruism

I have argued that through friendship an individual's happiness becomes extended to include the happiness of others. To have a friend as 'another self' thus entails a conception of good living that is in some significant way shared. I shall examine shortly the way in which this common pursuit does not jeopardize the separateness of individuals. But first I want to contrast friendship with a wider sense of altruism.

Altruistic sentiments such as goodwill (*eunoia*), kindness (*charis*), and pity (*eleos*) are constitutive of various virtues in Aristotle's scheme, e.g. generosity (*eleutheriotēs*), magnificence (*megaloprepeia*), and magnanimity (*megalopsuchia*). The definition of kindness in *Rh.* 2.7 is useful for our purposes. It is there defined as a willingness to give 'assistance [*hupourgia*] toward someone in need' (1385a18), and 'is great if it is shown towards someone in great need, or in need of what is important or what is difficult to get, or someone who has need in a crisis, or if the helper is the only one or first one or the most important one' (1385a19–21). Accordingly, in acting out of kindness, our sympathy goes out to an individual because of the circumstances, and not because of *who* the individual happens to be. The situation is different in friendship, when we act out of a specific concern for a *particular* person; because it is *that* person who is in need (and not another), what we can do and are willing to do, and what others count on us to do, is often greater (cf. *NE* 1169a18–34).

These remarks might suggest the following objection: that when we act out of kindness rather than friendship, we somehow *overlook* the person who is the object of our goodwill and consider her merely as an occasion for the exercise of our virtue. We might even seem, in a priggish way, to care more for our virtue than for the particular person towards whom it is being expressed.[13] But on Aristotle's view, I act for

[12] Though Aristotle's distinction between shame felt for 'conventional' and 'genuine' faults (*ta pros ton nomon, ta pros alētheian, Rh.* 1384b25) may be of some help. I am grateful here again to Geoffrey Sayre-McCord.

[13] The objection might be answered if we say that I act not for the sake of my virtue, but for the sake of this person *because* of my virtue. That is, my virtue explains why I am motivated to make this person the object of my concern. Cf. Herman, 'Rules, Motives and Helping Actions', 370–71.

the sake of the beneficiary, whether or not I have an enduring or prior attachment to her. Even though in wider cases of altruism the beneficiary is in a sense intersubstitutable with others, this does not diminish my concern for *this person now*. Aristotle makes the point as follows: to be a friend is to wish another well and desire good things for her, 'for her sake and not for your own' (*Rh.* 1380b37; cf. 1381b37). Equally, kindness outside of friendship depends upon offering assistance 'not in return for something, nor for some advantage to the helper himself, but for that of the one helped' (*Rh.* 1385a18–19).[14]

Thus both friendship and goodwill require the noninstrumentality of our beneficence. But friendship goes further in so far as its objects are not easily substituted by others. I may have a well-cultivated sense of altruism or even be a friendly sort of person who treats others with warmth and affection, but the exercise of these virtuous states does not itself secure for me the good of friendship. For that, I have to become attached to a particular person, and another person to me, in a way that displays mutual regard and affection (*NE* 1155b28–1156a5), and commitment to joint activity. Moreover, while virtuous states of character depend upon external conditions for their exercise, the absence of favourable conditions does not necessarily destroy them. But this is not so in the case of friendship. For friendship is more an activity than a state of character, and a virtuous activity, unlike other virtuous activities, that depends upon a specific person, as its external condition.[15] In the absence of that person, there is no friendship.

A Friend as Another But Separate Self

As we said earlier, a virtue friend is 'another self' (*allos autos*), 'another me' (*allos egō*) as Aristotle strikingly puts it in the *Magna Moralia* (1213a13, 1213a24, *NE* 1170b7, *EE* 1245a30). To some modern ears, the notion has a paternalistic ring to it, and suggests a lack of boundaries that adequately delimit the autonomous self. While a Kantian notion of autonomy is clearly alien to Aristotle, I want to suggest, none

[14] The difference for Aristotle between the two cases is not that I treat a friend more for his own sake than I do a stranger, but that when I fail to help a friend, I commit a deeper wrong and show a greater failing of character. As Aristotle says, 'a wrong becomes intensified in being exhibited towards those that are more fully friends, so that it will be a more terrible thing to defraud a friend than a fellow citizen, and more terrible not to help a brother than a stranger, and more terrible to wound a father than anyone else' (*NE* 1160a4–6).

[15] Aristotle does not explicitly say this, leaving it open at 1155a4 as to whether friendship is a virtue or something (e.g. activity) accompanied by virtue. It is also noteworthy that at 1105b22 Aristotle lists *philia* as a passion, but here he seems to have in mind friendly feeling as opposed to friendship.

the less, that the relationship between virtue friends exhibits some mindfulness both of the differences between friends and of their sep- arateness. This entails that such friends promote each other's good in a privileged way (as only another self can), but in a way that is still respectful of the mature rational agency of each. Given the similarity of virtue friends and the exclusiveness of the relationship, each is in a position to know how best to help the other, and how to help in a way that most reassures and pleases. In those cases where decisions are not joint, intimate knowledge of each other's abiding interests puts each in a position to offer counsel and support over the sort of choices that give real shape to each other's lives. Yet within this extended and inter- woven life, the individuals none the less retain their separateness. In this regard, there may be some significance in Aristotle's choice of words at *EE* 1245a35, where he says that a friend is 'a separate self' (*autos diairetos*). But we need to consider further evidence.

Aristotle's notion of self-sacrifice, and what an agent can legitimately forfeit to another, is of some help here. On Aristotle's view, friendship is marked by a level of practical concern and willingness to help that is otherwise uncommon. One comes to count on an intimate friend in a way one cannot count on a stranger or mere acquaintance (*NE* 8.9). Aid is given without even having to ask (*Rh.* 1381b35), and often without a return expected. But what is sacrificed, as Aristotle clearly indicates in *NE* 9.8 (and *MM* 2.13), are external goods, such as money, power, and opportunity (*NE* 1168b15 ff, 1169a20–30); in short, they are the sort of distributable (and scarce) goods one can give away, while still secur- ing for oneself, through that choice, the intrinsic good of fine action. Indeed, what is especially valuable to a self, and the basis for a proper conception of self-love, namely the capacities of practical reason (1168b28–1169a3), are exhibited in the action, so that even when the sacrifice involves dying for a friend, the action will express what is fine.[16] In this sense, Aristotle says, the good man 'seems to assign to himself the greater share in what is fine' (1169b1). The point is not that his desire to help is voided when he himself cannot be the agent (see 1169a33–4); that sort of priggish sense of self is not part of his notion of self-love. Rather, it is that when his agency *is* required, and he acts, his action secures for him the finest sort of good. Even when the choice literally ends in the death of reason, the sacrifice will not compromise his sense of self.

Implicit in this regard for one's own rational agency is a reciprocal regard for the friend. In so far as a friend is another self, in helping a

---

[16] For the proper qualifications of Aristotle's claim that the self is to be identified with reason, see *The Fabric of Character*, ch. 3, sect. 6, and nn. 48 and 57. On the sacrifice of life for the sake of the fine, see 1117b1–20.

friend an individual cannot pre-empt that friend's rational agency, or desire to make choices that will violate his agency. For it is just because that other individual values virtue and practical reason that he has been chosen as a friend and someone with whom a life can be spent. They are virtue friends, in part, because they are capable of living in relation to one another in a way that does not make one the slave of the other.[17] The result is that such individuals promote each other's interests only in certain ways—not by directly making choices for each other (unless these are jointly deliberated choices or *homonoia*), but by giving each greater opportunities for choice, and greater means for the realization of ends. These means may include scarce (*perimachēta*) material resources, as Aristotle suggests here, but they may also include sought for psychological goods, such as support and esteem and confidence in our endeavours. Aristotle remarks in the *Rhetoric* that it is characteristic of friends 'to praise the good qualities we possess, and especially those which we fear might not in fact belong to us' (1381a35–b1, 1381b10–14). We give friends support and confidence in these ways, without minimizing their separateness.

There is further evidence for the separateness of selves within character friendship. We can take up the issue by considering the possibility of virtuous characters having a diversity of ideals. On Aristotle's view, having a virtuous character implies possessing all the virtues, or complete virtue (*NE* 1145a1–2, 1098a17–18).[18] For the virtues imply one another and are inseparable. The pattern of unified virtues might, however, be different in different persons. So one individual might be especially honest, this virtue seeming to gain pre-eminence over others, while another individual might be particularly generous, her interactions being marked, above all, by a sense of bounty. Each individual has all the other virtues, and exercises them appropriately, as external conditions allow. But as a result of nature, development, and resources, certain virtues have gained greater expression and prominence in each individual's life. I believe this is consistent with Aristotle's notion of the unity of the virtues. My claim is not that the honest person *overlooks* the requirements of the other virtues (even though she *is* selective); it is rather that if we were to characterize her decency or goodness, her

---

[17] Here I draw on the implication of Aristotle's remarks at 1124b31 that the magnanimous person 'cannot live in relation to another, except a friend. For that would be slavish.' I have profited from T. H. Irwin's notes on this passage; see his translation of the *Nicomachean Ethics* (Hackett, 1985), 327.

[18] Aristotle's remarks can be understood as claiming that the virtues are in principle consistent, or, more strongly, that in actual cases of action, they can never contingently conflict. I understand him to be making the first, weaker claim.

honesty would deserve special mention. It mediates her goodness in a special way.[19]

Now individuals that come together as character friends might be similar yet different in the above sense that while they share virtue as an overall end, they often express it in ways that are distinct yet complementary. They are not mere look-alikes of one another. Aristotle suggests this thought at *EE*, 7. 12. In assessing the truth of the claim that a friend is another self, he comments:

> But the characteristics of a particular individual may be scattered, and it is difficult for all to be realized in one individual. For although by nature a friend is what is most similar, one individual may resemble his friend in body, one in character [*psuchē*], or one in one part of the body or character, and another in another. (1245a30–4)

Here Aristotle implies that friends bear varying degrees of similarity to each other. And this may in fact be important to the self-realization of each within the friendship. For if my friend has virtue *A* to a higher degree than I do, then I should want to strive to perfect that virtue to a greater degree in myself. I should want to emulate the good qualities he has and come to realize them in myself. In Aristotle's concluding remarks on friendship in *NE* 9 he alludes to precisely these differences and their role in adult ethical development:

> The friendship of good persons is good, being increased by their companionship; and they are thought to become better too by their activities and by improving each other; for from each other they take the mould of characteristics they approve. (1172a10–15)

The supposition is that character friends will realize to a different degree (and in a different manner) particular virtues. Each is inspired to develop himself more completely as he sees admirable qualities, not fully realized in himself, manifest in another whom he esteems. Remarks Aristotle makes about the notion of emulation in the *Rhetoric* are pertinent here. Emulation, he says, is felt most intensely 'before those whose nature is like our own and who have good things that are highly valued and are possible for us to achieve' (1388a31–2). Character

---

[19] Aristotle's remarks at *Pol.* 1329a9 ff., in which he suggests that different character traits gain pre-eminence at different times in an individual's life, might give limited support here. For a discussion of the sort of character who does *overlook* the more complete requirements of virtue, see my remarks on magnanimity in 'Common Sense and Uncommon Virtue', in *Midwest Studies in Philosophy*, 13 (University of Notre Dame Press, 1988).

friends, as extended yet different selves, are eminently suited as models to be emulated.

There are also implications for Aristotle's pivotal claim that through character friendships the parties gain in self-knowledge. In *NE* 9. 9, *EE* 7. 12, and *MM* 2. 15, Aristotle argues that a fundamental reason for including friendship within the happy life is that it enhances one's own awareness and understanding of one's agency and activities. The arguments in these texts are notoriously difficult (especially those in the *Nicomachean Ethics*), but the essential idea is something like this:[20] the good life requires excellent activity (1098a8), but since perception or understanding is a defining characteristic of human life (1170a16), to live that life in the fullest sense (*kuriōs*) requires self-perception of that activity (1170a17–19). Moreover, the pleasure that is intrinsic to that excellent activity (and essential for the good life) is enhanced through the pleasure and good of an awareness of it (1170b1–3). Friends are part of such a life in so far as through an awareness of their activities we see, in the striking words of the *Magna Moralia*, 'another me' (*heteros egō*) reflected, as it were, through 'a mirror' (1213a22–4). We learn about ourselves by having another self before us whose similar actions and traits we can study from a more detached and objective point of view: 'We can study a neighbour better than ourselves and his actions better than our own' (*NE* 1169b33–5). For in our own case, passion or favour at times blind our judgement (*MM* 1213a16–20). Through another just like us, yet numerically distinct, we can see ourselves from a point of view outside ourselves, and so at a distance.

But if another self need not be exactly similar, then self-knowledge might involve contrasting oneself with another, and considering how another would have felt or acted in the same circumstances given that individual's different point of view. This sort of transport of the imagination must, as we said earlier, be a part of friendship. Aristotle's introductory remarks in the *Metaphysics* have application here. Aristotle repeats in that celebrated passage the thought of *NE* 9. 9, that what characterizes human beings is their love of perception and knowledge. But here the emphasis is different:

All human beings desire to know by nature, and a sign of this is the delight we take in our senses . . . and above all else, the sense of

[20] The argument in these passages, esp. *NE*, 9. 9 (1169b30–1170b14), is tortuous. However, Irwin's simplification of the argument in his translation is of enormous help. Cooper's analysis of the contribution of friendship to self-knowledge ('Aristotle on Friendship') remains the best I know. Since I am in basic agreement with both their analyses of the argument, I refer the reader to their works.

sight . . . For this more than the other senses enables us to know and brings to light many distinctions between things. (980a22–8)

Self-knowledge, as a sub species of knowledge, requires the discrimination of what is peculiarly one's own. To overlook differences is ultimately to obscure an awareness of self.

Abbreviations

EE	*Eudemian Ethics*
MM	*Magna Moralia*
NE	*Nicomachean Ethics*
Poet.	*Poetics*
Pol.	*Politics*
Rh.	*Rhetoric*

[6]

The Problem of Total Devotion

Robert M. Adams

The Problem

"Hear, O Israel: The Lord our God, the Lord is one; and you shall love the Lord your God with all your heart, and with all your soul, and with all your might" (Deut. 6:4). This text, which holds a place of honor both in Judaism and in Christianity, expresses a demand for devotion—for total devotion—which is central to theistic religion quite generally. The problem that I mean to discuss can be seen as arising when this demand is paired, as it is by Jesus, with another familiar commandment of religious ethics: "You shall love your neighbor as yourself" (Lev. 19:18; Matt. 22:39). If love to God is to occupy all our heart and soul and strength, what will be left to love or care about our neighbor? This problem has troubled many religious thinkers, notably including St. Augustine, who states it by saying that when God commanded us to love him "with the whole heart, the whole soul, the whole mind, he left no part of our life that should be free and (as it were) leave room to want to enjoy something else."[1]

There may be something misleading about this formulation of the

This essay was originally published in *Rationality, Religious Belief, and Moral Commitment,* ed. Robert Audi and William J. Wainwright (Ithaca: Cornell University Press, 1986).

I am indebted to several groups with whom I have discussed versions of this material. Laura L. Garcia, Philip L. Quinn, and Edward Sankowski provided full written comments, which have been most helpful. Others whose comments have led to identifiable changes in the chapter are William P. Alston, José Benardete, Christopher Hughes, John Ladd, and Peter van Inwagen. The support of a fellowship at the Center of Theological Inquiry in Princeton during the writing of the paper is gratefully acknowledged.

[1] Aurelius Augustinus, *De doctrina Christiana* I, xxii, 21. I translate from the text in *Corpus scriptorum ecclesiasticorum latinorum,* vol. 80, ed. William M. Green (Vienna: Hoelder-Pichler-Tempsky, 1963). A widely available English translation is by D. W. Robertson, Jr., *On Christian Doctrine* (New York: Liberal Arts Press, 1958).

problem, although Augustine is not the only thinker to have posed it in these terms.[2] The heart, after all, is not like a dwindling reserve of petroleum, and love cannot be conserved by hoarding it. We might be tempted to think the whole problem merely verbal, a sophistical trick, because in some contexts 'with all your heart' can be a synonym of 'wholeheartedly', signifying only an unconflicted enthusiasm, which does not imply that one has no emotional force left to sustain any distinct and independent motive.

Nevertheless, I believe there is a real problem here. Religious devotion is more than wholeheartedness or unconflicted enthusiasm. It is supposed to occupy a person's life so fully that nothing is left outside the realm in which it reigns.. The history of spirituality affords many testimonies to the sweeping character of the claims of devotion to God—not least in the frequency with which independent interests in finite things have been seen as rivals and threats to religious devotion and, figuratively speaking, as a form of "idolatry," offering to the creature what properly belongs to God alone. The problem, then, is not essentially one of the distribution of scarce emotional resources. The problem is rather how a genuine and serious interest in something finite (such as love for one's neighbor) can be a part of one's life that at the same time expresses love for God—as it must, if one's whole life is to be devoted to God.

When I say that the problem of total devotion is a real problem, I do not mean that it is an open question whether devotion to God is compatible with love for one's neighbor. Many (perhaps all) theistic traditions can point to saints who have manifested both qualities in exemplary fashion. St. Francis and Gandhi and Mother Teresa come quickly to mind. Typically the saints themselves would deny that they have arrived at the point of loving God with absolutely all their heart and soul and strength or at the point of loving their neighbor perfectly as themselves. But it would be quite implausible to suppose that their love of neighbor only slips through the gaps left by the imperfection of their love for God. On the contrary, their love of neighbor seems to be highly integrated with, and supported by, their love of God and not in conflict with it. Our problem, then, is not one of establishing the possibility of the union of these loves but of understanding how it is possible.

Maybe the best way of reaching this understanding would be to study the lives of the saints, but I shall follow a more abstract approach here. First I will present and criticize an influential solution offered by St. Augustine. Then other possible contributions to a solution will be considered, culminating in those that seem to me most satisfying.

[2] Cf. Charles Hartshorne, *The Logic of Perfection and Other Essays in Neoclassical Metaphysics* (Lasalle, Ill.: Open Court, 1962), p. 40.

Augustine's Teleological Solution

"Whoever rightly loves a neighbor," according to St. Augustine, ". . . . loving him as himself, pours back all the love of himself and of the neighbor into that love of God which suffers no stream to be led away from it by whose diversion it might be diminished."[3] The problem, of course, is how this is to be done. Augustine's clearest answer is in terms of the subordination of means to end. He distinguishes between *enjoying* something and *using* it. "For to enjoy is to cling with love to some thing for its own sake [*propter se ipsam*]; whereas to use is to apply what is used to the obtaining of that which you love (provided it ought to be loved)."[4] What is used, in other words, is treated as a means to the end of enjoyment. Augustine introduces this distinction in order to make the point that God is to be enjoyed but other things, his finite creatures, ought only to be used. He likens us, in a memorable image, to exiles returning to their native land, in which alone they can find happiness. In such a case we would have to use various means of transport and other provisions in order to complete our trip. But "the pleasures of the journey" present a temptation: if we were "converted to enjoying those things that we ought to use," we would wish to prolong our travels instead of hastening home. In this way we would be alienated from our true country. "Thus, away from the Lord as wanderers in this mortal life, if we want to return to our own country where we can be blessed, we ought to use this world and not enjoy it."[5] St. Augustine explicitly applies this schema to the love of one's neighbor: "For it is commanded us to love each other; but it is a question whether man is to be loved by man for his own sake or for the sake of something else. For if for his own sake, we enjoy him; if for the sake of something else, we use him. But it seems to me that he is to be loved for the sake of something else. For as for what should be loved for its own sake, the blessed life consists in that. . . . But cursed is he who puts his hope in man."[6]

What does it mean, in this context, to speak of "using" one's neighbor and loving him "for the sake of" God? The most natural interpretation is in terms of a desire-plus-belief pattern of teleological reasons for desires. You desire a state of affairs S for the sake of an end E if you desire S because you desire E and believe that S would be conducive to E. If you desire S for its own sake, on the other hand, your motivation is not entirely of this sort; you desire S at least partly as an end in itself

---

[3] *De doctrina Christiana* I, xxii, 21.
[4] Ibid., I, iv, 4.
[5] Ibid., I, iv, 4.
[6] Ibid., I, xxii, 20.

and not only because you desire E and believe that S would be conducive to E. Augustine clearly conceives of love as at least largely a matter of desire. If we love our neighbor, we will desire his well-being and will desire some relationship with him. If we love our neighbor for his own sake, we will desire these states of affairs for their own sake; whereas we will desire them only because we desire some divine end to which we believe them conducive if we love our neighbor only for God's sake, as St. Augustine thinks we ought. Thus we are to use our neighbor, desiring nothing regarding him except as a means or way of realizing the divine end. What is the divine end? Most of what Augustine says suggests that it is one's own enjoyment of God, and I shall assume that here. Other possibilities will be canvassed later.

This solution to the problem of total devotion, with St. Augustine's sponsorship, has had a powerful—and I think a baneful—influence on Western religious thought and practice. It has molded a great deal of asceticism, both Catholic and Protestant. A brief—and vivid—example is Jonathan Edwards's youthful resolution "that no other end but religion shall have any influence at all on any of my actions."[7] It would be unfair to suppose that these views are fully representative of Augustine. Much that he says about love, for instance, in his beautiful homilies on 1 John, seems to proceed from a more attractive conception of the relation between neighbor love and devotion to God. Nonetheless, he does endorse the doctrine that God is to be enjoyed and all other beings are to be used only as means to the enjoyment of God; to the best of my knowledge, he gives us no other solution to the problem of total devotion that is so clearly articulated as this one. I shall refer to it as "Augustine's teleological solution."

Its clarity is doubtless one reason for the influence it has enjoyed, as is the centrality of means-end relationships to so much thinking about motivation. But there is also a profounder reason. Augustine's teleological solution of the problem of total devotion is rooted in his vision of human life as a quest for infinite satisfaction, fueled by a torrent of desire that cannot rest in anything less. This vision, which animates Augustine's famous narrative of his own life, is the very center of his apologetics, his case for theistic religion. Countless readers have found in it a persuasive picture of their own need and aspiration. And the great danger that attends the quest for infinite satisfaction, as Augustine sees it, is idolatry; it is the danger that we shall seek our infinite satisfaction, not in our invisible Creator, but in his visible creatures, who are by no means equipped to provide it. Experience testifies of

---

[7] *The Works of President Edwards: With a Memoir of His Life,* vol. 1, ed. Sereno Dwight (New York: S. Converse, 1829), p. 71.

this danger. How often do we seek from career or marriage, parents or children, a satisfaction that, if not infinite, is at least far more than they could ever give. We demand of them what only God could give and the results are unhappy. Augustine links this with the problem of total devotion in his statement that "as for what should be loved for its own sake, the blessed life consists in that." The implication is that, if we loved another human being for his or her own sake and not merely as a means to the enjoyment of God, we would be seeking our infinite satisfaction (idolatrously) in that fellow human. I do not think that is true, but if it were, Augustine's teleological solution of the problem of total devotion would be virtually forced on the theist.

The solution has unacceptable consequences, however. In the first place, if taken seriously, it imposes absurd restrictions on the enjoyment of the simple pleasures of life. Suppose I am offered the choice of eating either strawberries or apples, at equal cost and with a trusted physician's assurance of equal benefit to my health. Could Augustine approve of my choosing the strawberries just because I like their flavor better? Not in accordance with his theory of enjoying and using. For if I do choose the strawberries just because I prefer their flavor, I will be enjoying them, adhering to them for their own sake (or to their flavor for its own sake) and not just using them as means to the enjoyment of God.

Far more important for Christian ethics than sensory pleasures is the love of one's neighbor. The gravest disadvantage of Augustine's teleological solution of the problem of total devotion is that it does not allow for anything that really deserves the name of *love* of one's neighbor. For it implies that the neighbor is not to be loved for his own sake. His well-being and our fellowship with him are to be desired only as a means to our enjoyment of God. But what is really loved must be loved for its own sake. Where something is regarded only as a means or instrument, we can say that we "value" it but not that we "love" it. I do not *love* my car, for example, unless it means something to me that transcends its resale value and its usefulness for transportation. Similarly, if I do not desire the neighbor's well-being, or any relationship with him, except because I believe it will help me to enjoy God as I desire, I do not love my neighbor. This is reason enough to reject Augustine's teleological solution to the problem of total devotion.

It is also reason to reject other solutions that differ from it only in the specification of the religious end to which all other ends are to be subordinate as mere instruments or means. Whether the end that dominates in this way be the vision of God or Christian perfection or the coming of God's Kingdom, there will in any case be no room for the neighbor really to be loved. If I desire your well-being or my relationship with you only because I believe it will be conducive to one of these divine ends, then I do not really love you. That is at least partly due to the fact that these ends do not essentially involve you. I could in principle see God or attain Christian perfection without you, and the Kingdom of God could come without you. If I am seeking nothing, at bottom, except in order to realize one of these ends, then it does not matter, except incidentally, that *you* are involved.

Love's Religious Desires

What about divine ends that do essentially involve particular neighbors? Might they afford a more satisfactory solution to the problem of total devotion? Two such ends come to mind. The first, a version of the neighbor's well-being, is that the neighbor enjoy God. The second, a relationship that I might desire with the neighbor, is that we enjoy God together. The second of these, at least, is a divine end for the sake of which St. Augustine seems in some passages to think the neighbor might be loved.[8] Desiring these ends for their own sake, we could love God *in* loving the neighbor. On the one hand, the neighbor could truly be loved in this way, because he is not incidental to these ends but essentially involved in them. We would be desiring his well-being and a good relationship with him for their own sake. On the other hand, God also would be loved in these desires; for a desire that those I love should enjoy God and that it should be God that we enjoy together expresses love for God no less than would a desire that I myself should enjoy God. Moreover, these are desires that we would in any event expect to find in one who loves both God and her neighbor, and they do commonly characterize the love that serious theists have for other people. Love for God will naturally give a certain shape to what we envisage and desire as good for people that we love and for our relationship with them.

The desire that the neighbor enjoy God with us illustrates a point about the sharing of love that deserves comment here. When we think of love's desire for relationships, we often think only of two-membered, one-to-one relationships. This is romantically appealing but unrealistic. To love another person is not necessarily to want to be alone in the universe with her. The relationships that we desire and prize with other people are not only two-person relationships but also three-person, four-person, and in general many-person relationships. We may arrange a dinner party because we want to relate to all of a specific

[8] *De doctrina Christiana* I, xxix, 30.

group of people at the same time and to participate in their relation to each other. And when a person leaves a family or working unit or circle of friends, by divorce or taking a different job or going away to college, one feels sad, not just for the loss of a two-membered relationship, but for the loss of a many-membered relationship involving that person. Even where the one-to-one relationship can be maintained outside the group and the *n*-membered relationship in the group can be restructured as an *n*-minus-one-membered relationship, one is still apt to miss the specific *n*-membered relationship of which that person was an essential member. In such a case one does prize the individual person for her own sake, but the relationship one desires, while involving some one-to-one interaction, is a relationship of which other people are members, too.

To be unable to prize many-person relationships in this way, to insist exclusively on one-to-one relationships, would typically be evidence of possessiveness or jealousy. The possessive lover wants to limit the life of the beloved to their two-membered relationship with each other. A nonpossessive lover wants the beloved to live a larger life and wants to share it with him. Hence the nonpossessive lover will want to be part of many-membered relationships with the beloved and will prize them when they arise. As possessiveness is no virtue in love, there is no reason to suppose that either God or the neighbor is less perfectly loved if we desire to enjoy God with the neighbor than if we desired to enjoy either to the exclusion of the other.

This approach to the problem of total devotion, in terms of desires for religious ends that essentially involve the particular neighbor, differs in its structure, and not only in the religious ends proposed, from Augustine's teleological solution. For it does not subordinate the neighbor or the neighbor's good or our relationship with the neighbor as a means to a higher end. It does not provide a desire-plus-belief reason for loving the neighbor or desiring the neighbor's good, and it makes no use of the contrast between enjoying and using.

I think this approach to the problem is correct, as far as it goes, and provides the main point at which an understanding of love for God in terms of *desire* for a divine *end* can enter into an acceptable solution. But I hesitate for two reasons to call it a complete solution of the problem of total devotion. (1) This approach does not explain how I could be loving God in desiring for myself or my neighbor anything other than an explicitly divine end, such as the enjoyment of God, and therefore it does not show how total devotion could be compatible with prizing more mundane enjoyments (such as the taste of strawberries) for their own sake, either for oneself or for one's neighbor. (2) It provides no way of tracing love for the neighbor to a root in love for God. It does show how love for God and love for the neighbor can unite in desire for the same state of affairs. Given that one loves God and the neighbor, one will naturally want the neighbor to enjoy God. But why love the neighbor at all? No answer to that question is provided here, although the ideal of total devotion suggests that love for the neighbor should spring from love for God. The desire that the neighbor enjoy God (and enjoy God with us) can be part of love for the neighbor, but it is not a reason for loving the neighbor.

Religious Reasons for Love

There certainly can be religious reasons, rooted in devotion to God, for loving the neighbor, but I think they are not to be understood in terms of desire for a divine end. One can love someone for her devotion to God or as a child of God or for the sake of the image of God in her, just as one can love a person for her beauty or her courage or her human vulnerability. These reasons indicate characteristics that one finds attractive in the person. To say that you love a person for such a characteristic is not to say that you have a general desire or liking for it that you think she is a way of satisfying. You need not like or desire vulnerability to find it appealing, and your interest in the beauty or the religious devotion of a person you love is quite different from your interest in the beauty or religious devotion of a stranger. Loving someone for the sake of the image of God in her does not imply a desire for one more image of God than you would have without her. Perhaps you know enough images of God not to care about one more or less as such, but you prize her for the sake of the image of God in her. To love a person for reasons like these is not to regard her as a means or way to the satisfaction of an ulterior end. Yet such reasons for loving someone can be an expression of love for God.

To show that loving someone for religious reasons is not necessarily regarding her as a means or way to an ulterior end is to show that having religious reasons is compatible with loving someone as an end in herself and to that extent for her own sake. When we say that we want to be loved for our own sake, however, we may have something more in mind. The objection to being loved for one's money rather than for one's own sake is indeed very apt to be an objection to being regarded as a mere means to the enjoyment of one's possessions. But being loved for one's own sake (or "for oneself," as we might rather say in this context) can also be contrasted with being loved for one's looks or one's cheerfulness, without any implication that the latter entails being regarded as a means to an ulterior end. The complaint is rather that what is valued in one is too small or peripheral or accidental a part of oneself. It is not obvious what reasons for love would be exempt from this complaint. Even moral character is sufficiently accidental and changeable that being loved only for one's moral virtues might be contrasted with being loved for oneself. By the same token, loving someone solely for her religious devotion might not amount to loving her for herself, in one sense that concerns us. Loving someone for the sake of the image of God in her is an interesting case. It may seem comparatively safe from this criticism, in view of the central, important, and essential place that the image of God is thought to occupy in the constitution of human selfhood. On the other hand, it could seem too much like "loving" someone for her similarity to her mother, which hardly counts as loving her for herself. Probably you are loved for yourself if you are loved for the intrinsic glories of the image of God in you and not just for the relation of similarity to God—but how much does loving you for the first of this pair of reasons express a love for God?[9]

For these and other reasons it is not clear how much religious reasons for love can help with the problem of total devotion. Perhaps a complete solution based on such reasons would require us to take it as an ideal to have religious reasons for *all* our loves. That is not obviously unacceptable. But would we have to go further and take it as an ideal to have *only* religious reasons for our loves? And would that be acceptable? Surely it would be "too pious" to make it an ideal never to have it as a reason for loving someone that he is cute or that he is your son. In at least some cases one might have religious versions of such reasons. Instead of loving your son simply because he is your son, for instance, you might love him because God has given him to you as a son. Maybe a sense of having received a gift and a trust (and from whom, if not from God?) is in fact often implicit in loving a child because it is one's own. Probably, however, it would be objectionably artificial to divinize *all* reasons for love in this way.

I conclude that religious reasons for love are likely to provide at best a partial solution to our problem. Fortunately, other approaches remain to be explored. In this exploration the next two sections will be devoted to making sure that we do not overlook the obvious.

[9] I have had to deal very briefly here with issues about the meaning of 'for the sake of', 'for one's own sake', and 'for oneself', and about what it is to have a reason for loving someone. I hope to publish a fuller discussion of these issues elsewhere.

Putting God First

One thing certainly demanded in devotion to God is that one put God first in one's life. This is often characterized as loving God more than anything else. As a popular hymn puts it,

> Jesus calls us from the worship
>   Of the vain world's golden store,
> From each idol that would keep us,
>   Saying, "Christian, love me more,"[10]

Putting God first can also be understood more narrowly, and perhaps more clearly, as the most stringent of loyalties—a loyalty that one will not go against for the sake of any desire or other loyalty. If one is prepared to abandon, disobey, or slight God in order to please or obey or pamper a parent, spouse, child, teacher, boss, or friend, then one has made an idol of that person. Whenever any other interest conflicts with loyalty to God, one must decide for God.

Of course, other interests do not always conflict with loyalty to God. They may incline us to the same action that is demanded by loyalty to God or at least to actions not forbidden by God. This suggests a simple solution to the problem of total devotion. Why not say that love for one's neighbor and for other creatures is compatible with perfect devotion to God, provided that one loves God more and thus is fully prepared and disposed to set aside any desire arising from one's love of creatures if it should conflict with loyalty to God?

There is something right about this suggestion. Putting God first, in this sense, is a part—the most obvious and maybe the most important part—of the ideal of total devotion. But it is not the whole of it, and therefore this solution to the problem is not completely satisfying. Devotion to God is not conceived of simply as the absolutely first among a number of independent interests. It is supposed to be more encompassing, so that other good motives must find their place within it and all of life can be a worship of God. The idea that one should be loving God in loving the neighbor is very deeply rooted.

How this idea can be understood, I will continue to explore in the remaining sections of this paper. In the present section I will dwell on a more specific difficulty with the suggested simple solution to the problem of total devotion. The difficulty is that putting God first does

---

[10]"Jesus Calls Us," by Cecil Frances Alexander (1852), quoted from *The Hymnal* (Philadelphia: Presbyterian Board of Christian Education, 1939), no. 223.

not suffice to exclude idolatry. 'Idolatry' signifies here not just worshiping an image of a deity but, more broadly, giving to a creature what belongs only to God.

What belongs only to God? Not love, desire, or enjoyment as such. I am arguing that it is compatible with theistic devotion to have these affections for creatures. Theists likewise generally suppose that it is right to admire, trust, and even obey creatures in various ways on various occasions. What belongs only to God is indeed a sort of love, praise, trust, and obedience; but it is a very special sort. It is called "worship"; but that may not clarify very much, because what is meant is not a particular sort of easily recognized religious behavior, such as attending church or synagogue, but something more comprehensive and life encompassing.

One thing that clearly is meant is indeed the most stringent of loyalties. But what belongs to God alone is more than just a kind of loyalty. It is more broadly a type of importance in the believer's life. One is to "center one's life in God," to find one's principal identity in being a child of God and one's principal security in being loved by God. This is quite different from any desirable sort of love for one's neighbor. By contrast with this, idolatry would be found, not in loving another human being very much, but in feeling that life would be meaningless without him; not in the most intense enjoyment of philosophy, but in feeling that one would not be oneself if one could not do philosophy; not in liking other people and wanting to be their friend, but in feeling that one would be worthless if rejected by them.

In these examples we can see two reasons why putting God first does not suffice to exclude idolatry. First, loving God more is not enough, because the love that belongs to God differs more than quantitatively from the love that may properly be directed toward creatures. It occupies a different place in the organization of life. One does not arrive at idolatry simply by intensifying a proper love for creatures but by depending on them as one should depend on God. Because idolatry is not a merely quantitative matter, it can subsist even where one loves God still more than the idol. Indeed, one does not necessarily love the idol at all. The danger of idolatry lurks at least as much in authority and envy as in beauty and desire. To organize one's life around pleasing a boss or winning the respect of a professional rival is idolatrous, even if one neither likes nor loves that person.

Second, the most stringent loyalty to God is not enough, for one could still organize the meaning of one's life idolatrously around a finite object even if one were fully resolved and disposed to sacrifice it if loyalty to God should require—indeed, even if one actually had sacrificed it. It can be argued, for example, that that is exactly what the "knight of infinite resignation" is doing in Kierkegaard's *Fear and Trembling*. He has "concentrate[d] the whole substance of his life and the meaning of actuality into one single desire,"[11] for a particular beloved person, and then has renounced her for the sake of God. But he keeps the concentrated passion for the human beloved ever "young"[12] in his heart, for that is what makes his resignation "infinite" and thus constitutes it a relation to God. This outward renunciation of the beloved does not abolish but shelters the "knights" idolatry of her—shelters it from the vicissitudes and banalities of marriage, for instance—so that he can still define in relation to her the meaning of his life and even of his devotion to God. His passion for her still crowds out interests in other finite things and defines the possibility (or rather, impossibility) of happiness for him.[13] This is an idolatry that can remain in the organization of the heart even when God is voluntarily preferred to the idol.

Obedience

Another solution to the problem of total devotion is suggested by the following argument:

God commands love for the neighbor.
Obedience to God's commands is an expression of love for God.
Therefore love for the neighbor is an expression of love for God.

There is something right about this, as we shall see, but there are also serious objections to it.

The argument presupposes that, since God commands love for the neighbor, love for the neighbor can be a form of obedience to God. But that seems wrong. In loving our neighbor we are to desire her well-being. To say that this desire is a form of obedience to God is to say that it is motivated by a certain reason of a desire-plus-belief or resolution-plus-belief pattern. It is to say that we desire our neighbor's well-being because we want (or are resolved) to do what God commands and we believe that he commands us to desire her well-being. But this is not a reason for the desire for the neighbor's well-being: it is only a reason for wanting or trying to have this desire. For this reason commends, not the neighbor's well-being, but the desire for it; whereas a reason

---

[11] Søren Kierkegaard, *Fear and Trembling and Repetition*, ed. and trans. Howard V. Hong and Edna H. Hong (Princeton: Princeton University Press, 1983), p. 43.
[12] Ibid., p. 44.
[13] Ibid., p. 50.

for a desire must commend the object of the desire, rather than the desire itself. In a desire-plus-belief reason for desiring S, it is S that must be believed conducive to E, or a way of realizing E. But what is here believed to be a way of doing what God commands is not the neighbor's well-being but the desire for it. Commending a desire could provide a reason for the desire only if the desire had itself as part of its aim or object. But the desire in this case is no part of its own aim or object; its whole object is the neighbor's well-being. Therefore this desire cannot be a form of obedience.[14]

Still, it might be replied, the desire for the neighbor's well-being could be motivated in another way by reverence for the will of God. For God wills the neighbor's well-being as well as our desire for it. This suggests another reason that could be a reason for the desire, because it commends the object of the desire. We could desire the neighbor's well-being because we desire that God's will be done and believe that God wills the neighbor's well-being. Similarly, we could desire a good relationship with the neighbor because we believe that God wills that, and we desire that God's will be done. But this suggestion falls prey to substantially the same difficulty as Augustine's teleological solution of the problem of total devotion. If we desired the neighbor's well-being and a good relationship with her *only* out of a desire that God's will be done, we would not desire them for their own sake. It would not matter to us whether God's will be fulfilled by those states of affairs rather than by any others that he might have willed instead. And in this case we would not love the neighbor. Of course we may desire these states of affairs *partly* out of a desire that God's will be done and partly for their own sake, out of love for the neighbor. But then the love for the neighbor is not a form or expression of reverence for God's will but a separate motive for desiring some of the same states of affairs.

There are certain desires from which, of their very nature, there is

---

[14] If the desire for our neighbor's well-being cannot be a form of obedience, it might be thought to follow that it cannot be commanded; but I do not mean to draw that conclusion. The fact that it cannot be fulfilled with the motivational pattern characteristic of obedience certainly implies that the command to love one's neighbor as oneself is not a *typical* command and cannot function exactly as commands typically do. Nevertheless it is demanded of us by society—and, most theists would say, by God—that we desire our neighbor's well-being for its own sake. This demand is backed by the informal authority of society—and by the divine authority, as theists believe. And if it becomes clear that we have no desire for our neighbor's well-being for its own sake, persons concerned may rightly react with disapproval, reproach, and a sense of grievance. (In "Involuntary Sins," *Philosophical Review* 94 [1985], pp. 3–31, I have discussed much more fully our liability to blame for states, such as desire, that are not directly voluntary.) For that reason, I think it makes sense to regard ourselves as *commanded* to desire our neighbor's well-being for its own sake. In the same way I think we are rightly said to *promise* to love our spouses, even though one cannot exactly love *out of* a desire to keep one's promise.

no direct path to their fulfillment. Consider the desire to be unconcerned about one's motivational state. The keener it is, the farther it is from fulfillment. Likewise, if I want, for all the self-interested reasons in the world, to love another person unselfishly, a great gulf may still separate me from the love that I desire, for it is not the sort of thing that I can do for any of those reasons. The desire to live according to God's will is at least partly of this nature too, if God wills that we should love our neighbor. Its fulfillment involves caring, for their own sake, about things (such as the neighbor's well-being) that are quite distinct from one's own living according to whatever God's will may be. If one's desire to live according to God's will is so all-consuming as to prevent one from caring about anything else for its own sake, it will get in the way of its own fulfillment. The ideal of total devotion ought not to be an all-consuming desire of this sort. It should be something less self-concerned, and, as I shall explain below, I think it should not be entirely a matter of desire.

Nonetheless, realism will assign to self-conscious ethical choice an important role in the love of our neighbor. Without spontaneous desires and affections that are not forms of obedience, as I have argued, there is no love of the neighbor. But in practice we are not likely to love very well if we rely only on such spontaneity. We need to make voluntary efforts to pay attention to other people, to be helpful to them even when we do not feel like it, to study our own motives and actions self-critically, and so forth. These voluntary efforts can be obedience to God. They cultivate the soil in which less voluntary aspects of love can flourish. Thus love for the neighbor can be seen as growing out of devoted obedience to God—though that is still not quite the same as an explanation of how loving the neighbor can be a way of loving God.

Trust

My understanding of the problem of total devotion seems to resist any tidy reduction to one answer, but if I have a single chief constructive proposal to make, it is the following. Both the quest for God and enjoyment of God play a prominent part in St. Augustine's account of love for God, and rightly so. One loves God both in seeking fellowship with him and in actually having and enjoying fellowship with him. Of these two phases of love for God, Augustine's teleological solution to the problem of total devotion locates love for the neighbor and any other legitimate interest in creatures within the quest for God. This leads to the objectionable consequences of that solution. A more acceptable solution would find a rightful place for love of the neighbor and for other interests in creatures primarily in the other phase of love for God—in the realization and enjoyment of fellowship with him, rather than in the quest for it. That is my proposal, and the remainder of this paper will be devoted to it. In the present section I will discuss a relatively indirect way in which a trusting love for God, secure in the actuality of fellowship with him, can be reflected in love for creatures. Then, in the two following sections, I will go on to more direct connections between love for creatures and two aspects of the fulfillment of love for God—namely, the enjoyment of God and the inspiration that consummates the surrender of the heart to God.

A mundane model may help us to see how love for creatures can be a reflection of trusting love for God. We find that, among small children of the same age and in the same circumstances, some are much more inclined than others to cling closely to their mothers, to keep them always in sight, and to pester them for attention. The knowledgeable observer will not conclude that the more "clinging" children love their mothers more than the more independent ones. On the contrary, the more dependent children probably have a relationship with their mothers that, if not less loving, is at any rate weaker in certain respects. The more independent children are apt to be those that feel more secure in their mother's love and care, and they are therefore able to turn their attention with less anxiety to other things. This sense of security is, in part, a manifestation of their love for their mothers.

More precisely, the sense of security is a function of love for their mothers (and/or other persons on whom the child depends) plus trust or confidence that they are available when and if the child desires to turn to them. We might be tempted to say that the sense of security is a function not of the love but only of the trust. But that would be a mistake, for belief in the availability and beneficence of someone to whom the child was not attached would not have the same effect.

In this example the most important point for our present purpose is that the strength of a loving personal relationship can be reflected in attention to things other than the loved person. Paradoxical as this may sound in the abstract, it is plausible enough when we say that a child's sense of security in its mother's love frees it to pay attention to things other than the mother, whereas without this assurance its energies would be absorbed in seeking and clinging to maternal care or in coping with the lack of it. In empirical corroboration of this point, it has been observed that children of from one to three years of age are more apt to be absorbed in playing with toys and exploring their environment in their mother's presence than in her absence[15]—a finding

[15] See John Bowlby, *Separation*, vol. 2 of *Attachment and Loss* (New York: Basic Books, 1973), ch. 3. Much in Bowlby's three-volume work is relevant to my argument in this section.

that would not be expected on the assumption that interest in mother and independent interests in other objects simply compete for the child's attention and are not otherwise related.

The same point can be illustrated from adult life. Most of us would be able to concentrate more fully on the task of writing a paper on some impersonal subject, such as formal logic, if we felt secure in one or more love relationships than we would if we were experiencing disruption in a love relationship or felt that no one loved us. Of course this is not the only possible pattern of relationship between these types of interest. For both adults and children, it is possible to steel oneself to invest one's interest in other things, in the conviction that love is impossible. The point I want to make is just that there is a pattern—and obviously the happiest pattern—in which a lively and independent interest in other things reflects one's love for, and trust in, some person.

This point can be applied to the relation between love for God and love for creatures. If one both loves God and trusts in God's love, this will issue in an inner peace or sense of security. And this, as many religious thinkers have argued, will free one to take a lively interest in God's creatures for their own sake—to enjoy his gifts with un-self-conscious gratitude and to love one's neighbor. Here a love for God, combined with faith in him, provides an atmosphere of gladness and security in which a love for the creature can be encompassed.

Enjoyment

We have just explored a way in which trust in the fulfillment of one's love for God may permeate one's other interests, but rather indirectly—not as coinciding with them or providing a positive impulse toward them but as a source of freedom to have them or pursue them and as a frame of mind, a confidence, in which they can be pursued. I want now to focus on an idea that establishes a more direct connection between the two loves, by arguing that God can be enjoyed, with love, in enjoying creatures.

I mean to use the word "enjoy" in its ordinary sense and not necessarily according to Augustine's definition. It is important to the argument, and I think also obviously true, that enjoying the beloved is one of the forms that love characteristically takes. This is not to say that love is always pleasant. Enjoyment is present in widely varying degrees in different loves and at different times. Nevertheless, enjoyment is an important aspect of love. And it is a familiar phenomenon that we can enjoy a person we love in enjoying something else.

We seek shared pleasures for the enhancement of our loves—a delicious meal, a great concert, a beautiful day at the beach or in the woods; or more personally, the joys of conversation or the physical pleasures of sex. Why are these seen as enhancing love? Perhaps at least partly because there is not a sharp line between enjoying something *with* another person and enjoying the other person. How do we enjoy other people? Most broadly, I suppose, by enjoying our experience of them. In particular, that includes enjoying our relationships with them, which includes enjoying what we do together.

Besides enjoying what we do together, we enjoy other people in our experience of their personal characteristics and what they do individually. We enjoy the sound of their voices, the look or the touch of their bodies. We enjoy their ideas and their feelings, whether explicitly expressed or read by us between the lines. We enjoy the grace of their gestures or the cuteness of their expressions, the wit and style or the candor and intensity of their conversation and letters. In all of this we enjoy the other people themselves: this is the sort of thing we mean when we speak of enjoying another person.

In many of these cases, however, we do not enjoy *only* the other person. This is most obviously true of the shared pleasures. We enjoy the caviar and the music for their own sake, too, and would very likely still enjoy them if eaten or heard alone. But even the other person's ideas and performances are apt to be enjoyed for themselves at the same time that we enjoy the person in enjoying them. The joke I heard her tell would still amuse me if it came to me impersonally in the pages of a magazine.

The usual word for the relationship between these enjoyments is that we enjoy the other person "in" enjoying something else—for instance, "in" enjoying the music. Several characteristics of this relationship may be noted: (1) If we enjoy another person in enjoying the music, we enjoy both the person and the music. If I say, "I enjoyed listening to the music with him," it makes sense to ask me, "What did you like about the experience?" For normally, if we enjoy an experience, we can give reasons for that by picking out features of the experience that we like. If I enjoyed the music, I can answer truly, "I liked the music." If I enjoyed the other person, I can answer truly, "I liked sharing it with him." If I enjoyed the other person in enjoying the music, I must have liked both of these distinguishable features of the experience. (2) Although the enjoyment of the music and of the other person are distinguishable in this way, they are so fused into a single experience that in some sense they are not separate. And (3) each enjoyment enhances the other. We would normally say, not that we like the music better, but that we enjoy it more, because we enjoy sharing the experience with someone else; and we would say that we enjoy the other person more because we enjoy the music that we hear together. (4) If we enjoy the other person in enjoying the music, we like the music and the sharing with the other person, each for its own sake, or at any rate not merely as a way or means to the other. The claim that I liked the music merely as a way or means to the sharing could be understood according to a liking-plus-belief pattern of reasons for liking (analogous to the desire-plus-belief pattern of reasons for desire discussed above) as meaning that I liked the music only because I liked sharing an experience with the other person and regarded listening to the music as a way of doing that (much as one might enjoy selling something only because one liked making money and saw the transaction as a way of making money). If I liked the music only for this reason, it would be misleading to list the music in addition to the sharing as something that I liked about the experience or to say that I enjoyed the other person "in enjoying the music."

Are there cases in which one enjoys another person alone and not in enjoying something else? I suppose so. One might enjoy an experience about which one did not particularly like anything except that it was an experience of seeing *her*. But such experiences can claim no preeminence. The enjoyment of conversation and of sexual intercourse, for instance, is not in general of this type, in view of the intellectual and sensory pleasures typically involved in them. It would be bizarre to take it as an ideal of love to enjoy the other person only alone and never in enjoying something else.

Similar things can be said about *enjoying God*. When people speak of it, they normally have in mind cases in which an experience of God is enjoyed. This should not be understood too subjectivistically, as if it were not God himself that is enjoyed but only a state of one's own mind. (A similar antisubjectivistic caution applies to what I said about enjoying other people in general by enjoying our experience of them.) But if someone said, "I have never experienced God, but I have often enjoyed him," one would wonder what was meant.

How does one experience God? Believers often say they experience the Creator in his works. Suppose one enjoys the sunlight on the autumn leaves and is the more excited because one catches there (as one believes) a glimpse of the beauty of the Creator at work. If this is indeed an experience of God, it seems right to say that it is one in which one enjoys God, enjoys what he does, *in* enjoying the light and the leaves. Likewise, if one experiences and enjoys God through a piece of religious literature or a religious liturgy, one would (at least in typical cases) be enjoying God *in* enjoying the literature or the liturgy. And most important here, if I experience the love of my friends as a manifestation of the love of God, that would normally be a case in which I

am enjoying both God and my friends in enjoying this social experience and am enjoying God *in* enjoying my friends. The creature is
enjoyed, in these cases, as something more than a means to the enjoyment of God. It is because one enjoys the light, the leaves, the friend,
and the friend's love for their own sake that one sees and appreciates in
them the glory of God, so as to praise him for them and enjoy him in
enjoying them.

It has been pointed out to me that in some cases it would be odd to
say that we enjoy a creator himself in enjoying his works. Do we enjoy
Rembrandt himself in enjoying his paintings? Perhaps not. Rembrandt
is gone and has left his works behind for us to enjoy. But God is not like
that. On theistic as opposed to deistic conceptions of creation, he has
not gone away and left his works behind; he remains unceasingly active
in them. To the example of the painter may be contrasted that of a
dancer, who cannot go away and leave his performance behind. (Or if
he leaves a motion picture of his work, there is nothing odd about
saying we enjoy him in enjoying the film.) Now, in a theistic as opposed
to a pantheistic view, God's creatures are more distinct from him than
the dance is from the dancer. But they are not as separable from him as
paintings are from the painter. God is neither as wholly immanent in
his works as the dancer in the dance nor as purely transcendent over
them as the painter in relation to his paintings. These reflections suggest that the immanent aspect of God's relation to his creation is important to the possibility of loving God in loving his creatures.[16]

It is not only in enjoying his creatures that God is enjoyed. There are
experiences in which God alone is enjoyed. I take that to be true of
some experiences of communion with God or of the presence of God,
where the experience is of nothing else. This is certainly an important
and valuable form of experience of God and enjoyment of God. But I
think it would be a mistake to take it as an ideal to enjoy God only in
this way, to the exclusion of enjoying him in enjoying his creatures.
With some trepidation, I am inclined to say that that would be to make
a sort of idol out of this type of experience, substituting too private a
deity for the Lord of all who shows his glory in many works and gifts.
Another way in which one may enjoy God alone is in his presence in
suffering, in which he is enjoyed the suffering is not. But clearly it
would be perverse to seek to enjoy God only in that way.

To the extent, therefore, that enjoyment can be a form of love, love
for God and love for creatures can coincide in enjoying God in enjoy-

---

[16] To this extent I agree with Hartshorne's treatment of the problem of total devotion
in *The Logic of Perfection*, pp. 40–41. But I am not prepared to carry the affirmation of
divine immanence as far as he does or to rely on it so completely for the solution of the
problem.

ing his creatures.[17] Perhaps one should aspire to such a religious consciousness that God would be enjoyed in *all* one's enjoyment of creatures. Before this suggestion can be accepted, however, we must
confront a possible protest against such an all-encompassing ideal of
religious devotion. It would be objectionably possessive, as was noted
above in the section "Love's Religious Desires," to want your beloved's
life to be limited to a two-person relationship with you. You should be
able to enjoy many-person relationships with each other. But you
might think it perfectly appropriate to want your beloved *also* to concentrate, some of the time, on *you alone,* and not to enjoy you *only in*
enjoying your children or your friends. "Two's company, but three's a
crowd," we say, meaning that we want time to be alone in twosomes. A
religious ideal that would have us always conscious of God's involvement in every situation—or even a belief in God's omnipresence and
omniscience—might therefore seem to threaten a desirable intimacy
with the intrusion of a third party.

It must be acknowledged, I think, that there is a sense of being
absolutely alone with another human being (or indeed of being absolutely alone with oneself) that may, not unreasonably, be welcomed by
nontheists but that is hardly compatible with theistic faith. But theists
need not regret the loss of this particular solitude. We do not (or
should not) want to take our parents along on our honeymoon—but
God is different. Theists must say that we should want to "take him
along" even (or perhaps especially) on our honeymoon. God's immanence helps in understanding the relevant difference here between
him and our human parents. A continuing relation to him is built into
the structure of our selfhood and of any relationship between human
persons. I do not have to look away from my human partner to see
God, and you do not grasp my true selfhood better by abstracting from
my relation to God. For this reason I am inclined to say that God could
appropriately be enjoyed in all legitimate enjoyment of creatures.

Inspiration

It is a truism that shared interests make a friendship more perfect.
When we speak of sharing interests, we mean being interested in the
same things for their own sake; we do not mean just being interested in
the friend's interests for the sake of the friendship. Thus, if my wife
loves tennis and I have never cared about it, I might play tennis with

[17] And perhaps in enjoying the creatures *in* enjoying God, as Philip Quinn has suggested that I should say.

her and even "cultivate an interest" in tennis, for the sake of our relationship; but as long as that is my sole motive in the matter, we do not yet share an interest in tennis. That occurs only when I too am interested in tennis for its own sake.

Similarly, it is plausible to suppose that fellowship with God would be perfected by sharing God's interests, loving and hating what he loves and hates. One will be more fully in tune with God if one loves fidelity and hates lying as he does and if one loves one's neighbor as he does. "God is love, and he who abides in love abides in God, and God abides in him" (1 John 4:16).

God loves the neighbor for the neighbor's own sake. So if my only interest in the neighbor is that I would like to have a better relationship with God and think that loving the neighbor would contribute to that, I do not yet share God's interest in the matter, as I do not yet love the neighbor. That occurs only if I love the neighbor for his own sake.

If this line of thought is right, then those who desire fellowship with God have reason to want to love their neighbor for their neighbor's own sake. But this is one of those desires that I discussed above, whose nature permits no direct path from the desire to its fulfillment because the fulfillment involves having a motivation that is not based on the desire. Such desires have in some measure to let go if they are to enjoy full satisfaction. That is generally true of the desire for friendship, and much in the history of humankind's wrestling with grace suggests that it is also true of the desire for friendship with God.

If sharing God's love for the neighbor enhances fellowship with God, that constitutes an important connection between love for God and love for the neighbor. Can we go further and say that, if in fellowship with God one shares God's love for the neighbor, the love for the neighbor is a form or part or expression of one's love for God? We do seem to think that shared love for a third object can be manifestation of love for a friend. Perhaps "Love me, love my dog" is rarely meant as a serious statement about love, but it is surely no accident that people do not say only "Love me, put up with my dog." We test people's love for us by their appreciation and concern, not only for us, but also for what they see us love and care about. A lack of love for the children of one's marriage not only is a sin against them but also is rightly apt to be seen as a deficiency in one's love for one's spouse. Conversely, we think that the shared love of parents for their children ought to be in some way an expression of their love for each other. (Of course, one might have strong and good reasons for not sharing some interests of the beloved. Perhaps he has some interests that are bad, base, or even wicked. I do not say it would be a test of love to share such interests.)

Why do we take the actual sharing of acceptable interests as a test of love? Why is it not enough that the lover *wants* to share the beloved's interests? The main reason, I suspect, is that the failure to enter into the desires and affections of the other person suggests that one's heart is closed against her in a way that seems to us unloving. I will develop this point in connection with a solution to the problem of total devotion gleaned from Anders Nygren's great book *Agape and Eros*.

Rejecting Augustine's teleological solution, Nygren holds that the relation between love for God and love for the neighbor should be conceived nonteleologically. "God is not the end, the ultimate object, but the starting-point and permanent basis of neighborly love. He is not its *causa finalis* but its *causa efficiens*. . . . It is not as being loved, but as loving, that God sets love in motion."[18]

This fits nicely with Nygren's conception of love for God as surrender rather than quest. I think Nygren goes, indeed, to an indefensible extreme in excluding the theme of quest from the Christian type of love for God, but my interest here is in what he does include in that love. "Man's love for God signifies that man, moved by [the] Divine love, gratefully wills to belong wholly to God."[19] According to Nygren's interpretation of Jesus, "To have love for God means . . . exactly the same as to be possessed by God, to belong absolutely to Him. . . . Love towards God . . . is the *free*—and in that sense spontaneous—surrender of the heart to God."[20]

To be possessed by God is to have God acting in us and through us. If we are possessed by God, then "our" love for the neighbor can be God's love for the neighbor, for the neighbor's own sake, at work in us. And that is how Nygren thinks it is with Christian neighbor-love: "In the life that is governed by Agape, the acting subject is not man himself; it is—as Paul expresses it—God, the Spirit of God, the Spirit of Christ, the Agape of Christ. . . . The Christian has nothing of his own to give; the love which he shows to his neighbor is the love which God has infused into him."[21] Nygren could have added (though I have not found that he did) that this love for the neighbor is a part of one's love for God. For letting God do this in one is part of one's willingly being possessed by God, which Nygren identifies with love for God.

Nygren's position bristles with problems, but I will try to show that the approach it exemplifies is plausible. One problem is that, like many other theologians, Nygren often seems to have a straightforwardly causal understanding of what it is to be possessed by God. On this

[18] Andres Nygren, *Agape and Eros*, trans. Philip S. Watson (New York: Harper & Row, 1969), p. 216.
[19] Ibid., p. 213.
[20] Ibid., p. 94.
[21] Ibid., p. 129.

understanding, God inspires us or infuses his love for our neighbor into us simply by causing us to love the neighbor. But it is hard to see how God's causing that neighbor-love in me could constitute a part or form or expression of my loving God—any more than it would constitute my loving a brain surgeon if the surgeon caused me to share her feelings for a third person by stimulating my brain with an electrode.

There is another way of thinking about being inspired or possessed by God, however, which makes it easier to see that state as a form of love for God. Although divine inspiration undoubtedly has unique characteristics, we can find a model for this way of thinking in very mundane cases in which we say that one person's feeling, desire, or other state of mind is "inspired" by another person's. In such inspiration there is certainly an influencing that is broadly speaking causal. But if an emotion is inspired in me in this way, I am engaged in the process in a way in which I would not be if the other person were simply operating on me. I know, or at some level sense, his emotion and respond to it, and it is in my apprehending and responding that he influences me. In this my heart is not closed against him but open to him; and because we expect this of love, sharing the beloved's interests can be a test of love—though I am not denying that inspiration can also take place without love.

Because the one who is inspired participates in the process in this way, there is a place in this model for Nygren's description of love toward God as free and spontaneous surrender of the heart to God and as *willing* to belong to God—though 'willing' is not quite the right word for it, because this is not a straightforwardly voluntary process. Desires and emotions inspired in us by those of another person are not in general voluntarily adopted. Opening one's heart to a friend in the sense that now concerns us is not a voluntary action; it is not something one does by consciously trying. It does not even come about primarily as a result of wanting to do it. The heart may remain closed, though one wants very much to open it, if one is too distrustful. This opening of the heart is therefore an aspect of love that does not fit very well in a conception of love that focuses too exclusively on the passionate quest. It is a matter of letting the other person in, so to speak, rather than going out and grabbing him. It is a trusting rather than a controlling aspect of love—but it is nonetheless love. If our love for the neighbor is inspired by God's in this way—that we believe in God's love for the neighbor, or sense it, and respond to it by loving the neighbor ourselves, for the neighbor's own sake—then our love for the neighbor is a response to God as well as to the neighbor, and it can be an expression of love for God.

This position invites an objection that will be worth thinking about.

Let us imagine a friendship between Tom and Joe such that Tom's likes, dislikes, desires, affections, and so on vary with Joe's and are "carbon copies" of Joe's. In that case we want to say that Tom's affections are not *genuine;* Tom does not genuinely love what Joe loves. Why should we not conclude that our love for our neighbor is not genuine if it is inspired by God's love for the neighbor—and more generally, that desires, emotions, and attitudes inspired by someone else's are not genuine?

The key to a response to this objection is the difference between *imitation* and *inspiration.* The way Tom's affections are described in the proposed counterexample, we take them to be imitative, and imitative feelings are not genuine. But affections and desires do not have to be original or unconventional in order not to be imitative. People can be at once very conventional and very genuine in their love for their family, for example. There are also many cases in which genuine feelings and interests that are not particularly conventional are inspired by those of other people. One can quite genuinely "imbibe a deep love of Mozart" from one's father or "catch" one's roommate's "infectious" enthusiasm for political action.

What makes the difference, then, between imitative phoniness and inspired genuineness? The most crucial difference is that in imitation one is responding only to what one imitates and not (except very superficially) to the ostensible object of the supposed affection or feeling; whereas in inspiration there is a much deeper interplay of response to the object and to the other person by whom one is inspired. In imitation, in other words, one copies the other person; whereas in inspiration one enters into the other person's response to the object.

A connected point is that inspired affections and interests are not as dependent as imitative ones on a continued sense of the affections and interests of the person from whom we got them. They are not fickle, as imitative responses are. Inspiration, in the present sense, changes the person who receives it. If my "love" for Mozart disappeared as soon as I thought my father's did, that would be a strong reason for saying that it was imitative and not a genuine love. If I had really imbibed a love of Mozart, I would now be responding to the music for its own sake and not solely to my father, and my love for it would not be so dependent on my perception of my father.

This point might be thought to conflict with claims that we ought to be so possessed by God as to be instantly responsive to his inspiration and totally plastic under the impressions of his Spirit. But I believe this objection involves a theological misconception. In the ideal of surrendering the heart to God there is a place for a response to God that is immediate and variable, but also a place for permanent transformation (which often takes a long time). God is not fickle in his loves and has no desire for a devotion that readies itself to join him in fickleness. The love for one's neighbor that is a fruit of God's Spirit is precisely one that will retain much of its vigor when one is gripped by doubts about God or angry at him or feeling religiously dry.

I do not want to leave the impression that I think the inspiration of human love by divine love is as ordinary and unmysterious as the mundane models I have been using might suggest. In this connection I will make the following observations. We do not love our neighbor as ourselves. Reflecting on the pervasiveness of self-centered motivation, perhaps all of us have sometimes wondered whether we really loved anyone at all. I know how needy and how grasping, when it comes to love, I and others close to me are. And yet it is my experience that from time to time (fairly often, thank God!) we give each other a love that is purer and better than anything we have to give.[22] I cannot prove that this is not an illusion, but I am sure it is not. I take it to be an experience of God—of God loving us, in us and through us—and that is not the least of the reasons for prizing the experience.

In this context I can begin to give an acceptable sense to Nygren's claim that "in the life that is governed by Agape, the acting subject is not man himself" but "the Spirit of God." Yet this is only half the truth. God's love would not be experienced as it is in such a case if the human subject were not loving too—much less perfectly, but nonetheless really. Here the human love participates in the divine, not just causally as its product, but sacramentally as its vehicle.

[22] Cf. Karl Barth, *Church Dogmatics,* vol. I/2, trans. G. T. Thomson and Harold Knight (Edinburgh: T. & T. Clark, 1956), pp. 450–54.

[7]

Kant on Friendship

H. J. Paton

I

It is not uncommonly believed that in his ethics Kant is cold and even inhuman—blind to the varieties of human nature and insensitive to the complexity of personal relations. Without decisively endorsing such criticism, Professor Hodges[1] has argued that Kantian ethics are at least inadequate; and in support of this view he calls attention to three interesting types of human relationship—his list is not meant to be exhaustive. These types are: (1) the relation between 'strangers' or casual acquaintances, where the governing moral principle is one of *courtesy* and *helpfulness;* (2) the relation between 'associates', that is, between those who co-operate for some common purpose, the guiding principle here being a principle of *justice* or a rough balance of interests between the associates; and (3) the relation between 'fellows', which is based on affinity and ranges 'through the different levels of friendship to the deepest levels of love and intimacy.' Rather hesitatingly, he takes the governing principle here to be a principle of *love*, although he suggests that the kind of love he means is one which Kant himself might describe as respect. The Kantian ethic on his view gives an excellent analysis of 'associate' morality, but goes wrong in offering this as an account of morality *sans phrase*. The reason why it is felt to be cold and inhuman is that it neglects or overlooks the distinctive nature of 'fellowship' morality.

Now it is true that Kant dislikes a romantic type of morality which gushes forth in warm emotion and encourages its practitioners to

This essay was originally published in *Proceedings of the British Academy* (1956) and is reprinted here by permission of The British Academy.
[1] Aristotelian Society, Supplementary Volume xxii, pp. 197 ff.

think what noble fellows they are, when they are only doing their duty and that most imperfectly. It is also true that he dislikes even more the opposite extreme: he has no use for a system of ethics which reduces morality to mere expediency or calculated self-interest. If he is wrong in these two attitudes, then he is wrong, but at least his position is clear. So far, I hope, Professor Hodges would not be unsympathetic, but he would still insist that Kant's account of morality is at the very least incomplete in so far as it fails to account for the special duties appropriate to fellowship. If we are to assess the truth of such criticisms, it may not be unprofitable to consider some of the things that Kant actually says about friendship—a relationship at least closely akin to that which Professor Hodges has in view.

But before we begin to consider the details, we must look at the problem more generally if we are to follow Kant's discussion in its context. We must recognize that for him moral action has a common form however much its matter varies. Formal moral laws or imperatives, which alone are discussed in the *Groundwork of the Metaphysic of Morals*, must, as formal, be one and the same in all moral relationships between men *as such* whether they are mere acquaintances or mere associates or what Professor Hodges calls fellows. If we want a very rough analogy, these formal laws may be compared to the physical laws which must apply to every body even if it happens to be an organism and so subject to biological laws as well.

To recognize the common form of moral action need in no way blind us to its varying matter, that is, to its different ends. Moral action considered as regards both form and matter is the topic of the *Metaphysic of Morals* published by Kant towards the end of his long life. The same topic is treated also in his *Lectures on Ethics*,[2] although in a more popular and less authoritative way. In the interests of brevity I will concentrate on what is said about friendship in the *Metaphysic of Morals*. The general neglect of this work is one of the main reasons why Kant's ethics are so often misunderstood.

The *Metaphysic of Morals* is concerned with the laws of freedom (not of nature), and it is divided into two parts. The first part, the *Doctrine of Right,* has played a great role in continental jurisprudence; in this country it has played none. It is concerned with the laws of *external* freedom and so with *legal* obligation, which lies outside our present inquiry. In it we take men simply as having the aims and interests they do in fact have, and we try to determine what kind of laws are necessary if the external freedom of the individual is to be compatible with the

[2] *Eine Vorlesung Kants über Ethik,* edited by Menzer (1924) and translated into English by Infield. I refer to it as *V.* and cite the page of the original followed by the equivalent page of the translation (referred to as *L*).

external freedom of others. These laws, the laws of the State, are laws that can be enforced by others, and they are concerned only with outer actions, not with inner motives. We may also have a moral duty to obey these laws, but with this the State as such has no concern. Here we may seem to have something like Professor Hodges's morality of mere associates, the guiding principle of which is justice; but such a claim would require many qualifications.

For our immediate purpose we have to deal only with the second part of the *Metaphysic of Morals*, the *Doctrine of Virtue*—that is, with ethical as opposed to legal obligation, with the laws of internal freedom which, as duties, have to be enforced by each man himself: they cannot be enforced by the physical power of the State. Ethical obligation is concerned, not simply with actions, but with their inner motive or maxim; and because of this there is in our moral choices a certain playroom or latitude, which, if extended to our legal obligations, would cause us trouble with the police. Different kinds of ethical duties are associated with different kinds of virtue and vice.

It is often said that in his ethics Kant recognizes only one duty—the duty of acting for the sake of duty or (in the language used by others but never by Kant) the duty of conscientiousness. This error springs from a neglect of Kant's technical terms. Our one formal ethical obligation (*Tugendverpflichtung, obligatio ethica*) is to act out of respect for the *law* as such. But our material ethical duties or offices (*Tugendpflichten, officia ethica*) are the pursuit of certain *ends* which are also duties. The form of moral action is one; its ends and offices are many. Reverence for law as such, he tells us, does not yet establish an end as a duty.[3]

[Friendship manifestly belongs to the sphere of ethics, not of law; and even if it is something more than a duty and more than a virtue, it is connected with our duty towards others rather than with our duty towards ourselves, which must here be ignored. According to Kant, ethical duties towards others fall into two main classes: (1) duties of *love*, such as kindness, gratitude, sympathy; and (2) duties of *respect*, such as the avoidance of arrogance, backbiting, and mockery. Friendship has to be treated separately because in it love and respect are combined on an equal footing.]

Kant's treatment of this topic, it should be said at the outset, is subject to certain limitations which some may find unsatisfactory. This is not merely because his discussion tends to be more and more telescoped the farther he proceeds in this work of his old age so that it almost seems as if he were becoming tired. Even in his applied ethics,

---

[3] T. 410. '*T*' refers to the *Tugendlehre* (or Doctrine of Virtue). The page number both for this and for other works refers to the edition published by the Berlin Academy.

so far as it is a metaphysic of ethics and not a kind of casuistry, he
believes it proper to restrict his remarks to situations which arise between human beings *as such*. Thus in discussing our duty to others he
does not think it his function to examine the problems raised by differences of rank, age, sex, riches, and poverty, and so on;[4] and this must
apply also to friendship. He may be too optimistic in supposing that if
he confines himself to situations common to all mankind, it will be
possible to work out an *a priori* division of virtues and vices which can
be regarded as complete; but even if we hold that any division must to
some extent be a matter of convenience, differing for different types
of society, his self-denial at least makes his discussion more compact;
and if he insists on the need for logical abstraction in philosophical
thinking, this should not be confused either with coldness of moral
outlook or with indifference to facts.

II

Friendship (considered in its perfection) is defined by Kant in the
Metaphysic of Morals as *an association of two persons through equal and
mutual love and respect.* He takes it to be an ideal of the practical and
emotional concern[5] displayed by each in the well-being of the other. In
other words it is an ideal of what he calls '*humanity*' both in action and
in feeling[6]—a characteristic which can belong to man in so far as he is
an animal endowed with reason and not merely a rational being as
such. In such a humane friendship the friends are united through a
morally good will. Friendship of this type may not be the source of all
the happiness in life, but it always carries with it worthiness to be happy
and so has to be regarded as a duty.

It is not wholly clear what Kant means by speaking of friendship in
its perfection (or purity or completeness). He may use the phrase
vaguely to indicate that he is concerned only with ideal friendship, or
he may wish to suggest that the friendship in question is complete
inasmuch as it is not only practical but also emotional. I suspect, however, that he is referring, directly or indirectly, to the perfect or complete friendship of Aristotle—to that friendship of good men which is
based on goodness, not on pleasure or utility, and yet carries with it
both pleasure and utility. In his *Lectures on Ethics*[7] Kant himself recognizes three types of friendship: (1) friendship based on need, (2)

[4] Compare *T*. 469.
[5] *T*. 469. *Ein Ideal der Teilnehmung und Mitteilung.*
[6] *Humanitas practica* and *humanitas aesthetica. T*. 456–7.
[7] *V*. 257 ff. = *L*. 203 ff.

friendship based on taste, and (3) friendship based on moral attitude.[8] These are fairly close to the three types recognized by Aristotle; but in the present passage, perhaps because it belongs to a metaphysic of morals, the inferior kinds of friendship are ignored. This gives us no ground for supposing Kant to have held that a perfect friendship must necessarily be devoid of advantage and destitute of taste.

Aristotle, it will be remembered, already regards friendship as mutual goodwill and insists that it must involve a rather complicated kind of equality. Kant adds to this that in ideal friendship we must have equal respect as well as equal love. Even this insistence on the need for respect is not altogether new—something very like it is to be found in the *De Amicitia* of Cicero—but it is highly characteristic of Kant.

If we consider friendship to be a duty, there would appear to be a difficulty, and perhaps a special difficulty for Kant, in treating it as an association through love and respect; for love and respect seem to be emotions and, as we are often reminded, emotions cannot be summoned up as motives and so must lie beyond the sphere of duty altogether.

Kant is not unaware of these difficulties. Love, he tells us,[9] is a matter of feeling, not of volition. I cannot love because I will to love, and still less because I ought to love. Hence a duty to love is an absurdity (*ein Unding*). But, unlike some of his critics, Kant does not suppose that this leaves no more to be said.

In the first place, love, even as a natural emotion, is—he tells us—one of the subjective conditions without which our minds would be incapable of receiving the concept of duty. It is indeed absurd to regard it as an emotion which we ought to feel, but it is, nevertheless, a natural predisposition which every man has and in virtue of which he can be subject to duty.[10]

In the second place, besides love as an emotion (*amor complacentiae*) there is also a practical love (*amor benevolentiae*), a kind of goodwill which as issuing in action is subject to the laws of duty. It is our duty to do men kindnesses to the best of our ability whether we feel love for them or not, and even if we recognize that many of them are not conspicuously lovable.[11]

This, it will be said, merely gives the position away: Kant's so-called practical love consists in doing cold services to others for the sake of duty. But this view again is a misunderstanding of what he means. The two kinds of love, emotional and practical, are for him not uncon-

---

[8] *Gesinnung.*
[9] *T.* 401.
[10] *T.* 399.
[11] *T.* 401–2.

nected. Emotional love is, as I have said, a predisposition necessary for the concept of practical love as a duty. Furthermore, we have a duty to cultivate this emotional love so that we may display it in our acts of kindness and friendship; and the continual practice of kindness to our fellow men will in the end lead us 'really to love them.'[12] Surely this is not cold inhumanity but sheer common sense.

Similar considerations apply to the respect which we ought to show to our friends, but here the problem is rather more complicated. Kant uses the rather colourless German word '*Achtung*' in different, but not unconnected, senses. We might say that he uses it almost as a technical term for different grades in what he takes to be fundamentally the same emotion. These grades seem to range from what I call 'reverence' to what I call 'respect', or even 'consideration'. The Latin words employed by Kant are *reverentia* and *observantia*, and we have to remember that these refer, not merely to emotion, but to emotion which issues in action and can so far be subject to rules.

First of all there is reverence for the *law* as such. Kant believes, perhaps with too much confidence, that this emotion will be roused in any man who has not entirely ruined his capacity for intellectual abstraction if only he will contemplate the moral law and 'behold virtue in her proper shape.'[13] This reverence is extended to *men* and *actions* when these seem, as it were, to embody the law or to manifest virtue in a high degree. But even when men are far from being saints or heroes, they still have a right, not perhaps to reverence but at least to respect, simply in virtue of their humanity. Merely as human beings they contain the law in themselves at least potentially—that is, they are aware (or at least can be aware) that they ought to obey the law and so must assume themselves free to do so. This is what constitutes the dignity of man, which we have a duty to respect both in ourselves and in others. Every man has a corresponding right to be respected in his dignity as a man. The duties of love do not give rise to such a corresponding right; for no man can have a right to be loved.

As will have been noticed, the emotion of respect or reverence in all its grades springs either directly or indirectly from our consciousness of the moral law and of our duty (and freedom) to obey it. As a feeling Kant takes respect or reverence to be unique: it does not seem to be connected, as even love is, with the satisfaction of our natural inclinations. In one place[14] he does appear to suggest that it may be at least akin to the natural feeling of a child for its parents, a pupil for his teacher—a feeling which arises from comparing our own worth with

[12] *T.* 402. See also *V.* 247–8 = *L.* 196–7.
[13] *Gr.* 426 n. = 61 n.
[14] *T.* 449.

that of another—but perhaps we should not make too much of this. The essential point is that we can have no duty to feel reverence or respect, yet unless we had a predisposition to feel it we could have no concept of duty, and so no duty, at all. Furthermore, it is a feeling which we do have and which it is our duty to cultivate. This can be done, I take it, partly by contemplating moral goodness and its examples in real life, and still more by acting in accordance with the law by which the feeling is aroused.

Love and respect are thus, in one aspect, feelings which accompany[15] and facilitate the fulfilment of certain duties; but in defining the duties they accompany we have to abstract from their emotional aspect. It cannot be our duty to have feelings of love and respect, but only to cultivate them and to act on them. Hence the duty to love my neighbour must be defined as the duty to act on the maxim of making the ends of others my own (so far as these ends are not immoral). The duty of respecting my fellow man is defined as the duty to act on the maxim of never degrading another to be merely a means for the attainment of my own ends. This does not mean that the fulfilment of these duties is free from emotion, and still less that it ought to be. On the contrary, if we had no predisposition to the emotions of love and respect, the duties could not even arise.

The duty of loving one's neighbour is therefore positive, while the duty of respecting one's neighbour is taken to be negative: it restrains my actions within their proper limits. Duties of love may be described as meritorious in a technical sense because they are not the fulfilment of a right, and because they put others under an obligation to show gratitude. Duties of respect are obligatory but not meritorious since they merely conform to the rights of others and so impose upon them no new obligation.

Considered merely as feelings, the love and respect present in the exercise of our duties may be found in separation: we may love a man who seems little worthy of respect, and we may respect a man who seems little worthy of love. Nevertheless, if we consider love and respect as practical duties, they are always bound together, not merely in friendship but in every duty to others, although in different duties now one and now the other may constitute the main principle so that love may be subordinate to respect or respect to love. Thus it is a duty of love to help a man in need, but we have at the same time a duty of respect; for in order not to wound his self-esteem we ought to act as if we were only giving him his due or performing a service of little merit.[16] Kant may not be an emotional moralist, but he cannot be accused

[15] *T.* 448.
[16] *T.* 448–9.

of forgetting the duty to consider most scrupulously the feelings of others.

In friendship as in other human relations love and respect may be regarded as analogous to the principles of attraction and repulsion in the material world. Love draws men together, while respect keeps them at a fitting distance. It is respect which prevents even the best of friends from being too familiar and so making their friendship cheap.[17] Respect, one might say, is a safeguard against that possessiveness which is the bane of so many friendships, especially of love between men and women and between parents and children.

We may not be prepared to accept all the details of Kant's psychology, but in the main his ethical doctrine is surely sound. The relation of friendship, and even of love, as I hope Professor Hodges would agree, does not exempt men from their ethical duties to one another—or even from their legal duties, though these may be performed from a more generous motive so that the prohibitions and sanctions of the law become less conspicuous. Friendship is, so to speak, an added grace; but—in spite of the views and behaviour sometimes reported in the Sunday newspapers—it gives no one a right to cheat or assault or murder the beloved, or even to withhold kindness, gratitude, and sympathy. And although Kant may seem to speak in too negative a way, is it not a condition of the most perfect friendship that it should be founded, not only on love, but also on a respect which does not cease to show regard for the dignity of every human person as such?

III

We must now turn to the difficulties of friendship.[18] Kant has a dislike of spurious emotion, and he knows well that friendship is a hobby horse for romantic novelists or—as he puts it in his *Lectures*—for rhetorical moralists, of whom he is emphatically not one. As soon as he has defined perfect friendship, he goes on at once to warn us that it is merely an Idea—an ideal which, although morally obligatory, is unattainable in practice: our duty is only to strive towards it as the maximum of mutual love and respect. In his account of the obstacles we have to meet I seem to detect an undercurrent of that satirical humour which, as we know, he commonly displayed with a perfectly straight face in ordinary conversation; but it is usually so dry that most readers take him to be deadly serious. Here he is engaged in bringing a romantic ideal down to earth.

[17] *T.* 470 and 449.
[18] *T.* 469 ff.

The first difficulty arises from the equality in love and respect which is said to belong to friendship. How can a man know that the love he feels for his friend is equal to the love his friend feels for him? Indeed how can he know how far his own love for his friend is balanced by an equal respect? And how can he know whether the very warmth of his affection may not result in a loss of the other's respect? All this, as Kant says, makes it hard to attain the equilibrium of ideal friendship on its subjective or emotional side.

The second difficulty is this. Morally speaking it is the duty of a friend to call attention to the other's faults; for this is in his best interests and so is a duty of love. Unfortunately the friend thus favoured may take a different view. He may think he is being treated with a lack of respect; that this scrutiny and criticism may mean he has already lost the esteem of his friend or is about to lose it; or even that to be thus scrutinized and admonished is an insult in itself. Kant leaves the problem at that.

The next point is that it is most desirable to have a friend in need; that is, provided he is ready to help at his own expense. On the other hand, it is hard on the friend if he is to be weighed down by the needs of another, and chained to somebody else's fate. Hence friendship cannot be an association aiming at reciprocal advantage. The help each friend may count on receiving from the other must not be the motive and end of friendship; for, if it were, each would lose the other's respect. As Kant puts it in his *Lectures,* the delicacy of friendship cannot consist in my seeing that there is a shilling for me in somebody else's money box.[19] I may be confident that my friend will give me help if I am in need, but I should not think that I am entitled to demand it: such help must be understood only as an outer manifestation of inner kindness in the heart, and it is dangerous to put it to the test. Each friend must be generous enough to bear his own burdens and even to conceal them from the other. If he does accept a service from the other, he may be right in counting on equality in the other's affection, but perhaps not in his respect. Kant has always a proper regard for individual independence.

The conclusion of all this seems to be that we should distrust excessive emotion in friendship. Certainly the love in friendship cannot be a sudden overwhelming passion (*Affekt*); for this is blind in its choice and is likely to go up in smoke. It may indeed be sweet to enjoy a reciprocal possession bordering on complete fusion into one person; but friendship based purely on emotion is too delicate a thing to last, and mutual love must be limited by mutual respect. Kant has no use for lovers who

[19] *V.* 259 = *L.* 204.

live in a succession of squabbles in order to enjoy the sweetness of reconciliation.

IV

Having deflated the romantic ideal so precious to *die schöne Seele* Kant turns to a more practicable kind of friendship. He calls it, rather oddly, 'moral friendship' and defines it as *the complete confidence of two persons in disclosing to one another their secret thoughts and feelings, so far as such disclosure is compatible with mutual respect.*

It is not too easy to see how this fits in with the rest of the discussion. This moral friendship is obviously distinct from the friendship of mere emotion—from aesthetic friendship, as Kant calls it here. But it appears also to be distinct from perfect friendship, both because it is defined differently, and also because, as he tells us later, it can in fact be realized, although only rarely. Yet perfect friendship, as we have seen, is also moral: we have a duty to strive towards it as an ideal. It might be suggested that he is now considering perfect friendship in abstraction from its emotional side, but this is unsatisfactory. The definition of moral friendship seems too narrow to cover even the practical side of perfect friendship. Furthermore, it would appear that even moral friendship in this narrow and almost technical sense must still be bound up not only with respect, but presumably also with love, as well as with confidence or trust. It looks as if Kant is singling out for special emphasis that relationship between friends which can be subject to definite moral principles rather than to vague emotions and so can be more readily achieved.

When we come to think of it, we may be inclined to agree that the most fundamental, and the most precious, element in friendship—so to speak, the very core of friendship—is the free intercourse of mind with mind. At any rate those of us who are at all reflective have a need, which must be specially urgent in an authoritarian State, to talk freely with a kindred spirit, as Kant says, about our acquaintances, about religion, and about the government; and in so doing to display, if not to discuss, our own weaknesses and failings. In this way we can escape from the prison in which our thoughts and feelings would otherwise be bottled up. It is not wholly clear how far this moral friendship includes within itself also what in the *Lectures* Kant describes as the friendship of taste, which in certain respects is akin to the friendship described by Aristotle as aiming at the pleasant and yet as being also comprehended within a perfect friendship which aims at the good. If we may judge by the *Lectures*[20] moral friendship (or something very like it) does at least exhibit, not only such qualities as confidence and candour, but also amiability, liveliness, and cheerfulness. On the other hand, the friendship of need does appear to be excluded, as pragmatic or prudential, from moral friendship.[21] This is sound enough so far as an association is *merely* pragmatic; but Kant also appears to exclude, or at least to distinguish, from moral friendship the friendship which burdens itself with the needs of others even out of love. This seems inconsistent with what has gone before, and such a friendship would not be merely pragmatic unless its sole aim were to satisfy some natural inclination and so to attain the individual's own happiness; but in that case the burden would surely cease to be a burden. In his *Lectures*[22] Kant says expressly that the friendship of need is presupposed in every friendship, not in the sense that each friend demands help from the other, but in the sense that each is confident of receiving help, if this should be necessary. The reason why it is here excluded is apparently that it is too vague to be brought under precise rules. As an ideal it knows no limits, but in human experience it must be very limited indeed.

Moral friendship, as defined by Kant, clearly demands a similarity of outlook both intellectual and moral—as he puts it elsewhere,[23] friends must have similar intellectual and moral principles. Otherwise he thinks that at least the friendship of taste depends more on variety. A professor is more likely to enjoy a friendship with a soldier or a merchant than with another professor, since what one professor knows the other will know also.[24] This fully accords with Kant's own practice and with his rule that philosophy should never be talked at dinner.

Although moral friendship can be realized, even if only seldom, the difficulties are not ignored. If our friend is not equally candid, we may be in danger of losing his respect. He may even be ignoble enough to use our confidences to our detriment, or he may be unable to distinguish between what can be repeated to others and what not—he may suffer from indiscretion. No secrets should be passed on to a third party, however supposedly trustworthy, unless express permission has been given to do so. In choosing friends to confide in we have to exercise care and common sense.

Kant fully recognizes that friendship may be too narrow and exclusive: we must regard the limited circle of our friends as only a part of

[20] *V.* 263 = *L.* 207.
[21] *T.* 472.
[22] *V.* 258 = *L.* 204.
[23] *V.* 263 = *L.* 207.
[24] *V.* 260 = *L.* 205.

that wider circle which includes all those who seek to live as citizens of the world; but it is only human nature to begin with the particular and proceed to the universal.[25] We cannot in fact be friends with everybody, but some men are *capable* of being friends with everybody, and it is these we describe as citizens of the world and friends of man: they are willing to put the best interpretation on everything, and they combine goodheartedness with intelligence and taste. The term 'friend of man' is to be preferred to words like 'philanthropist' or 'benefactor' since it contains the notion of equality and respect which these words lack. Kindness ought to be shown with the humility characteristic of a friend of man—not with the pride that comes too easily to those who are rich enough to be philanthropists.

V

Since the relationship between strangers was one of those which Kant is supposed by Professor Hodges to neglect, it should be added that Kant is no more blind to the virtues necessary in casual social intercourse than he is to the deeper virtues of friendship. He adds to his account of friendship a brief appendix[26] on what he calls the homiletic virtues: these are not concerned, as the name might suggest, with sermons, but with the ordinary duties of politeness and sociability. It is our duty to cultivate not only *humanitas practica* but also *humanitas aesthetica* and in this way to associate virtue with the Graces.

The formal manners and outer decorum of a gentleman, which Kant manifested so conspicuously and yet so modestly in his own life— in spite of his contempt for the excessive formalism of his time he was known even in his indigent youth as *der elegante Magister*[27]—are judged by him to be only the outworks and by-products of virtue; but they produce the illusion of a beauty akin to virtue and so bring virtue itself into vogue. Although they may be only the small change of social intercourse, nevertheless, if we practise them sincerely by showing ourselves approachable, affable, polite, hospitable, and gentle (for example, in being able to contradict without wrangling), they can develop into genuine virtue in their practitioner and can impose on others an obligation to follow his example. In the *Lectures*[28] he speaks of them,

[25] *V.* 265 = *L.* 209.

[26] *T.* 473.

[27] The best account of Kant's life in his earlier days is to be found in *Kant und Königsberg* by the late Professor K. Stavenhagen.

[28] *V.* 251 = *L.* 198.

not only as a preparation for the surer exercise of virtue, but even as virtue itself though practised only in miniature.

VI

In this discussion we have been concerned, not so much with the Critical philosopher as with the sage of Königsberg—almost, one might say, with Kant in slippers; and what we have found is not a full-scale treatise on the ethics of friendship but a brief and challenging sketch. From the examination of this limited topic I have sought only to suggest that neither in his life nor in his teaching was he so cold and inhuman and blind as is commonly supposed, although he had a rooted dislike for what I may call gush and portentousness in moral thinking. Professor Hodges gave me my starting-point only because his views are so clear, so ingenious, and on the whole so sympathetic. If I had been looking for really crude misunderstandings, they could easily have been found. When Kant insists throughout that his applied ethics, as opposed to his jurisprudence, is concerned solely with the ends which are also duties, it is almost incredible that so many of his critics should suppose him to be interested only in abstract principles and wholly indifferent to the ends of moral action. This can happen only if we fail to understand what he is doing in the *Groundwork* and proceed on this basis to a fanciful construction of what he must have thought instead of reading what he actually says in the *Metaphysic of Morals*.

May I in conclusion raise a more general question? Apart from the *particular* example of the discussion on friendship—and I might per-haps have chosen a better one for my purpose—what is this *kind* of discussion worth and how far does it belong to the task of philosophy?

Most philosophers today would regard reflections of this type as lying wholly outside the province of philosophy. It is interesting, how-ever, to note that at the end of last year Mr. Nowell-Smith, in a talk on the Third Programme about what he called the unhappy divorce be-tween ethics and psychology, took a different view. As I have not seen this in print, I hope he will forgive me if I have failed to understand him, but I think he put forward three main contentions. First, it is absurd of philosophers to disclaim interest in psychology and refuse to trespass on what they regard as somebody else's territory. Secondly, philosophers ought to discuss the nature of different virtues and vices. And thirdly, they ought to examine and expound the rules of right conduct.

Unfortunately, besides defending these general principles, he went out of his way to assert that their neglect by modern philosophers springs mainly from the influence of Immanuel Kant. He suggested therefore that it would be better for us to go back to the older tradition of Plato and Aristotle.

As there is something to be said against *a priori* history, even when it is written by professed empiricists, perhaps I may be allowed to put on record the following facts.

In the first place Kant did not regard psychology as forbidden ground. On the contrary, he lectured on it for some thirty years and considered this to be among the activities incumbent upon him as a teacher of pure philosophy.[29]

In the second place, as I hope I have already made clear, he discussed systematically the nature of the different virtues and vices.

In the third place the whole *Metaphysic of Morals* may be described as an attempt to formulate the rules of right conduct not only for individuals, but also for States.

No doubt it is possible to argue that the effect of these endeavours was to make his successors want to do the precise opposite—just as some thinkers, notably Professor Dewey, have argued that Kant, in spite of being a consistent opponent of tyranny and whole-hearted advocate of freedom, was responsible for the excesses of Nazi Germany.[30] But such contentions should rest on empirical evidence. So far as I know, there is no evidence that philosophers influenced by Kant have been conspicuous in departing from his example. T. H. Green, for example, was notably interested in the discussion of particular virtues and vices.

If we set aside this lapse into history, what is there to be said about Mr. Nowell-Smith's general principles? Any answer suggested here must be summary, but I hope not unsympathetic.

So far as Kant's own application of these principles is concerned, there can be little doubt that, at least in his university teaching, what he did was well worth while. He was addressing students most of whom were little more than schoolboys, and probably rather rough ones at that; and we know that on them, and indeed on the soldiers and officials who sometimes came to his lectures, he made a lasting impression, both intellectual and moral, which remained as a kind of inspiration throughout their lives. His easiest and most popular lectures were, as we can well imagine, those on Anthropology and Physical Geography, subjects which he regarded as necessary for that knowledge of the

---

[29] *Anthropologie, Vorrede,* 122.

[30] This strange contention has been dealt with faithfully by Professor Julius Ebbinghaus (*Philosophical Quarterly,* April 1954).

world and of human nature without which the 'ought' prescribed by reason cannot on his view be put into practice.[31] In his lectures on Ethics he was obliged to comment on the dry-as-dust textbooks of Baumgarten; but even through the imperfect notes of his pupils we can still see how he could break away and talk frankly about moral problems and moral ideals.

We live in a more sophisticated age, but I am sure Mr. Nowell-Smith is right in saying that a moral philosopher ought to have some knowledge of psychology, as indeed also of economics and of social science. I would only add that thinking about ultimate moral principles should, as Kant always insisted, be sharply distinguished from thinking about their application with the help of psychology, and that both should be distinguished from the study of psychology itself. In order to be comprehensive it is not necessary to be confused.

The real difficulties begin when we have to consider the place that should be assigned in ethics to the study of particular virtues and vices and the study of particular moral rules. All such study should be general, though it may profitably be illustrated by examples. No attempt should be made to work out a system of rules to cover all possible exceptional cases. If we study possible exceptions, it should be in order, as Kant held, to exercise and sharpen moral judgement so that we may be better prepared to decide for ourselves what we ought to do when the moment of crisis comes.

As regards the general rules which have to be formulated in any discussion of virtues and vices, uplift and exhortation, and above all romantic emotion, should be avoided by philosophers, who cannot allow their thinking to be blurred by a haze, however golden, and would at once lose the respect of their more intelligent pupils if they yielded to this temptation. Even a more detached discussion may be put down as tedious moralizing, and it may be thought that philosophers are not qualified for this kind of thinking, which should be left to practical men. Few of us have any ambition to follow in the footsteps of Seneca; and I must admit that when I sought to compare Kant's discussion of friendship with the longer disquisitions of Aristotle and Cicero, I was not greatly encouraged by their example. Aristotle, as always, is dispassionate and acute, if a little flat and over-occupied with minutiae. Cicero—or perhaps in this connexion I should call him Tully—is more inclined to exhortation and not so conspicuously sincere. Perhaps I skimmed through them in too great a hurry, but such enlightenment as I received was not unaccompanied by tedium. On the other hand, it is only fair to Aristotle to say that his account of friendship is less interest-

---

[31] *Physische Geographie, Einleitung,* § 2. 158.

ing than his account of the virtues. And as for Cicero, in spite of his eighteenth-century reputation, he is not a philosopher of the first rank, if he is a philosopher at all.

Although there are difficulties in the way of a moral philosopher who becomes also a moralist, he can hardly be said to understand his own principles if he has no idea how they are to be applied in action; and as even he may also be human, there is a practical problem for him as a man—a problem which is specially acute when difficult moral adjustments have to be made in a rapidly changing society, and when traditional standards are questioned in theory as well as neglected in practice. If he is unable to offer any guidance, who will? Are the problems of action to be left to prophets and priests, or are we to rely on journalists and politicians and men of the world? To some men the exhortations of the prophets may appear as unbalanced or even hysterical, and the instructions of priests as in danger of becoming hide-bound and hag-ridden. As for those who dabble casually in these matters, they are sometimes sentimental, sometimes cynical, generally superficial, and nearly always confused. The ears of youth are assailed by a buzz of conflicting voices. As an American student said to me after a lecture—I hope not because of it: 'Where are we to find out what we ought to do? We are all lost.'

In a democracy it is proper that all sorts of voices should be heard in these debates, and philosophers would be false to their profession if they claimed to speak with special authority. Yet, whatever their limitations, they may perhaps hope to speak with clearer principles and with more consistency than others. By their very detachment they may have fewer axes to grind and less liability to be swept by emotion into folly and fanaticism. They have a tradition, even if it is not always accepted today, of trying to see life steadily and to see it whole. Although they are not infallible, they may do something to dispel the muddles, and cool the emotions, present in popular controversy—I think, for example, of the late Professor Field's little book on *Pacifism and Conscientious Objection* and Professor Hart's wireless talk on capital punishment. If this is possible in dealing with particular topics, there may be good reasons why some philosophers should once again examine practical problems more systematically in their moral and political philosophy. At least they should not be deterred from this by a fear that their reputations will be for ever tarnished if their clearer thinking should also happen to promote more intelligent moral action. Hence I should like to support the plea of Mr. Nowell-Smith against a narrow specialism and against too sharp a separation between theoretical and practical problems; but perhaps he will forgive me for adding that if he wants to sample earlier attempts at doing what he thinks should be done, he might do worse than consult some of the more neglected writings of Immanuel Kant.

Postscript

Since a man's own words throw more light on his personality than any amount of talk about him, I venture to add, even at the cost of some repetition, a translation of the few short sections in the *Metaphysic of Morals* which have formed the chief basis of my discussion. They are taken from Part II, *The Doctrine of Virtue*, pp. 468–74. My renderings are rather more free than they would have been if I had been writing, so to speak, an official translation of the whole book. The text in places is corrupt, and I have sometimes followed the second edition, although it was published without any active co-operation from Kant.

The Ethical Duties We Owe to Other Men, Not Simply as Men, But as Men of Different Sorts and Conditions

§45

Duties of this kind give no occasion for a special chapter in a system of pure ethics: since they are not determined by principles of mutual obligation between men as such, they cannot properly constitute a *part* of the *metaphysical* rudiments of ethical doctrine. All they can offer us is rules for *applying* the principle of virtue (the formal factor) to cases that arise in experience (the material factor)—rules that are adjusted to differences in the persons concerned. Hence, as happens in all empirical divisions, they do not admit of any classification that can be guaranteed to be complete. Nevertheless, just as we require that there should be a passage, with its own special rules, from a metaphysic of nature to physics, so too we may rightly demand something similar from a metaphysic of morals—namely, that by applying pure principles of duty to cases furnished by experience these principles should, as it were, be *schematized* and set out in such a way as to be ready for practical use in moral action.

Consider, for example, questions like the following: How should we behave to men according as they are in a state of moral purity or moral corruption? How ought we to treat them in virtue of their civilized or barbarous condition? How should we conduct ourselves towards the learned or the unlearned? How should we deal with the learned if they handle their science as scholars and men of the world or as narrow specialists and pedants—if they seek practical results or aim rather at wit and taste? How should our treatment of others vary according to their differences of rank, age, sex, health, riches and poverty, and so on? All these questions are concerned, not with so many *kinds* of ethical *obligation* (for there is only *one* kind of ethical obligation, that of virtue as such), but merely with different kinds of *application* (corollaries). These are not to be treated as integral parts of ethics or as members in the *division* of a system (which must arise *a priori* from a concept of reason): they belong only to an appendix.

None the less this application is necessary if the exposition of an ethical system is to be complete.

The Intimate Union of Love and Respect in Friendship

§46

Friendship (considered in its perfection) is an association of two persons through equal and mutual love and respect.

It is easy to see that this is an ideal whereby friends are united through a morally good will in such a way that each is concerned, both practically and emotionally, with the well-being of the other; and even if it does not produce the whole happiness of life, those who adopt this ideal in their attitude to one another are so far worthy of happiness. Hence friendship among men can easily be seen to be their duty.

Yet it is also easy to perceive that such friendship is a mere Idea (although one that is morally necessary): to strive after it (as the maximum of goodness in their attitude towards each other) is a duty imposed by reason—not indeed an ordinary duty, but one which carries honour with it—and yet it is in practice unattainable. For in his relations to his neighbour how can a man make sure that one of the factors requisite for this duty (for example, an attitude of mutual kindness) is *equal* in one friend to what it is in the other? What is more, how can he find out even in the same person what relation holds between the feeling connected with one duty and the feeling connected with the other (for example, the feeling connected with kindness and the feeling connected with respect)? And how can he be sure that if one of the two friends is more ardent in *affection*, he may not because of this lose something of the other's *respect*? Does not this imply that subjectively love and esteem in both parties can hardly be brought into that symmetry of equipoise which none the less is required for friendship?

In this equipoise love can be regarded as attraction and respect as repulsion: if the principle of love bids friends come closer together, the principle of respect requires them to keep one another at a fitting distance. This limitation in intimacy is expressed in the rule that even the best of friends should not make themselves *too familiar* in their relations to one another. Here we find a maxim that holds, not merely for the superior in relation to the inferior, but also *vice versa*. Otherwise the superior may unexpectedly feel his pride hurt: he may wish the respect of the inferior to be for a moment suspended, but not ended. Once respect is impaired, it is lost beyond recovery, so far as inner feeling is concerned, even if its outer marks in the way of manners may be restored.

Friendship conceived as attainable in its purity or completeness (as between Orestes and Pylades or Theseus and Peirithous) is the hobby horse of those who write romances. Contrast with this the saying of Aristotle: 'My dear friends, there is no such a thing as a friend.' The following observations may draw our attention to the difficulties of perfect friendship.

From a moral point of view it is admittedly the duty of a friend to call the other's attention to his faults; for this is in his best interests and so is a duty of love. His partner, however, sees in this a lack of the respect on which he counted: he believes that he has already sunk in the esteem of his friend or that he is in continual danger of losing it altogether because of such scrutiny and secret criticism; and even the mere fact that he is to be scrutinized and admonished will seem to be an insult in itself.

How welcome it is to have a friend in need—provided always that he is an active friend ready to help at his own expense! Yet it is also a heavy burden to feel chained to the fate of another and weighed down with someone else's need.

Hence friendship cannot be an association aiming at mutual advantage—the association must be purely moral. The help each friend may count on receiving from the other in case of need must not be regarded as the end and motive of his friendship—this would mean that he would lose the other's respect: it must be understood only as an outer manifestation of inner kindness in the heart, and should not be put to the test, which is always dangerous. Each friend, that is to say, must be generously intent on sparing the other his own burden, on carrying it solely by himself, and even on concealing it altogether from the other; and yet at the same time he can congratulate himself that in case of need he would be able to count with assurance on the other's help. If one of them does accept a *service* from the other, although he can perhaps rightly count on equality in affection, he may not be able to count on equality in respect; for he sees himself manifestly a stage lower, as put under an obligation without being able to impose any obligation in return.

Sweet as it is to feel a reciprocal possession verging on complete fusion into one person, friendship is a thing so *delicate* (*teneritas amicitiae*) that it is never for a moment safe from *rifts* if we let it rest on emotions and fail to subject reciprocal sympathy and self-surrender to principles—that is, to rules for preventing over-familiarity and for limiting mutual love by the requirements of respect. Such rifts are common among the uneducated, although they do not always lead to a final *rupture* (the rabble brawl and make it up). People of this type cannot abandon one another and yet they cannot come to terms; for they need to squabble in order to relish the sweetness of unity in reconciliation.

At all events the love in friendship cannot be a sudden overwhelming *passion* (*Affekt*); for this is blind in its choice, and in the end it goes up in smoke.

§47

Moral friendship (as distinct from emotional friendship) is the complete confidence of two persons in disclosing to one another their secret thoughts and feelings, so far as such disclosure is compatible with mutual respect.

Man is a being meant for society (though he is also an unsociable one); and in cultivating social qualities he feels powerfully the need to *disclose* himself to others (even without having any further end in view). On the other hand, since he is also cramped and forewarned by the fear that others might misuse this revelation of his thoughts, he sees himself constrained to *lock up* in himself a good part of his opinions (especially those about other people). He would like to discuss with someone else what he thinks about his acquaintances, about the government, about religion, and so on; but he dare not risk it, partly because the confidant might use this to his detriment, while cautiously holding back his own views, and partly because, if he himself exposes his defects while the confidant conceals his own, he might forfeit the other's respect by exhibiting himself with complete candour.

If he finds a man of understanding with whom he need not fear this danger but can unbosom himself in complete confidence—a man too who shares his way of looking at things—he can then air his views; he is no longer entirely *alone* with his thoughts as in a prison, but enjoys a freedom which he cannot have among the common herd, where he must shut himself up in himself. Every man has his secrets and dare not confide blindly in others; for most of them have an ignoble tendency to use his confidences to his disadvantage, and many have not enough common sense to appreciate and distinguish what can be repeated and what not—they suffer from indiscretion. It is rare to find the requisite combination of qualities in one person (*rara avis in terris, nigroque simillima cygno*), especially as the closest friendship demands that this understanding and trusted friend should also feel bound not to impart the secrets confided to him to any other, however supposedly trustworthy, unless express permission has been given to do so.

This kind of friendship (friendship conceived solely as moral) is no mere ideal: like the black swan it does exist here and there in its perfection. The other kind of friendship (the pragmatic), which harasses itself with the ends of other men, although out of love, can have neither the purity nor the requisite completeness that is demanded if a maxim is to determine action precisely: it is an ideal set by our wishes, which knows no limits as a concept of reason, but in experience must be very limited indeed.

A *friend of man* as such (that is, a friend of the whole human race) is one who sympathizes with the well-being of all men: he shares their joy in it and will never disturb it without deep regret. Yet the expression 'a *friend* of man' is of somewhat narrower meaning than a term like '*philanthropist*'—that is, one who merely loves his fellow men. For in the expression 'a friend of man' there is also thought and regard for the *equality* of men—the Idea that in putting others under an obligation by our kindness we are under an obligation ourselves; as if we were brothers under one universal father who seeks the happiness of us all.

Thus the relation of a patron, as benefactor, to his protégé, as a beneficiary obliged to be grateful, may indeed be a relation of mutual love, but not of friendship; for the respect due from each to the other is not equal. The duty of showing kindness as a friend of man is a necessary humbling of oneself, and regard for this helps to save us from the pride so apt to overcome those who are fortunate enough to possess the means for being benefactors.

Appendix: The Virtues of Social Intercourse
(*virtutes homileticae*)

§48

It is a duty both to ourselves and to others to display moral excellence in our social relations (*officium commercii, sociabilitas*)—not to *isolate* ourselves (*separatistam agere*); and while we ought to make ourselves a fixed centre of our principles, we should regard the circle thus drawn around us as also a part of the wider circle which comprehends all those who seek to be citizens of the world. The aim here is not to further the highest good of the world as an end, but only to cultivate the means that lead indirectly to this end. Among such means are agreeableness in society, considerateness, mutual love and respect (amiability and good manners, *humanitas aesthetica et decorum*). By cultivating these we associate virtue with the Graces, and to do this is itself an ethical duty.

All these are indeed only *outworks* or by-products (*parerga*) which give the illusion of a beauty akin to virtue; but it is not an illusion that deceives us since everybody knows how it ought to be taken. Although we have here only the small change of intercourse, yet it does promote the feeling for virtue itself by an effort to bring this illusion as near as possible to the truth, when we show ourselves *approachable, affable, polite, hospitable,* and *gentle* (for example, in being able to contradict without wrangling). Even as the purely formal manners of society all these attitudes show what is obligatory and put others under a like obligation: they make for a virtuous state of mind in so far as they at least bring virtue into *vogue.*

The question then arises: Is it right to cultivate relations with the vicious? We cannot avoid meeting them—in order to do so we should have to retire from the world; and besides we are not competent to judge them.

But where vice becomes a scandal, that is, a public exhibition of contempt for the strict laws of duty, and so brings with it open dishonour, then, even if it is not punishable by the laws of the land, the association that formerly existed must be broken off or avoided as much as possible. To continue the association further robs virtue of all honour and puts it up for sale to any one rich enough to bribe the toadies of this world with the delights of self-indulgence.

[8]

Personal Love and Kantian Ethics
in *Effi Briest*

Julia Annas

One of the most striking aspects of Kant's moral philosophy is the way in which he takes himself to be articulating ordinary moral consciousness and providing a metaphysical basis for judgments that we are naturally inclined to make anyway. (At the end of chapter 1 of the *Groundwork of the Metaphysics of Morals,* he even questions whether philosophy might do more harm than good in disturbing the innocence of the ordinary person's moral reasoning.) This raises some difficulties for the parallels Kant wants between practical and theoretical reason (since the everyday use of theoretical reason, unstirred to philosophical self-consciousness, is not so innocent), yet Kant still insists that, while the presupposition of moral thinking, namely freedom to act, is problematic,[1] there is no great problem about what moral thinking is. It is the recognition that there are demands on us which are categorical—which do not depend on any desire or interests that we have—and which are impartial, applying to anyone in relevantly similar circumstances, individual characteristics and particular commitments being discarded as irrelevant.[2] Kant realizes, of course, that we do not *act* morally all or even most of the time; but "even children of moderate age" can recognize, he claims, what is obvious to anybody

This essay was originally published in *Philosophy and Literature* 8, 1 (1984): 15–31. Reprinted by permission of The Johns Hopkins University Press.

I have been helped by discussion with Martha Nussbaum, Margaret Jacobs, Anthony Lloyd and Ralph Walker.

[1] Kant's claims about the kind of freedom which morality presupposes are riddled with difficulty, and he shifts in his view of the relation between freedom and morality. See R. C. S. Walker, *Kant* (London: Routledge and Kegan Paul, 1978), pp. 147–50.

[2] This is a rather tidied-up representation of Kant's claims about the universality of moral judgment. He is somewhat vague on this (see Walker, pp. 151–59, esp. n. 2). I take it that Kant's intentions are captured by the thought that a moral judgment must be impartial in the sense of favoring no individual as such.

prepared to use their reason, namely that morality is a matter of doing one's duty regardless of one's own interests or desires, and abstracting totally from any personal considerations.[3]

The most telling modern criticism of Kant is that he was just wrong in his claim to be articulating what morality is. It is all too obvious to us now that Kant was overimpressed by the consensus among moral views uttered by the members of the society in which he lived; that the religious background giving those views support has largely disappeared;[4] and that for many people morality simply cannot be regarded in Kant's way without fiction and pretense.[5] It can no longer seem obvious to us that the Categorical Imperative is the manifest principle of morality, the only serious problem about this being how it is possible. And not only is the unconditional force Kant ascribes to morality not easily available to us, we are also all too aware of the dangers implicit in regarding morality as essentially a matter of impartiality.[6] At best we can regard Kant as having highlighted something of importance in *some* areas of morality, and having then taken himself wrongly to have characterized the whole of it.[7]

Modern criticisms of Kant, then, spring from the fact that we have to adjust to a situation in which we no longer find moral imperatives categorical and have difficulty in seeing impartiality as definitive of the moral point of view. We no longer have the moral consciousness that Kant was confident of finding even in children of moderate age; and we have to live with that fact in moral philosophy as well as in everyday moral life.[8]

---

[3] Prussian Academy edition, pp. 410–11; p. 75 of the translation of the *Groundwork of the Metaphysics of Morals* in H. J. Paton, *The Moral Law* (London: Hutchinson, 1948).

[4] See. E. Anscombe, "Modern Moral Philosophy," *Philosophy* (1958): 1–19; reprinted in *The Definition of Morality*, eds. G. Wallace and A. Walker (London: Methuen, 1970), pp. 211–34.

[5] This view is strongly argued by P. Foot in *Virtues and Vices* (Oxford: Blackwell, 1978) and also in *Philosophy as It Is*, eds. T. Honderich, and M. Burnyeat (London: Penguin, 1979), pp. 12–28.

[6] This has been powerfully argued by Bernard Williams, mostly in his attacks on utilitarianism. The article in which the relevance of these arguments to Kantianism is most strongly brought out is "Persons, Character and Morality," in *The Identities of Persons*, ed. A. O. Rorty (Berkeley: University of California Press, 1976), pp. 197–216. Williams's arguments show that the differences between Kantian and utilitarian theories are small compared with their fundamental agreement that morality requires impartiality, and that personal needs and individual projects are by definition not moral considerations.

[7] See the perceptive criticisms of Kant's claims to be articulating "the moral point of view" in L. Blum, *Friendship, Altruism and Morality* (London: Routledge and Kegan Paul, 1980), esp. chap. 3.

[8] Confusions often arise in moral argument because of uncertainty as to whether the moral point of view is what Kant claims it is, but personal projects matter also (or more), or whether Kant was wrong to exclude personal projects from the moral point of view. Blum has several criticisms of Williams on this score; see pp. 212–13 and 223–24. For an

Because of this we may fail to ask another question, which is itself of deep interest: does Kant's account of the structure of morality do justice even to the actual moral lives of people who did respond, in a way we no longer can, to the call of Duty stripped of all possible appeal to any other motive? Kant separates morality and its motive from all actual concerns of the agent. What are the results of this in someone who responds to this notion of morality, and understands it in a Kantian way? It is hard to ask about the consequences to ourselves of having Kant's view of morality, for we cannot unselfconsciously have this viewpoint. Our moral universe is, from the Kantian point of view, dislocated and pluralistic, and the question does not arise of the consequences to the agent of holding the Kantian point of view artlessly and in confident innocence of alternatives.

Effi Briest is of exceptional interest to anyone interested in Kant's moral philosophy because in it we see people who think of Duty as Kant assumed everyone does, and we can see the further effects of this in their moral thinking and moral personalities in a way no contemporary book could bring out. Fontane is, of course, writing about Bismarck's Prussia of the 1890s. Since Kant's time Prussian imperialism has flourished, Berlin has become an important capital and there have been vast social changes. Nevertheless, Fontane is writing about a severely Protestant Prussian society in which, although Kant is never mentioned in the novel, a Kantian view of morality, and its religious background, prevails. Duty is thought of as being sharply opposed to any of the agent's desires, needs or interests, and is grasped by abstracting from all personal considerations. Fontane's characters differ from us in that these are ideas that they are brought up on and live by; for them Duty really does have a categorical Kantian role, and they see any opposition to it in themselves as being mere self-interest. And we can ask in their case the question that we cannot realistically ask in our own: What kind of person is it who thinks in this kind of way?

I

Effi Briest is, of course, far more than a case study of people who impose a Kantian framework on their moral lives. It is a moving and

---

extreme, but revealing, statement of the view that Kant was right about morality but that just gives us good reason to suspect the notion, see Joan Didion, *Slouching towards Bethlehem* (London: Penguin, 1979), especially the final paragraph: "Because when we start deceiving ourselves into thinking not that we want something or need something, not that it is a pragmatic necessity for us to have it, but that it is a *moral imperative* that we have it, then is when we join the fashionable madmen, and then is when the thin whine of hysteria is heard in the land, and then is when we are in bad trouble."

very skillful work, deservedly one of the most famous examples of the nineteenth-century realist novel. The central character is a woman and the central theme adultery, another respect in which Fontane's preoccupations are typical of his time, adultery being the situation where the effects of society's attitudes are more marked as limitations on how individuals can perceive their own lives. Once more, the way Effi's life is destroyed by others' attitudes after the divorce has clear parallels with the fate of Anna Karenina.[9] In picking out as a single theme the effects on people's lives of seeing morality in Kantian terms, I am conscious of being highly selective. For one thing I shall not concentrate directly on Effi herself, since she is the character in the book who least thinks in a Kantian way. I shall simply assume here, without attempting to defend it, my assumption that there is nothing arbitrarily subjective in giving one of many possible readings of a rich and complex book.

I shall not be claiming, either, that my reading necessarily reconstructs Fontane's own intentions in writing the book. For, even if this were possible, and a proper critical task (both highly contentious), it would not have decisive weight in the present issue. What is at stake is the effect on the characters of a moral outlook which everyone takes for granted, and in a novel exploiting the conventions of realism this can be studied in its own right as distinct from any authorial judgment that we might be able to distill out. Further, Fontane's attitudes to Prussia, to the social conventions prominent in this novel, and to adultery, are complex and often ambivalent.[10] As one reads *Effi Briest* it is hard not to think of the author as endorsing what I shall claim to be a strong implicit criticism of the Kantian view of morality. But Fontane did not write novels to illustrate moral themes; and in other contexts he was capable of highly Kantian sentiments. At Frederick William I's memorably horrible act of forcing his son, Frederick the Great, to watch the execution of his friend Katte, Fontane once remarked that far from being a blot on the Hohenzollern escutcheon it shone like a precious stone—even though it was a bloodstone. Whatever Fontane's own intentions, we can hardly fail to see this remark as a terrible distortion of Kant's claim that even in the most difficult of circumstances the good will shines like a precious stone; no doubt it did take

[9] See J. P. Stern, "*Effi Briest, Madame Bovary, Anna Karenina,*" *Modern Language Review* 52 (1957): 363–75. This article, however, shows at points an odd understanding of morality.

[10] Fontane's earlier novel *L'Adultera*—translated by G. Annan as *The Woman Taken in Adultery* (Chicago: University of Chicago Press, 1979)—deals with the same theme as *Effi Briest* in a quite different and untragic way.

strong will and devotion to duty to get Frederick William to do that to his son.[11]

II

Effi Briest is a novel of adultery, but the actual adultery is all offstage: what we see are rather its effects in people's lives. Most of the book describes the background to and development of an affair the revelation of which six years later creates utter wreckage in the lives of the characters whom the book has made familiar to us.

As the book opens we see Effi, a healthy and vigorous sixteen-year-old girl, playing childish games with her friends and waiting without interest for her parents' distinguished visitor. Half an hour later she is engaged to him. Baron von Innstetten is a middle-aged bureaucrat, well launched on a successful career. In his youth he was in love with Effi's mother, but the match did not come off because he had not achieved enough in his career; she married a much older, successful man, exactly as Effi in turn is now to do. Sentiment has led Innstetten, when ready to marry, to his old love's daughter, and Effi's parents welcome him.

It is a situation which one would think very likely to lead to disaster, and the Briests are, in fact, once Effi is safely married, disarmingly realistic about it, and frank about expressing their beliefs. They know that there is no romantic love on either side, that Innstetten is too staid for a restless, curious and immature girl, and that there is something odd about their own feelings in the matter. "Now *you* would have been able to cope," says Briest to his wife. "You would have been altogether

---

[11] "Unsere Zeit einerseits in Verweichlichung, anderseits in Oberflächlichkeit, die nicht tief genug in den Fall eindringt, hat in dem Geschehen einen *Fleck* auf dem blanken Schilde der Hohenzollern erkennen wollen; ich meinerseits sehe darin einen *Schmuck*, einen Edelstein. Dass es ein Blutkarneol ist, ändert nichts" (*Westf. Monatshefte* 1879, p. 723). I owe the reference to Professor A. C. Lloyd who found it copied in a MS. slip of Levin Schücking. Kant's well-known passage, at the opening of the first chapter of the *Groundwork* (Academy edition, p. 395): "Wenn gleich durch eine besondere Ungunst des Schicksals, oder durch kärgliche Ausstattung einer stiefmütterlichen Natur es diesem Willen gänzlich an Vermögen fehlte, seine Absicht durchzusetzen; wenn bei seiner grössten Bestrebung dennoch nichts von ihm ausgerichtet würde, und nur der gute Wille (freilich nicht etwa als ein blosser Wunsch, sondern als die Aufbietung aller Mittel, so weit sie in unserer Gewalt sind) übrig bliebe; so würde er wie ein Juwel doch für sich selbst glänzen, als etwas, das seinen vollen Werth in sich selbst hat." In *Effi Briest*, Frederick's fate is mentioned sympathetically by Wüllersdorf, when trying to comfort Innstetten for the emptiness of his life: "Or drive out to Potsdam . . . where Kaiser Friedrich is buried. . . . And while you're standing there just think what *his* life was like, and if that doesn't reassure you, then you're beyond all help" (p. 261).

more suited to Innstetten than Effi."[12] (Effi later has exactly the same thought: "Oh, I'm not really any good as a grand lady. Now mother would have fitted in here" [p. 71].). Effi's mother sees the problem exactly:

> Her vanity will be satisfied, but will her love of fun, her love of adventure? I doubt it. Where day-to-day entertainment and excitement are concerned, all those little things that keep away boredom, that deadly enemy of clever young women, Innstetten will be a very poor help. . . . And the worst thing is that he won't even try properly to tackle the question of how he should set about it. They'll jog along like that for a while without much harm being done, but finally she'll notice it and then she'll feel hurt. And then I don't know what will happen. Because although she's so gentle and easy-going, there's also a touch of the devil in her and she can take lots of risks. (pp. 43–44)

The forecast is absolutely right. Effi gets along well enough with Innstetten, but after a year of marriage neither sex nor motherhood have woken her up to a new life; her exalted social position forces her to behave in a sophisticated fashion, but she has not matured. She is still happiest when she can get away to her parents' house and play her old games with her childhood friends; the new role she has to play constrains her, but answers to nothing in her nature. Stuck in a boring, provincial northern port, sustaining, as provincial governor's wife, a stifling social round visiting bigoted and philistine local gentry, Effi becomes easy prey for Major Crampas, a cynical (and rather stagy) seducer. He has no advantages of an obvious kind over her husband (he is even older, for example) but it is clear that he desires her sexually, whereas Innstetten's desires are rather placid. Effi does not love or admire him, but she drifts and is drawn by sexual forces that are feared and unfamiliar. "Although she was capable of strong feelings, she was not a strong character, she lacked endurance . . . and so, she drifted on, one day because she felt unable to change anything, the next because she didn't want to. . . . Sometimes she was shocked to realize how easy she found it" (p. 157). Innstetten is promoted and they move to Berlin; she regards this as her salvation from danger. The affair is over; it never meant much to Crampas, and it turns out that it has positively helped Effi's marriage. She no longer feels the need to court risk, many of her tensions have been resolved, and she settles down to six happy years of marriage. Innstetten and she turn out to be well-matched and to suit each other well; the affair is forgotten.

[12] Theodor Fontane, *Effi Briest*, trans. Douglas Parmée (London: Penguin Classics, 1967), p. 41. All references are to this edition and will be inserted parenthetically in the text.

Then by accident Innstetten discovers the six-year-old incriminating letters from Crampas to Effi, which she has kept. ("What are stoves and fireplaces for?" remarks a cynical friend [p. 235]. We have no doubt that Crampas has destroyed hers.)

What is Innstetten to do? He does his duty. He challenges Crampas to a duel and kills him, and he divorces Effi.

But what he does hardly exhausts our interest; we want to know what lies behind these actions, how he responds, and feels he has to respond, to this knowledge.

III

Innstetten is a man of principle. At her engagement the local minister tells Effi so admiringly. She is worried. "I think Niemayer even said later on that he was a man of fundamental principles, too. . . . And I'm afraid that I . . . that I haven't got any" (p. 39). After the divorce, she finds that she was right to be worried; the Minister's wife, saying that she will try to persuade Innstetten to let Effi see their daughter, says that "it won't be an easy task for us. Your husband—forgive me if I refer to him as I used to—is not a man who acts according to moods and whims but according to principles, and he'll find it hard to give them up or even to relax them temporarily. . . . Anything that is hard on you he considers right and proper" (p. 245).

When Innstetten reads the letters, he feels no hatred or desire for revenge; he loves his wife and can understand all too well why she was tempted at the time, and how unimportant the affair was in their lives. Above all, the lapse of time has removed passions about it (p. 214). With the knowledge that has come from living with her for many years, Innstetten has an understanding of Effi that blocks and breaks up simple, crude emotional responses. His personal feelings and desires all lead him to wish to leave things as they are. He loves his wife and child and has every wish not to wreck their lives as well as his own.

Still, he acts. Why? "It's got to be done. I've no choice, I must do it" (p. 215). The reason Innstetten gives is that, while individuals can forgive, society cannot; and individuals cannot escape society: "society will despise us and finally we will despise ourselves and not be able to bear it and blow our brains out" (p. 215). And he tells his friend Wüllersdorf that what forces him to act is the fact that now somebody else knows. As long as he alone knew, he could have acted or not, but he cannot live with the thought that another knows and must judge him accordingly, even a single friend (pp. 215–16). Neither reason, however, really explains Innstetten's action. Since he does not really respect society's rules, he does not really feel the pressures he talks about: "All that high-falutin' talk about 'God's judgment' is nonsense, of course, and we don't want any of that, yet our own cult of honour on the other hand is idolatry" (p. 216). Innstetten is not an empty bureaucrat like Karenin; his resources are inner. His patriotic feelings, for example, are private and he dislikes public jingoism (pp. 142, 145). He does not, as his words to Wüllersdorf suggest, lack the moral courage to act as he thinks right regardless of others, and we do not really believe him when he says that his opinion of himself depends utterly on his friend's opinion of his wife.

The trouble is deeper. If he does not do his duty, Innstetten cannot live with himself, regardless of other people. After killing Crampas, he feels revulsion and wishes he had acted differently. But, revealingly, he sees only one alternative: "I should have burnt the letters. . . . And when she came to me, all unsuspecting, I should have said to her, 'There's where you belong' and cut myself off from her. Inwardly, not in the eyes of the world. There are so many lives that aren't real lives and so many marriages that aren't real marriages, either. . . . And my happiness would have come to an end . . ." (p. 222). So, in spite of what he said, Innstetten did really have a choice whether or not to kill Crampas, and divorce Effi; but he did not have a choice whether or not to reject her inwardly. It may be the knowledge that another person has which impels him to public action; but it is the knowledge that he has, regardless of others, that has already destroyed his happiness, because it has forced him to divorce Effi in his heart. (It is clear to him that such an inner separation would have destroyed their happiness as effectively as the public action he does take.)

How can Innstetten understand Effi as well as he does, feel no anger or desire for revenge, feel so little commitment to society's conventions on the issue, and yet be unable to forgive her and accept what she has done? It is because he is a man of principle. His understanding of his wife becomes inert, unable to move him, because he cannot trust or accept feelings that go against his principles. When he believed Effi innocent he had a "good conscience" about loving her (p. 99). Now he can no longer have such a good conscience; he can only sustain feelings for her that are morally appropriate to what she has done, certified by principle. Five minutes' reading of the letters changes him from a devoted husband into a man who never sees his wife again and warns their daughter against her as a moral danger. And the frightening thing about this is the way it takes place in spite of all his natural feelings and his full recognition of the depth and significance of a shared life and mutual affection. His principles drive him not only to destructive action but to a rejection of every loving impulse towards

Effi; his sympathy with her and understanding of what she has done remain frozen, unable to motivate him to accept her.

Innstetten is a textbook example of Kant's man who acts out of respect for the moral law, without or indeed against all motives that arise from one's human nature. Kant's philanthropist begins to show his moral worth of character when he acts from duty rather than inclination; Innstetten, acting as an injured husband should in his society, does so from duty and against inclination. The six-year gap between lapse and discovery makes it clear to all, including him, that his actions are not motivated by feelings that would have been perfectly natural, like rage or jealousy. What then does motivate him?

Kant describes this type of motivation: "Now an action done from duty has to set aside altogether the influence of inclination, and along with inclination every object of the will; so there is nothing left able to determine the will except objectively the *law* and subjectively *pure reverence* for this practical law, and therefore the maxim of obeying this law even to the detriment of all my inclinations."[13] The imperative of duty has a content, but Innstetten does not reject Effi (publicly or inwardly) because that content has any appeal to him; it has none. His action thus involves, for Kant, no objectionable heteronomy of the will; his reaction to what he should do is purely formal, since, as Kant demands, the object of his reverence for the moral law is the law alone. Innstetten sees his duty as inescapable just because it is his duty and not imposed on him by any inclination. What he must do thus has for him the status of a categorical imperative which "must . . . abstract from all objects to this extent—they should be without any *influence* at all on the will so that practical reason (the will) may not merely administer an alien interest but may simply manifest its own sovereign authority as the supreme maker of law."[14]

Kant follows up the passage just quoted with the statement that one ought to promote others' happiness, not because one cares about it in any way, trivial or profound, but because it cannot be one's duty to be indifferent to it. Thus we are offered a roundabout and unconvincing moral reason for what we would normally take to be the province of our natural affections. If Innstetten had sought Effi's unhappiness because of jealousy or a sense of wounded honor, we would have at once understood (whether or not we approved). But like a good Kantian he does not act for any such reason. His duel with Crampas was "a bit of play-acting" inspired by no real hatred. "And now I must continue to play-act and send Effi away and ruin her life and mine as well" (p.

13 Academy edition, pp. 400–401; Paton, p. 66.
14 Academy edition, p. 441; Paton, p. 102.

222). Innstetten promotes his own, and Effi's, unhappiness out of pure duty, rising above every inclination in order to act out of pure reverence for the moral law.

Have we a criticism of Kantian ethics in this terrible example of living according to it? I think that we do; but we must be careful not to confuse it with different and ineffective criticisms that might be made.

Kant states that in moral philosophy we cannot argue from examples at all; but his reasons have no force here. He objects that we can never know that we have a *pure* example of what is supposedly displayed, and thus examples cannot be used to establish principles, since they presuppose them. But we are not trying to derive an exceptionless principle from this, or any, example; and it would be curious to suppose that this is the role examples ever play in moral philosophy. Kant himself admits that examples "set beyond doubt the practicability of what the law commands."[15] An example like the present one shows that it is not only practicable but in some ways questionable: from Innstetten's reverence for the moral law we draw some adverse conclusions about the kind of person his moral outlook makes him. Of course the example does not *prove* anything; we must inescapably use our judgment as to what in it is relevant and what is not. But why should there be anything surprising in that? It is only from an already accepted Kantian point of view that examples are limited to the trivial role of illustrating already established principles, or forced into the impossible role of proving principles all by themselves.

It is not a telling criticism of Kant to point out that Innstetten's action needlessly wrecks a lot of happiness for the sake of doing a duty that has no obvious point beyond itself. What he does, of course, produces negative utility on anybody's understanding of "utility"; but while this is, unsurprisingly, a knockdown objection for a utilitarian, it is not an objection that damages Kant in his own terms. Our reasoning faculties, he holds, are not limited to working out good or bad consequences; reason "can even reduce happiness to less than zero without proceeding contrary to its purpose"; reason has its own kind of satisfaction in fulfilling a purpose which is demanded by reason even at the expense of inclination.[16] Innstetten is perfectly aware that what he is doing has catastrophic consequences in destroying happiness, and this has already failed to move him. It is not enough for the utilitarian to claim that this is irrational, since he disagrees, finding it more rationally compelling to do his duty. And it is not enough either for the utilitarian then to say that the consequences *ought* to have moved him, for this is

[15] Academy edition, p. 409; Paton, p. 73.
[16] Academy edition, p. 396; Paton, p. 62.

just to disagree without offering any further grounds. (I shall ignore the puerile move of claiming that Innstetten *must* have been moved by the happiness of having done his duty.)

The serious objection is that Innstetten's action and its motivation provide no criticism of Kant, because the action fails by Kant's own standards to be a moral action.[17] Innstetten feels the force of the moral law, but in this case he has a wrong conception of what morality is: he has confused the sublime moral law with the social conventions of Bismarck's Berlin. Kant does not only teach that morality is distinct from any inclination; he also gives a test for the maxims of our actions if we wish to act morally: "Act only on that maxim through which you can at the same time will that it should become a universal law." And Innstetten's action fails this test; the resulting tragedy thus shows nothing wrong with thinking in a Kantian way, but at most something wrong with being insufficiently critical as to what morality is.

One might try to resist this objection by claiming that it is not clear that Innstetten's maxim of avenging his wrong as a husband *does* fail Kant's test. Innstetten is certainly being completely impartial in that he is not smuggling in any factor which favors himself. The reverse is true. He could certainly universalize the maxim that all injured husbands should avenge their wrongs. There is no inconsistency in willing this to hold as a universal law of nature. (Perhaps it is thought that he could not *will* this, because it is, like letting one's talents rot, not in accordance with our rational nature; but it is notoriously unclear just what this does and does not exclude.)[18]

But this does not succeed in meeting the objection. Innstetten is not being impartial in the relevant sense; certainly he is not favoring himself, but then neither is he motivated to defend anyone else's wounded honor as though it were his own. He reacts precisely as the particular man to whom a particular woman is married; in going along with society's demands he does not question whether they might lack real force just because they apply to him in virtue of that fact. Innstetten is at no point uncritical of the duel, or the divorce—or society's attitude to both—but his response is not to deliberate about what then *is* required of him as a rational agent; rather, he goes ahead with what society requires, though he does not endorse it and is quite detached

---

[17] A great deal depends on what kind of "test" we take Kant to be proposing. Ralph Walker in a most helpful discussion has suggested that Kant himself can be interpreted in a more sympathetic way than I propose (though my interpretation is the one usually made, and therefore presumably the one available to the characters in the novel).

[18] *The Lectures on Ethics* take it as obvious that it is not in accordance with our rational nature to will the performance of a great many kinds of actions where we might find the claim dubious, such as suicide and sodomy.

from it. As he and Crampas fight, in absurdly formalistic fashion, they are both aware of the absurdity of what they are doing and its total irrelevance to the way they both feel. After the duel, Innstetten imagines Crampas's last look as saying, "'Innstetten, always standing on principle . . . .' And perhaps he was right—I can hear myself saying something similar. True, if I'd felt deep hatred, if I'd had an irresistible urge for vengeance . . ." (p. 222). Innstetten's motivation is hollow and empty even to himself;[19] in its passivity towards society's demands it shows itself as not truly moral by Kantian standards as well as ours.

But even if Innstetten's maxim of action fails Kantian tests, this leaves undisturbed the really important objection against him as a Kantian moral agent, for this is an objection to the results of the *form* of Kantian moral thinking, and holds even for an agent who does not succeed in giving his maxims of action acceptable Kantian content. Innstetten is aware that he could have burned the letters, but could not, for all that, have forgiven Effi; and this is the heart of the matter. He could have altered things so that the knowledge that Effi was unfaithful need not have led him to kill Crampas; but he has no power over the effects of that knowledge within himself. He cannot avoid the force of his pure reverence for the moral law, which Kant describes with so much approval, and against which any other motivation is set as being merely inclination and deprived of all value. "And when she came to me, all unsuspecting, I should have said to her, 'There's where you belong' and cut myself off from her." Kantian morality is condemned not by Innstetten's legal murder of Crampas, which it need not endorse, but by the effects it has on Innstetten's way of thinking, which it must.

Why is Innstetten forced, unwillingly and against his better nature, to cut off all the feelings he has for Effi as his wife, companion, mother of his child? The novel poses this question very starkly, since the marriage was never a match of romantic love and the adultery long ago.

We find the answer in Kant's sharp separation of the motive to be moral on the one hand from all *inclinations* on the other; and this is the core of the defect in Kantian morality which Innstetten's tragedy shows up. For if the call of morality is different in kind from *any* other motive I have, it can make no difference, from the moral point of view, wheth-

---

[19] One could say that what motivates Innstetten and Crampas is not so much duty as their consciousness of themselves as dutiful people; this second-level motive works in the absence of any conviction in the first-level attitudes. This is what Williams calls the "reflexive deformation" of a moral attitude—"Utilitarianism and Moral Self-Indulgence" in *Contemporary British Philosophy*, 4th series, ed. H. D. Lewis (London: Allen and Unwin, 1976). In their case it is less self-indulgence than moral nihilism of a kind, a peculiar absurdist commitment to a principle in the conviction that no actual facts about the situation rationally compel to action.

er my motives were for self-gratification or for benefiting other people: benevolence or attachment to others, just because they are motives
that depend on particular objects, produce heteronomy of the will just
as much as the pursuit of one's own happiness. *Any* material object for
practical reasoning precludes the autonomy demanded by morality;
from the moral point of view, an attachment to the happiness of other
individuals merely because they are those individuals (one's family, for
example) is just as much a barrier to the true impartiality required by
morality as is an attachment to one's own happiness regardless of
others. Hence Kant's rightly notorious example of the philanthropist
whose character can be truly seen as moral only when he loses all
pleasure in benevolence; the benevolent character is itself denied all
moral worth and placed quite explicitly on a level with a shop-keeper's
concern for his profits. As Bernard Williams penetratingly puts it in
describing Kant's view:

> The deeply disparate character of moral and non-moral motivation, to-
> gether with the special dignity or supremacy attached to the moral, make
> it very difficult to assign to those other relations and motivations [based
> on attachments to individuals] the significance or structural importance
> which some of them are capable of possessing. Once one thinks about
> what is involved in having a character, one can see that the Kantians'
> omission of character is both a condition of their ultimate insistence on
> the demands of impartial morality, and also a reason for finding inade-
> quate their account of the individual.[20]

When one reads Kant, one is struck by the insistent way he always
opposes moral motivation to *self*-interest and love of *self*. The *only*
danger to the uninstructed moral reason is presented as being "needs
and inclinations" which present a "turbulent" opposition to dutiful-
ness; reverence for the moral law "is properly awareness of a value
which demolishes my self-love"; what is relative to universal human
inclinations and needs has a market *price*, but no dignity (all non-moral
motivations, again, are put on the level of the shop-keeper's); man as
unaware of his membership in the kingdom of ends "would have to be
regarded as subject only to the law of nature—the law of his own
needs."[21] Most disturbing of all is the well-known passage where love
which cannot be commanded, residing "in the propensions of feelings"
and "melting compassion" is labelled *pathological;*[22] it is an "inclination"

[20] Bernard Williams, "Persons, Character and Morality," pp. 198, 210.
[21] Academy edition, p. 405; Paton, p. 70; Academy edition, p. 401 n.; Paton, p. 67;
Academy edition, pp. 434–35; Paton, p. 96; Academy edition, pp. 439–40; Paton, p. 101.
[22] Academy edition, p. 399; Paton, p. 65. On Kant's view of the emotions see the
criticisms by Blum.

that one happens to have, like a disease. Because of Kant's great stress on the freedom that is presupposed by morality, *all* our particular attachments and commitments appear as mere inclinations with respect to which we are *passive;* they do not express anything significant about our moral personalities (there is no moral significance just in being a philanthropist rather than a profit-maker); and the choices between alternatives that they express and lead to are all morally indifferent. And because what matters is the great divide between pure reverence for the moral law and everything else, no importance is attached to the difference between caring for myself and caring for others. Reverence for the moral law expresses our rational nature, whereas inclinations do not. Why bother drawing distinctions between motivations, none of which are rational?

In Innstetten we see the results of this way of thinking. Once he knows that Effi is a moral offender, any impulses that oppose a strictly moral reaction to what she has done are thrust down to the level of self-indulgence, and treated as such. If what duty opposes is inclination, then what stands in the way of duty must be really, whatever the appearances, mere inclination; so forgiving and accepting Effi becomes regarded as weakness and failure, surrender to his own needs and inclinations—something a moral person cannot rationally do. Duty is seen as a value that demolishes *self*-love; Innstetten is unable to attach any *moral* importance to his marriage, or to differentiate between caring for it and giving in to selfish desires. From the moral, impartial point of view his marriage is a source merely of inclination, and once knowledge of the letters has forced him to take the moral point of view he is obliged to overcome inclination and to regard as such the destruction of his happiness and shared life. The fact that *another person's* happiness is destroyed too does not enter into his agonized thinking with any moral weight. What difference can there be between destroying Effi's happiness and destroying his own? They are both only inclinations; to give way to care for either would be irrational, since duty is what reason demands (and appears to us with the imperative force of a demand only because we are not fully rational). A Kantian man of principle cannot continue to love an erring wife; in taking the required impersonal view of her adultery he has already degraded his feelings of attachment to her, regarding them as something the properly moral point of view must ignore.[23]

---

[23] It may be objected that there is nothing in Kantian ethics *demanding* condemnation of the agent as well as condemnation of the act. Cannot a Kantian hate the sin and love the sinner as well as anyone else can? But even if it is undesired, the form of Kantian thinking makes it inevitable; the split between moral and all other reasoning demanded by Kantian rejection of the sin leaves inadequate resources for any love of the sinner to remain possible, since it excludes the notion of character that would be required.

I have called this the more profound objection, because it is quite distinct from problems over the actual principle on which Innstetten acts. Nowadays we have a different view of marriage, and do not sympathize with Prussian society's view of Effi's adultery; but this does not trivialize Innstetten's dilemma. For in imposing the Kantian framework of duty versus inclination on his own situation, he destroys part of himself. The call of duty, which he cannot oppose, compels him to put deep emotions and commitments on a level with trivial feelings, and to treat his love for his wife as part of his concern for himself. In doing so he is blotting out for himself her reality as a separate person. This is deeply ironical for Kantian ethics, which lays such stress on treating humanity always as an end in itself and never as a means to one's own ends. For this is only on the *moral* plane; the separateness of persons and respect for them as livers of distinct lives disappears when they are seen as sources of any motivation distinct from the moral. What Innstetten does to Effi brings about her death, and both of them know this; but he has tried not to treat her *morally* as a means to his ends.

Before she dies, Effi forgives Innstetten for everything he has done, even turning her child against her—"Because he had a great deal of good in his nature and was as fine a man as anyone can be who doesn't really love" (p. 266).[24] This is not sentimental; it is a profound recognition of Innstetten's tragedy. Committed to principle, classifying anything that conflicts with this as mere inclination, Innstetten has deformed his whole inner life, and Effi is right to trace this to his failure to commit himself truly to another person. In showing himself able to treat his love for his wife as merely a part of his self-love, his concern for her as merely a pathological inclination of his own, he has failed the marriage in a much deeper way than Effi's adultery ever did. Everything worldly has been taken from Effi, but her capacity to love and to attach herself to others has not been destroyed; in the end she emerges as the stronger character, forgiving him. We end up judging him her moral inferior, not because these days we take adultery less seriously but because of the way his conception of what morality requires has amputated not just his capacity for happiness but most sources of moral worth. He has blinded himself to vital differences between deep and trivial emotions, between commitment to others and self-interest. Effi has been punished by the world, but Innstetten has punished himself.

We last see him receiving honors in which he has lost interest, dutifully killing his child's feelings for her mother and, as the Minister's wife says, judging right and proper anything that is hard on her. A

---

[24] The German is more expressive: "Denn er hatte viel Gutes in seiner Natur und war so edel, wie jemand sein kann, der ohne rechte Liebe ist."

letter from Roswitha the maid awakens in him the realization that his present life is worthless and meaningless compared with his family life in the past, but there is nothing that he can do about it, no way to remake his devastated capacities for love and attachment. "I've lost all pleasure in everything. The more distinctions I earn, the more I feel that it's been valueless. I've made a mess of my life" (p. 259). All that survives from the wreckage of his personality is the recognition that he, not Effi, made a mess of his life; his love was not profound enough to resist the way that duty claimed to put it on a level with inclination and self-love. Wüllersdorf sees that he is right and that there is no real consolation; they just have to manage with "makeshift constructions" (p. 261). Their monotonous lives are brightened by theatre visits and drinks with cynical acquaintances (p. 261). It is rather strongly implied that Innstetten's loneliness is comforted by the maid Joanna, but he finds her presence in his "empty, bare" life merely depressing (p. 259). He had a shared life full of developing and worthwhile interests and pleasures; now he is alone with his moral rectitude and a furtive liaison. It is a neat symbol for the pure autonomy of the will, which, refusing to distinguish self-interest from concern for others, is by its very success left in a world where there are no deep attachments to other people, but only the lonely will itself and desires that the agent sees as passive and pathological. Innstetten's life has become what he thought it ought to be: freely chosen duty opposed to self-gratification, with no deep commitment to others. His tragedy is intensified by the fact that he is still sensitive enough to see clearly that such a life contains nothing that can make it worth living, no concerns that carry one along without the constant thought that one might as well be dead (pp. 258–59). For, as Williams puts it:

> My present projects are the condition of my existence, in the sense that unless I am propelled forward by the conatus of desire, project and interest, it is unclear why I should go on at all; the world, certainly, as a kingdom of moral agents, has no particular claim on my presence, or, indeed, interest in it. . . . Now the categorical desires which propel one on do not have to be even very evident to consciousness, let alone grand or large; one good testimony to one's existence having a point is that the question of its having a point does not arise, and the propelling concerns may be of a relatively everyday kind such as certainly provide the ground of many sorts of happiness.[25]

These words might have been written to describe Innstetten: having rejected the concerns which did in fact make his life worthwhile, on the

---

[25] Bernard Williams, "Persons, Character and Morality," p. 208.

grounds that they were really self-gratification, he finds out too late that a life that really is a combination of duty and self-gratification is a parody of a life, and clearly so to the agent.

Joanna, the maid who ends up with such an ambiguous place in Innstetten's life, was "full of high principles and with a strong sense of decorum" (p. 207). She prides herself on knowing "what is fit and proper and all about honour" (p. 225). The other maid, Roswitha, lacks a strong sense of principle; she does not think of herself as entitled to a strong moral viewpoint, being an unmarried mother and a despised peasant Catholic in a society of high-minded urban Protestants.[26] She nevertheless perceives and acts on others' needs in a way that Joanna never does; without question or reproach she comes to stay with Effi after the divorce and shares her lonely life. She is not intelligent, and it is obvious that she is very limited; but we admire the warmth of her feelings and can see that she has them in large part because unlike Joanna she is not concerned with high principles.

IV

Effi's parents are principled too. Even on her deathbed her mother reminds her that her misfortunes are her own fault (p. 265); and, although perceptive about Effi's character (pp. 41–44, 197–98), she can think of no deeper comment than that things would have been better if Effi had been brought up more strictly and by a minister with more robust religious beliefs (p. 267). When she hears of Effi's long-past affair, she writes the following to her:

> You'll be living a lonely life. . . . You'll be excluded from the society in which you've been moving up till now. And the saddest thing for us and for you . . . is that you will be excluded from our house, too. We can't afford to offer you any asylum in Hohen-Cremmen, there can be no refuge for you in our house, because that would mean cutting ourselves off from everyone we know and this we are emphatically not inclined to do. Not because we are particularly worldly and would look upon it as

[26] Her position is similar, one imagines, to that of an Irish peasant Catholic in Protestant England of the same date. Officially Effi is repelled by Catholic beliefs, but there is an undertow of feeling that Protestantism leaves out something important in its banishment of ritual and superstitious practices that engender a feeling of security in the world (pp. 110, 190–91). This kind of sympathy with Catholic practices (*not* dogma) emerges also in Fontane's *Schach von Wuthenow*, translated by E. M. Valk as *A Man of Honor* (New York: Ungar, 1975). Victoire, raised in a milieu where her aunt is horrified at the presence in a church of pre-Reformation images (even unpainted, pp. 45, 53) ends up finding real support and comfort from the ultimate painted devotional doll, the Bambino in the Aracoeli church in Rome (pp. 192–93).

completely unbearable to have to say good-bye to so-called "society." No, that's not the reason, but simply because we want to make our position plain and show the whole world that we condemn—I'm afraid I must use this word—your actions—the actions of our only daughter, the daughter whom we loved so dearly . . . . (p. 232)

If one read this letter out of context, one would assume that it was a satire, a showing-up of heartless people pretending that their cruelty is painful duty. What is horrifying is that it is not; it *is* painful duty. The Briests do love their daughter; they mean every word. Like Innstetten, they feel that they must do their duty, and that anything that makes it hard to do one's duty must be weakness and self-indulgence, and therefore to be resisted at all costs. They cannot, any more than their son-in-law, discriminate morally between pain inflicted on themselves and pain inflicted on another. We see the same deformation of character: the more the offender is loved, the more that love is seen only as a dangerous source of indulgence of self, opposing duty. And, as in Innstetten's case, what is repulsive in their reaction is the form it takes rather than its content; we are not so much horrified that people can get so upset about adultery as horrified and saddened that they can impose such a structure on their own feelings, can see morality (whatever its content) as so sharply distinct from the rest of practical reasoning that, within the latter, a deeply rooted and natural love is degraded to the status of a gratification of the self.

But whereas Innstetten is strong, and survives in the desert he has made of his inner life, the Briests are, in their own terms, weaker. When Dr. Rummschüttel asks them to take Effi back—though even then he has to claim that he is arguing from duty (p. 250)—they do, though it is not easy for them. "I love her as much as you do, perhaps more," says Luise von Briest to her husband (and it is important that she is both sincere and right). "But we've not been sent into the world just to be weak and forbearing and show respect for all that's against the laws of God and man . . . ." Briest replies: "Oh really, Luise. One thing's more important . . . . Parents' love for their children" (p. 251). He does not mean that parents are morally permitted to love their children, which could hardly have much weight against their moral condemnation of Effi's actions, and anyway would be a classic case of what Williams aptly calls having "one thought too many,"[27] weakening the force of a natural attachment by giving it a roundabout and unconvincing justification from the impartial point of view. Rather, he realizes belatedly that it cannot be right to see morality as assimilating deep love and commitment to pathological weakness and self-indulgence.

---

[27] Bernard Williams, "Persons, Character and Morality," pp. 214–15.

The Briests continue to think of themselves as obscurely self-indulgent in loving their erring child, but by the end of the book are beginning to glimpse a better view. Perhaps, after all, morality is not so sharply cut off from mere fact; perhaps it was morally relevant that Effi was too young when they married her off; perhaps the passing of time can make a moral difference. When Effi dies her parents bury her where they can constantly see her grave; unlike Innstetten they have not cut her out of their lives, and because of it, their lives will not be as empty and hard to bear as his. They allow themselves to be reminded of the importance of things that are levelled to unimportance when the "natural dialectic" of practical reasoning is taken to be either pure reverence for the moral law or "a disposition to quibble with these strict laws of duty."[28] Innstetten, unable to look beyond the Kantian framework of duty versus selfish inclination, has destroyed three lives. But the novel's final scene shows us the growth rather than the absence of love; her parents' love came too late to save Effi, and still leaves them uneasy, but it is there. It can hardly prove, but it does suggest, that to live successfully by the Kantian ethic is to risk destroying one's sources of love and concern for others, and that this not only hurts the others but leaves one's own life bare and meaningless too. And it also suggests that to reject the Kantian demand by standing by one's love and care for others is not weakness, but a realistic recognition that there are moral values that are not discerned from the impartial point of view.

[28] Academy edition, p. 405; Paton, p. 70.

[9]

Was Effi Briest a Victim
of Kantian Morality?

Marcia Baron

Kant's moral philosophy has in recent years seen a revival of interest on the part of both sympathizers and opponents. Perhaps the most interesting and serious criticism is one which claims that a Kantian approach to ethics—and indeed to life—is deeply destructive of all that is most valuable to human existence. In Julia Annas's words, "To live successfully by the Kantian ethic is to risk destroying one's sources of love and concern for others, and . . . this not only hurts the others but leaves one's own life bare and meaningless too."[1] Annas's "Personal Love and Kantian Ethics in *Effi Briest*" provides a powerful and eloquent defense of this claim. Arguing that Effi, herself quite unKantian, lives in a society in which "a Kantian view of morality . . . prevails" (p. 157) and, in particular, that Effi's husband, Geert Innstetten, is extremely Kantian, Annas suggests that an examination of the "moral universe" in Fontane's novel discloses just how damaging Kantian ethics is.

My aim is to evaluate the extent to which the tragedies of *Effi Briest* can be traced to a Kantian view of morality. More specifically, I will question whether Innstetten is as Kantian as Annas suggests and whether a Kantian view of morality really does prevail in the narrow, cold, and harsh social environment of late nineteenth-century Prussia

This essay was originally published in *Philosophy of Literature* 12 (1988): 95–113. Reprinted by permission of The Johns Hopkins University Press.

This article has benefited from comments from Thomas Pogge and from discussions with students in my graduate seminars at Stanford University and the University of Illinois (1985). I especially want to thank Peter Simonson and Elizabeth Dimm for their insightful comments on Julia Annas's paper. Thanks, too, to the American Council of Learned Societies for its support in 1984–85, when I began writing this article.

[1] Julia Annas, "Personal Love and Kantian Ethics in *Effi Briest*," Chapter 8 in this volume. Page references will be inserted parenthetically in the text.

as depicted by Fontane. In doing so I hope to correct some common misunderstandings of just what a Kantian character would be.

I

That Innstetten is a man of principle is beyond dispute,[2] and this fact lends some support to Annas's claim that he "is a textbook example of Kant's man who acts out of respect for the moral law" (p. 163). But a man of what type of principle? And in what way a man of principle? What we need to determine is whether the concept of duty which plays a prominent motivational role in Innstetten's conduct is one and the same as, or at least very similar to, what Kant means by "duty."

We may begin by guarding against some tempting misconceptions concerning what counts as evidence that an agent has a Kantian concept of duty and, more broadly, a Kantian moral outlook. It is sometimes supposed that the fact that a person acts with grim determination and contrary to inclination (or what we would hope would be his inclination) is evidence that he acts as a Kantian. This assumption seems to lurk behind a curious remark in Annas's paper. Fontane, she observes, "was capable of highly Kantian sentiments," and she supports her assertion as follows:

> Of Frederick William I's memorably horrible act of forcing his son, Frederick the Great, to watch the execution of his friend, Katte, Fontane once remarked that far from being a blot on the Hohenzollern escutcheon it shone like a precious stone—even though it was a bloodstone. Whatever Fontane's own intentions, we can hardly fail to see this remark as a terrible distortion of Kant's claim that even in the most difficult of circumstances the good will shines like a precious stone; no doubt it did take strong will and devotion to duty to get Frederick William to do that to his son. (p. 158)

Assuming that her claim is not that Fontane must have been thinking of Kant (and, moreover, attributing Kantian motivation to Frederick William I) since he used the phrase "shone like a precious stone," I take her to be asserting that Frederick William must have been acting from devotion to duty, in Kantian fashion, and that Fontane must have been admiring the act as an act done from duty. While this is one possible explanation for Frederick William I's conduct, it is a curious one, since there is nothing in Kant's ethics to suggest that he would regard so macabre an act as a duty. Nor is there anything in the anecdote, as told

---

[2] As will emerge in Section IV, even this claim needs qualification.

here, to support the claim that his motive was that of duty. And while it must have taken a strong will to do what Frederick William I did, there is no reason to think that it took a good will—a will obedient to practical reason—rather than a wayward will; and there is good reason to suspect it was the latter. Grim determination and firm resolve *may* constitute evidence of a sense of duty, but they are just as likely to evidence any of a diverse set of motives or motivational attitudes, e.g., hatred, rage, desire for revenge; an obsessive desire to become wealthy or powerful, or not to be thought weak and "effeminate"; a single-minded pursuit of some more specific goal.[3] In sum, grim determination alone is no evidence of Kantian motivation, except negatively, in that it indicates that the agent is not acting out of direct desire.

A second common pitfall is to suppose that anyone harsh and rigid, especially anyone who adheres rigidly to rules, is probably a Kantian. The supposition is tempting, in part because Kant's moral philosophy is so frequently, almost ubiquitously, described as an ethic of rules. But, if Kant's is an ethic of rules at all—and this is debatable—it is not an ethic of rules in the usual sense of the word "rules." It is not an ethic of rules for "external" action. His concern is with inward principles, with character. This is particularly plain in *Religion Within the Limits of Reason Alone*, *Education*, and the *Doctrine of Virtue*, but the *Foundations of the Metaphysics of Morals* and the *Critique of Practical Reason* provide strong clues as well. The concept of duty, Kant writes in the *Foundations*, contains that of the good will. (It is easy to forget this when our ordinary use of the term "duty" leads us to think of duty as tied to institutional rules, and to action much more than to character.)[4] Moreover, the Categorical Imperative does not test the morality of actions, but that of maxims.[5] It tests the principles on which we act, our fundamental intentions or policies.

Even if one argued that Kant did have an ethic of rules (since, after

[3] The goal might be a lofty, putatively moral one, e.g., the impeachment of President Reagan, or it could be an extremely self-centered goal, e.g., to become Miss America. But by its very single-mindedness the single-minded pursuit of any goal is barred from qualifying as acting from duty. When one acts from duty, one takes into account all competing moral considerations, or at least does not dismiss them as not to be considered. Yet to pursue something single-mindedly is to refuse to think about the question of what one really ought to do. Indeed, one does not regard the matter as open for consideration. I discuss this in "On Admirable Immorality," *Ethics* 97 (1986).

[4] I discuss this in "The Ethics of Duty/Ethics of Virtue Debate and Its Relevance to Educational Theory," *Educational Theory* 35 (1985): 135–49.

[5] To distinguish *the* categorical imperative, which is formal, from the particular material imperatives that Kant says can be derived from it, I use upper-case "C" and "I." The importance of the distinction is brought out nicely by Allen Buchanan in "Categorical Imperatives and Moral Principles," *Philosophical Studies* 31 (1977): 249–60; and by H. J. Paton in *The Categorical Imperative: A Study in Kant's Moral Philosophy* (London: Hutchinson's University Library, 1947; rpt. Philadelphia: University of Pennsylvania Press, 1971).

all, general rules of *some* sort might be generated from the results of applying the Categorical Imperative to various maxims), it would be quite another matter to show that he has an ethic of rigid, unreflective adherence to rules, adherence usually grounded on no consideration other than the fact that they are dictated by social conventions. Kant speaks out repeatedly against blind adherence to norms or the views of authorities as, for instance, in "What is Enlightenment?": "*Immaturity* is the inability to use one's understanding without guidance from another. . . . If I have a book to serve as my understanding, a pastor to serve as my conscience, a physician to determine my diet for me, and so on, I need not exert myself at all. I need not think, if only I can pay: others will readily undertake the irksome work for me."[6]

A third error is to associate with Kantian ethics a tendency to be judgmental. Since the Kantian takes morality seriously, we imagine her evaluating the conduct of others—and almost always coming up with a negative verdict. Yet Kant's writings very strikingly emphasize self-evaluation and in particular forward-looking reflection on one's conduct; not assessment of the conduct of others. As Onora O'Neill has pointed out, the Categorical Imperative is primarily a test for agents to apply to their own maxims.[7]

Kant's antimoralism emerges most strikingly in the *Doctrine of Virtue*, where we learn that our two obligatory ends are the happiness of others and our own perfection.[8] Lest we think that Kant simply forgot (or perhaps saw as secondary) the perfection of others, he explicitly denies that the perfection of others is an obligatory end.[9] I am not to make it my business to lead others to virtue and to manipulate them to care for this but not that. This is already quite antimoralistic, but Kant goes farther and claims that we ought not merely refrain from preaching, but also embrace others' ends. The duty to adopt as my end the happiness of others entails adopting their ends as mine, on his view. Only their permissible ends, to be sure; I am not to "give the lazy fellow

[6] Kant, "An Essay on the Question, 'What is Enlightenment?'" in *Perpetual Peace and Other Essays*, trans. Ted Humphrey (Indianapolis: Hackett, 1983), p. 41.

[7] Onora O'Neill, "Consistency in Action" in *Morality and Universality: New Essays on Ethical Universalizability*, edited by Nelson Potter and Mark Timmons (Dordrecht: D. Reidel, 1985), pp. 159–86. I am very much indebted in this section to O'Neill's work (although my position concerning what it is that the Categorical Imperative is to test differs from hers). See also her "Kant After Virtue," *Inquiry* 26 (1983): 387–406.

[8] See also Thomas Hill Jr.'s "Kant's Anti-Moralistic Strain," *Theoria* 44 (1978): 131–41, which argues that Kant has an antimoralistic strain with respect to punishment.

[9] "For the perfection of another man, as a person, consists precisely in *his own* power to adopt his end in accordance with his own concept of duty; and it is self-contradictory to demand that I do (make it my duty to do) what only the other person himself can do." Kant, *The Doctrine of Virtue*, trans. Mary J. Gregor (Philadelphia: University of Pennsylvania Press, 1964), pp. 44–45.

a soft cushion so that he [may] pass away his life in sweet idleness" or "see to it that the drunkard is never short of wine . . . ,"[10] but apart from refraining from aiding in immorality, I am not to engage in the moral management of my friends, offering aid only when I regard their ends as sufficiently worthy. Nor may I turn up my nose at the "trivial" concerns of others. Their ends must be taken seriously, since their happiness must be taken seriously.

With this is mind, let us consider what reasons there are, beyond superficial similarities, for thinking that a Kantian view of morality prevails in *Effi Briest*. It should be clear that the harshness and tendency to condemn others which typify the people in whose midst Effi lives do not manifest a Kantian outlook. This is so both because a judgmental stance towards others is something which Kant opposes (and which his theory in no way requires) and because the standards by which they judge are mere social mores, mindlessly accepted. But are these people Kantian in some other respect? Annas writes that in *Effi Briest* "we see people who think of Duty as Kant assumed everyone does," elaborating that "Duty is thought of as being sharply opposed to any of the agent's desires, needs or interests, and is grasped by abstracting from all personal considerations" (p. 157). There is something, to be sure, which these people take very seriously. But is this something Duty? Is it what Kant means by *duty* or *morality*? To determine this, we need to examine the characters whose attitudes, commitments, and deliberation seem to mark them as Kantians. I follow Annas in focusing on Innstetten.

II

Innstetten's decision to challenge Major Crampas to a duel and to divorce Effi, after learning of Effi's affair with Crampas six years earlier, provides a strong case for Annas's claim. He feels no hatred or desire for revenge towards either Crampas or Effi; as he tells Wüllersdorf, he still loves Effi and feels "tempted to forgive her."[11] Nonetheless, he decides to divorce her and to challenge her ex-lover to a duel. Why?

Innstetten's deliberations before taking action suggest that his thinking is *not* particularly Kantian. Responding to Wüllersdorf's query ("If

---

[10] *The Doctrine of Virtue,* pp. 153–54.

[11] Theodor Fontane, *Effi Briest,* trans. Douglas Parmée (London: Penguin Classics, 1967), p. 214. All references are to this edition.

things are like that, Innstetten, then . . . why all this fuss?"), he reflects as follows:

> We're not isolated persons, we belong to a whole society and we have constantly to consider that society, we're completely dependent on it. If it were possible to live in isolation, then I could let it pass. I should then be bearing a burden that I had myself accepted, my true happiness would have disappeared, but so many people live without "true happiness" that I should have had to do so, too—and would have. . . . We don't necessarily have to rid the world of someone who has robbed us of our happiness. If we're turning our backs on the world, we can let him go on living too. But with people living all together, something has evolved that now exists and we've become accustomed to judge everything, ourselves and others, according to its rules. And it's no good transgressing them, society will despise us and finally we will despise ourselves and not be able to bear it and blow our brains out. (*EB,* p. 215)

This seems to be strong evidence that his motivation is *not* Kantian. The thought process has more affinity with the writings of Patrick Lord Devlin who, with hints of Hegel and of James Fitzjames Stevens, writes that "Society cannot tolerate rebellion" with respect to its common morality and institutions. The bonds of common morality hold society together. "The bondage is part of the price of society; and mankind, which needs society, must pay its price."[12]

But, Annas claims, Innstetten's reflections after killing Crampas suggest that the deliberations just cited provide an incomplete explanation, at best. In her words,

> After killing Crampas, he feels revulsion and wishes he had acted differently. But, revealingly, he sees only one alternative: "I should have burnt the letters. . . . And when she came to me, all unsuspecting, I should have said to her, 'There's where you belong' and cut myself off from her. Inwardly, not in the eyes of the world" (p. 222). So, in spite of what he said, Innstetten did really have a choice whether or not to kill Crampas, and divorce Effi; but he did not have a choice whether or not to reject her inwardly. (p. 162)

If Annas is right, what does this show? It shows, she says, that Innstetten "cannot avoid the force of his pure reverence for the moral law, which Kant describes with so much approval" (p. 166). This, she says, is

---

[12] Patrick Lord Devlin, *The Enforcement of Morals* (London: Oxford University Press, 1965), pp. 9–10.

the serious objection, for "Kantian morality is condemned not by Innstetten's legal murder of Crampas, which it need not endorse, but by
the effects it has on Innstetten's way of thinking, which it must" (p.
166). This is not very compelling. Whether Innstetten has "pure reverence for the moral law" is at issue. To appeal to an assumption that he
does is to beg the question.

But perhaps Annas is not making this assumption. She might be
arguing by process of elimination that this *was* the motive; alter-
natively, she may be relying on separate indications to support her
claim. Both arguments, thus understood, would begin as follows: Innstetten cannot have been moved solely or primarily by his concern
for society's demands, for society (he thinks) demands that he challenge Crampas to a duel, and yet he says later that he could have
forgone that. What rules out his also forgiving Effi? Here the arguments part ways, offering different answers to the question just posed.
First answer: the only remaining explanation is his devotion to doing
whatever morality requires (together with his belief that it would be
immoral to forgive her.) Second answer: careful examination of his
character (rather than simply an argument by elimination) discloses
that it was his commitment to morality that ruled out his forgiving Effi.

To evaluate this disjunctive argument let us first consider the evidence for the claim that Innstetten's commitment is a Kantian commitment to morality and then ask whether there are alternative explanations of his decision. Annas's arguments are complex and interwoven,
so it will be best to quote at some length. After objecting to "Kant's
sharp separation of the motive to be moral . . . from all *inclinations*,"
according to which, she says, "*all* our particular attachments and commitments appear as mere inclinations with respect to which we are
passive," she writes,

> In Innstetten we see the results of this way of thinking. Once he knows
> that Effi is a moral offender, any impulses that oppose a strictly moral
> reaction to what she has done are . . . treated as such. . . . Duty is seen as
> a value that demolishes *self*-love; Innstetten is unable to attach any *moral*
> importance to his marriage. . . . From the moral, impartial point of view
> his marriage is a source merely of inclination, and once knowledge of the
> letters has forced him to take the moral point of view he is obliged to
> overcome inclination and to regard as such the destruction of his happi-
> ness and shared life. The fact that *another person's* happiness is destroyed
> too does not enter into his agonized thinking with any moral weight. What
> difference can there be between destroying Effi's happiness and destroy-
> ing his own? They are both only inclinations. . . . A Kantian man of
> principle cannot continue to love an erring wife; in taking the required
> impersonal view of her adultery he has already degraded his feelings of

attachment to her, regarding them as something the properly moral point
of view must ignore. (p. 168)

Annas is correct to say that Kant sharply separates the motive to be
moral from all inclinations, but her claim that our attachments and
commitments (and the happiness of others, which I discuss below)
appear as mere inclinations is mistaken; and this mistake underlies the
arguments in the passage just cited. Kant is in fact at pains to contrast
mere inclinations, towards which we are passive, with our ends, which
we choose (or approve or ratify). We are not passive towards attachments and commitments. While we cannot force ourselves to *cease right
now* to be attached to a particular person or activity, we can and do
slowly detach ourselves or deepen an attachment (without, of course,
any guarantee of success). Commitments are still less compatible with
passivity. If I am committed to someone (as a friend, a spouse, a parent,
or as a co-worker on a particular project), how could my commitment
be something towards which I am passive? Agency plays a central role;
I commit myself. And how could my commitment be subsumed under
inclinations? Crucial to the notion of a commitment is that it binds me;
it is not just a matter of what inclines me, but rather it constrains my
conduct specifically with respect to feelings which may change, and
towards which I am relatively passive.

The point of Kant's much maligned distinction between the practical
and the pathological is not, as is often thought, to denigrate feelings
and emotional attachments but to contrast the raw feeling, towards
which we are passive, with our attitude and orientation, towards which
we are not.[13] Insofar as attachments, commitments and, more generally, ends are not immoral, they are, unlike inclinations, accorded a
positive value. They have this positive value in virtue of being the
objects of being chosen by any of us, beings with the power to set ends.
As Christine Korsgaard explains, rational choice—the power to set
ends—confers values on the ends chosen (though not, of course, unconditional value). For this reason, treating humanity or rational nature as an end in itself prohibits moralism: if "you view yourself as
having a value-conferring status in virtue of your power of rational
choice, you must view anyone who has the power of rational choice as
having, in virtue of that power, a value-conferring status." We must
view the ends of others, as well as our own ends, as possessing value
unless they are immoral (i.e., not "harmonious with what another can
make good by means of her rational choice").[14]

[13] See Susan Mendus's "The Practical and the Pathological," *The Journal of Value Inquiry*
19 (1985): 235–43 for a discussion of these issues.
[14] Christine M. Korsgaard, "Kant's Formula of Humanity," *Kant-Studien* 77 (1986): 196.

Because attachments and commitments are not, for Kant, on a level with inclinations, it is difficult to see why one's marriage would appear from "the moral, impartial point of view" as "a source merely of inclination," "lacking in moral importance," and why the same point of view would oblige someone in Innstetten's circumstances to "overcome inclination and to regard as such the destruction of his happiness and shared life." It is not as if impartiality requires an absence of inclination; so why would it require that Innstetten overcome inclination? To be sure, if one's inclination were, under the circumstances, in *conflict* with the requirements of morality, then morality as Kant sees it would require that the agent overcome inclination (not in the sense of ridding oneself of inclination, but simply of not allowing it to move one to act accordingly).[15] If, for instance, it were morally impermissible to love (forgive, remain married to) an erring wife, then morality would require Innstetten to overcome inclination (though not to regard as such the destruction of his happiness and shared life). [Is it in this sense that a Kantian is thought to see duty as a value that demolishes self-love?] But there is no such position in Kant's ethics;[16] indeed, there is reason to believe that Kant would sharply oppose terminating a love relationship solely to punish the other for wrongs long past or, less punitively but very smugly, in order to remove oneself from impure company.[17]

[15] "Natural inclinations, *considered in themselves*, are *good*, that is, not a matter of reproach, and it is not only futile to want to extirpate them but to do so would also be harmful and blameworthy. Rather, let them be tamed and instead of clashing with one another they can be brought into harmony in a wholeness which is called happiness." Kant, *Religion Within the Limits of Reason Alone*, trans. Theodore M. Greene and Hoyt H. Hudson (New York: Harper & Row, 1960), p. 51.

[16] Throughout this article I assume that a distinction may be drawn between the positions in Kant's ethics and views which he happened to hold, where his holding them seems to have little to do with his ethical theory and a great deal to do with the culture of which he was a part. For this reason, I do not explore the possibility that his own attitudes towards women and marriage would be supportive of Innstetten's decision. This is an assumption about proper methodology for the history of philosophy, not a point about Kant's ethics in particular. It is admittedly controversial, but it is difficult to deny it without trivializing the history of philosophy by conflating it with the (intellectual) biography of philosophers. Of course, it is not easy to determine whether a philosopher's particular moral views bear on and illuminate his or her theory, and the assumption I make may well strike some as an all too convenient tool for defending one's favorite philosopher. In some instances, however, it seems appropriate to bracket the philosopher's moral views rather than regard them as central to the theory. I have in mind instances where the particular views, which strike us as appalling today, were dominant in the era in which the philosopher lived, especially if the views strike us as less "enlightened" than the theory, and if the views were not openly and vigorously contested at the time.

[17] Cf. Kant, *Lectures on Ethics*, trans. Louis Infield (New York: Harper & Row, 1963), pp. 66–67. I quote from this section in the next paragraph. Admittedly Kant does say in the *Doctrine of Virtue*, in connection with the question as to "whether we may . . . keep company with the vicious," that "if the vice is a scandal—that is, a publicly given example of contempt for the strict laws of duty, which brings infamy with it—then even if the laws

It is possible that Annas is equating a moral point of view, or a "strictly moral reaction," with a moralistic, judgmental view. As was mentioned above, there is no basis for this equation with respect to Kant's ethics. Indeed, Kant warns against being judgmental and advocates a curious asymmetry: "*Fragilitas* and *infirmitas humana* ought to be taken into account in judging of the actions of others, but not by way of excuses for our own misdeeds."[18] "Eagerness to discover faults in others betrays malice and envy of the morality we see shining in others when we are conscious of its absence in ourselves."[19] There is reason to think that Innstetten would not impress Kant, who admonished that "every man must guard against moral self-conceit."[20]

Nor is it the case that the happiness of others, or its destruction through my actions, is to have no moral weight for Kant. Here too there is an asymmetry: as noted earlier, promoting the happiness of others (in a nonpaternalistic manner) is an obligatory end. Kant nowhere dismisses the happiness of others as a "mere inclination." But even if he did, this would not have the implications that Annas suggests it has. It is perfectly permissible to act to satisfy inclinations, one's own or someone else's. It is just that if there is a conflict between satisfying someone's inclinations and the requirements of morality, morality is always proclaimed the winner.

But this might seem to have some sting to it; for doesn't Kantian morality, with its insistence on impartiality, require that one ignore one's personal preferences, loves, attachments, "projects" (in Bernard Williams's sense)?[21] Doesn't it, as Annas suggests at the end of the long quotation, oblige Innstetten to ignore his feelings of attachment to his wife? No. Impartiality (of this type; there are other types, but none relevant to our discussion) requires that Innstetten not treat himself as a special case. This means that his own attachment to Effi cannot serve as a justification for his own conduct unless someone else's attachment

---

of the country do not punish the vice, we must break off the existing association or avoid it as much as possible." For, he explains, "the further continuation of it does away with all the honour of virtue and puts it up for sale to anyone who is rich enough to bribe parasites with the pleasures of luxury" (p. 146). I take it that this would not be an apt description of the situation in *Effi Briest*.

18 *Lectures*, p. 67.

19 *Lectures*, p. 66.

20 *Lectures*, p. 246. See also Kant, *Religion*, pp. 42 ff. There Kant emphasizes that no matter how grave one's depravity, one can improve oneself through "a change of heart," "a kind of rebirth." This provides further reason for thinking that far from requiring Innstetten to divorce Effi (inwardly and/or outwardly), Kant's ethics would oppose such a decision. It would ask him to consider seriously the possibility that she has changed since her affair with Crampas six years earlier (and in fact Innstetten seems to realize that she has).

21 See B. A. O. Williams, "Persons, Character and Morality" and "Moral Luck," both in his *Moral Luck* (Cambridge: Cambridge University Press, 1981).

to his spouse can equally serve as a justification for his conduct—
provided the situations are relevantly similar. One may object that this
says too little,[22] but that would go no way towards showing that impartiality demands too much. It does not demand that one ignore and
thus disparage one's own projects; it demands only that one not take
the stand, "Because they're mine, they're important," unless one is
ready to allow that everyone take the same stand.

III

Annas's arguments fail to provide good reason to think that Innstetten's commitment is a Kantian commitment to morality. In addition,
there are a number of indications that he is not very Kantian (or else is
a failure as a Kantian). It is common to associate Kant with stern
prohibitions on particular types of action: lying, making a false
promise—one might add to this list extramarital sex, although Kant
mentions this relatively infrequently. Measured against these standards—Does he lie, etc.?—Innstetten may seem to pass the "test" (although his postmarital relationship with Joanna, the maid, might dis-
qualify him). But if we look beyond Innstetten's "outer actions" to the
character that they express, the clash between his conduct and Kantian
ethics is striking.

Kant's rather stiff prohibition on lying and making false promises is
typically conceived as disapproval primarily of the acts themselves.
This is, I think, a misconception. What Kant objects to is the *manipula-
tive* stance that these acts represent. In lying to someone—or, an equally bad act, deceiving another without lying—I fail to respect her as a
person, even if I lie to her "for her own good." Deception and manipulation are paradigmatic violations of the categorical imperative, whether or not the acts of deception or manipulation violate a highly specific,
"clear-cut" rule such as "Don't lie." Indeed, one might argue that compared to lies, subtle acts of manipulation or deception tend to afford
the subject less opportunity to discern the abuse and to confront the
deceiver with the misdeed, and thus tend to deny or cripple the other's
agency more than lies do.

That Innstetten nurtures and exploits Effi's fear of the Chinaman's
ghost is not mentioned in Annas's paper. Yet this feature of his character disturbs Effi greatly, alienating her from him and contributing to
her willingness to drift into an affair with Crampas. Almost a year after

[22] I do not mean to suggest that the requirement is trivial. Attention to international
relations, for example Reagan's foreign policy, provides striking proof that the requirements of impartiality are frequently violated.

the night she woke in terror, thinking she had seen the "Chinaman from upstairs," Effi is still troubled by her husband's unsympathetic and unreassuring reaction. "He didn't say yes or no and I didn't know what he thought," she explains to Crampas. When Crampas explains Innstetten's conduct in terms of his passion for being a pedagogue, and the utility that such a "ghost" has for a man whose position frequently requires him to leave his young wife alone for several days, her unease turns into deep resentment: "That Innstetten was cultivating the ghost in order not to live in a completely commonplace house could be accepted . . . ; but the other thing, that he was using the ghost as a means of education, was horrible and almost insulting. And she realized quite clearly that the expression 'means of education' was not really the half of it; what Crampas had meant was much more than that, a sort of calculated means of inspiring fear" (*EB*, p. 126).

There are many other anti-Kantian facets of Innstetten's personality: he is insensitive to the needs of others, and cannot be said (particularly in the early and difficult years of their marriage) to embrace Effi's ends. (Their honeymoon was a tour of the great art galleries of Europe. The bridegroom either didn't notice that his wife had no keen interest in art or didn't care.) Indeed, he is the prototype of a sort of person who worries Kant and motivates Kant's distinction between the practical and the pathological (between *humanitas practica* and *humanitas aesthetica*): the person who contents or even prides himself on having the right sentiments and does not bother to act accordingly.[23] Innstetten "felt that he loved Effi, and his good conscience in this respect led him to neglect making any special effort to show it" (p. 99). In addition, Innstetten is quite unreflective, not given to probe his character or consider whether he acts as he should towards Effi.[24] Rather than enumerate all of his anti-Kantian qualities, I will discuss just one more: his ambition.

Ambition is not ordinarily thought of as something disapproved of by Kant; and by itself it would not be objectionable. It is when it becomes a passion, narrowing one's vision, making one self-centered and rather single-minded that it is a character flaw. In the *Anthropology* Kant writes,

> The ambition of a person may always be an inclination whose direction is sanctioned by reason; but the ambitious person desires, nevertheless, to

[23] *Critique of Practical Reason*, trans. Lewis White Beck (Indianapolis: Bobbs-Merrill, 1956), pp. 88 and 159. See Mendus's discussion of this.

[24] The "first command of all duties to oneself . . . is *know* (scrutinize, fathom) *yourself.* . . . Moral self-knowledge, which requires one to penetrate into the unfathomable depths and abyss of one's heart, is the beginning of all human wisdom" (Kant, *Doctrine of Virtue*, p. 107).

be loved by others also; he needs pleasant relations with others, maintenance of his assets, and so forth. But if he is, however, passionately ambitious, then he is blind to those other purposes which his inclinations also
offer to him. . . . This is foolishness (making one's partial purpose the
whole of one's purpose) which even in its formal principle smacks reason
right in the face.[25]

Of course ambition is not unique in this respect; as Kant recognizes,
many passions have this quality. Innstetten's ambition, it just happens,
blinds him in roughly the way that Kant describes. It is only one of his
"purposes," but his vision is so narrow that he fails to notice how
unhappy Effi is in the beginning of her marriage. His disaffection
years later, after the divorce, is a reaction against the intensity and the
destructive single-mindedness of his earlier passion:

As far as climbing higher up the ladder was concerned, since that morning in Kessin when Crampas had taken leave of him with a look that was
ever before his mind's eye, Innstetten had become somewhat critical in
such matters. Since then, his standards of judgment had changed and he
saw things in a different light. What was distinction, after all? . . . however true it may have been that honours and favours from the highest
quarters meant a great deal to him, or, at least, had meant a great deal in
the past, he now realized the equal truth that there was little to be gained
from this splendid outward display and that what people call 'happiness',
if it exists at all, is something different from such display. (*EB*, p. 258)

IV

Annas argues that despite Innstetten's appeal to society's rules in his
pivotal exchange with Wüllersdorf ("It's no good transgressing them,
society will despise us and finally we will despise ourselves and not be
able to bear it and blow our brains out"—p. 215), this was not his real
reason for acting as he did. If it were, then why, she asks, when he later
repudiates his decision to challenge Crampas to a duel and to divorce
Effi, does he nonetheless think that he should have cut himself off
from her inwardly? That he does think this shows, Annas believes, that
he really was bound by a Kantian sense of duty. His sense of duty
required that he not forgive Effi.

I have argued that there is no reason to think that a Kantian conception of duty would require that. More importantly, there is no evidence

[25] Kant, *Anthropology from a Pragmatic Point of View*, trans. Victor Lyle Dowdell (Carbon-
dale: Southern Illinois University Press), pp. 173–74.

that Innstetten's concern with duty is with duty in anything like the Kantian sense or, more generally, that he thinks and behaves as Kant's ethics enjoins. But how, then, are we to understand Innstetten's momentous decision?

The explanation is much closer to the one that Innstetten provides than Annas allows. While the problem she cites warrants attention, it is not decisive evidence against his explanation. For one, the reasons why he challenges Crampas to a duel and divorces Effi need not be identical with the reasons why, had he not done so, he would nonetheless have divorced her inwardly. For another, there is no reason to assume that because he is tempted to forgive her, his refusal to do so reveals that he takes it to be his duty, in the full-blown Kantian sense, not to forgive her. Indeed, that explanation is implausible for reasons given earlier: there is no Kantian prohibition on forgiving or loving one who has acted wrongly, even very wrongly. And there are other possible explanations. The most plausible, I think, is that while Innstetten is able to imagine keeping Effi's adultery a secret and thus refraining from publicly acting out the role of the man who must defend his honor, he cannot imagine ignoring these considerations altogether. Privately, if not publicly, he must punish Effi; he must, as a "born educator," show her that what she has done is unforgivable.[26]

The problem that Annas cites thus turns out to be less serious than she suggested, and against the preponderance of textual evidence that Innstetten is motivated by a concern to abide by society's conventions, it does not provide a weighty counterargument. Innstetten's own explanation is, however, incomplete. To fill it out we need to take into account his attachment to his reputation and, intertwined with it, his ambition; and we need to examine the nature of his attachment to social rules and mores.

Throughout the novel we see Innstetten deeply concerned not about morality but about what people will think—and about his reputation. One might call this concern a sense of duty, provided that it is borne in mind that it is not a Kantian sense of duty; but even there it should be noted that his devotion or respect, and not just its object, is quite unKantian. He respects society's rules only half-heartedly; a large part of his concern for them is prudential. But his attitude toward society and its rules is more complex than this, and interestingly ambivalent. It is a mixture of cynicism and a sort of clinging, as if without them, he

---

[26] Cf. J. P. Stern, "*Effi Briest, Madame Bovary, Anna Karenina*," *Modern Language Review* 52 (1957): 363–75. Stern writes that Innstetten "forces himself to do what he conceives to be his duty according to the code in which he believes" and notes that by "calling it 'Götzendienst,' Wüllersdorf intimates (and von Instetten [sic] agrees) that the code is different from true morality, that society does not embody morality" (p. 370).

would have no identity. He nods in agreement when Wüllersdorf says, "The world is how it is and things don't go the way we want but the way that others want. All that high-falutin' talk about 'God's judgment' is nonsense, of course, and we don't want any of that, yet our own cult of honour on the other hand is idolatry. But we must submit to it, as long as the idol stands" (p. 216). While he can step back from social rules and regard them as merely conventional, he nonetheless holds that "it's no good transgressing them, society will despise us and finally we will despise ourselves and not be able to bear it. . . . So once again, there's no hatred or anything of that sort and I don't want to have blood on my hands merely for the sake of the happiness I've been deprived of, but that something which forms society—call it a tyrant if you like—is not concerned with charm or love, or even with how long ago a thing took place. I've no choice, I must do it" (p. 215).

His ambivalence towards social norms does not leave him in the grip of doubt and indecision. Concern for his reputation, proud awareness of his position, and plans to move "up the ladder" easily resolve his ambivalence—at least prior to killing Crampas.

Manifestations of Innstetten's concern for his reputation are so abundant that Fontane could scarcely have included more without tedium. When Effi asks that he not leave her alone overnight, he responds, "I don't leave you alone because I'm inconsiderate or just because I feel like it, but because I have to. I have no choice, I'm an official, I can't just say to the Prince or Princess: 'Your Excellency, I can't come, my wife feels lonely.'" Effi then proposes that they move to a different house, one in which she feels more at ease. She receives the same reply: "I can't have the people here in the town saying: Governor Innstetten is selling his house because his wife saw beside her bed the ghost of a little Chinaman . . . . It would be fatal, Effi. I should never recover from the ridicule" (pp. 78–79).

Effi quickly comes to view him accordingly. Years later, after seeing their daughter for the first time since Innstetten divorced her three years earlier, she articulates her anger towards him as follows: "I thought he had a noble heart and I've always felt small beside him but now I know it's he who is small. . . . *He* taught the child that; he always was a schoolmaster. . . . Too much is too much. He was always thinking of his career and nothing more. Honour, honour, honour . . ." (p. 249).[27]

It is not *only* his reputation that prompts Innstetten to take social conventions so seriously; he values them and is perturbed to see them violated, or even indirectly challenged, by liberalism and "the poi-

[27] Cf. also pp. 81, 114, and 120.

sonous dragon's head of revolution" (p. 211; see also p. 99). As his exchange with Wüllersdorf reveals, he feels that if we do not guide our lives by social rules, in some sense we cannot get on—and not just collectively, but even as individuals. The stakes are self-hatred.

Innstetten later repudiates his cult of honor. Upon learning that he has been awarded a once longed-for promotion, he is pleased but not elated by the news, for "What was distinction, after all?" (p. 257). After reading his other letter, from Roswitha, Effi's maid ("Innstetten was sufficiently a Civil Servant to open the letter from 'His Excellency' first"), he reflects bitterly to Wüllersdorf, "The more distinctions I earn, the more I feel that it's been valueless. I've made a mess of my life and so I've been thinking to myself I ought to have absolutely nothing to do with ambition and vanity and everything connected with them . . ." (p. 259). He now recognizes the extent to which his obsession with reputation and distinction contributed to his ruin.

My claims about Innstetten's character and his momentous decision gain further support if we ask, looking at other characters in *Effi Briest*, what goodness is opposed to. In Effi's parents (especially her mother) and in Joanna we see harshness and a stern attachment to principle, as we do in Innstetten. But on careful examination it emerges that what is criticized is not a Kantian commitment to morality, and a stern attachment to the principles entailed by such a commitment, but rigid adherence to society's rules—and a quickness to judge others and cut them off accordingly. When, upon reading Roswitha's letter Innstetten sees her goodness ("She's worth more than we are," Wüllersdorf says, and Innstetten agrees) and at the same time sees his own deep character flaws, he denounces not morality but honor, distinctions, ambition, and vanity (pp. 259–60). Likewise when Effi's parents decide to take her back. Hesitating, her mother queries: "Then the catechism and morality and the claims of society are to be brushed aside?" "Oh, Luise," Effi's father replies, "you can quote the catechism as much as you like but don't quote society" (pp. 251).[28]

The lively contrast between Effi's two maids, Joanna and Roswitha, provides added insight into a basic opposition in the novel between "frank kindheartedness" with not "a trace of superiority or reproach, nothing but true human sympathy" (p. 244) and smugness, vanity, competitive moralism, malice, intolerance, and a lack of understanding. Roswitha is an extreme example of frank kindheartedness with an absence of a proper "outward display." Joanna is all that Roswitha is

---

[28] Luise still isn't convinced. In words reminiscent of Innstetten (whom she would have married if he'd been older and more established at the time that he courted her) she remarks, "It's difficult to get along without society."

not: attractive, sophisticated, and "proper"; but also malicious, judgmental, lacking in compassion, and vain. When they learn of the duel
and the impending divorce, Joanna becomes enraged at Roswitha's
sympathy for their mistress and for Crampas. Because she, unlike
Roswitha, has "always been in service with distinguished families,"
Joanna tells her, she knows "what is fit and proper and all about honour." She explains that "if the master hadn't done anything, then all
the 'right people' would have cut him" (pp. 225–26). Even more than
Innstetten, she tends to conflate what others think with what is right;
and like him, she is intensely interested in her social position.[29]

V

I have focused on many of the same aspects of the novel as Annas:
the same passages, the same contrasts among the characters. But we
see them differently. She takes the chief flaw in Innstetten, Joanna, and
Effi's parents to be that they are too principled. I have tried to show
that the problem is not simply that of being a person of principle but of
adhering to the wrong sorts of principles and being harsh and judgmental. In Innstetten's case (and to some extent in Joanna's, too), other
flaws of character enter in: ambition, vanity, a sense of superiority and
its usual concomitant, excessive concern to be thought superior by the
relevant others.

Of course Annas also believes that Innstetten adheres to the wrong
sorts of principles. Her concern, however, is not with his adherence to
society's rules, but to principle cut off from compassion and love, as she
thinks principles must be for a Kantian. I have tried to show that her
view is based on a misunderstanding of Kant's ethics, though I did not
have the space to say all on this subject that needs to be said.[30]

Although I do not think that *Effi Briest* provides reason for believing
that "to live successfully by the Kantian ethic is to risk destroying one's
sources of love and concern for others," it does perhaps point up a
different problem with Kant's ethics. Kant is too confident that anyone,
no matter how lacking his sensibilities, how defective his feelings towards others, and how tied he is to social conventions, will be able to
determine what he ought, morally, to do. In his later ethical writings

---

[29] "Full of high principles and with a strong sense of decorum, she based her life on
her convictions as servant in a good family and her feeling of superiority over Roswitha"
(*EB*, p. 207).

[30] For further discussion see Mendus, Barbara Herman, "Integrity and Impartiality,"
Monist 66 (1983): 233–50, and my as yet untitled book, forthcoming from Cornell
University Press.

Kant shows signs of recognizing the value of sentiment; he sees that it is wrong to be malicious or resentful whether or not one acts accordingly, and notes that our "sympathetic moral feelings" may aid us in "participating actively in the fate of others . . . from moral principles."[31] But he does not ever appear to notice the role that our sentiments play in enabling us to be morally perceptive and thus better able to determine how we should act.

It might be that some people do better not to act from their sense of duty; Innstetten might be such a person. (But not Dr. Rummschüttel, whose sense of duty prompted him to write to Effi's parents and urge them to take her back; and not Effi's parents, who might have prevented the entire tragedy by engaging in moral reflection before encouraging her to accept Innstetten's proposal of marriage, and who surely had the resources, at the time that they learned of her infidelity, to react more thoughtfully than they did.) This is a tricky matter; for how am I to know which, a sense of duty or an emotive response, will be the better guide in the circumstances at hand? If I have the resources to know this, it seems likely that I would be able to incorporate such insight into my moral reflections, and thus to act wisely from duty after all. Moreover, it is implausible to suggest that someone whose feelings are deficient would do better to act from desire than from principle. If the point has application, it applies to someone like Roswitha, or Huck Finn, who, if they act on what they think of as moral principles, are more likely to act wrongly than if they flout the principles. But this hardly indicts moral principles; rather, it indicts the common misconceptions (co-optation?) of morality and moral principles.

These are the sorts of questions that might be pursued by someone who shares Annas's view that *Effi Briest* portrays the dangers of Kantian ethics. I doubt that further examination of them would show Kantian ethics to be as deeply misguided as she thinks, but it might shore up insights into circumstances in which acting on principle is not to be recommended.

[31] *The Doctrine of Virtue*, p. 126.

[1 0]

Friendship as a Moral Phenomenon

Lawrence Blum

I

It is entirely appropriate, as we have seen, that a friend act for the benefit of his friend for his own sake and without apprising himself of other possibilities for his beneficence. Not only is this appropriate but, I will argue in this chapter, it is also morally good. Clearing out of the way the concern with impartiality opens up a realm of moral inquiry which includes the altruistic emotions in general, and friendship as a particular relationship which embodies them. In this chapter I will examine friendship as a moral phenomenon in its own right, and will discuss conceptions of friendship which would deny its moral significance.

Friendship is a largely unfamiliar territory for modern moral philosophy, dominated as it has been by Kantian concerns or with utilitarianism, neither of which is hospitable to particular relationships which are both personally and morally significant. For example, contemporary emphasis on conduct which is morally required of us, or on considerations which we are required to take into account, does not easily allow for a focus on friendship as an arena for morally good, yet not morally obligatory, behavior and sentiments.

Let me begin with two central claims. The first is that, other things being equal, acts of friendship are morally good insofar as they involve acting from regard for another person for his own sake. This does not mean that every altruistic act within a friendship is morally admirable or praiseworthy. Some forms of considerateness towards one's friend, or willingness to help, are such that their absence would constitute a

This essay is excerpted from Lawrence Blum, *Friendship, Altruism, and Morality* (Northway, Andover, U.K.: Routledge, 1980). Reprinted by permission of Routledge.

moral failure, and their presence merely something which is to be expected of a friend. So acts can be morally significant though not morally praiseworthy, and this is what I mean by saying that any action done out of regard for the friend for his own sake is morally good. It is analogous to saying that every dutiful act is morally good although some are such that performing them is only what is to be expected, whereas failure to perform them is blameworthy.

Second, the deeper and stronger the concern for the friend—the stronger the desire and willingness to act on behalf of the friend's good—the greater the degree of moral worth (again, other things being equal). Thus a friendship which involves a very deep and genuine regard for the friend's good is a morally excellent relationship.

The argument that friendship is, or can be, a source of moral excellence begins best with an example of what such a friendship might look like. Kate and Sue are friends. Both are clerical workers in the same large insurance firm. Sue is a quiet, thoughtful and somewhat moody person; Kate is cheery and outgoing.

Sue and Kate enjoy each other's company. They enjoy talking about people they know and events that take place in the office. They appreciate and value qualities they see in each other. Kate feels she learns a lot from Sue.

Kate cares very much for Sue. Sue has a tendency to get depressed quite often. Kate has learned how to make Sue feel better when she is in such moods. Sue is not naturally or readily open about what is bothering her; but Kate has learned how to draw her out when she feels that Sue wants to talk. Sometimes she pushes Sue too hard and is rebuffed by her, in a not especially sensitive way. Kate is hurt by such rebuffs. But more often Sue is glad to have such a good friend to talk to, and is grateful for Kate's concern for her, and for Kate's initiative in getting her to talk. Sometimes Kate can cheer Sue up just by being cheerful herself (as she naturally is anyway), but she often senses when such a mood would not be appropriate.

Kate and Sue are comfortable with each other. They feel able to 'be themselves' with each other, more so than with most other people. They trust each other and do not feel that they need to 'keep up a good front' with one another. The women trust each other with personal matters which they do not usually discuss with their husbands. They know that the other will treat the matter seriously, and will not breach the confidence involved. They know each other well and know how to be helpful to the other in discussing intimate personal matters. They care deeply for each other, and they know this about each other, though they do not express it to each other explicitly. Each one appreciates the care and concern which she knows the other has for her. This is part of what enables them to be so open with each other—the knowledge that the response will be a caring one, even when it is not directly helpful in a practical sense.

Kate and Sue are willing to go to great lengths to help each other out. They readily do favors for each other—helping shop, picking up something at the cleaners, making excuses and covering for each other at work, taking care of each other's children.

When Kate is troubled about something Sue is concerned too; and vice versa. Sue thinks about how to help Kate out. For example, she helps her to think about how to deal with her horrible boss.

The relationship between Sue and Kate was not always so close. They came to know each other gradually. Their different temperaments kept them from taking to each other immediately. In addition, Kate often felt, and still sometimes feels, shut out by Sue's reserve, and her rebuffs. She was anxious to please Sue, to have Sue like her, and this often made her forget her own desires and needs. In her insecurities in the relationship she would also not be able to focus attention on Sue's own needs, feelings, and situation. In struggling with Sue, and with herself, to reach a deeper level of commitment, she worked through these insecurities. She was thereby enabled to distinguish more clearly Sue's needs and feelings from her own, to overcome tendencies to distort.

I have attempted here to describe a friendship which is both realistic (i.e., not involving saints) and yet which has reached a high degree of moral excellence. I mean to have brought out the following features: the concern, care, sympathy, and the willingness to give of oneself to the friend which goes far beyond what is characteristic and expected of people generally. The caring within a friendship is built up on a basis of knowledge, trust, and intimacy. One understands one's friend's good through knowing him well, much better than one knows non-friends, hence much better and more deeply than one knows their good. One is more sensitive to one's friend's needs and wants than one is to non-friends. In genuine friendship one comes to have a close identification with the good of the other person, an occurrence which is generally much rarer and at a much shallower level with other people.

In addition one gives much of oneself, unselfishly, to one's friend, as part of caring for him. One takes this for granted and does not typically regard it as a sacrifice; this is because one does care about the friend, and not because one is motivated by self-interest. The level of self-giving is generally much greater, though also of a different nature, than with non-friends. All these aspects of friendship are of great moral worth and significance. I will refer to these aspects generally as 'deep caring and identification with the good of the other.'

The caring in such a friendship ranges over a period of time and involves a commitment into the future. Kate and Sue know that neither one will simply drift away from the other. They will stick by each other. Their caring means that if trouble arises between them, they will try to work it through. Of course they know that, human existence being what it is, there is always a possibility of some kind of breach that would drive them apart. But this possibility is not translated into any actual distancing of themselves from one another, or into self-protection through 'lowering one's expectations.' In fact, each expects the other's care, concern, and commitment to extend into the foreseeable future; this is a source of deep comfort and joy to both of them, though they are seldom aware of it explicitly.

It is not the willing self-giving which is by itself the ground of the moral excellence oᶠ friendship, but only the self-giving which takes place within a relationship in which one genuinely understands and knows the other person, and understands one's separateness from him. For under the influence of a romantic passion one might be willing to do all sorts of things for the other person, to sacrifice for him. But this passion, and its associated disposition to act for the sake of the other, might be superficial, though very intense. It is not grounded in a real knowledge and understanding of the other, and of one's relationship to the other, such as exists in the example of Kate and Sue. In such a passion one not only gives of oneself—which is morally meritorious—but one, as it were, gives oneself away. And, as many writers have pointed out, this giving oneself away—failing to retain a clear sense of the other's otherness and of one's own separateness and integrity as a person—can stem not only from romantic passion or infatuation, but can be an integral part of long-standing and stable relationships, and can be a settled tendency within an individual's way of relating to others.[1]

We can say, in summary, that the moral excellence of friendship involves a high level of development and expression of the altruistic emotions of sympathy, concern, and care—a deep caring for and identification with the good of another from whom one knows oneself clearly to be other.

II

Let us consider some conceptions of friendship which would deny its moral significance.

---

[1] On this issue see Anna Freud, 'A Form of Altruism,' in *The Ego and the Mechanisms of Defense*, rev. ed. (New York: International Universities Press, 1966); Max Scheler, *The Nature of Sympathy*, trans. Werner Stark (London: Routledge & Kegan Paul, 1965), pp. 42–43 and *passim;* and Blum et al., 'Altruism and Women's Oppression,' in C. Gould and M. Wartofsky, eds., *Women and Philosophy* (New York: Putnam, 1976).

On the first conception, friendship is pictured as a sort of natural process, as something which merely happens to one. In one's life one runs across certain people whom one likes and is drawn to, and some of these people become one's friends. This happens to virtually everyone. There is nothing special about it, rather it is simply a natural part of human life, not a particular achievement or a matter of something which one works at.

Moreover, the course of friendship is largely a matter of the vagaries of our emotions. It is thus not really something over which we have control.

> Personal relations cannot be controlled by morality because they cannot be controlled at all. . . . they are not the sort of thing of which it makes sense to speak of making them different. They exist or occur; they are lived, experienced, and they change; but they are not controlled.[2]

Thus friendship cannot be a moral excellence, because it is not the sort of thing on which we exercise moral control and agency.

There are several things deeply wrong with this picture of friendship and of personal relationships generally. Most fundamentally, not everyone does have friends in the same way. People have very different relationships to their friends and treat their friends differently, and some of these differences are morally significant. In particular the levels of caring for and giving of oneself to one's friends are very different among different people (and within the same person's friendships).

I might have a genuine friend, someone whom I genuinely like to be with and to do certain kinds of things with, yet I might not care for and about him very deeply. I wish him well, hope for good things for him, and am willing to do some things for him, even if they inconvenience me to some extent. But I do not give much of myself to him. Perhaps I do not even know him very well, and do not make an effort to do so. I do not in any very significant way identify with his goals and aspirations, nor substantially desire his good for its own sake.

There is not necessarily anything wrong with this friendship. Perhaps, even if I could care more about my friend, I do not wish to do so. We understand each other's feelings and neither would want the relationship to be more than it is. There is nothing blameworthy here.

Nevertheless, this friendship is evidently not at the personal and moral level of Kate and Sue's friendship. It involves much less in the way of caring, of the giving of oneself to the other; of the transcen-

---

[2] Bernard Mayo, *Ethics and the Moral Life* (London: Macmillan, 1958).

dence of self involved in the deep identification with the other's good; of the level of considerateness, sympathy, and concern involved in Kate and Sue's friendship.

We all, I would think, can recognize that we have friendships at differing levels of commitment, care, and concern. Though all genuine human caring has moral worth and significance, is it not evident that a deeper level of caring involves greater moral worth? Such caring, far from being a natural process, is difficult to achieve, and is not really so common. It involves getting outside oneself, being able to focus clearly on and to know another person. It involves being willing to give of oneself, and in a way which is not simply experienced as self-sacrifice or self-denial. It involves overcoming within oneself obstacles, defenses, or distortions which prevent the deep caring for the other. (And this will generally involve some kind of shared process with the other person.)

Not only are there variations of moral level within one's own friendships; but it is also true that people may vary greatly among themselves in this regard. Some people are generally more caring, giving, helpful, and considerate towards their friends than are others.

III

Thus some people may have no friendships of a high level of moral excellence. And, as Aristotle recognized, some people may actually be incapable of such friendships. A truly selfish person could not have friends in the fullest sense. If he were genuinely able to care for another person for his own sake, if he were able to give much of himself to the other freely and for his own sake, based on a genuine understanding of him, then he would not be selfish.

It is true that selfish people can be very attached to one or another person, e.g., a spouse or friend. But it seems that such a friendship could not be a friendship of the most morally excellent kind. The attachment or friendship would be too grounded in self-centered considerations. Thus a selfish man could be very attached to his wife, dote on her, and in some ways do a lot for her. But this does not mean that he really cares for her for her own sake. His behavior would be compatible with his caring for her, so to speak, for her willingness to serve him, to be at his command, to flatter his ego. His giving could be either a minor concession for her serving him or even a further expression or assertion of his power over her and of her dependence on him. If he were truly selfish then something like this would be the most likely explanation of his 'beneficent' behavior. That a person should care very genuinely and fully for only one person while basically being very selfish seems an impossibility.[3]

Nevertheless, it would be wrong to say that a selfish person cannot really have friends at all, in any sense of the term. For first of all there are important aspects of friendship besides caring for the other, i.e., enjoying being with the other person or sharing certain kinds of activities with him, liking the other person. So a selfish man can have friends, in that there are people whom he likes and enjoys sharing certain activities with. Second, even a selfish person can wish another well, be well-disposed towards another. (Here we have to keep in mind the difference between a humanly selfish person and a sociopath.) It is only caring in the full sense which is incompatible with selfishness.[4]

Thus there are very different levels of friendship, levels which are understood in moral terms, in terms of how fully one cares for the other. If this is so then there is something wrong with the conception that friendships happen, so to speak, naturally, without our moral intervention, and that friendships are of a uniform moral type. Friendship always involves a giving of self to the other and a valuing of the other for his own sake. Friendship thus involves an orientation of our (moral) selves towards another person, rather than a process which merely happens to us and which (in Mayo's word) cannot be 'controlled.' On a more general level, personal relations are not merely 'lived' and 'experienced,' nor is their 'change' a merely natural process unrelated to moral aspects of ourselves, as Mayo implies. Rather friendship is an expression of moral activity on our part—of a type of

[3] This line of thought should make one suspicious of an interesting argument put forward by Bernard Williams in *Morality: An Introduction to Ethics* (New York: Harper & Row, 1972), chapter 1, that a person who is generally selfish but who cares for just one person could be led to extend his caring to others, the transition from one to many being a fairly natural one (a matter of quantity rather than quality), and the gap between one and many being much smaller than that between none and one. If my own argument is right, then the kind of caring which a selfish person has for only one person is likely to be minimal and deficient, and not such as could be readily extended to a genuine caring for others.

I am not denying here that a person could care genuinely and deeply about only one person, but only that such a person could be a fundamentally selfish person, essentially unresponsive to the weal and woe of others.

[4] A selfish person will have many relationships which are not friendships at all, but which are sustained solely by his deriving some pleasure or advantage from them. If he does not wish the other well at all, nor really like him or enjoy being with him, then there is no friendship. But if these elements do exist, then even if the man's primary concern with the other is the advantage he derives from him there is still some sort of friendship. And so the basically selfish person can have friendships of a minimal sort. (I follow Aristotle's account of friendship here: *Nichomachean Ethics,* trans. J. A. K. Thomson [Baltimore: Penguin, 1955], books 8 and 9; and in particular John Cooper's reconstruction of that account in 'Aristotle on the Forms of Friendship," *Review of Metaphysics* [June 1977].)

regard for another person, a giving of oneself, and a caring for another for his own sake.

IV

In the case of Kate and Sue, the 'moral activity' involved in the friendship is especially evident. For I have described the deep level of caring between the women as an outcome of effort and struggle, and hence as a kind of moral achievement. Certainly, attaining a deep level of friendship, in which the parties mean a great deal to one another and care deeply for one another, often involves obstacles and difficulties, the overcoming of which requires effort. One friend disappoints the other, or feels let down by him; they misunderstand each other; they quarrel and feel that there are insuperable barriers between them. Such happenings within the history of a friendship can lead to a distancing and weakening of the bonds between the friends. Or they can constitute tests of the relationship, which ultimately strengthen the ties and deepen the meaning of the friendship. The friends can make the effort to rectify or to correct a misunderstanding, to struggle to achieve the greater mutual understanding which will prevent such disappointments and misunderstandings in the future.

It is difficult to conceive of a deep friendship which does not involve some such effort and struggle. Nevertheless, it is not such effort and struggle in its own right which grounds the moral significance of friendship. For one thing, friendships which involve something like the same level of caring do differ in the amount of effort and struggle which has gone into them, and, I would argue, it is not the effort and struggle but the level of caring itself which primarily determines the level of moral value in the friendship. It is the genuine care for another person which constitutes a moral activity of the self, not primarily the exertion of will or effort which might have gone into the development of that caring. In caring we as it were go out from ourselves to another person; we give of ourselves; we affirm the friend in his own right. These processes cannot be portrayed as something which merely happens to us, or which we simply experience, as is, e.g., finding ourselves attracted to someone. And so effort and will are not required for the activity essential to morality.[5] This is not to exclude the possibility, however, that effort and will could be a further source of moral value

---

[5] Part of the problem here is that the language and antitheses of 'activity/passivity,' 'doing something/something happening to one,' are ill-suited to express how our friendship is a reflection of ourselves morally.

in a friendship beyond (though also requiring as a condition of this moral value) the caring involved.

Thus in a friendship in which the parties care deeply for each other but in which the relationship has developed without much pain, difficulty, effort, and struggle, there is still great moral merit in the caring.[6]

V

Another conception of friendship which conduces to failing to see its moral significance pictures friendship, or rather doing good for one's friends, as a kind of extension of the self, so that when one acts for the other one is simply promoting what is in a'sense one's own good. This self-centredness would exclude friendship from being a moral good, much less a moral excellence.

Our discussion can help us to see what is wrong with this conception as a general characterization of friendship. For a genuine friend truly cares for the other for his own sake. He is willing to give of himself to promote the other's good; he understands the other in his own being and interests, and can distinguish the other's interests from his own, even while he is able to care deeply for their realization and in that sense identify with the friend and his good. He grieves for the friend's sorrows. He is happy for him at his good fortune or successes in valued endeavors; he is sad for him at his losses and disappointments. It is his human growth and happiness which he desires—and for the friend's own sake, not his own.[7]

Thus the sense of identification involved in genuine friendship is not a matter of self-interest at all, and caring for the friend is not simply an extension of caring for oneself. This mistaken conception of friendship trades on an ambiguity within the notion of 'identification,' which can have either an egoistic or a non-egoistic sense. Even in the non-egoistic sense described above, the one who identifies gets pleasure from the good accruing to the one with whom he identifies. But this pleasure is not the motive of his beneficent action; in fact it is a sign of the degree to which he cares for the other as other than himself and in his own right.

The conception of friendship as extended self-interest is more appropriate to a kind of symbiotic attachment to another person (in

[6] The previous and following sections owe their existence to some well-taken criticisms by Jennifer Radden of a previous draft. I fear, however, that I have inadequately addressed the issues raised in those criticisms.

[7] This conception of caring is powerfully spelled out by M. Mayerhoff in *On Caring* (New York: Perennial Library, 1971).

which one has no clear sense of a self separate from the other, and in which one lives through the other so that, in that sense, his pleasures are one's own). Such an attachment can be of great importance to the person, of great emotional intensity, and can take on some of the forms of friendship—but is not at all friendship in the fullest sense.[8]

In arguing that Kate cares for her friend Sue for Sue's sake and not for Kate's own, that Kate is aware of Sue in her otherness from herself, and that Kate gives of herself to Sue, I am not arguing that Kate sacrifices herself for Sue. Nor am I arguing that when she acts for Kate's good, she acts in a manner unconnected with her own interests. She acts altruistically in the sense that her actions are motivated by genuine concern for her friend's weal and woe for its own sake; but not in the (more familiar) sense in which it implies acting in disregard of or contrary to one's own interests. But this is, partly, to say that the terms 'egoism' and 'altruism' as usually understood serve us ill in describing acting from friendship. Let us explore this further.

Friendship involves persons being bound up with one another. The different sorts of emotions and feelings which the friends have towards one another get their meaning and significance from the entire relationship of which they are a part.[9] In caring about the weal and woe of my friend Dave it is integral to the nature of this caring that it be for someone whom I like, whom I know likes me, who cares about my weal and woe, whom I trust, who is personally important to me, who cares about our friendship, etc. In acting from friendship towards Dave I express my acknowledgement of a relationship which includes all these feelings and attitudes. This is why the caring and the acts of beneficence in friendship are not separate from my own interests, from what is personally a good to me; it is not, in that sense, 'disinterested.' In fact friendship is a context in which the division between self-interest and other-interest is often not applicable. The friendship itself defines what is of importance to me, and in that sense what is in my interest. In that sense I do not generally sacrifice my own interest in acting for the good of my friend. I act with a sense of the friendship's importance to me, even though it is the friend whose benefit I directly aim at (i.e., which is my motive for acting), and not my own.

It is not that in acting for the friend's good I am acting from a combination of altruistic and egoistic motives, e.g., that I am both disinterestedly concerned with my friend's good, yet I also enjoy acting to help him. Nor am I acting from the former motive in combination

---

[8] This unhealthy form of pseudo-friendship is described by Scheler, *The Nature of Sympathy*, p. 42.

[9] See Blum, *Friendship, Altruism, and Morality*, chapter 3, pp. 55–57, concerning good to others within and outside of friendship.

with acting in order to preserve the friendship (which I am conceiving to be of benefit to me), nor in combination with the thought that my friend will be led to be more likely to benefit me in the future. These latter three portrayals involve possible motivations, which can be seen as a combination of an egoistic and an altruistic motive; but they are not accurate portrayals of our typical beneficent acts of friendship.

The way in which the value to me of my friendship with Dave figures into my acting for his good is not as a consideration for the sake of which I act. Nor is my liking of Dave a liking to do or enjoy doing every action which promotes his good. Rather, these figure in as a context of meaning of my action. They are background conditions of my being motivated to act for the sake of Dave's good. I am not doing less than acting fully for the sake of his good, and in that sense altruistically.

The notion of sacrifice implies an interest which the agent forgoes in order to promote something which is not an interest of his. It implies a clear separation between the interest he forgoes and the one for the sake of which he acts. It is the absence of such a separation in the case of friendship which means that it is not true as a general characterization of acting from friendship that in acting for the good of one's friend one is sacrificing for him. (Nevertheless in some particular actions it would be true to say that we sacrificed something of what we wanted in order to help our friend.)[10]

VI

Even if the notion that friendship is a kind of extended self-interest is abandoned, the previous discussion indicates what might be thought

[10] The general inapplicability of the notion of self-sacrifice and the limitations of the concepts of egoism and altruism in the context of friendship have wider implications for moral and social philosophy. For it can be argued that such concepts are misleading in the context of any genuinely cooperative endeavor, i.e., one in which there is a shared goal among the participants, a goal regarded by them as a good, and thus a good which is in essence shared rather than being merely an aggregate of individual and private goods. Such a cooperative enterprise, even if it can be seen also as fostering the individual and private interests of its participants, becomes a context of meaning which is essential to understanding the significance of actions which individuals take within that common endeavor. Acting for the sake of the good-of-cooperation is here analogous to acting out of friendship. (In fact friendship can be seen as a type of cooperative relationship, on this definition.) It cannot typically be seen as involving self-sacrifice; nor, on the usual understanding, can concepts of egoism and altruism be usefully applied. For a discussion of this perspective, on the concepts of egoism and altruism see Alasdair MacIntyre, 'Egoism and Altruism,' in Paul Edwards, ed., *Encyclopedia of Philosophy*, vol. 2 (New York: Macmillan, 1967). In 'Community,' chapter 5 of *The Poverty of Liberalism* (Boston: Beacon Press, 1968), R. P. Wolff makes an important beginning to defining concepts necessary for conceptualizing cooperative relationships and endeavors.

to be a moral deficiency in the kind of concern involved in friendship, namely that one would not have the concern if the other were not one's friend. The friendship, with all it involves, is a necessary condition for the concern, even if the concern is granted to be directed genuinely towards the friend for his own sake. Let us call this 'conditional altruism.'

Conditional altruism might be thought to be deficient precisely because it is not a universal form of concern. It is not directed towards the friend simply in virtue of his humanity but rather only in virtue of some relationship in which he stands towards oneself. This line of thinking, which I will call 'universalist,' is given a particularly stringent expression in Kierkegaard's *Works of Love*. He says that love of one's friend (one's beloved) has no moral value except insofar as it stems from a love which one would have for 'one's neighbor,' i.e., for any human being; and so, for example, if one saves a drowning person because he is one's friend—i.e., one would not do so if he were not one's friend—one's act would not have moral significance. Kierkegaard does not say there is anything wrong with loving one's friend and acting out of love for him; he says only that such love has no moral significance.[11]

A weaker view would be that love or concern for one's friend, though not without moral significance altogether, is yet in important ways deficient as a moral attitude towards another person. Though Kant himself does not say this in his own discussions of friendship (which are generally sensitive and sensible),[12] it can be seen as an extension of some themes within the Kantian outlook, in particular the focus on universality and impartiality in the moral attitudes we take towards others. On this view conditional altruism would be, though not without value, yet without the full moral value that a universalistic altruism would have.

The consequences of this challenge to conditional altruism go far beyond the moral significance of friendship itself. For there are many sorts of special attachments, connections, and relationships between people—such as family member, neighbor (in the non-Christian sense), fellow worker, comrade, fellow member (of various organizations), member of same ethnic group or community, regular frequenter of the same pub, fellow citizen or countryman—which can be sources of a stronger sympathy, concern, and willingness to help one

[11] Søren Kierkegaard, *Works of Love*, trans. Howard Hong and Edna Hong (New York: Harper & Row, 1962), part 1, chapter 2B.
[12] Immanuel Kant, *The Doctrine of Virtue*, trans. Mary Gregor (New York: Harper & Row, 1964), pp. 140–46: 468–73; and *Lectures on Ethics*, trans. L. Infield (New York: Harper & Row, 1963), pp. 200–209.

another than might exist in their absence.[13] The special connection or relationship is a condition of the altruism, which is therefore not purely universalistic.

Thus the issue here is at the core of the moral significance of the altruistic emotions themselves. For these special connections give rise to sympathy, compassion, and concern, and on the view which I am putting forth here these are morally good, independent of how they have arisen and whether they would exist towards the person in question in the absence of those special circumstances or relationships.

VII

Let us then examine the universalist challenge to all conditional altruism, or altruism based on special relationships. On my view, such conditional altruism does involve concern for the other for his own sake. The fact that if he were not our friend we would not have this concern for him does not mean that it is not for his own sake that we care about him. What detracts from such concern is only if the regard to the other's good stems primarily from self-concern. One could be concerned about one's friend Joe primarily because how Joe is doing reflects on oneself in the eyes of others. One could be involved in helping poor persons who are members of one's ethnic group primarily because one feels that the existence of such persons reflects badly on the group as a whole, and therefore on oneself. These examples would be excluded by my own formulation, of caring for the good of the other for his own sake, for they involve a primary concern with oneself rather than with the other.

On the other hand, if an Italian is dedicated to helping poor Italians, and is genuinely concerned for their welfare, then, even if he would not be so concerned if the persons were not Italians, he is still concerned genuinely for them for their own sakes; and, on my view, that attitude (and the actions stemming from it) have moral value.

Conditional altruism might be thought to be defective because concern with those in special relationships to oneself often takes the form primarily of hating, being opposed to, or denying the legitimacy of the interests of those outside the relationship in question. These are the familiar phenomena of chauvinism and provincialism. (It is less clear

[13] John Cooper, 'Aristotle on the Forms of Friendship,' *Review of Metaphysics* (June 1977), p. 620, has argued that Aristotle uses the concept of friendship (*philia*) to refer to many different forms of social connection between people ('civic friendship'), all of which are different ways in which, or contexts in which, we come to care about another for his own sake.

how this would work in regard to friendship; perhaps jealousy is an analogous phenomenon in that one's energies are directed against someone outside the relationship rather than towards one's friend or towards strengthening or enriching the relationship itself.)

There are two negative aspects of this chauvinism, which can exist independently of one another. The first is the opposition to those outside the relationship, an attitude bad in itself. The second is that the outside focus may mean a deficiency in one's concern for those within the relationship; one may be not so much genuinely concerned with their good as with hating or opposing those outside it. (Yet this connection is not an invariable one. It is quite possible for someone to be genuinely concerned with a group to which he is attached—to really care about their well-being—and yet also to have despicable attitudes towards those outside of his group.)

These are deficiencies within conditional altruism. But my view allows for the condemning of the despicable attitude towards those outside the special relationship, and also accords no moral value to the attitude towards those within it which does not consist in a genuine regard for the weal and woe of the persons in question. My view does, however, say that if the concern is genuine then it is *ceteris paribus* morally good; and if it is accompanied by a despicable attitude towards those outside then it is this accompanying attitude which is condemned and not the conditional altruism itself.

There may be some tendency on the part of a universalist outlook to think that conditional altruism always involves a negative attitude towards those who do not satisfy the condition. If this were true it would be a reason for regarding conditional altruism as a whole as fundamentally defective. But it clearly is not true. A person may be deeply devoted to the welfare of the Italian community without being suspicious of, or wishing the harm of, non-Italians. He may even wish well for non-Italian communities and recognize the worthiness of their aspirations, though he does not have the actual concern for them which he has for his own community. Sympathy for the interests of other groups could fairly naturally grow from concern for the interests of one group. Conditional altruism merely implies not being as concerned about the good of those who do not satisfy the condition as one is about those who do. It does not necessarily involve having an attitude towards those who do not which is in itself morally deficient.

It is important to recognize that genuine devotion to a particular group—family, neighborhood, ethnic community, ethnic group, club— is in itself morally good, and becomes morally suspect only when it involves a deficient stance towards others. It is morally good in that it involves (among other things) an admirable degree of sympathy, compassion, and concern for others. Moral philosophy ought to be able to give expression to the moral value of such an attitude, and an exclusively universalist perspective cannot do so.

On the other hand, the pitfalls of such conditional altruism should not be ignored. The connection between concern for those who satisfy the condition and opposition to those who do not is often no mere coincidence. For example, in a situation of scarce resources, devotion to one group competing for those resources can well mean opposition to others, and this can easily involve blameworthy attitudes towards these other people. (It should be noted, however, that merely competing against other groups for resources which one desires for one's own is not in itself reprehensible. It becomes so only if one either competes in an unfair or despicable way, or if, as is unfortunately too natural, one comes to develop unjustified and negative attitudes towards the other group.) Moreover, in some situations alleged devotion to the welfare of one group can, as things stand, mean little more than hatred or opposition to groups outside. Devotion to the welfare of whites as whites in America would be an example of this; there is virtually no room for this to be a genuinely altruistic attitude, or for it really to be other than opposition to non-whites.

VIII

On the universalist view, one cares for the other in a fully morally appropriate manner only when one cares for him simply as a human being, i.e., independent of any special connection or attachment one has with him. On my view one's concern need only be genuinely for the other and not, directly or indirectly, for the sake of oneself. Whether one would care about the other in the absence of the special connections does not detract from its full moral value.

This is in no way to deny that it is morally good to have altruistic attitudes towards those with whom one has no special relationship; indeed such attitudes must be central to any moral view which places emphasis on the altruistic emotions. But it is to say that whatever factors encourage the development of genuinely altruistic attitudes are themselves to be regarded favorably, from a moral point of view. In addition, this is to be realistic in our moral outlook; for in general we do care more about those to whom we stand in some special relationship than about those to whom we do not. These relationships involve a deeper identification with the other's good than is customary in their absence; and it is entirely proper that they do so. It is true that some persons can develop a quite deep sense of identification with the good of others, or of particular groups of others (e.g., oppressed Chileans, people suffering from a certain disease) to whom they stand in no (prior) special relationship; and such an attitude does seem more morally admirable than conditional altruism of (if we might speak this way) the same strength. But such attitudes are too rare for a moral outlook to be built entirely around them (although in my view their moral value is still able to be given full articulation), and, in any case, their exceptional moral value is not a reflection of a deficiency in the moral value of conditional altruism.

The tradition of which Kierkegaard is a representative places sole emphasis on altruistic attitudes towards strangers, or towards others in abstraction from the special relationships in which we stand to them. This must be an incomplete conception of love or concern for others, though a conception (such as Aristotle's or those of Greek philosophers generally) which gives little or no place to the notion of concern for others simply as human beings is similarly incomplete. For both are significant forms of our concern for others for their own sake, and it is this which has moral value.[14]

IX

This chapter has investigated friendship as a moral phenomenon. The full moral dimensions of friendship are difficult, if not impossible, to focus on within a Kantian framework, with its emphasis on obliga-

---

[14] Some reference to C. D. Broad's 'Egoism as a Theory of Human Motives," *Hibbert Journal* 48 (October 1949–July 1950) is in order here. Broad is one of the few writers I have run across who distinguishes conditional altruism as a particular type of motive. He calls it 'self-referential,' distinguishing it from 'self-regarding' motives. The former are genuinely altruistic, he acknowledges, though their operation is dependent on an 'egoistic motive-stimulant,' such as a pre-existing relationship to the other person.

Yet Broad confuses the issue by implying that it is useful to group self-referential motives together with self-regarding ones to yield a possible and plausible definition of psychological egoism (i.e., the view that all motives are either self-regarding or self-referential—see pp. 109, 111, 112). He thus implies, seemingly contrary to his original definition, that self-referential motives are best seen as in some way egoistic.

It may be that Broad believes that all self-referential motives are as a matter of fact accompanied by egoistic motives of the self-regarding kind (see, e.g., p. 108). As a matter of empirical fact this does not seem true, and Broad's support for it seems weak. For example Broad is certainly wrong (as well as sexist) in saying that a mother's desire for her child's happiness is always accompanied by 'the desire that other women shall envy her as the mother of a happy, healthy, and popular child' (p. 108). In any case, even if the general claim were true, it would not make the self-referential motive itself any less genuinely altruistic.

Broad's discussion seems to involve, though not consistently, a kind of universalist bias—a tendency to class other-regarding motives which are not grounded in universal considerations (e.g., love or duty to human beings simply *qua* human beings) as somehow egoistic or otherwise morally deficient.

tory conduct, on impersonal considerations, on universal attitudes. I have been particularly concerned to show that friendship can be morally excellent and not merely morally legitimate. But, in addition, all friendships are morally good to the extent that they involve a genuine concern with the good of another for his own sake (and, in that sense, involve self-transcendence).

In emphasizing, in contrast to the Kantian view, the moral dimensions of friendship, I want to avoid on the other side an overmoralized view of friendship, and of its personal and human significance. One such view sees the concern for the friend's good as the central element in friendship, downplaying or neglecting the liking of the friend, the desire to be with him, the enjoyment of shared activities, etc.[15]

A second overmoralized view sees friendship, or at least the highest forms of it, as having its grounds, its object, or the source of connection between the friends primarily in the friend's moral qualities and character; Aristotle, for example, seems to hold this view in his discussion in *Nichomachean Ethics*.

I argued in *Friendship, Altruism, and Morality* (chap. 2) that it is no defect of personal feelings that they fail to have such moral grounding. The same argument holds for friendships. To make the friend's moral character the central feature of friendship is to neglect too much the shared liking and caring (and mutual recognition of these by the friends) and the shared activities in which these are expressed. These features, though not unrelated to a person's moral character, are not primarily grounded in them either.

One does not need to regard someone as a virtuous person in order to care for him as a friend; nor, in caring for him for his own sake need one focus primarily on whatever morally virtuous qualities he has.[16]

The arguments of this chapter and the previous one have also borne, directly and indirectly, on the altruistic emotions in general. Most obviously, friendship is a relationship in which sympathy and concern

[15] Charles Fried's discussion of love (which he sees as very akin to friendship, differing primarily in intensity) in *Anatomy of Values* (Cambridge: Harvard University Press, 1970) illustrates this false view. Fried explains love almost entirely in terms of the willingness to give of oneself to the other beyond what is deserved (pp. 77–80). He gives insufficient emphasis to the role of liking, enjoying being with the other, etc. Henry Sidgwick in his discussion of love warns against precisely this error: *The Methods of Ethics*, 7th ed. (Chicago: University of Chicago Press, 1962), pp. 244–45.

[16] Nor, I would add, is a friendship in which the friend's moral virtue is the grounds of the friendship necessarily a morally superior form of friendship. Such a grounding does not seem to me what we mean by 'caring for another for his own sake.' If this is right it seems to me a point against Aristotle's view of friendship; but I cannot be certain of this, for the interpretation of what he means by love (*philia*) for another for his own sake is not entirely clear to me. On this see Cooper, 'Aristotle on the Forms of Friendship'; and 'Friendship and the Good in Aristotle,' *Philosophical Review* (July 1977), 290–315.

flourish, and an argument that beneficence prompted by friendship is morally good is an argument that beneficence prompted by altruistic emotion is morally good. Related to this, the argument that conditional altruism or altruism stemming from special relationships is morally good bears directly on many, though by no means all, forms of altruistic emotion. In the background of these arguments is my argument in *Friendship, Altruism, and Morality* (chap. 3), refuting the Kantian view that the impartial perspective is required of us in all our actions. Clearing this argument out of the way is a necessary condition for building towards a positive view of the moral value of altruistic emotions.

In addition to providing a context for the altruistic emotions, friendship also can serve as a metaphor for them, in relation to the Kantian view. For the two conceptions of friendship which I have discussed as contradicting the view that friendship involves moral excellence have direct analogies to Kantian views of altruistic emotions. Analogous to the 'natural process' view of friendship (pp. 196–99) is the Kantian view that altruistic emotions, and emotions in general, are like natural processes over which we, as moral beings, have no control, and for which we cannot be blamed, praised, or morally assessed. Analogous to the 'extended self-interest' conception of friendship (pp. 200–202) is the Kantian view that acting from altruistic emotion—or, rather, acting from feeling or emotion in general—is acting out of a kind of self-interest, in that it involves acting to gratify an inclination or desire.

In *Friendship, Altruism, and Morality* (chap. 8) I counter the former view of altruistic emotions and feelings. There I argue that we are not passive with respect to our feelings and emotions. They cannot be regarded as natural processes external to our moral agency, for which we cannot be morally assessed. Rather they are an expression of our moral being, just as the quality of a person's friendships is partly an expression of his moral being or character.

I do not counter the 'egoist' view of altruistic emotions directly in this book, partly because so much philosophic argument has gone into showing that this fairly crude form of psychological egoism is false.[17] If one accepts that acting from altruistic emotion involves acting genuinely altruistically then these well-known arguments will support my viewpoint here. In addition, in chapter 2 of *Friendship, Altruism, and Morality*, I have tried to show that acting from altruistic emotions does

---

[17] The arguments of Joseph Butler in *Fifteen Sermons Preached at the Rolls Chapel* (New York: Bobbs-Merrill, 1950), especially the Preface and sermon; and of Broad in 'Egoism as a Theory of Human Motives' seem to me particularly worthy of note here. These arguments are not, however (in my opinion), conclusive against more subtle forms of egoism, such as in 'self-realization' theories.

not necessarily involve acting from inclination, but on the contrary can involve acting contrary to it; and that in fact it is a necessary feature of the altruistic emotions that they involve a willingness to sacrifice some of our own interests, comfort, or convenience, for the sake of another's good.

[1 1]

Alienation, Consequentialism,
and the Demands of Morality

Peter Railton

Introduction

Living up to the demands of morality may bring with it alienation—
from one's personal commitments, from one's feelings or sentiments,
from other people, or even from morality itself. In this article I will
discuss several apparent instances of such alienation, and attempt a
preliminary assessment of their bearing on questions about the accep-
tability of certain moral theories. Of special concern will be the question whether problems about alienation show consequentialist moral
theories to be self-defeating.

I will not attempt a full or general characterization of alienation.
Indeed, at a perfectly general level alienation can be characterized only
very roughly as a kind of estrangement, distancing, or separateness
(not necessarily consciously attended to) resulting in some sort of loss
(not necessarily consciously noticed).[1] Rather than seek a general anal-

This essay was originally published in *Philosophy and Public Affairs* 13,2. Copyright ©
1984 by Princeton University Press. Reprinted by permission of Princeton University
Press. I am grateful to a number of people for criticisms of earlier drafts and helpful
suggestions for improvement. I especially thank Marcia Baron, Stephen Darwall, William K. Frankena, Allan Gibbard, Samuel Scheffler, Rebecca Scott, Michael Stocker,
Nicholas Sturgeon, Gregory Trianoski-Stillwell, and Susan Wolf.

[1] The loss in question need not be a loss of something of value, and *a fortiori* need not
be a bad thing overall: there are some people, institutions, or cultures alienation from
which would be a boon. Alienation is a more or less troubling phenomenon depending
upon what is lost; and in the cases to be considered, what is lost is for the most part of
substantial value. It does not follow, as we will see in Section V, that in all such cases
alienation is a bad thing on balance. Moreover, I do not assume that the loss in question
represents an actual *decline* in some value as the result of a separation coming into being
where once there was none. It seems reasonable to say that an individual can experience
a loss in being alienated from nature, for example, without assuming that he was ever in
communion with it, much as we say it is a loss for someone never to receive an education

ysis I will rely upon examples to convey a sense of what is involved in the sorts of alienation with which I am concerned. There is nothing in a word, and the phenomena to be discussed below could all be considered while avoiding the controversial term 'alienation.' My sense, however, is that there is some point in using this formidable term, if only to draw attention to commonalities among problems not always noticed. For example, in the final section of this article I will suggest that one important form of alienation in moral practice, the sense that morality confronts us as an alien set of demands, distant and disconnected from our actual concerns, can be mitigated by dealing with other sorts of alienation morality may induce. Finally, there are historical reasons, which will not be entered into here, for bringing these phenomena under a single label; part of the explanation of their existence lies in the conditions of modern "civil society," and in the philosophical traditions of empiricism and rationalism—which include a certain picture of the self's relation to the world—that have flourished in it.

Let us begin with two examples.

I. John and Anne and Lisa and Helen

To many, John has always seemed a model husband. He almost invariably shows great sensitivity to his wife's needs, and he willingly goes out of his way to meet them. He plainly feels great affection for her. When a friend remarks upon the extraordinary quality of John's concern for his wife, John responds without any self-indulgence or self-congratulation. "I've always thought that people should help each other when they're in a specially good position to do so. I know Anne better than anyone else does, so I know better what she wants and needs. Besides, I have such affection for her that it's no great burden—instead, I get a lot of satisfaction out of it. Just think how awful marriage would be, or life itself, if people didn't take special care of the ones they love." His friend accuses John of being unduly modest, but John's manner convinces him that he is telling the truth: this is really how he feels.

Lisa has gone through a series of disappointments over a short period, and has been profoundly depressed. In the end, however, with the help of others she has emerged from the long night of anxiety and melancholy. Only now is she able to talk openly with friends about her state of mind, and she turns to her oldest friend, Helen, who was a

---

or never to appreciate music. Regrettably, various relevant kinds and sources of alienation cannot be discussed here. A general, historical discussion of alienation may be found in Richard Schacht, *Alienation* (Garden City, N.Y.: Doubleday, 1971).

mainstay throughout. She'd like to find a way to thank Helen, since she's only too aware of how much of a burden she's been over these months, how much of a drag and a bore, as she puts it. "You don't have to thank me, Lisa," Helen replies, "you deserved it. It was the least I could do after all you've done for me. We're friends, remember? And we said a long time ago that we'd stick together no matter what. Some day I'll probably ask the same thing of you, and I know you'll come through. What else are friends for?" Lisa wonders whether Helen is saying this simply to avoid creating feelings of guilt, but Helen replies that she means every word—she couldn't bring herself to lie to Lisa if she tried.

II. What's Missing?

What is troubling about the words of John and Helen? Both show stout character and moral awareness. John's remarks have a benevolent, consequentialist cast, while Helen reasons in a deontological language of duties, reciprocity, and respect. They are not self-centered or without feeling. Yet something seems wrong.

The place to look is not so much at what they say as what they don't say. Think, for example, of how John's remarks might sound to his wife. Anne might have hoped that it was, in some ultimate sense, in part for *her* sake and the sake of their love as such that John pays such special attention to her. That he devotes himself to her because of the characteristically good consequences of doing so seems to leave her, and their relationship as such, too far out of the picture—this despite the fact that these characteristically good consequences depend in important ways on his special relation to her. She is being taken into account by John, but it might seem she is justified in being hurt by the way she is being taken into account. It is as if John viewed her, their relationship, and even his own affection for her from a distant, objective point of view—a moral point of view where reasons must be reasons for any rational agent and so must have an impersonal character even when they deal with personal matters. His wife might think a more personal point of view would also be appropriate, a point of view from which "It's my wife" or "It's Anne" would have direct and special relevance, and play an unmediated role in his answer to the question *"Why* do you attend to her so?"

Something similar is missing from Helen's account of why she stood by Lisa. While we understand that the specific duties she feels toward Lisa depend upon particular features of their relationship, still we would not be surprised if Lisa finds Helen's response to her expression of gratitude quite distant, even chilling. We need not question whether she has strong feeling for Lisa, but we may wonder at how that feeling finds expression in Helen's thinking.[2]

John and Helen both show alienation: there would seem to be an estrangement between their affections and their rational, deliberative selves; an abstract and universalizing point of view mediates their responses to others and to their own sentiments. We should not assume that they have been caught in an uncharacteristic moment of moral reflection or after-the-fact rationalization; it is a settled part of their characters to think and act from a moral point of view. It is as if the world were for them a fabric of obligations and permissions in which personal considerations deserve recognition only to the extent that, and in the way that, such considerations find a place in this fabric.

To call John and Helen alienated from their affections or their intimates is not of itself to condemn them, nor is it to say that they are experiencing any sort of distress. One may be alienated from something without recognizing this as such or suffering in any conscious way from it, much as one may simply be uninterested in something without awareness or conscious suffering. But alienation is not mere lack of interest: John and Helen are not *uninterested* in their affections or in their intimates; rather, their interest takes a certain alienated form. While this alienation may not itself be a psychological affliction, it may be the basis of such afflictions—such as a sense of loneliness or emptiness—or of the loss of certain things of value—such as a sense of belonging or the pleasures of spontaneity. Moreover, their alienation may cause psychological distress in others, and make certain valuable sorts of relationships impossible.

However, we must be on guard lest oversimple categories distort our diagnosis. It seems to me wrong to picture the self as ordinarily divided into cognitive and affective halves, with deliberation and rationality belonging to the first, and sentiments belonging to the second. John's alienation is not a problem on the boundary of naturally given cognitive and affective selves, but a problem partially constituted by the bifurcation of his psyche into these separate spheres. *John's* deliberative self seems remarkably divorced from his affections, but not all psyches need be so divided. That there is a cognitive element in affection—that affection is not a mere "feeling" that is a given for the deliberative self but rather involves as well certain characteristic modes of thought and perception—is suggested by the difficulty some may have in believing that John really does love Anne if he persistently thinks about her in

---

[2] This is not to say that no questions arise about whether Helen's (or John's) feelings and attitudes constitute the fullest sort of affection, as will be seen shortly.

the way suggested by his remarks. Indeed, his affection for Anne does seem to have been demoted to a mere "feeling." For this reason among others, we should not think of John's alienation from his affections and his alienation from Anne as wholly independent phenomena, the one the cause of the other.[3] Of course, similar remarks apply to Helen.

III. The Moral Point of View

Perhaps the lives of John and Anne or Helen and Lisa would be happier or fuller if none of the alienation mentioned were present. But is this a problem for *morality*? If, as some have contended, to have a morality is to make normative judgments from a moral point of view and be guided by them, and if by its nature a moral point of view must exclude considerations that lack universality, then any genuinely moral way of going about life would seem liable to produce the sorts of alienation mentioned above.[4] Thus it would be a conceptual confusion to ask that we never be required by morality to go beyond a personal point of view, since to fail ever to look at things from an impersonal (or nonpersonal) point of view would be to fail ever to *be* distinctively moral—not immoralism, perhaps, but amoralism. This would not be to say that there are not other points of view on life worthy of our attention,[5] or that taking a moral point of view is always appropriate—one could say that John and Helen show no moral defect in thinking so impersonally, although they do moralize to excess. But the fact that a particular morality requires us to take an impersonal point of view

---

[3] Moreover, there is a sense in which someone whose responses to his affections or feelings are characteristically mediated by a calculating point of view may fail to know himself fully, or may seem in a way unknowable to others, and this "cognitive distance" may itself be part of his alienation, I am indebted here to Allan Gibbard.

[4] There is a wide range of views about the nature of the moral point of view and its proper role in moral life. Is it necessary that one actually act on universal principles, or merely that one be willing to universalize the principles upon which one acts? Does the moral point of view by its nature require us to consider everyone alike? Here I am using a rather strong reading of the moral point of view, according to which taking the moral point of view involves universalization and the equal consideration of all.

[5] A moral point of view theorist might make use of the three points of view distinguished by Mill: the moral, the aesthetic, and the sympathetic. "The first addresses itself to our reason and conscience; the second to our imagination; the third to our human fellow-feeling," from "Bentham," reprinted in *John Stuart Mill: Utilitarianism and Other Writings*, ed. Mary Warnock (New York: New American Library, 1962), p. 121. What is morally right, in his view, may fail to be "loveable" (e.g., a parent strictly disciplining a child) or "beautiful" (e.g., an inauthentic gesture). Thus, the three points of view need not concur in their positive or negative assessments. Notice, however, that Mill has divided the self into three realms, of "reason and conscience," of "imagination," and of "human fellow-feeling"; notice, too, that he has chosen the word 'feeling' to characterize human affections.

could not sensibly be held against it, for that would be what makes it a morality at all.

This sort of position strikes me as entirely too complacent. First, we must somehow give an account of practical reasoning that does not merely multiply points of view and divide the self—a more unified account is needed. Second, we must recognize that loving relationships, friendships, group loyalties, and spontaneous actions are among the most important contributors to whatever it is that makes life worthwhile; any moral theory deserving serious consideration must itself give them serious consideration. As William K. Frankena has written, "Morality is made for man, not man for morality."[6] Moral considerations are often supposed to be overriding in practical reasoning. If we were to find that adopting a particular morality led to irreconcilable conflict with central types of human well-being—as cases akin to John's and Helen's have led some to suspect—then this surely would give us good reason to doubt its claims.[7]

For example, in the closing sentences of *A Theory of Justice* John Rawls considers the "perspective of eternity," which is impartial across all individuals and times, and writes that this is a "form of *thought and feeling* that rational persons can adopt in the world." "Purity of heart," he concludes, "would be to see clearly and act with grace and self-command from this point of view."[8] This may or may not be purity of heart, but it could not be the standpoint of actual life without radically detaching the individual from a range of personal concerns and commitments. Presumably we should not read Rawls as recommending that we adopt this point of view in the bulk of our actions in daily life, but the fact that so purely abstracted a perspective is portrayed as a kind of moral ideal should at least start us wondering.[9] If to be more

[6] William K. Frankena, *Ethics*, 2d ed. (Englewood Cliffs, N.J.: Prentice-Hall, 1973), p. 116. Moralities that do not accord with this dictum—or a modified version of it that includes all sentient beings—might be deemed alienated in a Feuerbachian sense.

[7] Mill, for instance, calls the moral point of view "unquestionably the first and most important," and while he thinks it the error of the moralizer (such as Bentham) to elevate the moral point of view and "sink the [aesthetic and sympathetic] entirely," he does not explain how to avoid such a result if the moral point of view is to be, as he says it ought, "paramount." See his "Bentham," pp. 121f.

Philosophers who have recently raised doubts about moralities for such reasons include Bernard Williams, in "A Critique of Utilitarianism," in J. J. C. Smart and B. Williams, *Utilitarianism: For and Against* (Cambridge: Cambridge University Press, 1973), and Michael Stocker, in "The Schizophrenia of Modern Ethical Theories," *Journal of Philosophy* 73 (1976): 453–66.

[8] John Rawls, *A Theory of Justice* (Cambridge: Harvard University Press, 1971), p. 587, emphasis added.

[9] I am not claiming that we should interpret all of Rawls' intricate moral theory in light of these few remarks. They are cited here merely to illustrate a certain tendency in moral thought, especially that of a Kantian inspiration.

perfectly moral is to ascend ever higher toward *sub specie aeternitatis* abstraction, perhaps we made a mistake in boarding the moral escalator in the first place. Some of the very "weaknesses" that prevent us from achieving this moral ideal—strong attachments to persons or projects—seem to be part of a considerably more compelling human ideal.

Should we say at this point that the lesson is that we should give a more prominent role to the value of non-alienation in our moral reasoning? That would be too little too late: the problem seems to be the way in which morality asks us to look at things, not just the things it asks us to look at.

IV. The "Paradox of Hedonism"

Rather than enter directly into the question whether being moral is a matter of taking a moral point of view and whether there is thus some sort of necessary connection between being moral and being alienated in a way detrimental to human flourishing, I will consider a related problem the solution to which may suggest a way of steering around obstacles to a more direct approach.

One version of the so-called "paradox of hedonism" is that adopting as one's exclusive ultimate end in life the pursuit of maximum happiness may well prevent one from having certain experiences or engaging in certain sorts of relationships or commitments that are among the greatest sources of happiness.[10] The hedonist, looking around him, may discover that some of those who are less concerned with their own happiness than he is, and who view people and projects less instrumentally than he does, actually manage to live happier lives than he despite his dogged pursuit of happiness. The "paradox" is pragmatic, not logical, but it looks deep nonetheless: the hedonist, it would appear, ought not to be a hedonist. It seems, then, as if we have come across a second case in which mediating one's relations to people or projects by a particular point of view—in this case, a hedonistic point of view— may prevent one from attaining the fullest possible realization of sought-after values.

However, it is important to notice that even though adopting a hedonistic life project may tend to interfere with realizing that very pro-

[10] This is a "paradox" for individual, egoistic hedonists. Other forms the "paradox of hedonism" may take are social in character: a society of egoistic hedonists might arguably achieve less total happiness than a society of more benevolent beings; or, taking happiness as the sole social goal might lead to a less happy society overall than could exist if a wider range of goals were pursued.

ject, there is no such natural exclusion between acting for the sake of another or a cause as such and recognizing how important this is to one's happiness. A spouse who acts for the sake of his mate may know full well that this is a source of deep satisfaction for him—in addition to providing him with reasons for acting internal to it, the relationship may also promote the external goal of achieving happiness. Moreover, while the pursuit of happiness may not be the reason he entered or sustains the relationships, he may also recognize that if it had not seemed likely to make him happy he would not have entered it, and that if it proved over time to be inconsistent with his happiness he would consider ending it.

It might be objected that one cannot really regard a person or a project as an end as such if one's commitment is in this way contingent or overridable. But were this so, we would be able to have very few commitments to ends as such. For example, one could not be committed to both one's spouse and one's child as ends as such, since at most one of these commitments could be overriding in cases of conflict. It is easy to confuse the notion of a commitment to an end *as such* (or *for its own sake*) with that of an *overriding* commitment, but strength is not the same as structure. To be committed to an end as such is a matter of (among other things) whether it furnishes one with reasons for acting that are not mediated by other concerns. It does not follow that these reasons must always outweigh whatever opposing reasons one may have, or that one may not at the same time have other, mediating reasons that also incline one to act on behalf of that end.

Actual commitments to ends as such, even when very strong, are subject to various qualifications and contingencies.[11] If a friend grows too predictable or moves off to a different part of the world, or if a planned life project proves less engaging or practical than one had imagined, commitments and affections naturally change. If a relationship were highly vulnerable to the least change, it would be strained to speak of genuine affection rather than, say, infatuation. But if members of a relationship came to believe that they would be better off without it, this ordinarily would be a non-trivial change, and it is not difficult to imagine that their commitment to the relationship might be contingent in this way but nonetheless real. Of course, a relationship involves a shared history and shared expectations as well as momentary experiences, and it is unusual that affection or concern can be changed overnight, or relationships begun or ended at will. Moreover, the sorts of affections and commitments that can play a decisive role in shaping one's life and in making possible the deeper sorts of satisfactions are

---

[11] This is not to deny that there are indexical components to commitments.

not those that are easily overridden or subject to constant reassessment or second-guessing. Thus a sensible hedonist would not forever be subjecting his affections or commitments to egoistic calculation, nor would he attempt to break off a relationship or commitment merely because it might seem to him at a given moment that some other arrangement would make him happier. Commitments to others or to causes as such may be very closely linked to the self, and a hedonist who knows what he's about will not be one who turns on his self at the slightest provocation. Contingency is not expendability, and while some commitments are remarkably non-contingent—such as those of parent to child or patriot to country—it cannot be said that commitments of a more contingent sort are never genuine, or never conduce to the profounder sorts of happiness.[12]

Following these observations, we may reduce the force of the "paradox of hedonism" if we distinguish two forms of hedonism. *Subjective hedonism* is the view that one should adopt the hedonistic point of view in action, that is, that one should whenever possible attempt to determine which act seems most likely to contribute optimally to one's happiness, and behave accordingly. *Objective hedonism* is the view that one should follow that course of action which would in fact most contribute to one's happiness, even when this would involve *not* adopting the hedonistic point of view in action. An act will be called *subjectively hedonistic* if it is done from a hedonistic point of view; an act is *objectively hedonistic* if it is that act, of those available to the agent, which would most contribute to his happiness.[13] Let us call someone a *sophisticated*

---

[12] It does seem likely to matter just what the commitment is contingent upon as well as just how contingent it is. I think it is an open question whether commitments contingent upon the satisfaction of egoistic hedonist criteria are of the sort that might figure in the happiest sorts of lives ordinarily available. We will return to this problem presently.

Those who have had close relationships often develop a sense of *duty* to one another that may outlast affection or emotional commitment, that is, they may have a sense of obligation to one another that is less contingent than affection or emotional commitment, and that should not simply be confused with them. If such a sense of obligation is in conflict with self-interest, and if it is a normal part of the most satisfying sorts of close relationships, then this may pose a problem for the egoistic hedonist.

[13] A few remarks are needed. First, I will say that an act is available to an agent if he would succeed in performing it if he tried. Second, here and elsewhere in this article I mean to include quite "thick" descriptions of actions, so that it may be part of an action that one perform it with a certain intention or goal. In the short run (but not so much the long run) intentions, goals, motives, and the like are usually less subject to our deliberate control than overt behavior—it is easier to say "I'm sorry" than to say it and mean it. This, however, is a fact about the relative availability of acts to the agent at a given time, and should not dictate what is to count as an act. Third, here and elsewhere I ignore for simplicity's sake the possibility that more than one course of action may be maximally valuable. And fourth, for reasons I will not enter into here, I have formulated objective hedonism in terms of actual outcomes rather than expected values (relative to the information available to the agent). One could make virtually the same argument using an expected value formulation.

hedonist if he aims to lead an objectively hedonistic life (that is, the happiest life available to him in the circumstances) and yet is not committed to subjective hedonism. Thus, within the limits of what is psychologically possible, a sophisticated hedonist is prepared to eschew the hedonistic point of view whenever taking this point of view conflicts with following an objectively hedonistic course of action. The so-called paradox of hedonism shows that there will be such conflicts: certain acts or courses of action may be objectively hedonistic only if not subjectively hedonistic. When things are put this way, it seems that the sophisticated hedonist faces a problem rather than a paradox: how to act in order to achieve maximum possible happiness if this is at times—or even often—*not* a matter of carrying out hedonistic deliberations.

The answer in any particular case will be complex and contextual—it seems unlikely that any one method of decision making would always promote thought and action most conducive to one's happiness. A sophisticated hedonist might proceed precisely by looking at the complex and contextual: observing the actual modes of thought and action of those people who are in some ways like himself and who seem most happy. If our assumptions are right, he will find that few such individuals are subjective hedonists; instead, they act for the sake of a variety of ends as such. He may then set out to develop in himself the traits of character, ways of thought, types of commitment, and so on, that seem common in happy lives. For example, if he notes that the happiest people often have strong loyalties to friends, he must ask how he can become a more loyal friend—not merely how he can seem to be a loyal friend (since those he has observed are not happy because they merely seem loyal)—but how he can in fact be one.

Could one really make such changes if one had as a goal leading an optimally happy life? The answer seems to me a qualified *yes,* but let us first look at a simpler case. A highly competitive tennis player comes to realize that his obsession with winning is keeping him from playing his best. A pro tells him that if he wants to win he must devote himself more to the game and its play as such and think less about his performance. In the commitment and concentration made possible by this devotion, he is told, lies the secret of successful tennis. So he spends a good deal of time developing an enduring devotion to many aspects of the activity, and finds it peculiarly satisfying to become so absorbed in it. He plays better, and would have given up the program of change if he did not, but he now finds that he plays tennis more for its own sake, enjoying greater internal as well as external rewards from the sport. Such a person would not keep thinking—on or off the court—"No matter how I play, the only thing I really care about is whether I win!"

He would recognize such thoughts as self-defeating, as evidence that his old, unhelpful way of looking at things was returning. Nor would such a person be self-deceiving. He need not hide from himself his goal of winning, for this goal is consistent with his increased devotion to the game. His commitment to the activity is not eclipsed by, but made more vivid by, his desire to succeed at it.

The same sort of story might be told about a sophisticated hedonist and friendship. An individual could realize that his instrumental attitude toward his friends prevents him from achieving the fullest happiness friendship affords. He could then attempt to focus more on his friends as such, doing this somewhat deliberately, perhaps, until it comes more naturally. He might then find his friendships improved and himself happier. If he found instead that his relationships were deteriorating or his happiness declining, he would reconsider the idea. None of this need be hidden from himself: the external goal of happiness reinforces the internal goals of his relationships. The sophisticated hedonist's motivational structure should therefore meet a *counterfactual condition:* he need not always act for the sake of happiness, since he may do various things for their own sake or for the sake of others, but he would not act as he does if it were not compatible with his leading an objectively hedonistic life. Of course, a sophisticated hedonist cannot guarantee that he will meet this counterfactual condition, but only attempt to meet it as fully as possible.

Success at tennis is a relatively circumscribed goal, leaving much else about one's life undefined. Maximizing one's happiness, by contrast, seems all-consuming. Could commitments to other ends survive alongside it? Consider an analogy. Ned needs to make a living. More than that, he needs to make as much money as he can—he has expensive tastes, a second marriage, and children reaching college age, and he does not have extensive means. He sets out to invest his money and his labor in ways he thinks will maximize return. Yet it does not follow that he acts as he does solely for the sake of earning as much as possible.[14] Although it is obviously true that he does what he does because he believes that it will maximize return, this does not preclude his doing it for other reasons as well, for example, for the sake of living well or taking care of his children. This may continue to be the case even if Ned comes to want money for its own sake, that is, if he comes to see the accumulation of wealth as intrinsically as well as extrinsically attractive.[15] Similarly, the stricture that one seek the objectively he-

---

[14] Michael Stocker considers related cases in "Morally Good Intentions," *The Monist* 54 (1970): 124–41. I am much indebted to his discussion.
[15] There may be a parallelism of sorts between Ned's coming to seek money for its own

donistic life certainly provides one with considerable guidance, but it does not supply the whole of one's motives and goals in action.

My claim that the sophisticated hedonist can escape the paradox of hedonism was, however, qualified. It still seems possible that the happiest sorts of lives ordinarily attainable are those led by people who would reject even sophisticated hedonism, people whose character is such that if they were presented with a choice between two entire lives, one of which contains less total happiness but nonetheless realizes some other values more fully, they might well knowingly choose against maximal happiness. If this were so, it would show that a sophisticated hedonist might have reason for changing his beliefs so that he no longer accepts hedonism in any form. This still would not refute objective hedonism as an account of the (rational, prudential, or moral) *criterion* one's acts should meet, for it would be precisely in order to meet this criterion that the sophisticated hedonist would change his beliefs.[16]

V. The Place of Non-Alienation among Human Values

Before discussing the applicability of what has been said about hedonism to morality, we should notice that alienation is not always a bad thing, that we may not want to overcome all forms of alienation, and that other values, which may conflict with non-alienation in particular cases, may at times have a greater claim on us. Let us look at a few such cases.

It has often been argued that a morality of duties and obligations may appropriately come into play in familial or friendly relationships when the relevant sentiments have given out, for instance, when one is exasperated with a friend, when love is tried, and so on.[17] 'Ought' implies 'can' (or, at least, 'could'), and while it may be better in human terms when we do what we ought to do at least in part out of feelings of love, friendship, or sympathy, there are times when we simply cannot

---

sake and a certain pattern of moral development: what is originally sought in order to live up to familial or social expectations may come to be an end in itself.

It might be objected that the goal of earning as much money as possible is quite unlike the goal of being as happy as possible, since money is plainly instrumentally valuable even when it is sought for its own sake. But happiness, too, is instrumentally valuable, for it may contribute to realizing such goals as being a likeable or successful person.

[16] An important objection to the claim that objective hedonism may serve as the *moral* criterion one's acts should meet, even if this means not believing in hedonism, is that moral principles must meet a *publicity* condition. I will discuss this objection in Section VI.

[17] See, for example, Stocker, "The Schizophrenia of Modern Ethical Theories."

muster these sentiments, and the right thing to do is to act as love or friendship or sympathy would have directed rather than refuse to perform any act done merely from a sense of duty.

But we should add a further role for unspontaneous, morally motivated action: even when love or concern is strong, it is often desirable that people achieve some distance from their sentiments or one another. A spouse may act toward his mate in a grossly overprotective way; a friend may indulge another's ultimately destructive tendencies; a parent may favor one child inordinately. Strong and immediate affection may overwhelm one's ability to see what another person actually needs or deserves. In such cases a certain distance between people or between an individual and his sentiments, and an intrusion of moral considerations into the gap thus created, may be a good thing, and part of genuine affection or commitment. The opposite view, that no such mediation is desirable as long as affection is strong, seems to me a piece of romanticism. Concern over alienation therefore ought not to take the form of a cult of "authenticity at any price."

Moreover, there will occur regular conflicts between avoiding alienation and achieving other important individual goals. One such goal is autonomy. Bernard Williams has emphasized that many of us have developed certain "ground projects" that give shape and meaning to our lives, and has drawn attention to the damage an individual may suffer if he is alienated from his ground projects by being forced to look at them as potentially overridable by moral considerations.[18] But against this it may be urged that it is crucial for autonomy that one hold one's commitments up for inspection—even one's ground projects. Our ground projects are often formed in our youth, in a particular family, class, or cultural background. It may be alienating and even disorienting to call these into question, but to fail to do so is to lose autonomy. Of course, autonomy could not sensibly require that we question all of our values and commitments at once, nor need it require us to be forever detached from what we are doing. It is quite possible to submit basic aspects of one's life to scrutiny and arrive at a set of autonomously chosen commitments that form the basis of an integrated life. Indeed, psychological conflicts and practical obstacles give us occasion for reexamining our basic commitments rather more often than we'd like.

At the same time, the tension between autonomy and non-alienation should not be exaggerated. Part of avoiding exaggeration is giving up the Kantian notion that autonomy is a matter of escaping determination by any contingency whatsoever. Part, too, is refusing to conflate

18 Williams, "Critique."

autonomy with sheer independence from others. Both Rousseau and
Marx emphasized that achieving control over one's own life requires
participation in certain sorts of social relations—in fact, relations in
which various kinds of alienation have been minimized.

Autonomy is but one value that may enter into complex trade-offs
with non-alienation. Alienation and inauthenticity do have their uses.
The alienation of some individuals or groups from their milieu may at
times be necessary for fundamental social criticism or cultural innova-
tion. And without some degree of inauthenticity, it is doubtful whether
civil relations among people could long be maintained. It would take
little ingenuity, but too much of the reader's patience, to construct here
examples involving troubling conflicts between non-alienation and virtually any other worthy goal.

VI. Reducing Alienation in Morality

Let us now move to morality proper. To do this with any definite-
ness, we must have a particular morality in mind. For various reasons, I
think that the most plausible sort of morality is consequentialist in
form, assessing rightness in terms of contribution to the good. In attempting to sketch how we might reduce alienation in moral theory
and practice, therefore, I will work within a consequentialist framework (although a number of the arguments I will make could be made,
mutatis mutandis, by a deontologist).

Of course, one has adopted no morality in particular even in adopting consequentialism unless one says what the good is. Let us, then,
dwell briefly on axiology. One mistake of dominant consequentialist
theories, I believe, is their failure to see that things other than subjective states can have intrinsic value. Allied to this is a tendency to reduce
all intrinsic values to one—happiness. Both of these features of classical utilitarianism reflect forms of alienation. First, in divorcing subjective states from their objective counterparts, and claiming that we seek
the latter exclusively for the sake of the former, utilitarianism cuts us
off from the world in a way made graphic by examples such as that of
the experience machine, a hypothetical device that can be pro-
grammed to provide one with whatever subjective states he may desire.
The experience machine affords us decisive subjective advantages over
actual life: few, if any, in actual life think they have achieved all that
they could want, but the machine makes possible for each an existence
that he cannot distinguish from such a happy state of affairs.[19] Despite

---

[19] At least one qualification is needed: the subjective states must be psychologically
possible. Perhaps some of us desire what are, in effect, psychologically impossible states.

this striking advantage, most rebel at the notion of the experience machine. As Robert Nozick and others have pointed out, it seems to matter to us what we actually *do* and *are* as well as how life *appears* to us.[20] We see the point of our lives as bound up with the world and other people in ways not captured by subjectivism, and our sense of loss in contemplating a life tied to an experience machine, quite literally alienated from the surrounding world, suggests where subjectivism has gone astray. Second, the reduction of all goals to the purely abstract goal of happiness or pleasure, as in hedonistic utilitarianism, treats all other goals instrumentally. Knowledge or friendship may promote happiness, but is it a fair characterization of our commitment to these goals to say that this is the only sense in which they are ultimately valuable? Doesn't the insistence that there is an abstract and uniform goal lying behind all of our ends bespeak an alienation from these particular ends?

Rather than pursue these questions further here, let me suggest an approach to the good that seems to me less hopeless as a way of capturing human value: a pluralistic approach in which several goods are viewed as intrinsically, non-morally valuable—such as happiness, knowledge, purposeful activity, autonomy, solidarity, respect, and beauty.[21]

---

[20] Robert Nozick, *Anarchy, State, and Utopia* (New York: Basic Books, 1974), pp. 42ff.

[21] To my knowledge, the best-developed method for justifying claims about intrinsic value involves thought-experiments of a familiar sort, in which, for example, we imagine two lives, or two worlds, alike in all but one respect, and then attempt to determine whether rational, well-informed, widely-experienced individuals would (when vividly aware of both alternatives) be indifferent between the two or have a settled preference for one over the other. Since no one is ideally rational, fully informed, or infinitely experienced, the best we can do is to take more seriously the judgments of those who come nearer to approximating these conditions. Worse yet: the best we can do is to take more seriously the judgments of those we *think* better approximate these conditions. (I am not supposing that facts or experience somehow entail values, but that in rational agents, beliefs and values show a marked mutual influence and coherence.) We may overcome some narrowness if we look at behavior and preferences in other societies and other epochs, but even here we must rely upon interpretations colored by our own beliefs and values. Within the confines of this article I must leave unanswered a host of deep and troubling questions about the nature of values and value judgments. Suffice it to say that there is no reason to think that we are in a position to give anything but a tentative list of intrinsic goods.

It becomes a complex matter to describe the psychology of intrinsic value. For example, should we say that one values a relationship of solidarity, say, a friendship, *because it is* a friendship? That makes it sound as if it were somehow instrumental to the realization of some abstract value, friendship. Surely this is a misdescription. We may be able to get a clearer idea of what is involved by considering the case of happiness. We certainly do not value a particular bit of experienced happiness because it is instrumental in the realization of the abstract goal, happiness—we value the experience for its own sake because it is a happy experience. Similarly, a friendship is itself the valued thing, the thing of a valued kind. Of course, one can say that one values friendship and therefore seeks friends, just as one can say one values happiness and therefore seeks happy experiences. But this locution must be contrasted with what is being said when, for example, one talks of seeking *things that make one happy*. Friends are not "things that make one achieve

These goods need not be ranked lexically, but may be attributed weights, and the criterion of rightness for an act would be that it most contribute to the weighted sum of these values in the long run. This creates the possibility of trade-offs among values of the kinds discussed in the previous section. However, I will not stop here to develop or defend such an account of the good and the right, since our task is to show how certain problems of alienation that arise in moral contexts might be dealt with if morality is assumed to have such a basis.

Consider, then, Juan, who, like John, has always seemed a model husband. When a friend remarks on the extraordinary concern he shows for his wife, Juan characteristically responds: "I love Linda. I even *like* her. So it means a lot to me to do things for her. After all we've been through, it's almost a part of me to do it." But his friend knows that Juan is a principled individual, and asks Juan how his marriage fits into that larger scheme. After all, he asks, it's fine for Juan and his wife to have such a close relationship, but what about all the other, needier people Juan could help if he broadened his horizon still further? Juan replies, "Look, it's a better world when people can have a relationship like ours—and nobody could if everyone were always asking themselves who's got the most need. It's not easy to make things work in this world, and one of the best things that happens to people is to have a close relationship like ours. You'd make things worse in a hurry if you broke up those close relationships for the sake of some higher goal. Anyhow, I know that you can't always put family first. The world isn't such a wonderful place that it's OK just to retreat into your own little circle. But still, you need that little circle. People get burned out, or lose touch, if they try to save the world by themselves. The ones who can stick with it and do a good job of making things better are usually the ones who can make that fit into a life that does not make them miserable. I haven't met any real saints lately, and I don't trust people who think they *are* saints."

If we contrast Juan with John, we do not find that the one allows moral considerations to enter his personal life while the other does not. Nor do we find that one is less serious in his moral concern. Rather, what Juan recognizes to be morally required is not by its nature incompatible with acting directly for the sake of another. It is important to Juan to subject his life to moral scrutiny—he is not merely stumped when asked for a defense of his acts above a personal level, he does not *just* say "Of course I take care of her, she's my wife!" or "It's Linda" and

---

friendship"—they partially constitute friendships, just as particular happy experiences partially constitute happiness for an individual. Thus taking friendship as an intrinsic value does not entail viewing particular friendships instrumentally.

refuse to listen to the more impersonal considerations raised by his friend. It is consistent with what he says to imagine that his motivational structure has a form akin to that of the sophisticated hedonist, that is, his motivational structure meets a counterfactual condition: while he ordinarily does not do what he does simply for the sake of doing what's right, he would seek to lead a different sort of life if he did not think his were morally defensible. His love is not a romantic submersion in the other to the exclusion of worldly responsibilities, and to that extent it may be said to involve a degree of alienation from Linda. But this does not seem to drain human value from their relationship. Nor need one imagine that Linda would be saddened to hear Juan's words the way Anne might have been saddened to overhear the remarks of John.[22]

Moreover, because of his very willingness to question his life morally, Juan avoids a sort of alienation not sufficiently discussed—alienation from others, beyond one's intimate ties. Individuals who will not or cannot allow questions to arise about what they are doing from a broader perspective are in an important way cut off from their society and the larger world. They may not be troubled by this in any very direct way, but even so they may fail to experience that powerful sense of purpose and meaning that comes from seeing oneself as part of something larger and more enduring than oneself or one's intimate circle. The search for such a sense of purpose and meaning seems to me ubiquitous—surely much of the impulse to religion, to ethnic or regional identification (most strikingly, in the "rediscovery" of such identities), or to institutional loyalty stems from this desire to see ourselves as part of a more general, lasting, and worthwhile scheme of things.[23] This presumably is part of what is meant by saying that secu-

---

[22] If one objects that Juan's commitment to Linda is lacking because it is contingent in some ways, the objector must show that the *kinds* of contingencies involved would destroy his relationship with Linda, especially since moral character often figures in commitments—the character of the other, or the compatibility of a commitment with one's having the sort of character one values—and the contingencies in Juan's case are due to his moral character.

[23] I do not mean to suggest that such identities are always matters of choice for individuals. Quite the reverse, identities often arise through socialization, prejudice, and similar influences. The point rather is that there is a very general phenomenon of identification, badly in need of explanation, that to an important extent underlies such phenomena as socialization and prejudice, and that suggests the existence of certain needs in virtually all members of society—needs to which identification with entities beyond the self answers.

Many of us who resist raising questions about our lives from broader perspectives do so, I fear, not out of a sense that it would be difficult or impossible to lead a meaningful life if one entertained such perspectives, but rather out of a sense that our lives would not stand up to much scrutiny therefrom, so that leading a life that *would* seem meaningful from such perspectives would require us to change in some significant way.

larization has led to a sense of meaninglessness, or that the decline of traditional communities and societies has meant an increase in anomie. (The sophisticated hedonist, too, should take note: one way to gain a firmer sense that one's life is worthwhile, a sense that may be important to realizing various values in one's own life, is to overcome alienation from others.)

Drawing upon our earlier discussion of two kinds of hedonism, let us now distinguish two kinds of consequentialism. *Subjective consequentialism* is the view that whenever one faces a choice of actions, one should attempt to determine which act of those available would most promote the good, and should then try to act accordingly. One is behaving as subjective consequentialism requires—that is, leading a *subjectively consequentialist life*—to the extent that one uses and follows a distinctively consequentialist mode of decision making, consciously aiming at the overall good and conscientiously using the best available information with the greatest possible rigor. *Objective consequentialism* is the view that the criterion of the rightness of an act or course of action is whether it in fact would most promote the good of those acts available to the agent. Subjective consequentialism, like subjective hedonism, is a view that prescribes following a particular mode of deliberation in action; objective consequentialism, like objective hedonism, concerns the outcomes actually brought about, and thus deals with the question of deliberation only in terms of the tendencies of certain forms of decision making to promote appropriate outcomes. Let us reserve the expression *objectively consequentialist act (or life)* for those acts (or that life) of those available to the agent that would bring about the best outcomes.[24] To complete the parallel, let us say that a *sophisticated consequentialist* is someone who has a standing commitment to leading an objectively consequentialist life, but who need not set special stock in any particular form of decision making and therefore does not necessarily seek to lead a subjectively consequentialist life. Juan, it might be argued (if the details were filled in), is a sophisticated consequentialist,

---

[24] Although the language here is causal—'promoting' and 'bringing about'—it should be said that the relation of an act to the good need not always be causal. An act of learning may non-causally involve coming to have knowledge (an intrinsic good by my reckoning) as well as contributing causally to later realizations of intrinsic value. Causal consequences as such do not have a privileged status. As in the case of objective hedonism, I have formulated objective consequentialism in terms of actual outcomes (so-called "objective duty") rather than expected values relative to what is rational for the agent to believe ("subjective duty"). The main arguments of this article could be made using expected value, since the course of action with highest expected value need not in general be the subjectively consequentialist one. See also notes 13 and 21.

Are there any subjective consequentialists? Well, various theorists have claimed that a consequentialist must be a subjective consequentialist in order to be genuine—see Williams, "Critique," p. 135, and Rawls, *Theory of Justice*, p. 182.

since he seems to believe he should act for the best but does not seem to feel it appropriate to bring a consequentialist calculus to bear on his every act.

Is it bizarre, or contradictory, that being a sophisticated consequentialist may involve rejecting subjective consequentialism? After all, doesn't an adherent of subjective consequentialism also seek to lead an objectively consequentialist life? He may, but then he is mistaken in thinking that this means he should always undertake a distinctively consequentialist deliberation when faced with a choice. To see his mistake, we need only consider some examples.

It is well known that in certain emergencies, the best outcome requires action so swift as to preclude consequentialist deliberation. Thus a sophisticated consequentialist has reason to inculcate in himself certain dispositions to act rapidly in obvious emergencies. The disposition is not a mere reflex, but a developed pattern of action deliberately acquired. A simple example, but it should dispel the air of paradox.

Many decisions are too insignificant to warrant consequentialist deliberation ("Which shoelace should I do up first?") or too predictable in outcome ("Should I meet my morning class today as scheduled or should I linger over the newspaper?"). A famous old conundrum for consequentialism falls into a similar category: before I deliberate about an act, it seems I must decide how much time would be optimal to allocate for this deliberation; but then I must first decide how much time would be optimal to allocate for this time-allocation decision; but before that I must decide how much time would be optimal to allocate for *that* decision; and so on. The sophisticated consequentialist can block this paralyzing regress by noting that often the best thing to do is not to ask questions about time allocation at all; instead, he may develop standing dispositions to give more or less time to decisions depending upon their perceived importance, the amount of information available, the predictability of his choice, and so on. I think we all have dispositions of this sort, which account for our patience with some prolonged deliberations but not others.

There are somewhat more intriguing examples that have more to do with psychological interference than mere time efficiency: the timid, put-upon employee who knows that if he deliberates about whether to ask for a raise he will succumb to his timidity and fail to demand what he actually deserves; the self-conscious man who knows that if, at social gatherings, he is forever wondering how he should act, his behavior will be awkward and unnatural, contrary to his goal of acting naturally and appropriately; the tightrope walker who knows he must not reflect on the value of keeping his concentration; and so on. People can learn to avoid certain characteristically self-defeating lines of thought—just

as the tennis player in an earlier example learned to avoid thinking
constantly about winning—and the sophisticated consequentialist may
learn that consequentialist deliberation is in a variety of cases self-
defeating, so that other habits of thought should be cultivated.

The sophisticated consequentialist need not be deceiving himself or
acting in bad faith when he avoids consequentialist reasoning. He can
fully recognize that he is developing the dispositions he does because
they are necessary for promoting the good. Of course, he cannot be
preoccupied with this fact all the while, but then one cannot be *preoccupied* with anything without this interfering with normal or appropriate patterns of thought and action.

To the list of cases of interference we may add John, whose all-
purpose willingness to look at things by subjective consequentialist
lights prevents the realization in him and in his relationships with
others of values that he would recognize to be crucially important.

Bernard Williams has said that it shows consequentialism to be in
grave trouble that it may have to usher itself from the scene as a mode
of decision making in a number of important areas of life.[25] Though I
think he has exaggerated the extent to which we would have to exclude
consequentialist considerations from our lives in order to avoid disastrous results, it is fair to ask: If maximizing the good were in fact to
require that consequentialist reasoning be *wholly* excluded, would this
refute consequentialism? Imagine an all-knowing demon who controls
the fate of the world and who visits unspeakable punishment upon
man to the extent that he does not employ a Kantian morality. (Obviously, the demon is not himself a Kantian.) If such a demon existed,
sophisticated consequentialists would have reason to convert to
Kantianism, perhaps even to make whatever provisions could be made
to erase consequentialism from the human memory and prevent any
resurgence of it.

Does this possibility show that objective consequentialism is self-
defeating? On the contrary, it shows that objective consequentialism
has the virtue of not blurring the distinction between the *truth-
conditions* of an ethical theory and its *acceptance-conditions* in particular
contexts, a distinction philosophers have generally recognized for theories concerning other subject matters. It might be objected that, unlike other theories, ethical theories must meet a condition of publicity,
roughly to the effect that it must be possible under all circumstances
for us to recognize a true ethical theory as such and to promulgate it
publicly without thereby violating that theory itself.[26] Such a condition

---

[25] Williams, "Critique," p. 135.
[26] For discussion of a publicity condition, see Rawls, *Theory of Justice*, pp. 133, 177–82,

might be thought to follow from the social nature of morality. But any such condition would be question-begging against consequentialist theories, since it would require that one class of actions—acts of adopting or promulgating an ethical theory—*not* be assessed in terms of their consequences. Moreover, I fail to see how such a condition could emanate from the social character of morality. To prescribe the adoption and promulgation of a mode of decision making regardless of its consequences seems to me radically detached from human concerns, social or otherwise. If it is argued that an ethical theory that fails to meet the publicity requirement could under certain conditions endorse a course of action leading to the abuse and manipulation of man by man, we need only reflect that no psychologically possible decision procedure can guarantee that its widespread adoption could never have such a result. A "consequentialist demon" might increase the amount of abuse and manipulation in the world in direct proportion to the extent that people act according to the categorical imperative. Objective consequentialism (unlike certain deontological theories) has valuable flexibility in permitting us to take consequences into account in assessing the appropriateness of certain modes of decision making, thereby avoiding any sort of self-defeating decision procedure worship.

A further objection is that the lack of any direct link between objective consequentialism and a particular mode of decision making leaves the view too vague to provide adequate guidance in practice. On the contrary, objective consequentialism sets a definite and distinctive criterion of right action, and it becomes an empirical question (though not an easy one) which modes of decision making should be employed and when. It would be a mistake for an objective consequentialist to attempt to tighten the connection between his criterion of rightness and any particular mode of decision making: someone who recommended a particular mode of decision making regardless of consequences would not be a hard-nosed, non-evasive objective consequentialist, but a self-contradicting one.

VII. Contrasting Approaches

The seeming "indirectness" of objective consequentialism may invite its confusion with familiar indirect consequentialist theories, such as rule-consequentialism. In fact, the subjective/objective distinction cuts

---

582. The question whether a publicity condition can be justified is a difficult one, deserving fuller discussion than I am able to give it here.

across the rule/act distinction, and there are subjective and objective forms of both rule- and act-based theories. Thus far, we have dealt only with subjective and objective forms of act-consequentialism. By contrast, a *subjective rule*-consequentialist holds (roughly) that in deliberation we should always attempt to determine which act, of those available, conforms to that set of rules general acceptance of which would most promote the good; we then should attempt to perform this act. An *objective rule*-consequentialist sets actual conformity to the rules with the highest acceptance value as his criterion of right action, recognizing the possibility that the best set of rules might in some cases—or even always—recommend that one not perform rule-consequentialist deliberation.

Because I believe this last possibility must be taken seriously, I find the objective form of rule-consequentialism more plausible. Ultimately, however, I suspect that rule-consequentialism is untenable in either form, for it could recommend acts that (subjectively or objectively) accord with the best set of rules even when these rules are *not* in fact generally accepted, and when as a result these acts would have devastatingly bad consequences. "Let the rules with greatest acceptance utility be followed though the heavens fall!" is no more plausible than "*Fiat justitia, ruat coelum!*"—and a good bit less ringing. Hence, the arguments in this article are based entirely upon act-consequentialism.

Indeed, once the subjective/objective distinction has been drawn, an act-consequentialist can capture some of the intuitions that have made rule- or trait-consequentialism appealing.[27] Surely part of the attraction of these indirect consequentialisms is the idea that one should have certain traits of character, or commitments to persons or principles, that are sturdy enough that one would at least sometimes refuse to forsake them even when this refusal is known to conflict with making some gain—perhaps small—in total utility. Unlike his subjective counterpart the objective act-consequentialist is able to endorse characters and commitments that are sturdy in just this sense.

To see why, let us first return briefly to one of the simple examples of Section VI. A sophisticated act-consequentialist may recognize that if he were to develop a standing disposition to render prompt assistance in emergencies without going through elaborate act-consequentialist deliberation, there would almost certainly be cases in which he would perform acts worse than those he would have performed had he stopped to deliberate, for example, when his prompt action is misguided in a way he would have noticed had he thought the matter

[27] For an example of trait-consequentialism, see Robert M. Adams, "Motive Utilitarianism," *Journal of Philosophy* 73 (1976): 467–81.

through. It may still be right for him to develop this disposition, for without it he would act rightly in emergencies still less often—a quick response is appropriate much more often than not, and it is not practically possible to develop a disposition that would lead one to respond promptly in exactly those cases where this would have the best results. While one can attempt to cultivate dispositions that are responsive to various factors which might indicate whether promptness is of greater importance than further thought, such refinements have their own costs and, given the limits of human resources, even the best cultivated dispositions will sometimes lead one astray. The objective act-consequentialist would thus recommend cultivating dispositions that will sometimes lead him to violate his own criterion of right action. Still, he will not, as a trait-consequentialist would, shift his criterion and say that an act is right if it stems from the traits it would be best overall to have (given the limits of what is humanly achievable, the balance of costs and benefits, and so on). Instead, he continues to believe that an act may stem from the dispositions it would be best to have, and yet be wrong (because it would produce worse consequences than other acts available to the agent in the circumstances).[28]

This line of argument can be extended to patterns of motivation, traits of character, and rules. A sophisticated act-consequentialist should realize that certain goods are reliably attainable—or attainable at all—only if people have well-developed characters; that the human psyche is capable of only so much self-regulation and refinement; and that human perception and reasoning are liable to a host of biases and errors. Therefore, individuals may be more likely to act rightly if they possess certain enduring motivational patterns, character traits, or *prima facie* commitments to rules in addition to whatever commitment they have to act for the best. Because such individuals would not con-

---

[28] By way of contrast, when Robert Adams considers application of a motive-utilitarian view to the ethics of actions, he suggests "conscience utilitarianism," the view that "we have a *moral duty* to do an act, if and only if it would be demanded of us by the most useful kind of conscience we could have," "Motive Utilitarianism," p. 479. Presumably, this means that it would be morally wrong to perform an act contrary to the demands of the most useful sort of conscience. I have resisted this sort of redefinition of rightness for actions, since I believe that the most useful sort of conscience may on occasion demand of us an act that does not have the best overall consequences of those available, and that performing this act would be wrong.

Of course, some difficulties attend the interpretation of this last sentence. I have assumed throughout that an act is available to an agent if he would succeed in performing it if he tried. I have also taken a rather simple view of the complex matter of attaching outcomes to specific acts. In those rare cases in which the performance of even one exceptional (purportedly optimizing) act would completely undermine the agent's standing (optimal) disposition, it might not be possible after all to say that the exceptional act would be the right one to perform in the circumstances. (This question will arise again shortly.)

sider consequences in all cases, they would miss a number of opportunities to maximize the good; but if they were instead always to attempt to assess outcomes, the overall result would be worse, for they
would act correctly less often.[29]

We may now strengthen the argument to show that the objective act-
consequentialist can approve of dispositions, characters, or commitments to rules that are sturdy in the sense mentioned above, that is,
that do not merely supplement a commitment to act for the best, but
sometimes override it, so that one knowingly does what is contrary to
maximizing the good. Consider again Juan and Linda, whom we imagine to have a commuting marriage. They normally get together only
every other week, but one week she seems a bit depressed and harried,
and so he decides to take an extra trip in order to be with her. If he did
not travel, he would save a fairly large sum that he could send OXFAM
to dig a well in a drought-stricken village. Even reckoning in Linda's
uninterrupted malaise, Juan's guilt, and any ill effects on their relationship, it may be that for Juan to contribute the fare to OXFAM
would produce better consequences overall than the unscheduled trip.
Let us suppose that Juan knows this, and that he could stay home and
write the check if he tried. Still, given Juan's character, he in fact will
not try to perform this more beneficial act but will travel to see Linda
instead. The objective act-consequentialist will say that Juan performed the wrong act on this occasion. Yet he may also say that if Juan
had had a character that would have led him to perform the better act
(or made him more inclined to do so), he would have had to have been
less devoted to Linda. Given the ways Juan can affect the world, it may
be that if he were less devoted to Linda his overall contribution to
human well-being would be less in the end, perhaps because he would
become more cynical and self-centered. Thus it may be that Juan
should have (should develop, encourage, and so on) a character such
that he sometimes knowingly and deliberately acts contrary to his objective consequentialist duty. Any other character, of those actually
available to him, would lead him to depart still further from an objec-

[29] One conclusion of this discussion is that we cannot realistically expect people's
behavior to be in strict compliance with the counterfactual condition even if they are
committed sophisticated consequentialists. At best, a sophisticated consequentialist tries
to meet this condition. But it should be no surprise that in practice we are unlikely to be
morally ideal. Imperfections in information alone are enough to make it very improb-
able that individuals will lead objectively consequentialist lives. Whether or when to *blame*
people for real or apparent failures to behave ideally is, of course, another matter.

Note that we must take into account not just the frequency with which right acts are
performed, but the actual balance of gains and losses to overall well-being that results.
Relative frequency of right action will settle the matter only in the (unusual) case where
the amount of good at stake in each act of a given kind—for example, each emergency
one comes across—is the same.

tively consequentialist life. The issue is not whether staying home would *change* .Juan's character—for we may suppose that it would not—but whether he would in fact decide to stay home if he had that character, of those available, that would lead him to perform the most beneficial overall sequence of acts. In some cases, then, there will exist an objective act-consequentialist argument for developing and sustaining characters of a kind Sidgwick and others have thought an act-consequentialist must condemn.[30]

VIII. Demands and Disruptions

Before ending this discussion of consequentialism, let me mention one other large problem involving alienation that has seemed uniquely troubling for consequentialist theories and that shows how coming to terms with problems of alienation may be a social matter as well as a matter of individual psychology. Because consequentialist criteria of rightness are linked to maximal contribution to the good, whenever one does not perform the very best act one can, one is "negatively responsible" for any shortfall in total well-being that results. Bernard Williams has argued that to accept such a burden of responsibility would force most of us to abandon or be prepared to abandon many of our most basic individual commitments, alienating ourselves from the very things that mean the most to us.[31]

[30] In *The Methods of Ethics*, bk. IV, chap. v, sec. 4, Sidgwick discusses "the Ideal of character and conduct" that a utilitarian should recognize as "the sum of excellences or Perfections," and writes that "a Utilitarian must hold that it is always wrong for a man knowingly to do anything other than what he believes to be most conducive to Universal Happiness" (p. 492). Here Sidgwick is uncharacteristically confused—and in two ways. First, considering act-by-act evaluation, an objective utilitarian can hold that an agent may simply be wrong in believing that a given course of action is most conducive to universal happiness, and therefore it may be right for him knowingly to do something other than this. Second, following Sidgwick's concern in this passage and looking at enduring traits of character rather than isolated acts, and even assuming the agent's belief to be correct, an objective utilitarian can hold that the ideal character for an individual, or for people in general, may involve a willingness knowingly to act contrary to maximal happiness when this is done for the sake of certain deep personal commitments. See Henry Sidgwick, *The Methods of Ethics*, 7th ed. (New York: Dover, 1966), p. 492.

It might be thought counterintuitive to say, in the example given, that it is not right for Juan to travel to see Linda. But it must be kept in mind that for an act-consequentialist to say that an action is not right is not to say that it is without merit, only that it is not the very best act available to the agent. And an intuitive sense of the rightness of visiting Linda may be due less to an evaluation of the act itself than to a reaction to the sort of character a person would have to have in order to stay home and write a check to OXFAM under the circumstances. Perhaps he would have to be too distant or righteous to have much appeal to us—especially in view of the fact that it is his spouse's anguish that is at stake. We have already seen how an act-consequentialist may share this sort of character assessment.

[31] Williams, "Critique," sec. 3

To be sure, objective act-consequentialism of the sort considered here is a demanding and potentially disruptive morality, even after allowances have been made for the psychological phenomena thus far discussed and for the difference between saying an act is wrong and saying that the agent ought to be blamed for it. But just *how* demanding or disruptive it would be for an individual is a function—as it arguably should be—of how bad the state of the world is, how others typically act, what institutions exist, and how much that individual is capable of doing. If wealth were more equitably distributed, if political systems were less repressive and more responsive to the needs of their citizens, and if people were more generally prepared to accept certain responsibilities, then individuals' everyday lives would not have to be constantly disrupted for the sake of the good.

For example, in a society where there are no organized forms of disaster relief, it may be the case that if disaster were to strike a particular region people all over the country would be obliged to make a special effort to provide aid. If, on the other hand, an adequate system of publicly financed disaster relief existed, then it probably would be a very poor idea for people to interrupt their normal lives and attempt to help—their efforts would probably be uncoordinated, ill-informed, an interference with skilled relief work, and economically disruptive (perhaps even damaging to the society's ability to pay for the relief effort).

By altering social and political arrangements we can lessen the disruptiveness of moral demands on our lives, and in the long run achieve better results than free-lance good-doing. A consequentialist theory is therefore likely to recommend that accepting negative responsibility is more a matter of supporting certain social and political arrangements (or rearrangements) than of setting out individually to save the world. Moreover, it is clear that such social and political changes cannot be made unless the lives of individuals are psychologically supportable in the meanwhile, and this provides substantial reason for rejecting the notion that we should abandon all that matters to us as individuals and devote ourselves solely to net social welfare. Finally, in many cases what matters most is *perceived* rather than actual demandingness or disruptiveness, and this will be a relative matter, depending upon normal expectations. If certain social or political arrangements encourage higher contribution as a matter of course, individuals may not sense these moral demands as excessively intrusive.

To speak of social and political changes is, of course, to suggest eliminating the social and political preconditions for a number of existing projects and relationships, and such changes are likely to produce some degree of alienation in those whose lives have been disrupted. To an extent such people may be able to find new projects and relationships as well as maintain a number of old projects and relationships, and thereby avoid intolerable alienation. But not all will escape serious alienation. We thus have a case in which alienation will exist whichever course of action we follow—either the alienation of those who find the loss of the old order disorienting, or the continuing alienation of those who under the present order cannot lead lives expressive of their individuality or goals. It would seem that to follow the logic of Williams' position would have the unduly conservative result of favoring those less alienated in the present state of affairs over those who might lead more satisfactory lives if certain changes were to occur. Such conservativism could hardly be warranted by a concern about alienation if the changes in question would bring about social and political preconditions for a more widespread enjoyment of meaningful lives. For example, it is disruptive of the ground projects of many men that women have begun to demand and receive greater equality in social and personal spheres, but such disruption may be offset by the opening of more avenues of self-development to a greater number of people.

In responding to Williams' objection regarding negative responsibility, I have focused more on the problem of disruptiveness than the problem of demandingness, and more on the social than the personal level. More would need to be said than I am able to say here to come fully to terms with his objection, although some very general remarks may be in order. The consequentialist starts out from the relatively simple idea that certain things seem to matter to people above all else. His root conception of moral rightness is therefore that it should matter above all else whether people, insofar as possible, actually realize these ends.[32] Consequentialist moralities of the sort considered here undeniably set a demanding standard, calling upon us to do more for one another than is now the practice. But this standard plainly does not require that most people lead intolerable lives for the sake of some

---

[32] I appealed to this "root conception" in rejecting rule-consequentialism in Section VII. Although consequentialism is often condemned for failing to provide an account of morality consistent with respect for persons, this root conception provides the basis for a highly plausible notion of such respect. I doubt, however, that any fundamental ethical dispute between consequentialists and deontologists can be resolved by appeal to the idea of respect for persons. The deontologist has his notion of respect—e.g., that we not use people in certain ways—and the consequentialist has *his*—e.g., that the good of every person has an equal claim upon us, a claim unmediated by any notion of right or contract, so that we should do the most possible to bring about outcomes that actually advance the good of persons. For every consequentially justified act of manipulation to which the deontologist can point with alarm there is a deontologically justified act that fails to promote the well-being of some person(s) as fully as possible to which the consequentialist can point, appalled. Which notion takes "respect for persons" more seriously? There may be no non-question-begging answer, especially once the consequentialist has recognized such things as autonomy or respect as intrinsically valuable.

greater good: the greater good is empirically equivalent to the best possible lives for the largest possible number of people.[33] Objective consequentialism gives full expression to this root intuition by setting as the criterion of rightness actual contribution to the realization of human value, allowing practices and forms of reasoning to take whatever shape this requires. It is thus not equivalent to requiring a certain, alienated way of thinking about ourselves, our commitment, or how to act.

Samuel Scheffler has recently suggested that one response to the problems Williams raises about the impersonality and demandingness of consequentialism could be to depart from consequentialism at least far enough to recognize as a fundamental moral principle an agent-centered prerogative, roughly to the effect that one is not always obliged to maximize the good, although one is always permitted to do so if one wishes. The prerogative would make room for agents to give special attention to personal projects and commitments. However, the argument of this article, if successful, shows there to be a firm place in moral practice for prerogatives that afford such room even if one accepts a fully consequentialist fundamental moral theory.[34]

IX. Alienation from Morality

By way of conclusion, I would like to turn to alienation from morality itself, the experience (conscious or unconscious) of morality as an external set of demands not rooted in our lives or accommodating to our perspectives. Giving a convincing answer to the question "Why should I be moral?" must involve diminishing the extent that morality appears alien.

Part of constructing such an answer is a matter of showing that abiding by morality need not alienate us from the particular commitments that make life worthwhile, and in the previous sections we have begun to see how this might be possible within an objective act-consequentialist account of what morality requires. We saw how in

[33] The qualification 'empirically equivalent to' is needed because in certain empirically unrealistic cases, such as utility monsters, the injunction "Maximize overall realization of human value" cannot be met by improving the lives of as large a proportion of the population as possible. However, under plausible assumptions about this world (including diminishing marginal value) the equivalence holds.

[34] For Scheffler's view, see *The Rejection of Consequentialism: A Philosophical Investigation of the Considerations Underlying Rival Moral Conceptions* (Oxford: Clarendon Press, 1982). The consequentialist may also argue that at least some of the debate set in motion by Williams is more properly concerned with the question of the relation between moral imperatives and imperatives of rationality than with the content of moral imperatives as such. (See note 42.)

general various sorts of projects or relationships can continue to be a source of intrinsic value even though one recognizes that they might have to undergo changes if they could not be defended in their present form on moral grounds. And again, knowing that a commitment is morally defensible may well deepen its value for us, and may also make it possible for us to feel part of a larger world in a way that is itself of great value. If our commitments are regarded by others as responsible and valuable (or if we have reason to think that others should so regard them), this may enhance the meaning or value they have for ourselves, while if they are regarded by others as irresponsible or worthless (especially, if we suspect that others regard them so justly), this may make it more difficult for us to identify with them or find purpose or value in them. Our almost universal urge to rationalize our acts and lives attests our wish to see what we do as defensible from a more general point of view. I do not deny that bringing a more general perspective to bear on one's life may be costly to the self—it may cause reevaluations that lower self-esteem, produce guilt, alienation, and even problems of identity. But I do want to challenge the simple story often told in which there is a personal point of view from which we glimpse meanings which then vanish into insignificance when we adopt a more general perspective. In thought and action we shuttle back and forth from more personal to less personal standpoints, and both play an important role in the process whereby purpose, meaning, and identity are generated and sustained.[35] Moreover, it may be part of mature commitments, even of the most intimate sort, that a measure of perspective beyond the personal be maintained.

These remarks about the role of general perspectives in individual lives lead us to what I think is an equally important part of answering the question "Why should I be moral?": reconceptualization of the terms of the discussion to avoid starting off in an alienated fashion and ending up with the result that morality still seems alien. Before pursuing this idea let us quickly glance at two existing approaches to the question.

Morality may be conceived of as in essence selfless, impartial, impersonal. To act morally is to subordinate the self and all contingencies concerning the self's relations with others or the world to a set of imperatives binding on us solely as rational beings. We should be moral, in this view, because it is ideally rational. However, morality thus

---

[35] For example, posterity may figure in our thinking in ways we seldom articulate. Thus nihilism has seemed to some an appropriate response to the idea that mankind will soon destroy itself. "Everything would lose its point" is a reaction quite distinct from "Then we should enjoy ourselves as much as possible in the meantime," and perhaps equally comprehensible.

conceived seems bound to appear as alien in daily life. "Purity of heart" in Rawls' sense would be essential to acting morally, and the moral way of life would appear well removed from our actual existence, enmeshed as we are in a web of "particularistic" commitments—which happen to supply our *raisons d'être.*

A common alternative conception of morality is not as an elevated purity of heart but as a good strategy for the self. Hobbesian atomic individuals are posited and appeal is made to game theory to show that pay-offs to such individuals may be greater in certain conflict situations—such as reiterated prisoners' dilemmas—if they abide by certain constraints of a moral kind (at least, with regard to those who may reciprocate) rather than act merely prudentially. Behaving morally, then, may be an advantageous policy in certain social settings. However, it is not likely to be the *most* advantageous policy in general, when compared to a strategy that cunningly mixes some compliance with norms and some non-compliance; and presumably the Hobbesian individual is interested only in maximal self-advantage. Yet even if we leave aside worries about how far such arguments might be pushed, it needs to be said that morality as such would confront such an entrepreneurial self as an alien set of demands, for central to morality is the idea that others' interests must sometimes be given weight for reasons unrelated to one's own advantage.

Whatever their differences, these two apparently antithetical approaches to the question "Why should I be moral?" have remarkably similar underlying pictures of the problem. In these pictures, a presocial, rational, abstract individual is the starting point, and the task is to construct proper interpersonal relations out of such individuals. Of course, this conceit inverts reality: the rational individual of these approaches is a social and historical *product.* But that is old hat. We are not supposed to see this as any sort of history, we are told, but rather as a way of conceptualizing the questions of morality. Yet why when conceptualizing are we drawn to such asocial and ahistorical images? My modest proposal is that we should keep our attention fixed on society and history at least long enough to try recasting the problem in more naturalistic terms.[36]

As a start, let us begin with individuals situated in society, complete with identities, commitments, and social relations. What are the ingre-

---

[36] I do not deny that considerations about pay-offs of strategies in conflict situations may play a role in cultural or biological evolutionary explanations of certain moral sentiments or norms. Rather, I mean to suggest that there are characteristic sorts of abstractions and simplifications involved in game-theoretic analysis that may render it blind to certain phenomena crucial for understanding morality and its history, and for answering the question "Why should I be moral?" when posed by actual individuals.

dients of such identities, commitments, and relations? When one studies relationships of deep commitment—of parent to child, or wife to
husband—at close range, it becomes artificial to impose a dichotomy
between what is done for the self and what is done for the other. We
cannot decompose such relationships into a vector of self-concern and
a vector of other-concern, even though concern for the self and the
other are both present. The other has come to figure in the self in a
fundamental way—or, perhaps a better way of putting it, the other has
become a reference point of the self. If it is part of one's identity to be
the parent of Jill or the husband of Linda, then the self has reference
points beyond the ego, and that which affects these references points
may affect the self in an unmediated way.[37] These reference points do
not all fall within the circle of intimate relationships, either. Among the
most important constituents of identities are social, cultural, or religious ties—one is a Jew, a Southerner, a farmer, or an alumnus of Old
Ivy. Our identities exist in relational, not absolute space, and except as
they are fixed by reference points in others, in society, in culture, or in
some larger constellation still, they are not fixed at all.[38]

There is a worthwhile analogy between meaning in lives and meaning in language. It has been a while since philosophers have thought it
helpful to imagine that language is the arrangement resulting when we
hook our private meanings up to a system of shared symbols. Meaning,
we are told, resides to a crucial degree in use, in public contexts, in
referential systems—it is possible for the self to use a language with
meanings because the self is embedded in a set of social and historical
practices. But ethical philosophers have continued to speak of the
meaning of life in surprisingly private terms. Among recent attempts
to give a foundation for morality, Nozick's perhaps places greatest
weight on the idea of the meaning of life, which he sees as a matter of
an individual's "ability to regulate and guide [his] life in accordance
with some overall conception [he] chooses to accept," emphasizing the
idea that an individual creates meaning through choice of a life plan;
clearly, however, in order for choice to play a self-defining role, the
options among which one chooses must already have some meaning
independent of one's decisions.[39]

[37] Again we see the inadequacy of subjectivism about values. If, for example, part of
one's identity is to be Jill's parents, then should Jill cease to exist, one's life could be said
to have lost some of its purpose even if one were not aware of her death. As the example
of the experience machine suggested earlier, there is an objective side to talk about
purpose.

[38] Here I do not have in mind identity in the sense usually at stake in discussions of
personal identity. The issue is not identity as principle of individuation, but as *experienced,* as a sense of self—the stuff actual identity crises are made of.

[39] Nozick, *Anarchy,* p. 49. (I ignore here Nozick's more recent remarks about the mean-

It is not only "the meaning of life" that carries such presuppositions. Consider, for example, another notion that has played a central role in moral discourse: respect. If the esteem of others is to matter to an individual those others must themselves have some significance to the individual; in order for their esteem to constitute the sought-after respect, the individual must himself have some degree of respect for them and their judgment.[40] If the self loses significance for others, this threatens its significance even for itself; if others lose significance for the self, this threatens to remove the basis for self-significance. It is a commonplace of psychology and sociology that bereaved or deracinated individuals suffer not only a sense of loss owing to broken connections with others, but also a loss in the solidity of the self, and may therefore come to lose interest in the self or even a clear sense of identity. Reconstructing the self and self-interest in such cases is as much a matter of constructing new relations to others and the world as it is a feat of self-supporting self-reconstruction. Distracted by the picture of a hypothetical, presocial individual, philosophers have found it very easy to assume, wrongly, that in the actual world concern for oneself and one's goals is quite automatic, needing no outside support, while a direct concern for others is inevitably problematic, needing some further rationale.

It does not follow that there is any sort of categorical imperative to care about others or the world beyond the self as such. It is quite possible to have few external reference points and go through life in an alienated way. Life need not have much meaning in order to go on, and one does not even have to care whether life goes on. We cannot show that moral skepticism is necessarily irrational by pointing to facts about

---

ing of life in his *Philosophical Explanations* [Cambridge: Harvard University Press, 1981].) The notion of a "rationally chosen life plan" has figured prominently in the literature recently, in part due to Rawls' use of it in characterizing the good (see Rawls, *Theory of Justice*, ch. VII, "Goodness as Rationality"). Rawls' theory of the good is a complex matter, and it is difficult to connect his claims in any direct way to a view about the meaning of life. However, see T. M. Scanlon, "Rawls' Theory of Justice," *University of Pennsylvania Law Review* 121 (1973): 1020–69, for an interpretation of Rawls in which the notion of an individual as above all a rational chooser—more committed to maintaining his status as a rational agent able to adopt and modify his goals than to any particular set of goals—functions as the ideal of a person implicit in Rawls' theory. On such a reading, we might interpolate into the original text the idea that meaning derives from autonomous individual choice, but this is highly speculative. In any event, recent discussions of rationally chosen life plans as the bearers of ultimate significance or value do not appear to me to do full justice to the ways in which lives actually come to be invested with meaning, especially since some meanings would have to be presupposed by any rational choice of a plan of life.

[40] To be sure, this is but one of the forms of respect that are of importance to moral psychology. But as we see, self-respect has a number of interesting connections with respect for, and from, others.

meaning, but a naturalistic approach to morality need no more refute radical skepticism than does a naturalistic approach to epistemology. For actual people, there may be surprisingly little distance between asking in earnest "Why should I take any interest in anyone else?" and asking "Why should I take any interest in myself?"[41] The proper response to the former is not merely to point out the indirect benefits of caring about things beyond the self, although this surely should be done, but to show how denying the significance of anything beyond the self may undercut the basis of significance for the self. There is again a close, but not exact parallel to language: people can get along without a language, although certainly not as well as they can with it; if someone were to ask "Why should I use my words the same way as others?" the proper response would not only be to point out the obvious benefits of using his words in this way, but also to point out that by refusing to use words the way others do he is undermining the basis of meaning in his own use of language.

These remarks need not lead us to a conservative traditionalism. We must share and preserve meanings in order to have a language at all, but we may use a common language to disagree and innovate. Contemporary philosophy of language makes us distrust any strict dichotomy between meaning, on the one hand, and belief and value, on the other; but there is obviously room within a system of meanings for divergence and change on empirical and normative matters. Language itself has undergone considerable change over the course of history, coevolving with beliefs and norms without in general violating the essential conditions of meaningfulness. Similarly, moral values and social practices may undergo change without obliterating the basis of meaningful lives, so long as certain essential conditions are fulfilled. (History does record some changes, such as the uprooting of tribal peoples, where these conditions were not met, with devastating results.)

A system of available, shared meanings would seem to be a precondition for sustaining the meaningfulness of individual lives in familiar sorts of social arrangements. Moreover, in such arrangements identity and self-significance seem to depend in part upon the significance of others to the self. If we are prepared to say that a sense of meaningfulness is a precondition for much else in life, then we may be on the way

---

[41] This may be most evident in extreme cases. Survivors of Nazi death camps speak of the effort it sometimes took to sustain a will to survive, and of the importance of others, and of the sense of others, to this. A survivor of Treblinka recalls, "In our group we shared everything; and at the moment one of the group ate something without sharing it, we knew it was the beginning of the end for him." (Quoted in Terrence Des Pres, *The Survivor: An Anatomy of Life in the Death Camps* [New York: Oxford University Press, 1976], p. 96.) Many survivors say that the idea of staying alive to "bear witness," in order that the deaths of so many would not escape the world's notice, was decisive in sustaining their own commitment to survival.

to answering the question "Why should I be moral?" for we have gone beyond pure egocentrism precisely by appealing to facts about the self.[42] Our earlier discussions have yielded two considerations that make the rest of the task of answering this question more tractable. First, we noted in discussing hedonism that individual lives seem most enjoyable when they involved commitments to causes beyond the self or to others as such. Further, we remarked that it is plausible that the happiest sort of lives do not involve a commitment to hedonism even of a sophisticated sort. If a firm sense of meaningfulness is a precondition of the fullest happiness, this speculation becomes still more plausible. Second, we sketched a morality that began by taking seriously the various forms of human non-moral value, and then made room for morality in our lives by showing that we can raise moral questions without thereby destroying the possibility of realizing various intrinsic values from particular relationships and activities. That is, we saw how being moral might be compatible (at least in these respects) with living a desirable life. It would take another article, and a long one, to show how these various pieces of the answer to "Why should I be moral?" might be made less rough and fitted together into a more solid structure. But by adopting a non-alienated starting-point—that of situated rather than presocial individuals—and by showing how some of the alienation associated with bringing morality to bear on our lives might be avoided, perhaps we have reduced the extent to which morality seems alien to us by its nature.

[42] One need not be a skeptic about morality or alienated from it in any general sense in order for the question "Why should I be moral?" to arise with great urgency. If in a given instance doing what is right or having the best sort of character were to conflict head-on with acting on behalf of a person or a project that one simply could not go against without devastating the self, then it may fail to be reasonable from the agent's standpoint to do what is right. It is always *morally* wrong (though not always morally blameworthy) to fail to perform morally required acts, but in certain circumstances that may be the most reasonable thing to do—not because of some larger moral scheme, but because of what matters to particular individuals. Therefore, in seeking an answer to "Why should I be moral?" I do not assume that it must always be possible to show that the moral course of action is ideally rational or otherwise optimal from the standpoint of the agent. (I could be more specific here if I had a clearer idea of what rationality is.) It would seem ambitious enough to attempt to show that, in general, there are highly desirable lives available to individuals consistent with their being moral. While we might hope for something stronger, this could be enough—given what can also be said on behalf of morality from more general viewpoints—to make morality a worthy candidate for our allegiance as individuals.

It should perhaps be said that on an objective consequentialist account, being moral need not be a matter of consciously following distinctively moral imperatives, so that what is at stake in asking "Why should I be moral?" in connection with such a theory is whether one has good reason to lead one's life in such a way that an objective consequentialist criterion of rightness is met as nearly as possible. In a given instance, this criterion might be met by acting out of a deeply felt emotion or an entrenched trait of character, without consulting morality or even directly in the face of it. This, once more, is an indication of objective consequentialism's flexibility: the idea is to *be* and *do* good, not necessarily to *pursue* goodness.

[1 2]

Values and Purposes: The Limits of
Teleology and the Ends of Friendship

Michael Stocker

In acting, we act for some end. This teleological commonplace has been elevated to a, if not the, standard understanding of action. Witness the desire-plus-belief accounts of action and the identifications of reasons for and values in action with purposes, goals, desires, and the like. What I shall here argue is that teleological considerations are not sufficient for understanding many significant sorts of acts. To understand them we must recur to their source, or *arche*, not simply their end, or *telos*. More exactly, character and other elements *we act from or out of* are critical for identifying, evaluating, and explaining many significant sorts of acts.

In arguing for this, I shall attempt both to illuminate the poorly understood and inadequately discussed notion of *acting from or out of* and also to show its central importance for ethics, moral psychology, and action theory. Thus, I will be concerned to help develop, as a contrast to a teleology of acts, an *archeology* of acts; and to show, as a contrast to the importance of the teleological for acts, the importance of the *archeological* for acts. Since the terms deriving from '*arche*' have already been claimed, I shall use 'the *out of*' as the name of what I am arguing in favor of: acting from or out of. It is meant to straddle both the elements we act from or out of and also acting from those elements, just as 'the teleological' straddles the elements we act for and also acting for them.

This essay was originally published in *Journal of Philosophy* 78 (December 1981): 747–65. Reprinted by permission of Michael Stocker and the *Journal of Philosophy*.

My thanks are owed to the Philosophy Departments of the University of Arizona, San Jose State University, the University of Texas at Austin, and the University of California at San Diego, where I read drafts of this paper. Along with those acknowledged below, I wish to thank Michael Bratman, Janet Broughton, Myles Burnyeat, Toni Carey, Dagfinn Føllesdal, Mark Johnston, Richard Kraut, and Gregory Vlastos.

In arguing for the importance of the *out of*, I am not denying the importance of the teleological for understanding action. What I am denying is that we can understand action by relying only on teleology. My argument for this focuses on sections II and III on friendly acts, and in section IV on other sorts of acts. In section V it is shown that teleological considerations also play a role, complementing that of the *out of*, in understanding these acts.

The acts I consider, such as acts of friendship, involve many philosophically significant areas of ethics, moral psychology, and action theory. Further, they have deep human importance. Nonetheless, they have received little philosophical attention recently. This lack of attention, we might note, is condoned if not also induced by a reliance on teleology. Correlatively, a failure to understand and appreciate friendly acts and the others considered here condones if it does not also induce a reliance on teleology. For teleology is unable to accommodate many features central to such acts, in particular the *out of*, e.g., acting out of friendship.[1]

I. Various Teleologies

To argue for the *out of*, I shall use as a stalking horse a particular sort of teleology: a psychologically based teleology of acts. Its positive thesis is that only an act's purposes, goals, ends, desires, and the like—taken as psychological "entities"—are critical for understanding action. Its negative thesis is that the *out of* is not critical for understanding action, unless the *out of* is reducible to the teleological. So, for example, it would hold that to understand a friendly act—to identify it as a friendly act, to evaluate it, and to explain its occurrence—only its purposes, goals, ends, desires, and the like are critical. Character and other elements we act out of are relevant, if at all, only because and to the extent they are reducible to teleological elements.

Many contemporary theorists at least seem to incline to this view. But I shall not pursue this issue of attribution. For psychologically based teleologies are presented only for their heuristic value: to show the importance and independence of the *out of*.

---

[1] These issues bring to mind Aristotle's ethics and moral psychology, where character and the *out of* are so important and friendship is treated so extensively, and where, following the usual interpretation, he treats these all teleologically, as suggested by the opening words of the *Nicomachean Ethics*. In another paper, I hope to question this teleological interpretation of Aristotle, and I shall not discuss it here. But, as will become clear, much of the present discussion is of topics important to understanding Aristotle's commitment to teleology.

To enhance this heuristic value, we should distinguish such teleologies from three other views called teleological. The first is composed of those ethical theories which contrast with deontologies by holding that goodness is prior to and grounds rightness.[2] There is at least no simple connection between such a teleology and the sort I am here concerned with. The latter might identify only rightness, or rightness primarily and goodness only derivatively, with teleological elements. A nondeontological theory could hold both that goodness is prior to and grounds rightness and also that teleological elements are irrelevant for goodness or rightness.[3] Nonetheless, there are connections between these different teleologies, and some of my arguments tell against both sorts.

The second sort of teleology I am not directly concerned with consists of those teleologies which do not find their ends psychologically, but, e.g., metaphysically or scientifically.[4] Not all claims about goals, purposes, . . . of the universe, the plant or animal kingdom, a particular plant or animal, and so on invoke some being who has the relevant goal, purpose, desire, and the like. The third sort consists of teleologies, not of acts, but of other things, perhaps organs, lives, species, and so on.

Various sorts of teleologies have been alluded to. Ultimately what is needed is a taxonomy of teleologies. This would be out of place now.[5]

---

[2] Cf. "A teleological theory says that the basic or ultimate criterion of what is morally right, wrong, obligatory, etc. is the nonmoral value of what is brought into being." William Frankena, *Ethics* (Englewood Cliffs, N.J.: Prentice-Hall 1963), p. 13. See too, my "Rightness and Goodness: Is There a Difference?", *American Philosophical Quarterly*, 10, 2 (April 1973): 87–98. It would be useful to trace the shift in the meaning of 'teleological' from purposive to nondeontological. Kant's moral psychology—especially the relations among concern for goodness, consequences, pleasure, and desire—plays a leading, if not decisive, role in this shift. It might seem ironic that we, who do not accept his moral psychology—perhaps because we do not accept it and do not even take note of it—have accepted its theoretical upshot: this use of 'teleological'. My thanks are owed to Alan Wood for discussing this with me. On these issues, see G. E. Moore's entry under 'teleology' in vol. II of J. M. Baldwin, ed., *The Dictionary of Philosophy and Psychology* (New York: Macmillan, 1902); and also Max Scheler, *Formalism in Ethics and Non-formal Ethics of Value* (Evanston, Ill.: Northwestern UP, 1973), passim, but see esp. pp. 5–7.

[3] Similar considerations show that neither sort of teleology bears any simple relation with, much less is identical to, consequentialism—the view that finds what is morally relevant, e.g., for act evaluations, in consequences. Cf. fn 19 and my "Consequentialism and Its Complexities", *American Philosophical Quarterly*, 6, 4 (October 1969): 276–289.

[4] On these distinctions and the taxonomy in fn 5, see Richard Sorabji, *Necessity, Cause, and Blame* (Ithaca, N.Y.: Cornell, 1980), esp. ch. x, e.g., p. 164 and pp. 168/9. Following the lead he gives on pp. 168/9, it might be better throughout this paper, including here, not to say simply "psychologically" but rather "psychologically as we—post-Cartesians—understand psychology".

[5] Several main lineaments of such a taxonomy are: First, the sort of entity said to be teleological, to have an end or *telos:* e.g., an act, life, species, . . . A second has to do with the sort of relation the teleology concerns: e.g., being intended, the object of a purpose

Here it should be sufficient to repeat that I am concerned with psychologically based teleologies of acts: views that find what is critical for identifying, evaluating, and explaining acts in and only in such psychological entities as purposes, goals, desires, and the like.[6] Henceforth, unless otherwise made clear, this is what I shall mean by 'teleology'.

II. Teleology and Friendly Acts

To see the critical importance of the *out of,* let us consider friendship and friendly acts. For simplicity, and even though the argument is the same in both cases, let us consider only those friendly acts done for a friend, with care and the like, and exclude those acts done out of general friendliness, amiability, or goodwill.[7]

I shall assume, not argue, that friendship and friendly acts can be, as such, good. This is not uncontroversial, of course. It goes against many recent ethical theories. G. E. Moore's of *Principia Ethica* is a notable exception. Were I to defend this assumption—e.g., against those who might hold that friendship is good only because of what it allows us to get from our friends—I would emphasize the sorts of lives and societies we can have only given friendship and friendly acts. It may well be possible for some people in some circumstances—e.g., religious anchorites—to live what can be acknowledged as a good life without society and sociality. But at least many other forms of good life constitutively require those forms of society and sociality which constitutively involve friendship and friendly acts.

Those who do not agree with me about this conception and valuation of friendship can consider this paper as having a limited compass: viz., examining how friendship and friendly acts stand to teleology, or more generally, what sorts of values can be accommodated by a psycho-

or desire, the ideal toward which something "naturally" tends, . . . A third, needed to give determinate sense to the second, is the sort of domain the second is found in, discerned by, described or understood in terms of: e.g., psychology, biology, metaphysics, . . . A fourth is the sort of enterprise guiding or constituting interest in and use of the teleology: e.g., identification, evaluation, explanation, . . .As is easily seen, at least some elements from one lineament can be combined with one or more of various elements from others to form a teleology. For reasons discussed in fn 2, this taxonomy makes no room for theories called teleological because they are nondeontological. My warmest thanks are owed to Amélie Rorty for discussing this taxonomy and much else in this paper with me.

[6] Henceforth, I will use any one of 'purpose', 'aim', 'goal', 'intended object', 'desire', and the like to stand indifferently for any or all, unless otherwise made clear. So too, I will use, e.g., 'the goal', 'part of the goal', 'a goal', and the like to stand indifferently for any or all, unless otherwise made clear.

[7] My thanks are owed to Joel Feinberg for discussing this and much else in this paper with me.

logically based teleology of acts. As suggested below, those goods cannot be handled by such a theory, unless taken as merely instrumental goods. My arguments that so taking them involves "missing" their real value may, I realize, leave many contemporary theorists unmoved. For, as just noted, they may see and value friendship and friendly acts only as instruments for, not also as constituents of, a good life.

Let us now consider a friendly act, e.g., my visiting Harry in the hospital to cheer him up. I will assume that this is a good act at least in part because it is a friendly act, done out of friendship for a friend.

Can this act be identified as a friendly act, evaluated, and explained by a psychologically based teleology? One way to answer this is to see whether friendship does or does not fit into the blank space in the schema 'acting in order to/for the sake of . . .' For in that space we should find what is relevant for such a teleology: purposes, aims, goals, desires, and the like.

My act can be descried by 'going to the hospital in order to cheer up Harry'. If that is the relevant description, our teleology should find the value, or the value-determining aspects, of the act in what is given by 'to cheer up Harry'. And certainly there is some plausibility in this suggestion. Harry's being cheered up is reasonably thought good.

But the phrase 'to cheer up Harry' in no way mentions or adverts to the friendship my act manifests nor to the friendliness of the act. This is not to deny that there are intimate connections between friendship and acts of cheering up friends. But, consistent with all that has so far been said, I could have gone to visit Harry, not out of friendship, but for any number of other reasons, even unfriendly ones. (Below I consider the licitness of the suggested correspondence between "out of . . ." and "with/for the reason . . .".) Thus 'to cheer up Harry' cannot be used to show that teleological considerations are sufficient to characterize friendly acts.[8]

Let us consider a new description of my act. Since the old description did not mention the friendship, let us consider 'I visit the hospital in order to cheer up my friend Harry'. Here we have adverted to the friendship. But the same problem remains. To say I do something for a friend leaves it open why I do so: e.g., whether I do the act in a way constitutive of being a friend or whether I am taking advantage of a

---

[8] For reasons given above, I shall ignore claims that, so far as the value of what I did is concerned, it is in principle irrelevant why I went to visit Harry. So too, I shall ignore whether those claims would be extended to hold that even for the identification of what I did, as a friendly act or not, it is in principle irrelevant why I went to visit Harry. On these issues, see my "Intentions and Act Evaluations," *Journal of Philosophy*, 67, 17 (Sept. 3, 1970): 589–602; and "Act and Agent Evaluations," *Review of Metaphysics*, 27, 1, 105 (September 1973): 42–61.

friend. In the last case, my act is hardly a friendly one, nor does it have the value peculiar to friendly acts.

What seems needed is that I visit Harry to cheer him up, where I do this for his sake, not for an ulterior reason. Benefiting him or doing what he wants must be an ultimate reason for acting. So now we might consider 'to visit my friend to cheer him up for his own sake' or more generally 'to benefit a friend for the friend's sake' as what might show that the value of this friendly act is teleological.

But this will not do for several reasons. First, it leaves open, once again, whether I have acted out of friendship. For the description so far given is compatible with other sorts of acts: e.g., rewarding a hero for valor, paying homage to a great person, treating someone like a member of the kingdom of ends. To be sure, such acts can be done in regard to a friend and even done from friendship. But they need not be. They can be done for reasons entirely independent of friendship, indeed even without friendship, for the person.

Second, there is so far no mention of an enduring friendship. And it seems plausible to hold that friendship must have a significant temporal duration: that it must last more than one minute, or one hour, or . . .

To use the first objection, which seems the more important one here, against the adequacy of 'to benefit a friend for the friend's sake' is, of course, to hold that the value of a friendly act is, as such, different from the value of an act of, say, treating someone like a member of the kingdom of ends. This does not require gainsaying the goodness of "respectful" acts or of people whose character issues in them. For one could—and, I think, should—hold that not all good acts or states are good simply because they supply some amount of an undifferentiated good, and more particularly that the good constituted by respect is, as such, different qua sort, not quantity, of good than that constituted by friendship.

Earlier we augmented the description of what might teleologically locate the value of my act from 'benefiting someone' to 'benefiting a friend', and that to 'benefiting a friend for the friend's sake'. Can we augment that last description so that it guarantees that the act is done out of friendship? The most obvious addition is simply 'done out of friendship', which would give us 'benefiting a friend for the friend's sake, done out of friendship'. And the act I did would be described by 'visiting my friend Harry to cheer him up for his sake, done out of friendship'.

This is what seems needed to give us a friendly act: an act as done by a friend, not simply an act as a friend would do. To be sure, it is not sufficient for a friendly act. We need, in addition, a way to preclude acts done out of what might be called a misplaced sense of friendship, acts which "are done out of friendship even if they are not friendly acts, e.g., the friend who feels that he must point out grave moral faults in his friend".[9] So too, we need a way to preclude acts the agent should have seen would harm the friend or would fail to satisfy the friend's desires. At the very least, then, if we want sufficient conditions for a friendly act, we must add yet another condition requiring that the person act well and with practical wisdom. But I shall not pursue this here. For my concern is not with giving an analysis of friendly acts. Rather, it is with exploring the consequences, especially for a psychologically based teleology, of its being necessary that a friendly act be done out of friendship.

The question is whether the inclusion of the phrase 'out of friendship' in the description of the friendly act can be used to satisfy such a teleology. Indeed, even though that phrase seems needed, can it legitimately be there? Is what it signals even part of the act's purpose? For remember, we are considering psychologically based teleologies, e.g., of value. According to them, values are locatable in the blank of 'acting in order to/for the sake of . . .' because what fills that blank is the act's purpose, goal, and the like.

The question of legitimacy is not over grammatical correctness. It has, rather, to do with the conceptual status of what 'out of friendship' signals. We can easily see that not every grammatically correct fill-in of that blank gives even part of the goal. First, a description of Harry can go there without supplying part of the goal: e.g., to visit Harry . . . who is on the run from the law. Second, an evoking condition can go there without supplying part of the goal: e.g., to visit Harry . . . having been told he was still in the hospital. Third, an opportunity condition can go there without supplying part of the goal: e.g., to visit Harry . . . since the game was postponed and I had some free time. There is no need to continue with such irrelevant fill-ins. The point is clear: grammatical position does not guarantee conceptual status.

There are, however, other fill-ins which, though not part of the goal, are intimately and importantly connected with it. Some of these have to do with being sensitive to various circumstances. For example, I see a colleague being harrassed by hoodlums. Her being a colleague is what engages my attention and explains my going to her aid rather than following my usual course of averting my eyes and "minding my own business".[10] But the phrase 'to aid a colleague' need not give even part of my goal.

[9] To quote a letter from Michael Slote.
[10] As David Wiggins says about a related point in Aristotle, "For a man to have a specific conception of eudaimonia just is for him to become susceptible to certain distinc-

Another sort of important fill-in is that of a sine qua non condition. For example, I would not now be using your boat unless I had asked permission. But I do not use it in order, e.g., not to trespass; though that is why I asked permission. So too, I would not use your boat were I to believe I would fall overboard. But I do not use it in order, e.g., to stay dry; though that may be why I use it rather than another boat. In both cases, 'sailing for excitement' may be a perfectly adequate description.[11]

Moral considerations, including those of the good, can also play these sensitivity and sine qua non roles: Had I not been concerned about my growing tendency toward selfishness—or had I not had a certain conception of a good life, including sociality—I might not even have thought of going to visit Harry. Were I not to believe that visiting him would be good, I would not visit him. Nonetheless, my goal in visiting him might be simply to cheer him up for his own sake, not to act for the sake of the good.[12]

Finally, of course, one's goal can go in the blank of 'acting in order to/for the sake of . . .'. Here we can construct cases from many of those mentioned above: I visit Harry in order to see someone on the run from the law, or in order to fill some free time, or in order to live up to my ideal of sociality, or for the sake of the good.

The question for us is which, if any, of these fill-ins of 'acting in order to/for the sake of . . .' is most like that of 'out of friendship' where the inclusion of that phrase ensures that the act so described is a friendly act. Does 'out of friendship' play the role required by a psychologically based teleology, viz., being at least part of a goal? I do not think it can—not if the act is a friendly one.

III. For the Sake of Friendship and Out of Friendship

One can, of course, act for the sake of friendship. Here the friendship is part of the act's goal. But as I shall argue, to act for such a goal is, as such, to do a different sort of act and an act with a different sort

---

tive and distinctively compelling reasons for acting in certain sorts of ways" (264). "Weakness of Will, Commensurability, and the Objects of Deliberation and Desire", *Proceedings of the Aristotelian Society*, suppl. vol. 52 (1978/9): 251–277.

[11] This is to reject the identification of one's goal in doing an act with the totality of the significant world one's act helps, or is believed to help, bring about. And it raises the difficult problem, which will here be discussed only indirectly, of how to separate one's goal from other aspects of the world, including those one values.

[12] For further discussion of this sine qua non condition, see my "Morally Good Intentions", *The Monist*, 54, 1 (January 1970): 124–141.

of value than is done when one acts out of friendship.[13] Indeed, when one acts out of friendship, friendship is not, as such, a goal, but rather it plays both a sensitivity and a sine qua non role. (This is discussed in section V.). Thus, teleology cannot accommodate friendly acts, acts done out of friendship.

What is it, then, to act where friendship is a goal of the act, e.g., to act for the sake of friendship or to act for the sake of acting out of friendship? Why are such acts not, as such, friendly acts? Why do they not, as such, achieve the good of friendly acts? The answer seems obvious: if I act for the sake of friendship—to take one case for all—then my aim in acting is to get, sustain, strengthen the friendship, rather than to act for the sake of the friend.

So, for example, I may court someone in order that we become friends. Or, valuing our friendship and believing that it will suffer if I do not do such-and-such, I do it to preserve our friendship. Or, not "really wanting" to do something you want me to, and not being moved by my liking you, by my feelings of friendship for you, and the like, I do the act because I realize that friendship requires me to do it.[14] In these and other cases where friendship is a goal, there is no suggestion that in acting the agent acts out of, or even with, liking of or concern for the other person. What is said to be operative is, rather, concern for the friendship. And, as should be clear, concern for the friendship is different from concern for the friend.[15]

To be sure, there concerns are importantly related, as will be discussed in section V. And in practice, it might be very rare indeed that one is found without the other. My present claim in no way denies these facts. Rather, it uses them to argue that there are two distinct things to be interrelated.

For, as should be clear, my claim is that to act out of friendship is,

[13] My argument, it should be noted, allows that acting for the sake of friendship, in particular, or for the sake of the good or virtue, in general, can be good. This corrects a claim made in "The Schizophrenia of Modern Ethical Theories," *Journal of Philosophy*, 73, 14 (Aug. 12, 1976): 453–466, where, discussing someone visiting a person in the hospital for the sake of the good, rather than out of friendship, I wrote, "Surely there is something lacking here—and lacking in moral merit or value" (462). As Michael Slote argues, what is, rather, true is that although one sort of moral merit or value is lacking, another is present. Further, there seems no plausible way to hold that one sort of merit or value is, as such, better than the other. We can construct cases going either way.

[14] Here, the requirement can be either descriptive or evaluative or both: descriptive in that so acting is constitutive of being a friend, evaluative in that being a friend creates and is created by certain moral or moral-like values, obligations, and the like.

[15] Contrary to what this paragraph might seem to suggest, such modalities as warmth, spontaneity, and the like cannot be used to distinguish between acting out of friendship and for the sake of friendship. I can be warm, spontaneous, . . . in regard to a friend or friendship or act (in any combination of the three); and I can be cool, deliberate, . . . in regard to a friend or friendship or act (in any combination of the three).

first, not reducible to acting for the sake of friendship, and, second, is not reducible to acting for the sake of anything.[16] I have, I believe, established the first and given good reason to accept the second. For as argued in regard to at least many plausible ends, one can seek those ends without acting out of friendship and without doing a friendly act. Those arguments do not, of course, prove that there are no ends in terms of which we can reduce acting out of friendship. But they do make this claim of nonreducibility plausible.

Its plausibility can be increased further by the following considerations. My argument so far has been that there are no ends, properly so-called—e.g., not essentially described by the phrase 'out of friendship'—the seeking of which is, as such, to do a friendly act. For there are no ends, properly so-called, the seeking of which is, as such, to act out of friendship. This is an argument about the nature of an act's purpose. To that extent, it is consistent with the claim that the character structure out of which friendly acts issue is, itself, somehow constructed out of, analyzable in terms of, complex nests of purposes, dispositions to have purposes, hypothetical purposes, and the like. Discussing this seemingly teleological move should help advance the issue.

To begin with, it is not at all clear that such a construction or analysis would aid our teleology, except by sharing the name 'teleological'. For a particular act would not be a friendly act because of its purposes, but rather because it issued from a certain complex of purposes and the like or a being qua possessor of such a complex. And it is notoriously difficult to give a teleologically acceptable understanding of this relation of *issuing from*.

However, we need not pursue the above issues. For the arguments already given against reducing acting out of friendship to acting for the sake of those ends considered above also suggest that this construction or analysis cannot succeed. If acting out of friendship is composed of purposes, dispositions to have purposes, and the like, where these are purposes properly so-called, and thus not essentially described by the phrase 'out of friendship', there seems, as before, no guarantee that a person, even with those collocated purposes, has friendship or acts out of it. For even with all those purposes, there is no guarantee that the person cares about and likes, has friendship for, the "friend". This consideration is developed further in section V, where it is shown that and how the character structure of friendship involves forms of directed attention and sensitivity. Here we can note that it is very difficult to see how such attention and sensitivity can be guaranteed or

---

[16] I shall not consider whether *acting for the sake of* is reducible in terms of *acting out of*: e.g., acting for the sake of friendship in terms of acting out of the desire to have a friend. (But is 'out of the desire . . .' nonteleological?) In any case, it is clear that acting for the sake of, e.g., friendship is not reducible to acting out of friendship.

captured by that construction out of, or analysis in terms of, purposes—unless those purposes are already understood as coming from such forms of attention and sensitivity.[17]

One further point about my claim of nonreducibility should be made. (It also explains the use, above, of 'as such'.) This claim does not deny that there are objects such that to seek them is to do a friendly act. Obviously there are such objects: e.g., my visiting Harry to cheer him up for his own sake, out of friendship, thus, from that structure of care, concern, liking. Indeed, for the act to be a friendly act, 'out of friendship, thus, from that structure of care, concern, and liking' must describe the act and its object. But as argued, that phrase does not describe it qua object—qua teleologically acceptable object—necessary for a friendly act.[18]

Thus, the goal one has in acting out of friendship is, as such, different from the goal of acting for the sake of friendship, as such, or indeed acting for the sake of any end, properly so-called, as such. Nonetheless, and this is why I here say "as such", they need not be incompatible. One can act successfully with both goals at once, thus doing both sorts of acts at once. For example, knowing that my friendship with you will thrive if I do a given act, I do it both out of friendship—thus, out of care, liking, . . . for you—and also for the sake of friendship—e.g., to strengthen it. So my point is not that if one acts out of friendship, one does not act for the sake of friendship. Nor is it that if one acts out of friendship, one does not act for the sake of some other end. Indeed, in section V it will be shown that to act out of friendship involves acting for the sake of some other end. Rather, my point is that to act for the sake of some end, e.g., friendship, is not, as such, to act out of friendship. Put more generally, my point is that to act for the sake of friendship or some other end is, as such—but only as such, not necessarily—to miss acting out of friendship, to miss doing a friendly act, and to miss the value of a friendly act.[19]

---

[17] This issue is similar to issues concerning reductions of the mental. However, purposes, which here might seem reducers of character, are themselves highly resistant to such reductions. Thus, even if character could be reduced teleologically, the import of that for those issues is unclear.

[18] Some relations between what is given by the phrase 'out of friendship . . . liking' and the object of a friendly act are discussed in sec. V.

[19] Thus, we can see that the question of the adequacy of psychologically based evaluative teleologies is not the same as the question of the adequacy of consequentialist theories. (Nor, as noted in sec. I, is either the same as the question over deontology.) For as argued about a related point in "Consequentialism and Its Complexities," we can accept what is given by 'pleasing a friend out of friendship' as a bona fide consequence of a friendly act and as what is morally relevant about the act, without missing its value as a friendly act. This shows what should be clear in any case: causal consequences are importantly different from aims, goals, and the like, especially as these figure in ethics, practical reasoning, and moral psychology.

Allowing that an act can be done both out of friendship and for the sake of an end, even friendship, in no way contradicts my argument for the independent importance of the *out of* and against the adequacy of teleology. For my claim is not that friendly acts have no teleological elements. Rather, it is that they have, also have, nonteleological elements that are critical for identifying, evaluating, and explaining them. And this, I believe, I have shown, thus showing that teleology is inadequate in regard to friendly acts.

IV. Missing Other Values

Teleology is inadequate in regard to many other goods besides friendly acts. This can be shown by noting how aiming at them or plausibly related ends misses them in just the ways that aiming at friendship or plausibly related ends misses friendly acts. Since the arguments are essentially the argument given above, I shall only indicate teleology's inadequacy in regard to only two other great goods: courage and right emotion or passion.

Courage is outside the ambit of a psychologically based teleology. One can act in order to show that one is courageous. But to act for that end need not be to act courageously, nor conversely. Rather, to act courageously constitutively involves acting from a certain appreciation of the situation's danger, a suitable handling of fear, and the like. And these features, among others, are not amenable to a teleological understanding. Thus, there is no goal, properly so-called, the seeking of which is, as such, to act courageously.

So too, having or acting with right emotion cannot be accommodated by a psychologically based teleology. Indeed, it is difficult to see how such a teleology could even deal with the emotions, since they and their expressions are often importantly lacking in purposes. To be sure, a typical expression of an emotion may well be an act done for a purpose: e.g., acting angrily in hitting someone to gain revenge. But, barring the sort of case discussed below, revenge here is not a goal one has in doing an angry act qua angry act. Rather, it is a goal for doing the act which "as it happens" is an angry act. Thus, revenge would not be a purpose of the emotion or its expression. Indeed, so far as we are concerned, there seems no need of any purpose at all. For what makes an act an angry act and what gives it the value peculiar to such acts is not purpose, but what the emotion or expression issues from and expresses, e.g., affective states, appreciation of the situation, and the like. The lack of need for a purpose is still clearer (if that is possible) in regard to emotions or emotional "episodes" than in regard to expressions of emotion.

Of course, some emotions or episodes are had, and some expressions are made, for a purpose: e.g., my making myself angry or allowing myself to remain angry to convince you I am fierce. Perhaps a psychologically based teleology could handle such cases, as it may be able to handle the parallel cases of acting for the sake of friendship or for the sake of courage. Nonetheless, at least many of what are clearly the most important cases of emotion are outside the competence of a psychologically based teleology, as are—and indeed for the same reasons as—the parallel cases of acting out of friendship and out of courage.

Psychologically based teleologies are confuted not only by various goods and virtues, but also by various "bads" and vices. And indeed, missing the goal by aiming at it is not limited to goods and virtues, but is shared by at least some bads and vices. For example, acting out of hatred and acting for the sake of hatred divide in the ways that acting out of friendship and for the sake of friendship divide. If I harm you for the sake of hatred—perhaps because I fear I am getting soft or that I am letting down my side of a vendetta—then I am, e.g., trying to create, sustain, or strengthen my hatred, or I am acting out of a sense of what my hatred requires. But if I act out of hatred for you, I care about you: to harm you. Just as acting for the sake of hatred misses acting out of hatred, acting for the sake of some other end also misses acting out of hatred. Thus again, psychologically based teleologies are shown inadequate.

Some other goods and bads, we should note, lack this feature. Some lack it because it is strictly irrelevant for what goal, if any, they are sought or achieved. Pleasure and pain, conceived of as by many utilitarians, viz., as feelings, suggest themselves immediately.[20] So do such other goods and bads as physical health and sickness; good or bad fortune; keeping or losing one's friends and family because of health, wars, and the like; living in a just or unjust society. And so do at least many of the duties, obligations, and the like which so occupy recent ethical theorists.[21]

Now, however, is not the time to canvass various and sundry goods

[20] As Henry Sidgwick and others argue, the deliberate aiming at pleasure or happiness may prevent our attaining it. This seems, at least mainly, either a causal problem, say, of distraction, or a problem of having to specify the end more concretely. Such problems, I suggest, can be overcome by various strategies of indirection, which allow one to act with the same goal really. These are clearly not remedies for the sort of problem I am here concerned with. I am greatly indebted to Alfred MacKay for discussing this and much else in this paper with me.

[21] On this, see the articles mentioned in fns 2, 8, and 13, and also G. E. M. Anscombe "Modern Moral Philosophy", *Philosophy*, 33, 124 (January 1958): 1–19; Edmund Pincoffs, "Quandary Ethics," *Mind*, 80, 320 (October 1971): 552–571; and Bernard Williams, "A Critique of Utilitarianism", esp. ch. 5, "Integrity" in J. J. C. Smart and Williams, *Utilitarianism, For and Against* (New York: Cambridge, 1973).

and bads to see how and why they are in the relevant ways like friendship, courage, emotion, and hatred, on the one hand, or like pleasure
and pain, on the other.[22] Ultimately, of course, this must be done to see
whether we can find other significant categories—e.g., doing (*praxis*)
and producing (*poiesis*)—that are associated with these features. Here it
is sufficient to appreciate the critical and independent importance the
moral sciences must accord to character and the *out of*, and the bearing
of this on psychologically based teleologies.

V. Teleological and Nonteleological Elements

Such teleologies are inadequate for the moral sciences. Nonetheless,
desire, purpose, and the like are important for understanding action
and are, indeed, connected both genetically and constitutively with the
out of, as suggested below.

It seems reasonable to ascribe some role in the acquisition of a character to acting with the goal of acquiring that character and its forms of
values, interests, abilities, and so on. More particularly, Aristotelian
habituation seems to play some genetic role in such acquisition.[23] For
in doing and redoing an activity, urged on with praise and blame, with
explanations of the point, . . . , the person often comes to see and
"feel" the point of the activity, and more importantly to value the
activity itself. Doing the activity in those circumstances can effect a
transfer of evaluative allegiance to the activity, we could well say. In
friendship, clearly, there is a transfer of evaluative allegiance to the
friend, who becomes a value or source or focus of value.

Once the character is formed and the evaluative allegiances established, there may be no further need to act for the sake of those
activities, values, abilities, and the like. Thus, a friendly person can act
out of friendship without at the same time acting for the sake of
friendship. Indeed, it might seem, first, that friendship with a given
person should drop out of the repertory of goals of somebody already
a friend of that person; and second, that a person can do a friendly act
only when friendship and friendly acts are not sought, but are had or
done "naturally", simply expressing one's character.[24]

---

[22] "The Schizophrenia of Modern Ethical Theories" argues that many ethical theories
are committed to much the same sort of missing as are psychologically based teleologies.
For to act for the values, reasons, and the like countenanced by these ethical theories is to
miss the value of friendly and other acts discussed here.

[23] On habituation, see the *Nicomachean Ethics*, Bk. II, chs. 1–4.

[24] We should note the parallels between this claim and certain Zen claims about acting
naturally and directly, and thus the parallels between Plato's and Aristotle's person of
perfect virtue and the Zen master. I am indebted to Aryeh Kosman for developing this in
discussion and in an unpublished paper on *sophrosyne* in the *Charmides*. I am also indebted to him for discussing much else in this paper with me.

Even if these last two suggestions are well taken, possessed values remain constitutively important for their possessor. First, reflecting on one's values and on whether one's life and actions conform and conduce to them is of central importance for leading a good life.[25] These values now can play significant sensitivity and sine qua non roles: e.g., one is now sensitive to the needs and wants of the friend and to the requirements of friendship; and one would be moved not to do an act were one to believe it would harm the friend or violate one's conception of friendship.

Second, these values are teleologically important, as can be seen by the following. The character of a person who has become friendly has changed. The person now "naturally" values friends or this friend. But to value a friend is not simply to attend contemplatively to the friend. It also involves acting for the sake of the friend.[26] Thus, purposive or teleological action is constitutive of friendship and friendly acts. So too, for at least many other goods and virtues and their acts or activities: e.g., to act courageously one must act for the sake of, say, one's country.

However, these constitutive acts occur only because of and out of a "background" provided by the requisite character. This background provides a general focus—here, the friend—for purposive acts. Also, it helps constitute the acts as the sort they are—here, friendly acts.

Given the character structure of friendship and thus the valuing of the friend, one is naturally attentive to the good of the friend and what the friend wants. One's world of possible goals and actions is, thus, given a highly determinate content and direction by the friendship. To have those structure and values is, other things being equal, to have certain natural and inevitable goals—natural and inevitable given those structures and values.

But, of course, other things are often enough not equal. For those other things include many complex psychic structures, such as those of interest, energy, and mood. These structures can, if in certain states, stop a friendly person from acting out of friendship. For example, when emotionally drained, or suffused with a general hatred, or filled with self-doubt, . . . , a friendly person may only too naturally not act out of friendship for even a very good friend.[27]

Notwithstanding the vital role of that *ceteris paribus* clause, we must

[25] I am indebted to J. O. Urmson for emphasizing the role of such reflection and for discussing much else in this paper with me.

[26] This is so, I suggest, even where one acts out of friendship for someone one cannot affect, e.g., a dead friend. Thus, on my view, acting for the sake of someone out of friendship, say, need not involve an act that is consequentially evaluable. This issue is discussed in "Consequentialism and Its Complexities."

[27] This is argued for in my "Desiring the Bad: An Essay in Moral Psychology", *Journal of Philosophy*, 76, 12 (October 1979): 738–753.

still recognize the general intimate, if not conceptual, connections between the *out of* and the teleological—between, in short, character and purpose. To understand purpose, we must recur to character; and to understand character, we must recur to purpose.

Insofar as the *out of* and the teleological are so interconnected, several issues that arose earlier become clearer. First, we can now see more clearly why acting for the sake of friendship bears a systematic relation to acting out of friendship. To take only two points: there are systematic reasons why a person can and will do the same thing—taking 'same thing' one natural way—both for the sake of friendship and out of it: e.g., doing what the friend wants. And, by acting for the sake of friendship, one's evaluative allegiance to the friend may be strengthened or rekindled. For these reasons and others, we can see why a person might well find it useful to invoke friendship as a goal and act for its sake or in order to satisfy its requirements when, say, the springs of friendship are too dry.[28]

A second issue clarified by the interconnections of the *out of* and the teleological is the central issue of this paper. For we can now see in a systematic way why citing only the purposes of an act may be inadequate for evaluation, explanation, and identification.

The need to go beyond—or better, behind—purpose and teleology for evaluation and identification has been discussed above. Let us now turn briefly to the inadequacy of teleological explanation. If we keep in mind the interconnections between the *out of* and the teleological, we can see how various concerns with explanation and justification can be met from either the character "side" or the purpose "side" of action. Such questions as, "Why are you doing that?" can be answered by "Because of friendship" or "Because we are friends". Such answers can be taken as claims to be acting out of friendship. And so taken, they can explain or justify the act. Thus, we see that reasons for and justifications and explanations of acts can be given by the *out of*, that they need not make recourse to the teleological, to desires, purposes, intentions, goals, and the like.[29]

---

[28] This is a correlative of what was argued for in sec. II: acts of friendship cannot be identified by their purposes alone, the character structure must be given. That there are these correlatives constitutes a serious, even if necessary, social and moral ambiguity. The possibility of doing acts required by friendship, whether or not out of friendship, is important for maintaining civilized and "friendly" society. But to have that possibility is to have the possibility of false acts. And focusing on that may corrode relationships, e.g., by prompting such worries as whether seemingly friendly acts are done, not out of friendship, but only for the sake of friendship, and if so, why; or worse, whether they are merely calculated to gain or maintain a position of advantage; and so on. I thank Graeme Marshall for discussing this and much else in this paper with me.

[29] Cf. Wiggins, "Weakness of Will," p. 256. Since belief seems necessary for both teleological and nonteleological explanations, I shall not discuss it and its role here.

Moreover, in many cases, adverting to the *out of* may be more illuminating and determinate than adverting to the teleological. Compare "Because he is my friend" with "To help him" as answers to "Why are you doing that?" The latter leaves open what is attractive about the act, why the helping is taking place: whether it is out of friendship, because one was hired, . . .

To be sure, "Because he is my friend" also leaves open many possibilities, especially when we do not assume a background of a "normal", happy, energy-filled, . . . psyche. As is clear, in the absence of such a background, friends are often singled out for unfriendly, unhelpful action. When emotionally tired, one may take liberties with friends, perhaps hoping that they, of all people, will understand. And so on.

In these cases, we might want to say that "Because he is my friend" does not even suggest that the person is acting out of friendship. There are good reasons for taking this position. However, it requires that the notion of acting out of friendship be taken in a near-global way, to take account of all the various psychic features and structures which, in one way or another, help determine how one sees and acts in regard to friends because they are friends.

We should note that even such high-level and formal considerations as those of value, as such, need to be augmented by other psychic structures for them to serve as an adequate account of action. This can be seen by considering what may happen in a case of extreme *accidie:* one's values and what one values are, as such, detested and become repulsive and repugnant.[30] In such a case, acting for the sake of the good will hardly play the explanatory role frequently accorded it. In such a case, if I do an act that accords with my values, the correct account of my action almost certainly will not be in terms of my furthering those values. Rather, the account may advert precisely to my not having noticed that the act was in accord with them. Similarly, if in such a state, I knowingly aid someone I hate or hold in contempt, that may be explained in terms of my values, but only by taking them to have an "opposite polarity" than they normally have.

This claim about values, if correct, helps make an important point

---

Although the need for belief—e.g., in desire-plus-belief explanations—might formally tell against psychologically based teleologies, obviously I cannot exploit this need. For belief is no more in the camp of the *out of* than the teleological.

[30] On this see Aquinas, *Summa Theologica*, 2a2ae, Q. 35, "Of Sloth". We read in article 2 of "sorrow whereby one is displeased at" spiritual goods including "sorrow at the divine good, which is called sloth." In article 3, the effects of sloth reaching to reason, not just to sensuality, are listed as "dislike, horror, and detestation of the divine good." And in article 4, malice is characterized in terms of such detestation. But see 1a2ae, Q. 29, art. 5, and 2a2ae, Q. 34, art. 1. Citations above are taken from the translation of the Dominican Fathers of the English Province (New York: Benziger, 1947).

for this paper: values and evaluations are only one structure among possibly competing structures of the psyche.[31] Understanding a person or a person's action can require adverting to any or all of these structures—as well as to still other personal and extrapersonal factors.

Thus, this claim about values and the preceding claim about friendship show, if correct, that an adequate account of action, at least for many purposes, requires adverting to both the *out of* and the teleological. The *out of* we are now concerned with must be taken in at least a near-global way, for reasons sketched above.

Insofar as we are concerned with these more global structures, teleological elements come back into importance, but now against the background of those structures. For it is highly revealing to be told in answer to "Why are you doing that?", "He is my friend and I want to help him" or "He is my friend and I want to hurt him". Each, in its own way, allows us to make a good start at a good account of the act and of what the person is "about".

Accounts of action that advert to only the teleological or only some structures of the *out of* or even both, therefore, run the risk of serious inadequacy. If such accounts are successful, not simply out of luck, this would seem attributable to hidden assumptions about those other structures. (Those assumptions may often be hidden from the theorist offering the account.) To be sure, for some purposes it is perfectly legitimate to make assumptions about various structures. Even so, there is the danger for the various branches of the moral sciences of taking the success (or apparent success) of such partial accounts as showing that only those psychic structures adverted to are real psychic structures or the only structures we really need consider to understand people and action.

This, I suggest, is done by at least many philosophers and by others who rely on psychologically based teleologies. Indeed, one might ask, is this not exactly what is done by those who would account for action in terms of beliefs plus desires or values?[32]

Unless we take account of these various structures, there is little, if any, significant chance of our being able to understand action, purpose, character, value, and their interrelations. In particular, we will not be able to understand the complex nature of such goods as friend-

---

[31] This is argued for in "Desiring the Bad."

[32] Aristotle, it might be noted, offers a belief-plus-desire account of action, e.g., in *De Anima*, Bk. III, ch. 10, 439a9 sq. But he does not make this error, since his account of desire, unlike that of at least many contemporary theorists, is in terms of character and indeed the agent. See, for example, his claim in the *Nicomachean Ethics*, Bk. VI, ch. 2, 1139a32 sq that "The origin of action . . . is choice . . . and such an origin of action is a man."

ship and friendly acts—to see how, even though they have important teleological elements, they also have important nonteleological elements, and thus confute psychologically based teleologies. And in general, we may remain satisfied with psychologically based teleologies, which, if this paper is correct, are inadequate for evaluating, explaining, or identifying so many matters of great ethical and moral psychological moment.

PART III

FRIENDSHIP, SOCIETY,
AND POLITICS

[13]

Marital Slavery and Friendship:
John Stuart Mill's
The Subjection of Women

Mary Lyndon Shanley

John Stuart Mill's essay *The Subjection of Women* was one of the nine-teenth century's strongest pleas for opening to women opportunities for suffrage, education, and employment. Some contemporary femi-nists, however, have denigrated the work, questioning the efficacy of merely striking down legal barriers against women as the way to estab-lish equality between the sexes. These contemporary critics argue that Mill's failure to extend his critique of inequality to the division of labor in the household, and his confidence that most women would choose marriage as a "career," subverted his otherwise egalitarian impulses.[1]

I argue in this essay, however, that such critics have ignored an important aspect of Mill's feminism. *The Subjection of Women* was not solely about equal opportunity for women. It was also, and more fun-damentally, about the corruption of male-female relationships and the hope of establishing friendship in marriage. Such friendship was desir-able not only for emotional satisfaction, it was crucial if marriage were to become, as Mill desired, a "school of genuine moral sentiment."[2]

This essay was originally published in *Political Theory* 9, 2 (1981): 229–47. Copyright © 1981 Sage Publications, Inc. Reprinted by permission of Sage Publications, Inc.

I wish to thank Nannerl O. Keohane, Dennis F. Thompson, Eileen Sullivan, Ann Congleton, and Francis G. Hutchins for helpful comments on an earlier version.

[1] Contemporary authors who criticize Mill's analysis of equal opportunity for woman as not far-reaching enough are Julia Annas, "Mill and the Subjection of Women," *Philoso-phy* 52 (1977), 179–194; Leslie F. Goldstein, "Marx and Mill on the Equality of Women," paper presented at the Midwest Political Science Association Convention, Chicago, April 1978; Richard Krouse, "Patriarchal Liberalism and Beyond: From John Stuart Mill to Harriet Taylor," unpublished manuscript, Williamstown, MA; Susan Moller Okin, *Wom-en in Western Political Thought* (Princeton: Princeton University Press, 1979). From a different perspective, Gertrude Himmelfarb, *On Liberty and Liberalism: the Case of John Stuart Mill* (New York: Alfred Knopf, 1974) criticizes Mill's doctrine of equality as being too absolute and particularly takes issue with modern feminist applications of his theory.

[2] J. S. Mill, *The Subjection of Women* (1869) in Alice Rossi, ed., *Essays on Sex Equality*

The fundamental assertion of *The Subjection of Women* was not that equal opportunity would ensure the liberation of women, but that male-female equality, however achieved, was essential to marital friendship and to the progression of human society.

Mill's vision of marriage as a locus of sympathy and understanding between autonomous adults not only reforms our understanding of his feminism, but also draws attention to an often submerged or ignored aspect of liberal political thought. Liberal individualism is attacked by Marxists and neo-conservatives alike as wrongly encouraging the disintegration of affective bonds and replacing them with merely self-interested economic and contractual ties. Mill's essay, however, emphasizes the value of noninstrumental relationships in human life. His depictions of both corrupt and well-ordered marriage traces the relationship of family order to right political order. His vision of marriage as a locus of mutual sympathy and understanding between autonomous adults stands as an unrealized goal for those who believe that the liberation of women requires not only formal equality of opportunity but measures which will enable couples to live in genuine equality, mutuality, and reciprocity.

The Perversion of Marriage by
the Master-Slave Relationship

Mill's reconstruction of marriage upon the basis of friendship was preceded by one of the most devastating critiques of male domination in marriage in the history of Western philosophy. In *The Subjection of Women* Mill repeatedly used the language of "master and slave" or "master and servant" to describe the relationship between husband and wife. In the first pages of the book, Mill called the dependence of women upon men "the primitive state of slavery lasting on" (1: 130). Later he said that despite the supposed advances of Christian civilization, "the wife is the actual bond-servant of her husband: no less so, as far as legal obligation goes, than slaves commonly so called" (2: 158). Still later he asserted that "there remain no legal slaves, except the mistress of every house" (4: 217). The theme of women's servitude was not confined to *The Subjection of Women*. In his speech on the Reform Bill of 1867, Mill talked of that "obscure feeling" which members of Parliament were "ashamed to express openly" that women had no right

---

(Chicago: University of Chicago Press, 1970), ch. 2, p. 173. All references to *The Subjection of Women* will be to this edition and will be given in the body of the text using chapter and page, i.e., (2: 173).

to care about anything except "how they may be the most useful and devoted servants of some man."[3] To Auguste Comte he wrote comparing women to "domestic slaves" and noted that women's capacities were spent "seeking happiness not in their own life, but exclusively in the favor and affection of the other sex, which is only given to them on the condition of their dependence."[4]

But what did Mill mean by denouncing the "slavery" of married women? How strongly did he wish to insist upon the analogy between married women and chattel slaves? I believe that he chose the image quite deliberately. For Mill, the position of married women resembled that of slaves in several ways: the social and economic system gave women little alternative except to marry; once married, the legal personality of the woman was subsumed in that of her husband; and the abuses of human dignity permitted by custom and law within marriage were egregious.

In Mill's eyes, women were in a double bind: they were not free within marriage, and they were not truly free not to marry.[5] What could an unmarried woman do? Even if she were of the middle or upper classes, she could not attend any of the English universities, and thus she was barred from a systematic higher education.[6] If somehow she acquired a professional education, the professional associations usually barred her from practicing her trade. "No sooner do women show themselves capable of competing with men in any career, than that career, if it be lucrative or honorable, is closed to them."[7] Mill's depiction of the plight of Elinor Garrett, sister of Millicent Garrett Fawcett, the suffrage leader, is telling:

> A young lady, Miss Garrett, . . . studied the medical profession. Having duly qualified herself, she . . . knocked successively at all the doors through which, by law, access is obtained into the medical profession. Having found all other doors fast shut, she fortunately discovered one which had accidentally been left ajar. The Society of Apothecaries, it seems, had forgotten to shut out those who they never thought would

[3] Hansard, *Parliamentary Debates*, series 3, v. 189 (May 20, 1867), p. 820.
[4] Letter to August Comte, October, 1843, *The Collected Works of John Stuart Mill* (hereafter *C. W.*), v. XIII, *The Earlier Letters*, ed. Francis C. Mineka (Toronto: University of Toronto Press, 1963), p. 609, my translation.
[5] Mill's analysis of women's choice of marriage as a state of life reminds one of Hobbes' discussion of some defeated soldier giving his consent to the rule of a conquering sovereign. Women, it is true, could decide which among several men to marry, while Hobbes' defeated yeoman had no choice of master. But what could either do but join the only protective association available to each?
[6] A brief account of the struggle to provide for women's higher education in England can be found in Ray Strachey, *The Cause* (London: G. Bell, 1928), pp. 124–165.
[7] Hansard, v. 189 (May 20, 1867).

attempt to come in, and through this narrow entrance this young lady found her way into the profession. But so objectionable did it appear to this learned body that women should be the medical attendants even of women, that the narrow wicket through which Miss Garrett entered has been closed after her.[8]

Working-class women were even worse off. In the *Principles of Political Economy*, Mill argued that their low wages were due to the "prejudice" of society which "making almost every woman, socially speaking, an appendage of some man, enables men to take systematically the lion's share of whatever belongs to both." A second cause of low wages for women was the surplus of female labor for unskilled jobs. Law and custom ordained that a woman has "scarcely any means open to her of gaining a livelihood, except as a wife and mother."[9] Marriage was, as Mill put it, a "Hobson's choice" for women, "that or none" (1: 156).[10]

Worse than the social and economic pressure to marry, however, was women's status within marriage. Mill thoroughly understood the stipulations of the English common law which deprived a married woman of a legal personality independent of that of her husband. The doctrine of coverture or spousal unity, as it was called, was based on the Biblical notion that "a man [shall] leave his father and his mother, and shall cleave to his wife, and they shall be one flesh" (Genesis ii, 22–23). If "one flesh," then, as Blackstone put it, "by marriage, the husband and wife are one person in law." And that "person" was represented by the husband. Again Blackstone was most succinct: "The very being or legal existence of the woman is suspended during the marriage, or at least is incorporated and consolidated into that of the husband."[11] One of the most commonly felt injustices of the doctrine of spousal unity was the married woman's lack of ownership of her own earnings. As the matri-

---

[8] *Idem.* In the United States, one well-documented case in which a woman was prohibited from practicing law was Bradwell v. Illinois, 83 U.S. (16 Wall) 130 (1873).

[9] *The Principles of Political Economy* (1848) in *C. W.* II, p. 394 and III, pp. 765–766.

[10] Tobias Hobson, a Cambridge carrier commemorated by Milton in two Epigraphs, would only hire out the horse nearest the door of his stable, even if a client wanted another, *Oxford English Dictionary*, II, pp. 369.

[11] William Blackstone, *Commentaries on the Laws of England*, 4 vols. (Oxford: Clarendon Press, 1765–1769), Book I, ch. XV, p. 430. The consequences of the doctrine of spousal unity were various: a man could not make a contract with his wife since "to covenant with her would be to covenant with himself"; a wife could not sue without her husband's concurrence; a husband was bound to "provide his wife with necessaries . . . as much as himself"; a husband was responsible for certain criminal acts of his wife committed in his presence; and, as a husband was responsible for his wife's acts, he "might give his wife moderate correction . . . in the same moderation that (he is) allowed to correct his apprentices or children."

monial couple was "one person," the wife's earnings during marriage were owned and controlled by her husband.[12] During his term as a member of Parliament, Mill supported a Married Women's Property Bill, saying that its opponents were men who thought it impossible for "society to exist on a harmonious footing between two persons unless one of them has absolute power over the other," and insisting that England has moved beyond such a "savage state."[13] In *The Subjection of Women* Mill argued that the "wife's position under the common law of England [with respect to property] is worse than that of slaves in the laws of many countries: by the Roman law, for example, a slave might have his peculium, which to a certain extent the law guaranteed to him for his exclusive use" (2: 158–159). Similarly, Mill regarded the husband's exclusive guardianship over the married couple's children as a sign of the woman's dependence on her husband's will (2: 160). She was, in his eyes, denied any role in life except that of being "the personal body-servant of a despot" (2: 161).

The most egregious aspects of both common and statute law, however, were those which sanctioned domestic violence. During the Parliamentary debates on the Representation of the People Bill in 1867, Mill argued that women needed suffrage to enable them to lobby for legislation which would punish domestic assault:

> I should like to have a Return laid before this House of the number of women who are annually beaten to death, or trampled to death by their male protectors; and, in an opposite column, the amount of sentence passed. . . . I should also like to have, in a third column, the amount of property, the wrongful taking of which was . . . thought worthy of the same punishment. We should then have an arithmetical value set by a male legislature and male tribunals on the murder of a woman.[14]

But the two legal stipulations which to Mill most demonstrated "the assimilation of the wife to the slave" were her inability to refuse her master "the last familiarity" and her inability to obtain a legal separation from her husband unless he added desertion or extreme cruelty to

[12] The rich found ways around the common law's insistence that the management and use of any income belonged to a woman's husband, by setting up trusts which were governed by the laws and courts of equity. A succinct explanation of the law of property as it affected married women in the nineteenth century is found in Erna Reiss, *Rights and Duties of Englishwomen* (Manchester, 1934), pp. 20–34.

[13] Hansard, v. 192 (June 10, 1867), p. 1371. Several Married Women's Property Bills, which would have given married women possession of their earnings were presented in Parliament beginning in 1857, but none was successful until 1870.

[14] *Ibid.*, v. 189 (May 20, 1867), p. 826.

his adultery (2: 160–161). Mill was appalled by the notion that no matter how brutal a tyrant a husband might be, and no matter how a woman might loathe him, "he can claim from her and enforce the lowest degradation of a human being," which was to be made the instrument of "an animal function contrary to her inclination" (2: 160). A man and wife being one body, rape was by definition a crime which a married man could not commit against his own wife. By law a wife could not leave her husband on account of this offense without being guilty of desertion, nor could she prosecute him. The most vicious form of male domination of women according to Mill was rape within marriage; it was particularly vicious because it was legal. Mill thus talked not of individual masters and wives as aberrations, but of a legally sanctioned system of domestic slavery which shaped the character of marriage in his day.[15]

Mill's depiction of marriage departed radically from the majority of Victorian portrayals of home and hearth. John Ruskin's praise of the home in *Sesame and Lilies* reflected the feelings and aspirations of many: "This is the true nature of home—it is the place of Peace; the shelter, not only from all injury, but from all terror, doubt, and division. . . . It is a sacred place, a vestal temple, a temple of the hearth watched over by Household Gods."[16] Walter Houghton remarked that the title of Coventry Patmore's poem, *The Angel in the House,* captured "the essential character of Victorian love," and reflected "the exaltation of family life and feminine character" characteristic of the mid-nineteenth century.[17] James Fitzjames Stephen, who wrote that he disagreed with *The Subjection of Women* "from the first sentence to the last," found not only Mill's ideas but his very effort to discuss the dynamics of marriage highly distasteful. "There is something—I hardly know what to call it; indecent is too strong a word, but I may say unpleasant in the direction of indecorum—in prolonged and minute discussions about the relations between men and women, and the character of women as such."[18]

The Subjection of Women challenged much more than Victorian deco-

---

[15] Mill's outrage at women's lack of recourse in the face of domestic violence is reminiscent of the protests in the United States during the civil rights movement at token sentences pronounced by white juries against whites accused of assaulting Blacks in Southern states, and of Susan Brownmiller's argument in *Against Our Will: Men, Women and Rape,* that the desultory prosecution of rapists is itself a manifestation of violence against women.

[16] John Ruskin, "Of Queen's Gardens," in *Works,* ed. E. T. Cook and A. D. C. Wedderburn, 39 vols. (London: G. Allen, 1902–1912), XVIII, p. 122.

[17] Walter E. Houghton, *The Victorian Frame of Mind* (New Haven: Yale University Press, 1957), p. 344.

[18] James Fitzjames Stephen, *Liberty, Equality, Fraternity* (New York: Henry Holt, n.d.), p. 206.

rum, however; it was a radical challenge to one of the most fundamental and preciously held assumptions about marriage in the modern era, which is that it was a relationship grounded on the consent of the partners to join their lives. Mill argued to the contrary that the presumed consent of women to marry was not, in any real sense, a free promise, but one socially coerced by the lack of meaningful options. Further, the laws of marriage deprived a woman of many of the normal powers of autonomous adults, from controlling her earnings, to entering contracts, to defending her bodily autonomy by resisting unwanted sexual relations. Indeed, the whole notion of a woman "consenting" to the marriage "offer" of a man implied from the outset a hierarchical relationship. Such a one-way offer did not reflect the relationship which should exist between those who were truly equal, among beings who should be able to create together by free discussion and mutual agreement an association to govern their lives together.

In addition, Mill's view of marriage as slavery suggested a significantly more complicated and skeptical view of what constituted a "free choice" in society than did either his own earlier works or those of his liberal predecessors. Hobbes, for example, regarded men as acting "freely" even when moved by fear for their lives. Locke disagreed, but he in turn talked about the individual's free choice to remain a citizen of his father's country, as if emigration were a readily available option for all. In other of his works Mill himself seemed overly sanguine about the amount of real choice enjoyed, for example, by wage laborers in entering a trade. Yet Mill's analysis of marriage demonstrated the great complexity of establishing that any presumed agreement was the result of free volition, and the fatuousness of presuming that initial consent could create perpetual obligation. By implication, the legitimacy of many other relationships, including supposedly free wage and labor agreements and the political obligation of enfranchised and unenfranchised alike, was thrown into question. *The Subjection of Women* exposed the inherent fragility of traditional conceptualizations of free choice, autonomy, and self-determination so important to liberals, showing that economic and social structures were bound to limit and might coerce any person's choice of companions, employment, or citizenship.

Mill did not despair of the possibility that marriages based on true consent would be possible. He believed that some individuals even in his own day established such associations of reciprocity and mutual support. (He counted his own relationship with Harriet Taylor Mill as an example of a marriage between equals.)[19] But there were systemic

[19] On the relationship between John Stuart Mill and Harriet Taylor see F. A. Hayek,

impediments to marital equality. To create conditions conducive to a marriage of equals rather than one of master and slave, marriage law itself would have to be altered, women would have to be provided equal educational and employment opportunity, and both men and women would have to become capable of sustaining genuinely equal and reciprocal relationships within marriage. The last of these, in Mill's eyes, posed the greatest challenge.

The Fear of Equality

Establishing legal equality in marriage and equality of opportunity would require, said Mill, that men sacrifice those political, legal, and economic advantages they enjoyed "simply by being born male." Mill therefore supported such measures as women's suffrage, the Married Women's Property Bills, the Divorce Act of 1857, the repeal of the Contagious Diseases Acts, and the opening of higher education and the professions to women. Suffrage, Mill contended, would both develop women's faculties through participation in civic decisions and enable married women to protect themselves from male-imposed injustices such as lack of rights to child custody and to control of their income. Access to education and jobs would give women alternatives to marriage. It would also provide a woman whose marriage turned out badly some means of self-support if separated or divorced. The Divorce Act of 1857, which established England's first civil divorce courts, would enable women and men to escape from intolerable circumstances (although Mill rightly protested the sexual double standard ensconced in the Act).[20] And for those few women with an income of their own, a Married Women's Property Act would recognize their

---

John Stuart Mill and Harriet Taylor; their correspondence and subsequent marriage (Chicago: University of Chicago Press, 1951); Michael St. John Packe, *The Life of John Stuart Mill* (New York: Macmillan, 1954); Alice Rossi, "Sentiment and Intellect" in *Essays on Sex Equality* (Chicago: University of Chicago Press, 1970); and Gertrude Himmelfarb, pp. 187–238.

[20] The Matrimonial Causes Act of 1857, as the divorce measure was known, allowed men to divorce their wives for adultery, but women had to establish that their husbands were guilty of either cruelty or desertion in addition to adultery in order to obtain a separation. Mill was reluctant to say what he thought the terms of divorce should be in a rightly ordered society (see note 31), but he was adamant that the double standard was wrong in policy and unjust in principle.

Mill also spoke out sharply against that sexual double standard in his testimony before the Commission studying the repeal of the Contagious Diseases Act, an act which allowed for the arrest and forced hospitalization of prostitutes with venereal disease, but made no provision for the arrest of their clients. "The Evidence of John Stuart Mill taken before the Royal Commission of 1870 on the Administration and Operation of the Contagious Diseases Acts of 1866 and 1869" (London, 1871).

independent personalities and enable them to meet their husbands more nearly as equals.

However, Mill's analysis went further. He insisted that the subjection of women could not be ended by law alone, but only by law and the reformation of education, of opinion, of social inculcation, of habits, and finally of the conduct of family life itself. This was so because the root of much of men's resistance to women's emancipation was not simply their reluctance to give up their position of material advantage, but many men's fear of living with an equal. It was to retain marriage as "a law of despotism" that men shut all other occupations to women, Mill contended (1: 156). Men who "have a real antipathy to the equal freedom of women" were at bottom afraid "lest [women] should insist that marriage be on equal conditions" (1: 156). One of Mill's startling assertions in *The Subjection of Women* was that "[women's] disabilities [in law] are only clung to in order to maintain their subordination in domestic life: *because the generality of the male sex cannot yet tolerate the idea of living with an equal*" (3: 181, italics added). The public discrimination against women was a manifestation of a disorder rooted in family relationships. The progression of humankind could not take place until the dynamics of the master-slave relationship were eliminated from marriages, and until the family was instead focused on spousal equality.

Mill did not offer any single explanation or account of the origin of men's fear of female equality. Elsewhere, he attributed the general human resistance to equality to the fear of the loss of privilege, and to apprehensions concerning the effect of leveling on political order.[21] But these passages on the fear of spousal equality bring to a twentieth-century mind the psychoanalytic works about human neuroses and the male fear of women caused by the infant boy's relationship to the seemingly all-powerful mother, source of both nurturance and love and of deprivation and punishment.[22] But it is impossible to push Mill's text far in this direction. His account of the fear of equality was not psychoanalytic. He did, however, undertake to depict the consequences of marital inequality both for the individual psyche and for social justice. The rhetorical purpose of *The Subjection of Women* was not only to convince men that their treatment of women in law was unjust,

[21] For a discussion of Mill's views on equality generally, see Dennis Thompson, *John Stuart Mill and Representative Government* (Princeton: Princeton University Press, 1976), pp. 158–173.

[22] See, for example, Dorothy Dinnerstein, *The Mermaid and the Minotaur: Sexual Arrangements and Human Malaise* (New York: Harper and Row, 1976); Nancy Chodorow, *The Reproduction of Mothering: Psychoanalysis and the Sociology of Gender* (Berkeley: University of California Press, 1978); and Philip Slater, *The Glory of Hera* (Boston: Beacon Press, 1971) and the references therein.

but also that their treatment of women in the home was self-defeating, even self-destructive.

Women were those most obviously affected by the denial of association with men on equal footing. Women's confinement to domestic concerns was a wrongful "forced repression" (1: 148). Mill shared Aristotle's view that participation in civic life was an enriching and ennobling activity, but Mill saw that for a woman, no public-spirited dimension to her life was possible. There was no impetus to consider with others the principles which were to govern their common life, no incentive to conform to principles which defined their mutual activity for the common good, no possibility for the self-development which comes from citizen activity.[23] The cost to women was obvious; they were dull, or petty, or unprincipled (2: 168; 4: 238). The cost to men was less apparent but no less real; in seeking a reflection of themselves in the consciousness of these stunted women, men deceived, deluded, and limited themselves.[24]

Mill was convinced that men were corrupted by their dominance over women. The most corrupting element of male domination of women was that men learned to "worship their own will as such a grand thing that it is actually the law for another rational being" (2: 172). Such self-worship arises at a very tender age, and blots out a boy's natural understanding of himself and his relationship to others.

A boy may be "the most frivolous and empty or the most ignorant and stolid of mankind," but "by the mere fact of being born a male" he is encouraged to think that "he is by right the superior of all and every one of an entire half of the human race: including probably some whose real superiority he had daily or hourly occasion to feel" (4: 218). By contrast, women were taught "to live for others" and "to have no life but in their affections," and then further to confine their affections to "the men with whom they are connected, or to the children who constitute an additional indefeasible tie between them and a man" (1: 141).

[23] See also Mill's *Considerations on Representative Government* (1861) where he lambasted benevolent despotism because it encouraged "passivity" and "abdication of [one's] own energies," and his praise of the Athenian dicastry and ecclesia. *C. W.*, XIX, pp. 399–400, 411. During his speech on the Reform Bill of 1867, Mill argued that giving women the vote would provide "that stimulus to their faculties . . . which the suffrage seldom fails to produce." Hansard, v. 189 (May 20, 1867), 824.

[24] Mill's insight was like that which Virginia Woolf used in *A Room of One's Own*. Woolf, trying to explain the source of men's anger at independent women, stated that such anger could not be "merely the cry of wounded vanity"; it had to be "a protest against some infringement of his power to believe in himself." Women have served throughout history as "looking glasses possessing the magic and delicious power of reflecting the figure of a man at twice its natural size." Mill also argued that in order to create such a mirror, men had distorted women by education and had warped the reflection which women showed to men. Virginia Woolf, *A Room of One's Own* (New York: Harcourt Brace and World, 1929), p. 35.

The result of this upbringing was that what women would tell men was not, could not be, wholly true; women's sensibilities were systematically warped by their subjection. Thus the reflections were not accurate and men were deprived of self-knowledge.

The picture which emerged was strikingly similar to that which Hegel described in his passages on the relationship between master and slave in *The Phenomenology of Mind*.[25] The lord who sees himself solely as master, wrote Hegel, cannot obtain an independent self-consciousness. The master thinks he is autonomous, but in fact he relies totally upon his slaves, not only to fulfill his needs and desires, but also for his identity: "Without slaves, he is no master." The master could not acquire the fullest self-consciousness when the "other" in whom he viewed himself was in the reduced human condition of slavery: to be *merely* a master was to fall short of full self-consciousness, and to define himself in terms of the "thing" he owns. So for Mill, men who have propagated the belief that all men are superior to all women have fatally affected the dialectic involved in knowing oneself through the consciousness others have of one. The present relationship between the sexes produced in men that "self-worship" which "all privileged persons, and all privileged classes" have had. That distortion deceives men and other privileged groups as to both their character and their self-worth.[26]

No philosopher prior to Mill had developed such a sustained argument about the corrupting effects on men of their social superiority over and separation from women. Previous philosophers had argued either that the authority of men over women was natural (Aristotle, Grotius), or that while there was no natural dominance of men over women prior to the establishment of families, in any civil society such preeminence was necessary to settle the dispute over who should govern the household (Locke), or the result of women's consent in return for protection (Hobbes), or the consequence of the development of the

[25] G. W. F. Hegel, *The Phenomenology of Mind*, trans. J. B. Baillie (New York: Harper and Row, 1969). This paragraph is indebted to the excellent study of the *Phenomenology* by Judith N. Shklar, *Freedom and Independence* (Cambridge: Cambridge University Press, 1976), from which the quote is taken, p. 61. Mill's analysis also calls to mind Simone de Beauvoir's discussion of "the Other" and its role in human consciousness: in *The Second Sex*, trans. H. M. Parshley (New York: Random House, Vintage Books, 1974), pp. xix ff.

[26] Mill argued in addition that men's injustices to women created habits which encouraged them to act unjustly towards others. In *The Subjection of Women* Mill asserted that the habits of domination are acquired in and fostered by the family, which is often, as respects its chief, "a school of wilfulness, overbearingness, unbounded self-indulgeance, and a double-dyed and idealized selfishness" (2: 165). Virtue, for Mill, was not simply action taken in accordance with a calculus of pleasure and pain, but was habitual behavior. In *Considerations on Representative Government*, he lamented the effects "fostered by the possession of power" by "a man, or a class of men" who "finding themselves worshipped by others . . . become worshippers of themselves." *C. W.* XIX, p. 445.

sentiments of nurturance and love (Rousseau).[27] None had suggested that domestic arrangements might diminish a man's ability to contribute to public debates in the agora or to the rational governing of a democratic republic. Yet Mill was determined to show that the development of the species was held in check by that domestic slavery produced by the fear of equality, by spousal hierarchy, and by a lack of the reciprocity and mutuality of true friendship.

The Hope of Friendship

Mill's remedy for the evils generated by the fear of equality was his notion of marital friendship. The topic of the rather visionary fourth chapter of *The Subjection of Women* was friendship, "the ideal of marriage" (4: 233, 235). That ideal was, according to Mill, "a union of thoughts and inclinations" which created a "foundation of solid friendship" between husband and wife (4: 231, 233).

Mill's praise of marital friendship was almost lyrical, and struck resonances with Aristotle's, Cicero's, and Montaigne's similar exaltation of the pleasures as well as the moral enrichment of this form of human intimacy. Mill wrote:

> When each of two persons, instead of being a nothing, is a something; when they are attached to one another, and are not too much unlike to begin with; the constant partaking of the same things, assisted by their sympathy, draws out the latent capacities of each for being interested in the things . . . by a real enriching of the two natures, each acquiring the tastes and capacities of the other in addition to its own. (4: 233)

This expansion of human capacities did not, however, exhaust the benefits of friendship. Most importantly, friendship developed what Montaigne praised as the abolition of selfishness, the capacity to regard another human being as fully as worthy as oneself. Therefore friendship of the highest order could only exist between those equal in excellence.[28] And for precisely this reason, philosophers from Aristotle to Hegel had consistently argued that women could not be men's friends, for women lacked the moral capacity for the highest forms of friendship. Indeed, it was common to distinguish the marital bond from

[27] For excellent studies of each of these authors views on women (except for Grotius) see Okin. Grotius' views can be found in his *De Juri Belli ac Pacis Libri Tres [On the Law of War and Peace.]* (1625), trans. Francis W. Kelsey (Oxford: Clarendon Press, 1925), Bk. II, ch. V, sec. i, p. 231.

[28] Montaigne's essay "Of Friendship" in *The Complete Works of Montaigne*, trans. Donald M. Frame (Stanford: Stanford University Press, 1948), pp. 135–144.

friendship not solely on the basis of sexual and procreative activity, but also because women could not be part of the school of moral virtue which was found in friendship at its best.

Mill therefore made a most significant break with the past in adopting the language of friendship in his discussion of marriage. For Mill, no less than for any of his predecessors, "the true virtue of human beings is the fitness to live together as equals." Such equality required that individuals "[claim] nothing for themselves but what they as freely concede to every one else," that they regard command of any kind as "an exceptional necessity," and that they prefer whenever possible "the society of those with whom leading and following can be alternate and reciprocal" (4: 174–175). This picture of reciprocity, of the shifting of leadership according to need, was a remarkable characterization of family life. Virtually all of Mill's liberal contemporaries accepted the notion of the natural and inevitable complimentariness of male and female personalities and roles. Mill, however, as early as 1833 had expressed his belief that "the highest masculine and the highest feminine" characters were without any real distinction.[29] That view of the androgynous personality lent support to Mill's brief for equality within the family.

Mill repeatedly insisted that his society had no general experience of "the marriage relationship as it would exist between equals," and that such marriages would be impossible until men rid themselves of the fear of equality and the will to domination.[30] The liberation of women, in other words, required not just legal reform but a reeducation of the passions. Women were to be regarded as equals not only to fulfill the demand for individual rights and in order that they could survive in the public world of work, but also in order that women and men could form ethical relations of the highest order. Men and women alike had to "learn to cultivate their strongest sympathy with an equal in rights and in cultivation" (4: 236). Mill struggled, not always with total success, to talk about the quality of such association. For example, in *On Liberty*, Mill explicitly rejected von Humbolt's characterization of marriage as a contractual relationship which could be ended by "the declared will of either party to dissolve it." That kind of dissolution was appropriate when the benefits of partnership could be reduced to monetary terms. But marriage involved a person's expectations for the fulfillment of a "plan of life," and created "a new series of moral obligations . . . toward that person, which may possibly be overruled,

[29] Letter to Thomas Carlyle, October 5, 1833, *C. W.* XII, *Earlier Letters*, p. 184.
[30] Letter to John Nichol, August 1869, *C. W.* XVII, *The Later Letters*, ed. Francis C. Mineka and Dwight N. Lindley (Toronto: University of Toronto Press, 1972), p. 1634.

but cannot be ignored."[31] Mill was convinced that difficult though it might be to shape the law to recognize the moral imperatives of such a relationship, there were ethical communities which transcended and were not reducible to their individual components.

At this juncture, however, the critical force of Mill's essay weakened, and a tension developed between his ideal and his prescriptions for his own society. For all his insight into the dynamics of domestic domination and subordination, the only specific means Mill in fact put forward for the fostering of this society of equals was providing equal opportunity to women in areas outside the family. Indeed, in *On Liberty* he wrote that "nothing more is needed for the complete removal of [the almost despotic power of husbands over wives] than that wives should have the same rights and should receive the same protection of law in the same manner, as all other persons."[32] In the same vein, Mill seemed to suggest that nothing more was needed for women to achieve equality than that "the present duties and protective bounties in favour of men should be recalled" (1: 154). Moreover, Mill did not attack the traditional assumption about men's and women's different responsibilities in an ongoing household, although he was usually careful to say that women "chose" their role or that it was the most "expedient" arrangement, not that it was theirs by "nature."

Mill by and large accepted the notion that once they marry, women should be solely responsible for the care of the household and children, men for providing the family income: "When the support of the family depends . . . on earnings, the common arrangement, by which the man earns the income and the wife superintends the domestic expenditure, seems to me in general the most suitable division of labour between the two persons" (2: 178). He did not regard it as "a desirable custom, that the wife should contribute by her labour to the income of the family" (2: 179). Mill indicated that women alone would care for any children of the marriage; repeatedly he called it the "care which . . . nobody else takes," the one vocation in which there is "nobody to compete with them," and the occupation which "cannot be fulfilled by others" (2: 178; 3: 183; 4: 241). Further, Mill seemed to

---

[31] *C. W.*, XVIII, 300. Elsewhere Mill wrote, "My opinion on Divorce is that . . . nothing ought to be rested in, short of entire freedom on both sides to dissolve this like any other partnership." Letter to an unidentified correspondent, November 1855, *C. W.* XIV, *Later Letters*, p. 500. But against this letter was the passage from *On Liberty*, and his letter to Henry Rusden of July 1870 in which he abjured making any final judgments about what a proper divorce law would be "until women have an equal voice in making it." He denied that he advocated that marriage should be dissoluble "at the will of either party," and stated that no well-grounded opinion could be put forward until women first achieved equality under the laws and in married life. *C. W.*, XVII, *Later Letters*, pp. 1750–1751.

[32] *C. W.*, XVIII, p. 301.

shut the door on combining household duties and a public life: "like a man when he chooses a profession, so, when a women marries, it may be in general understood that she makes a choice of the management of a household, and the bringing up of a family, as the first call upon her exertions . . . and that she renounces . . . all [other occupations] which are not consistent with the requirements of this" (1: 179).

Mill's acceptance of the traditional gender-based division of labor in the family has led some recent critics to fault Mill for supposing that legal equality of opportunity would solve the problem of women's subjection, even while leaving the sexual division of labor in the household intact. For example, Julia Annas, after praising Mill's theoretical arguments in support of equality, complains that Mill's suggestions for actual needed changes in sex roles are "timid and reformist at best. He assumes that most women will in fact want only to be wives and mothers."[33] Leslie Goldstein agrees that "the restraints which Mill believed should be imposed on married women constitute a major exception to his argument for equality of individual liberty between the sexes—an exception so enormous that it threatens to swallow up the entire argument."[34] But such arguments, while correctly identifying the limitations of antidiscrimination statutes as instruments for social change, incorrectly identify Mill's argument for equal opportunity as the conclusion of his discussion of male-female equality.[35] On the contrary, Mill's final prescription to end the subjection of women was not equal opportunity but spousal friendship; equal opportunity was a means whereby such friendship could be encouraged.

The theoretical force of Mill's condemnation of domestic hierarchy has not yet been sufficiently appreciated. Mill's commitment to equality in marriage was of a different theoretical order than his acceptance of a continued sexual division of labor. On the one hand, Mill's belief in the necessity of equality as a precondition to marital friendship was a profound theoretical tenet. It rested on the normative assumption that human relationships between equals were of a higher, more enriching order than those between unequals. Mill's belief that equality was more

---

[33] Annas, 189.

[34] Goldstein, p. 8. Susan Okin makes a similar point, stating that "Mill never questioned or objected to the maintenance of traditional sex roles within the family, but expressly considered them to be suitable and desirable" (Okin, p. 237). Okin's reading of Mill is basically sound and sympathetic, but does not recognize the theoretical priority of Mill's commitment to marital equality and friendship.

[35] Of recent writers on Mill, only Richard Krouse seems sensitive to the inherent tension in Mill's thought about women in the household. Mill's own "ideal of a reformed family life, based upon a full nonpatriarchal marriage bond," Krouse points out, requires "on the logic of his own analysis . . . [the] rejection of the traditional division of labor between the sexes" (Krouse, p. 39).

suitable to friendship than inequality was as unalterable as his conviction that democracy was a better system of government than despotism; the human spirit could not develop its fullest potential when living
in absolute subordination to another human being or to government.[36]
On the other hand, Mill's belief that friendship could be attained and
sustained while women bore nearly exclusive responsibility for the
home was a statement which might be modified or even abandoned if
experience proved it to be wrong. In this sense it was like Mill's view
that the question of whether socialism was preferable to capitalism
could not be settled by verbal argument alone but must "work itself out
on an experimental scale, by actual trial."[37] Mill believed that marital
equality was a moral imperative; his view that such equality might exist
where married men and women moved in different spheres of activity
was a proposition subject to demonstration. Had Mill discovered that
managing the household to the exclusion of most other activity created
an impediment to the friendship of married women and men, *The
Subjection of Women* suggests that he would have altered his view of
practicable domestic arrangements, but not his commitment to the
desirability of male-female friendship in marriage.

The most interesting shortcomings of Mill's analysis are thus not
found in his belief in the efficacy of equal opportunity, but rather in his
blindness to what other conditions might hinder or promote marital
friendship. In his discussion of family life, for example, Mill seemed to
forget his own warning that women could be imprisoned not only "by
actual law" but also "by custom equivalent to law" (4: 241). Similarly, he
overlooked his own cautionary observation that in any household
"there will naturally be more potential voice on the side, whichever it is,
that brings the means of support" (2: 170). And although he had
brilliantly depicted the narrowness and petty concerns of contemporary women who were totally excluded from political participation, he
implied that the mistresses of most households might content themselves simply with exercising the suffrage (were it to be granted), a view
hardly consistent with his arguments in other works for maximizing
the level of political discussion and participation whenever possible.
More significantly, however, Mill ignored the potential barrier between
husband and wife which such different adult life experiences might
create, and the contribution of shared experience to building a common sensibility and strengthening the bonds of friendship.

Mill also never considered that men might take any role in the family
other than providing the economic means of support. Perhaps Mill's

[36] *Considerations on Representative Government, C. W.,* XIX, pp. 399–403.
[37] *Chapters on Socialism* (1879), *C. W.,* V, p. 736.

greatest oversight in his paean of marital equality was his failure to entertain the possibilities that nurturing and caring for children might provide men with useful knowledge and experience, and that shared parenting would contribute to the friendship between spouses which he so ardently desired. Similarly, Mill had virtually nothing to say about the positive role which sex might play in marriage. The sharp language with which he condemned undesired sexual relations as the execution of "an animal function" was nowhere supplemented by an appreciation of the possible enhancement which sexuality might add to marital friendship. One of the striking features of Montaigne's lyrical praise of friendship was that it was devoid of sensuality, for Montaigne abhorred "the Grecian license," and he was adamant that women were incapable of the highest forms of friendship. Mill's notion of spousal friendship suggested the possibility of a friendship which partook of both a true union of minds and of a physical expression of the delight in one's companion, a friendship which involved all of the human faculties. It was an opportunity which (undoubtedly to the relief of those such as James Fitzjames Stephen) Mill himself was not disposed to use, but which was nonetheless implicit in his praise of spousal friendship.[38]

One cannot ask Mill or any other theorist to "jump over Rhodes" and address issues not put forward by conditions and concerns of his own society.[39] Nevertheless, even leaving aside an analysis of the oppression inherent in the class structure (an omission which would have to be rectified in a full analysis of liberation), time has made it clear that Mill's prescriptions alone will not destroy the master-slave relationship which he so detested. Women's aspirations for equality will not be met by insuring equal civic rights and equal access to jobs outside the home. To accomplish that end would require a transformation of economic and public structures which would allow wives and husbands to share those domestic tasks which Mill assigned exclusively to women. Some forms of publicly supported day-care, parental as well as maternity leaves, flexible work schedules, extensive and rapid public transportation, health and retirement benefits for part-time employment are

---

[38] Throughout his writings Mill displayed a tendency to dismiss or deprecate the erotic dimension of life. In his *Autobiography* he wrote approvingly that his father looked forward to an increase in freedom in relations between the sexes, freedom which would be devoid of any sensuality "either of a theoretical or of a practical kind." His own twenty-year friendship with Harriet Taylor before their marriage was "one of strong affection and confidential intimacy only." *Autobiography of John Stuart Mill* (New York: Columbia University Press, 1944), pp. 75, 161. In *The Principles of Political Economy* Mill remarked that in his own day "the animal instinct" occupied a "disproportionate preponderance in human life." *C. W.*, III, p. 766.

[39] G. W. F. Hegel, *The Philosophy of Right*, ed. T. M. Knox (London: Oxford University Press, 1952), p. 11, quoted in Krouse, p. 40.

among commonly proposed measures which would make the choice of Mill's ideal of marriage between equals possible. In their absence it is as foolish to talk about couples choosing the traditional division of labor in marriage as it was in Mill's day to talk about women choosing marriage; both are Hobson's choices, there are no suitable alternatives save at enormous costs to the individuals involved.

Mill's feminist vision, however, transcends his own immediate prescriptions for reform. *The Subjection of Women* is not only one of liberalism's most incisive arguments for equal opportunity, but it embodies as well a belief in the importance of friendship for human development and progress. The recognition of individual rights is important in Mill's view because it provides part of the groundwork for more important human relationships of trust, mutuality and reciprocity. Mill's plea for an end to the subjection of women is not made, as critics such as Gertrude Himmelfarb assert, in the name of "the absolute primacy of the individual," but in the name of the need of both men and women for community. Mill's essay is valuable both for its devastating critique of the corruption of marital inequality, and for its argument, however incomplete, that one of the aims of a liberal polity should be to promote the conditions which will allow friendship, in marriage and elsewhere, to take root and flourish.

[14]

Feminism and Modern Friendship: Dislocating the Community

Marilyn Friedman

A predominant theme of much recent feminist thought is the critique of the abstract individualism which underlies some important versions of liberal political theory.[1] Abstract individualism considers individual human beings as social atoms, abstracted from their social contexts, and disregards the role of social relationships and human community in constituting the very identity and nature of individual human beings. Sometimes the individuals of abstract individualism are posited as rationally self-interested utility-maximizers.[2] Sometimes, also, they are theorized to form communities based fundamentally on competition and conflict among persons vying for scarce resources, communities held together by a social bond no deeper than that of instrumental relations based on calculated self-interest.[3]

First published in *Ethics* 99 (January 1989): 275–90, © 1988–1989 by The University of Chicago Press, and reprinted here by permission of The University of Chicago Press. The author has made slight changes for this volume.

[1] Cf. Carole Pateman, *The Problem of Political Obligation: A Critique of Liberal Theory* (Berkeley: University of California Press, 1979); Zillah Eisenstein, *The Radical Future of Liberal Feminism* (New York: Longman, 1981); Nancy C. M. Hartsock, *Money, Sex, and Power* (Boston: Northeastern University Press, 1983); Alison M. Jaggar, *Feminist Politics and Human Nature* (Totowa, N.J.: Rowman & Allanheld, 1983); Naomi Scheman, "Individualism and the Objects of Psychology," in Sandra Harding and Merrill B. Hintikka, eds., *Discovering Reality* (Dordrecht: D. Reidel, 1983), pp. 225–44; Jane Flax, "Political Philosophy and the Patriarchal Unconscious: A Psychoanalytic Perspective on Epistemology and Metaphysics," in Harding and Hintikka, eds., pp. 245–81; and Seyla Benhabib, "The Generalized and the Concrete Other: The Kohlberg-Gilligan Controversy and Moral Theory," in Eva Feder Kittay and Diana T. Meyers, eds., *Women and Moral Theory* (Totowa, N.J.: Rowman and Littlefield, 1987), pp. 154–77.

[2] Cf. David Gauthier, *Morals by Agreement* (Oxford: Oxford University Press, 1986).

[3] Cf. George Homans, *Social Behavior: Its Elementary Forms* (New York: Harcourt, Brace and World, 1961); and Peter Blau, *Exchange and Power in Social Life* (New York: Wiley, 1974).

Against this abstractive individualist view of the self and of human community, many feminists have asserted a social conception of the self.[4] This conception acknowledges the fundamental role of social relationships and human community in constituting both self-identity and the nature and meaning of the particulars of individual lives.[5] The social conception of the self has carried with it an altered conception of community. Conflict and competition are no longer considered to be the basic human relationships; instead they are being replaced by alternative visions of the foundation of human society derived from nurturance, caring attachment, and mutual interestedness.[6] Some feminists, for example, recommend that the mother-child relationship be viewed as central to human society, and they project major changes in moral theory from such a revised focus.[7]

Some of these anti-individualist developments emerging from feminist thought are strikingly similar to other theoretical developments which are not specifically feminist. Thus, the "new communitarians," to borrow Amy Gutmann's term,[8] have also reacted critically to various aspects of modern liberal thought, including abstract individualism, rational egoism, and an instrumental conception of social relationships. The communitarian self, or subject, is not a social atom but a being constituted and defined by its attachments, including the particularities of its social relationships, community ties, and historical context. Its identity cannot be abstracted from community or social relationships.

With the recent feminist attention to values of care, nurturance, and relatedness—values that psychologists call "communal"[9] and that have been amply associated with women and women's moral reasoning[10]— one might anticipate that communitarian theory would offer impor-

---

[4] Cf. my "Autonomy in Social Context," in James Sterba and Creighton Peden, eds., *Freedom, Equality, and Social Change: Problems in Social Philosophy Today* (Lewiston, N.Y.: Edwin Mellen Press, 1989), pp. 158–69.

[5] Cf. Drucilla Cornell, "Toward a Modern/Postmodern Reconstruction of Ethics," *University of Pennsylvania Law Review* 133 (January 1985): 291–380.

[6] Cf. Annette Baier, "Trust and Antitrust," *Ethics* 96, no. 2 (1986): 231–60; and Owen Flanagan and Kathryn Jackson, "Justice, Care, and Gender: The Kohlberg-Gilligan Debate Revisited," *Ethics* 97, no. 3 (1987); 622–37.

[7] Cf. Hartsock, *Money, Sex, and Power*, pp. 41–42; and Virginia Held, "Non-Contractual Society," in Marsha Hanen and Kai Nielsen, eds., *Science, Morality and Feminist Theory*, supplementary vol. 13 (1987) of *Canadian Journal of Philosophy*, pp. 111–38.

[8] Amy Gutmann, "Communitarian Critics of Liberalism," *Philosophy and Public Affairs* 14 (Summer 1985): 308–22.

[9] Cf. Alice H. Eagly and Valerie J. Steffen, "Gender Stereotypes Stem from the Distribution of Women and Men into Social Roles," *Journal of Personality and Social Psychology* 46 (1984): 735–54.

[10] Cf. Carol Gilligan, *In a Different Voice* (Cambridge: Harvard University Press, 1982).

tant insights for feminist reflection. There is considerable power in the model of the self as deriving its identity and nature from its social relationships, from the way it is intersubjectively apprehended, from the norms of the community in which it is embedded.

However, communitarian philosophy as a whole is a perilous ally for feminist theory. Communitarians invoke a model of community that is focused particularly on families, neighborhoods, and nations. These sorts of communities harbor social roles and structures which have been highly oppressive for women, as recent feminist critiques have shown. But communitarians seem oblivious to such difficulties and manifest a troubling complacency about the moral authority claimed or presupposed by these communities in regard to their members. By building on uncritical references to these sorts of communities, communitarian philosophy can lead in directions that feminists should not take.

This discussion is an effort to redirect communitarian thought so as to avoid some of the pitfalls which it poses, in its present form, for feminist theory and feminist practice. In the first part of the essay, I develop some feminist-inspired criticism of communitarian philosophy as it is found in writings by Michael Sandel and Alasdair MacIntyre.[11] My brief critique of communitarian thought has the aim of showing that communitarian theory, in the form in which it condones or tolerates traditional communal norms of gender subordination, is unacceptable from any standpoint enlightened by feminist analysis. This does not preclude agreeing with certain specific communitarian views—for example, the broad metaphysical conception of the individual, self, or subject as constituted by its social relationships and communal ties, or the assumption that traditional communities have some value. But the aim of Part I is critical: to focus on the communitarian disregard of gender-related problems with the norms and practices of traditional communities.

In the second part of this essay, I delve more deeply into the nature of certain sorts of communities and social relationships that communitarians largely disregard. I suggest that modern friendships, on the one hand, and urban relationships and communities, on the other, offer an important clue toward a model of community which usefully counterbalances the family-neighborhood-nation complex favored by communitarians. With that model in view, we can begin to transform the communitarian vision of self and community into a more congenial ally for feminist theory.

---

[11] In particular, Michael Sandel, *Liberalism and the Limits of Justice* (Cambridge: Cambridge University Press, 1982); and Alasdair MacIntyre, *After Virtue* (Notre Dame: University of Notre Dame Press, 1981).

The Social Self, in Communitarian Perspective

Communitarians share with most feminist theorists a rejection of the abstractly individualist conception of self and society so prominent in modern liberal thought.[12] This self—atomistic, pre-social, empty of all metaphysical content except abstract reason and will—is allegedly able to stand back from all the contingent moral commitments and norms of its particular historical context and assess each one of them in the light of impartial and universal criteria of reason. The self who achieves a substantial measure of such reflective reconsideration of the moral particulars of her life has achieved "autonomy," a widely esteemed liberal value.

In contrast to this vision of the self, the new communitarians pose the conception of a self whose identity and nature are defined by her contingent and particular social attachments. Communitarians extol the communities and social relationships, including family and nation, which comprise the typical social context in which the self emerges to self-consciousness. Thus, Michael Sandel speaks warmly of "those loyalties and convictions whose moral force consists partly in the fact that living by them is inseparable from understanding ourselves as the particular persons we are—as members of this family or community or nation or people, as bearers of this history, as sons and daughters of that revolution, as citizens of this republic."[13] Sandel continues:

> Allegiances such as these are more than values I happen to have or aims I 'espouse at any given time.' They go beyond the obligations I voluntarily incur and the 'natural duties' I owe to human beings as such. They allow that to some I owe more than justice requires or even permits, not by reason of agreements I have made but instead in virtue of those more or less enduring attachments and commitments which taken together partly *define the person I am.*[14]

---

[12] Contemporary liberals do not regard the communitarians' metaphysical claims (discussed below) as a threat to liberal theory. The liberal concept of the self as abstracted from social relationships and historical context is now treated, not as a metaphysical presupposition, but, rather, as a vehicle for evoking a pluralistic political society whose members disagree about the good for human life. With this device, liberalism seeks a theory of political process which aims to avoid relying on any human particularities that might presuppose parochial human goods or purposes. Cf. John Rawls, "Justice as Fairness: Political Not Metaphysical," *Philosophy and Public Affairs* 14, no. 3 (1985): 223–51; and Joel Feinberg, "Liberalism, Community, and Tradition," excerpted from *Harmless Wrongdoing*, vol. 4 of *The Moral Limits of the Criminal Law* (Oxford: Oxford University Press, 1988).

[13] Sandel, *Liberalism and the Limits of Justice*, p. 179.

[14] Ibid.; italics mine.

Voicing similar sentiments, Alasdair MacIntyre writes:

> we all approach our own circumstances as bearers of a particular social identity. I am someone's son or daughter, someone else's cousin or uncle; I am a citizen of this or that city, a member of this or that guild or profession; I belong to this clan, that tribe, this nation. Hence what is good for me has to be the good for one who inhabits these roles. As such, I inherit from the past of my family, my city, my tribe, my nation, a variety of debts, inheritances, rightful expectations and obligations. These constitute the given of my life, my moral starting point. This is in part what gives my life its own moral particularity.[15]

(An aside: It is remarkable that neither writer mentions sex or gender as a determinant of particular identity. Perhaps this glaring omission derives not from failing to realize the fundamental importance of gender in personal identity—could anyone really miss that?—but rather from the aim to emphasize what social relationships and communities contribute to identity, along with the inability to conceive that gender is a social relationship or that it constitutes a community.)

For communitarians, these social relationships and communities have a kind of morally normative legitimacy—they define the "moral starting points," to use MacIntyre's phrase, of each individual life. The traditions, practices, and conventions of our communities have at least a prima facie legitimate moral claim upon us. MacIntyre does qualify the latter point by conceding that "the fact that the self has to find its moral identity in and through its membership in communities such as those of the family, the neighborhood, the city and the tribe does not entail that the self has to accept the moral *limitations* of the particularity of those forms of community."[16] Nevertheless, according to MacIntyre, one's moral quests must begin by "moving forward from such particularity," for it "can never be simply left behind or obliterated."[17]

Despite feminist sympathy toward a social conception of the self and an emphasis on the importance of social relationships, at least three features of the communitarian version of these notions are troubling from a feminist standpoint. First, the communitarian's metaphysical conception of an inherently social self has little usefulness for normative analysis; in particular, it will not support a specifically feminist critique of individualist personality. Second, communitarian theory pays insufficient regard to the illegitimate moral claims which communities make on their members, linked, for example, to hierarchies of

[15] MacIntyre, *After Virtue*, pp. 204–5.
[16] Ibid., p. 205.
[17] Ibid.

domination and subordination. Third, the specific communities of
family, neighborhood, and nation—so commonly invoked by communitarians—are troubling paradigms of social relationship and communal life. I will discuss each of these points in turn.

First, the communitarians' metaphysical conception of the social self
will not support feminist critiques of ruggedly individualist personality
or its associated attributes: avoidance of intimacy, non-nurturance, social distancing, aggression, or violence. Feminist theorists have criticized our cultural norm of the highly individualistic, competitive, ag-
gressive personality type and have seen that personality type as more
characteristically male than female and as an important part of the
foundation for patriarchy.

Largely following the work of Nancy Chodorow, Dorothy Dinnerstein, and, more recently, Carol Gilligan,[18] many feminists have theorized that the processes of psycho-gender development, in a society in
which early infant care is the primary responsibility of women but not
men, result in a radical distinction between the genders in the extent to
which the self is constituted by, and self-identifies with, its relational
connection to others. Males are theorized to seek and value autonomy,
individuation, separation, and the moral ideals of rights and justice,
ideals which may seem to depend on a highly individuated conception
of persons. By contrast, females are theorized to seek and value connection, sociality, inclusion, and moral ideals of care and nurturance.

From this perspective, highly individuated selves are a problem.
They appear incapable of human attachments based on mutuality and
trust and unresponsive to human needs. They seem to approach social
relationships merely as rationally self-interested utility-maximizers, to
thrive on separation and competition, and to create social institutions
which tolerate, even legitimize, violence and aggression.

However, a metaphysical view that all human selves are constituted
by their social and communal relationships does not itself entail a
critique of these highly individualistic selves, nor does it yield any
indication of what degree of psychological attachment to others is desirable. On metaphysical grounds alone, there is no reason to suppose
that caring, nurturant, relational, sociable selves are better than more
autonomous, individualistic, and independent selves. All would be
equivalently socially constituted at a metaphysical level. Abstract individualism's failure would be not that it has produced asocial selves, for,
on the communitarian view, such beings are metaphysically impossible,

---

[18] Dorothy Dinnerstein, *The Mermaid and the Minotaur: Sexual Arrangements and Human
Malaise* (New York: Harper & Row, 1976); Nancy Chodorow, *The Reproduction of Mothering* (Berkeley: University of California Press, 1978); and Gilligan, *In a Different Voice*.

but, rather, that it has simply failed to acknowledge theoretically that selves are inherently social. And autonomy, independence, and separateness would become just a different way of being socially constituted, no worse or better than heteronomy, dependence, or connectedness.

If the communitarian conception of the social self is simply a metaphysical view about the constitution of the self (as it seems to be), it provides no basis for regarding nurturant, relational selves as morally superior to those who are highly individualistic. For this reason, it appears to be of no assistance to feminist theorists seeking a normative account of what might be wrong or excessive about competitive self-seeking behaviors or other seeming manifestations of an individualistic perspective. The communitarian "social self," as a metaphysical account of the self, is largely irrelevant to the array of normative tasks which many feminist thinkers have set for a conception of the self.

My second concern about communitarian philosophy has to do with the legitimacy of the communal norms and traditions which are supposed to define the moral starting points of community members. As a matter of moral psychology, it is common for persons to take for granted the moral legitimacy of the norms, traditions, and practices of their communities. However, this point about moral psychology does not entail that those norms and practices really are morally legitimate. It leaves open the question of whether, and to what extent, those claims might "really" be morally binding. Unfortunately, the new communitarians seem sometimes to go beyond the point of moral psychology to a stronger view, namely that the moral claims of communities really are morally binding, at least as "moral starting points." MacIntyre refers to the "debts, inheritances, *rightful* expectations and obligations"[19] which we "inherit" from family, nation, and so forth.

But such inheritances are enormously varied. In light of this variety, MacIntyre's normative complacency is quite troubling. Many communities practice the exclusion and suppression of non-group members, especially outsiders defined by ethnicity and sexual orientation.[20] Aren't there "rightful expectations and obligations" *across* community lines? Don't whites, for example, have debts to Blacks and native Americans for histories of exploitation? Didn't Jews, Gypsies, Poles, Czechoslovakians, and others have "rightful expectations" that Germany would not practice military conquest and unimaginable genocide? Didn't Germany owe reparations to non-Germans for those same

---

[19] MacIntyre, *After Virtue*, p. 205; italics mine.
[20] A similar point is made by Iris Young, "The Ideal of Community and the Politics of Difference," *Social Theory and Practice* 12 (Spring 1986): 12–13.

genocidal practices? If the new communitarians do not recognize legitimate "debts, inheritances, rightful expectations and obligations"
across community lines, then their views have little relevance for our
radically heterogeneous modern society. If there are such inter-
community obligations which override communal norms and practices,
then moral particularity is not accounted for by communal norms
alone. In that case, "the" community as such, that is, the relatively
bounded and local network of relationships which forms a subject's
primary social setting, would not singularly determine the legitimate
moral values or requirements which rightfully constitute the self's
moral commitments or self-definition.

Besides excluding or suppressing outsiders, the practices and traditions of numerous communities are exploitive and oppressive toward
many of their own members. This problem is of special relevance to
women. Feminist theory is rooted in a recognition of the need for
change in all the traditions and political practices which show gender
differentiation; many of these are located in just the sorts of communities invoked by communitarians, for example, families and nations.
The communitarian emphasis on communities unfortunately dovetails
too well with the current popular emphasis on "the family" and seems
to harken back to the repressive world of what some sociologists call
communities of "place"—the world of family, neighborhood, school,
and church, that so intimately enclosed women in oppressive gender
politics, the peculiar politics which it has been feminism's distinctive
contribution to uncover. Any political theory which appears to support
the hegemony of such communities—and which appears to restore
them to a position of unquestioned moral authority—must be viewed
with grave suspicion. I will come back to this issue when I turn to my
third objection to communitarian philosophy.

Thus, while admitting into our notion of the self the important
constitutive role played by social and communal relationships, we are
not forced to accept as binding on any particular subject the moral
claims made by the social and communal relationships in which that
subject is embedded or by which she is identified. Nor are we required
to say that any particular subject is herself morally obliged to accept as
binding the moral claims made on her by any of the communities
which constitute or define her. To evaluate the moral identities con-
ferred by communities on their members, we need a theory of communities—of their interrelationships and of their structures of power,
dominance, and oppression. Only such a theory would allow us to
assess the legitimacy of the claims made by communities upon their
members by way of their traditions, practices, and conventions of
"debts, inheritances, . . . expectations, and obligations."

The communitarian approach appears to celebrate the unavoidable interpersonal attachments of familial ties, and so forth. But some of these relationships compete with each other, and some communal attachments provide standpoints from which other such relationships in one's own life appear threatening or dangerous to one's self, one's integrity, or one's well-being. In such cases, simple formulas about the value of community provide no guidance. The problem is not simply how to appreciate community per se, but rather how to reconcile the conflicting claims, demands, and identity-defining influences of the various communities of which one is a part.

It is worth recalling that liberalism has always condemned, in principle if not in practice, the norms of social hierarchy and political subordination based on inherited or ascribed status. Where liberals have historically applied this tenet only to the public realm of civic relationships,[21] feminism seeks to extend it more radically to the "private" realm of family and other communities of place. These norms and claims of local communities which sustain gender hierarchies have no intrinsic legitimacy from a feminist standpoint. A feminist interest in community must certainly promote social institutions and relational structures which diminish and, finally, erase gender subordination.

Reflections such as these characterize the concerns of the modern self, the self who acknowledges no a priori loyalty to any feature of a situation or role, and who claims the right to question the moral legitimacy of any contingent moral claim.[22] We can agree with the communitarians that it would be impossible for the self to question all her contingencies at once, yet at the same time, unlike the communitarians, still strongly emphasize the critical importance of morally questioning various communal norms and circumstances one at a time.

A third problem with communitarian philosophy has to do with the sorts of communities evidently endorsed by communitarian theorists. Human beings participate in a variety of communities and social relationships, not only across time, but at any one time. However, when people think of "community," it is common for them to think of certain particular social networks, namely, those formed primarily out of family, neighborhood, school, and church.[23] These more typical communities also coincide with the substantive examples of community commonly invoked by Sandel and MacIntyre. Those examples fall largely into two groups. First, there are political communities which constitute

[21] John Stuart Mill's *The Subjection of Women* is a noteworthy exception. My thanks to L. W. Sumner for reminding me of this work.
[22] Cf. Cornell, "Toward a Modern/Postmodern Reconstruction of Ethics," p. 323.
[23] This point is made by Young, "The Ideal of Community and the Politics of Difference," p. 12.

our civic and national identities in a public world of nation-states. MacIntyre mentions city and nation, while Sandel writes of "nation or people, . . . bearers of this history, . . . sons and daughters of that revolution, . . . citizens of this republic."[24] Second, there are local communities centered around families and neighborhood that some sociologists call "communities of place." MacIntyre and Sandel both emphasize family, and MacIntyre also cites neighborhood along with clan and tribe.[25]

But where, one might ask, are the International Ladies Garment Workers' Union, the Teamsters, the Democratic Party, Alcoholics Anonymous, or Amnesty International? Although MacIntyre does mention professions and, rather archaically, "guilds,"[26] these references are anomalous in his work, which, for the most part, ignores such communities as trade unions, political action groups, associations of hobbyists, and so forth.

Some of the communities cited by MacIntyre and Sandel will resonate with the historical experiences of women, especially the inclusive communities of family and neighborhood. By contrast, political communities form a particularly suspect class from a woman's perspective. We all recall how political communities have, until only recently, excluded the legitimate participation of women. It would seem to follow that they have *not* historically constituted the identities of women in profound ways. As "daughters" of an American revolution spawned parthenogenically by the "fathers" of our country, we find our political community to have denied us the self-identifying heritage of our cultural *mothers*. In general, the contribution made to the identities of various groups of people by political communities is quite uneven, given that they are communities to which many are subject, but in which far fewer actively participate.

At any rate, there is an underlying commonality to most of the communities which MacIntyre and Sandel cite as constitutive of self-identity and definitive of our moral starting points. Sandel himself explicates this commonality when he writes that, for people "bound by a sense of community," the notion of community describes "*not a relationship they choose (as in a voluntary association) but an attachment they discover,* not merely an attribute but a constituent of their identity.[27] Not voluntary but "discovered" relationships and communities are what Sandel takes to define subjective identity for those who are bound by a "sense of community." It is the communities to which we

24 MacIntyre, *After Virtue*, p. 204; Sandel, *Liberalism and the Limits of Justice*, p. 179.
25 MacIntyre, ibid.; Sandel, ibid.
26 MacIntyre, ibid.
27 Sandel, *Liberalism and the Limits of Justice*, p. 150; italics mine.

are involuntarily bound to which Sandel accords metaphysical pride of place in the constitution of subjectivity. Most important here are not simply the "associations" in which people "cooperate" but the "communities" in which people "participate," for these latter "describe a form of life in which the members find themselves commonly situated 'to begin with,' their commonality consisting less in relationships they have entered than in attachments they have found."[28] Thus, the social relationships which one finds, the attachments which are discovered and not chosen, become the points of reference for self-definition by the communitarian subject.

For the child maturing to self-consciousness in her community of origin—typically a complex of family, neighborhood, school, and church—it seems incontrovertible that "the" community is found, not entered, discovered, not created. But this need not be true of an adult's communities of mature self-identification. Many communities are, for at least some of their members, communities of choice to a significant extent: labor unions, philanthropic associations, political coalitions, and, if one has ever moved or migrated, even the communities of neighborhood, church, city, or nation-state might have been chosen to an important extent. One need not have simply discovered oneself to be embedded in them in order that one's identity or the moral particulars of one's life be defined by them. Sandel is right to indicate the role of found communities in constituting the unreflective, "given" identity which the self discovers when first beginning to reflect on herself. But for mature self-identity, we should also recognize a legitimate role for communities of choice, supplementing, if not displacing, the communities and attachments which are merely found.

Moreover, the discovered identity constituted by one's original community of place might be fraught with ambivalences and ambiguities. Our communities of origin do not necessarily constitute us as selves who agree or comply with the norms which unify those communities. Some of us are constituted as deviants and resisters by our communities of origin, and our defiance may well run to the foundational social norms which ground the most basic social roles and relationships upon which these communities rest. Thus, poet Adrienne Rich writes about her experiences growing up with a Christian mother, a Jewish father who suppressed his ethnicity, and a family community which taught Adrienne Rich contempt for all that was identified with Jewishness. In 1946, while still a high school student, Rich saw, for the first time, a film about the Allied liberation of Nazi concentration camps. Writing about this experience in 1982, she brooded: "I feel belated

28 Ibid., pp. 151–52.

rage that I was so impoverished by the family and social worlds I lived in, that I had to try to figure out by myself what this did indeed mean for me. That I had never been taught about resistance, only about passing. That I had no language for anti-Semitism itself."[29] As a student at Radcliffe in the late forties, Rich met "real" Jewish women who inducted her into the lore of Jewish background and customs, holidays and foods, names and noses. She plunged in with trepidation: "I felt I was testing a forbidden current, that there was danger in these revelations. I bought a reproduction of a Chagall portrait of a rabbi in striped prayer shawl and hung it on the wall of my room. I was admittedly young and trying to educate myself, but I was also doing something that *is* dangerous: I was flirting with identity."[30] Most important, she was doing it apart from, indeed contrary to the wishes of, the family community in which her ambiguous ethnic identity originated.

For Sandel, Rich's lifelong troubled reflections on her ethnic identity might seem compatible with his theory. In his view, the subject discovers the attachments which are constitutive of its subjectivity through reflection on a multitude of values and aims, differentiating what is self from what is not-self. He might say that Rich discriminated among the many loyalties and projects which defined who she was in her original community, that is, her family, and discerned that her Jewishness appeared "essential"[31] to who she was. But it is not obvious, without question-begging, that her original community really defined her as essentially Jewish. Indeed, her family endeavored to suppress loyalties and attachments to all things Jewish. Thus, one of Rich's quests in life, so evidently not inspired by her community of origin alone, was to revitalize the identity found in that original context. The communitarian view that "found" communities and social attachments constitute self-identity does not, by itself, explicate the source of such a quest. It seems more illuminating to say that Rich's identity became, in part, "chosen"—that it had to do with social relationships and attachments which she sought out, rather than merely found, created as well as discovered.

Thus, the commitments and loyalties of our found communities, our communities of origin, may harbor ambiguities, ambivalences, contradictions, and oppressions which complicate as well as constitute identity and which have to be sorted out, critically scrutinized. In these undertakings, we are likely to utilize resources and skills derived from various communities and relationships, both those which are chosen or

[29] "Split at the Root: An Essay on Jewish Identity," in Adrienne Rich, *Blood, Bread, and Poetry* (New York: W. W. Norton, 1986), p. 107.

[30] Ibid., p. 108.

[31] This term is used by Sandel, *Liberalism and the Limits of Justice*, p. 180.

created, as well as those which are found or discovered. Thus, our theories of community should recognize that resources and skills derived from communities which are chosen or created may contribute equally well to the constitution of identity. The constitution of identity and moral particularity, for the modern self, may well require the contribution of radically different communities from those invoked by communitarians.

The whole tenor of communitarian thinking would change once we opened up the conception of the social self to encompass chosen communities, especially those which lie beyond the typical original community of family-neighborhood-school-church. No longer would communitarian thought present a seemingly conservative complacency about the private and local communities of place which have so effectively circumscribed, in particular, the lives of most women.

In the next part of this essay, I shall explore more fully the role of communities and relationships of "choice," which point the way toward a notion of community more congenial to feminist aspirations.

Modern Friendship, Urban Community, and Beyond

My goals are twofold: to retain the communitarian insights about the contribution of community and social relationship to self-identity, yet open up for critical reflection the moral particulars imparted by those communities, and to identify the sorts of communities which will provide nonoppressive and enriched lives for women.

Toward this end, it will be helpful to consider models of human relationship and community which contrast with those cited by communitarians. Modern friendship and urban community appear to offer us crucial insights into the social nature of the modern self. It is in moving forward from these relationships that we have the best chance of reconciling the communitarian conception of the social self with the longed-for communities of feminist aspiration.

Modern friendship and the stereotypical urban community share an important feature which is either neglected or deliberately avoided in communitarian conceptions of human relationship. From a liberal, or Enlightenment, or modernist standpoint, this feature would be characterized as voluntariness: these relationships are based partly on choice.

Let's first consider friendship as it is understood in this culture. Friends are supposed to be people one chooses on one's own to share activities and intimacies. No particular people are assigned by custom or tradition to be a person's friends. From among the larger number of one's acquaintances, one moves toward closer and more friendlike relationships with some of them, motivated by one's own needs, values, and attractions. No consanguineal or legal connections establish or maintain ties of friendship. As this relationship is widely understood in our culture, its basis lies in voluntary choice.

In this context, "voluntary choice" refers to motivations arising out of one's own needs, desires, interests, values, and attractions, in contrast to motivations arising from what is socially assigned, ascribed, expected, or demanded. Because of its basis in voluntary choice, friendship is more likely than many other relationships, such as those of family and neighborhood, to be grounded and sustained by shared interests and values, mutual affection, and possibilities for generating reciprocal respect and esteem.

Because of these features sustained by its voluntary basis, friendship, more so than many other relationships, can provide social support for people who are idiosyncratic, whose unconventional values and deviant lifestyles make them victims of intolerance from family members and others who are involuntarily related to them. In this regard, friendship has socially disruptive possibilities, for out of the unconventional living which it helps to sustain there often arise influential forces for social change. Friendship has had an obvious importance to feminist aspirations as the basis of the bond which is (ironically) called "sisterhood."[32] Friendship among women has consolidated not only the various historical waves of the feminist movement, but also numerous communities of women throughout history who defied local gender conventions and lived lives of creative disorder.[33] In all these cases, women moved out of their given or found communities into new attachments with other women by their own choice, that is, motivated by their own needs, desires, attractions, and fears rather than, and often in opposition to, the expectations and ascribed roles of their found communities.

Like friendship, many urban relationships are also based more on choice than on socially ascribed roles, biological connections, or other nonvoluntary ties. Urban communities include numerous voluntary associations, such as political action groups, support groups, associations of co-hobbyists, and so on. But while friendship is almost universally extolled, urban communities and relationships have been theorized in wildly contradictory ways. Cities have sometimes been taken as

---

[32] Martha Ackelsberg points out the ironic and misleading nature of this use of the term 'sisterhood' in "'Sisters' or 'Comrades'? The Politics of Friends and Families," in Irene Diamond, ed., *Families, Politics, and Public Policy* (New York: Longman, 1983), pp. 339–56.

[33] Cf. Janice Raymond, *A Passion for Friends* (Boston: Beacon Press, 1986), especially chaps. 2 and 3.

"harbingers" of modern culture per se,[34] and have been particularly associated with the major social trends of modern life, such as industrialization and bureaucratization.[35] The results of these trends are often thought to have been a fragmentation of "real" community, and the widely-lamented alienation of modern urban life: people seldom know their neighbors; population concentration generates massive psychic overload;[36] fear and mutual distrust, even outright hostility, generated by the dangers of urban life, may dominate most daily associations. Under such circumstances, meaningful relationships are often theorized to be rare, if at all possible.

But is this image a complete portrait of urban life? It is probably true, in urban areas, that communities of *place* are diminished in importance; neighborhood plays a far less significant role in constituting community than it does in non-urban areas.[37] But this does not mean that the social networks and communities of urban dwellers are inferior to those of non-urban residents.

Much evidence suggests that urban settings do not, as commonly stereotyped, promote only alienation, isolation, and psychic breakdown. The communities available to urban dwellers are different from those available to non-urban dwellers, but not necessarily less gratifying or fulfilling.[38] Communities of place are relatively nonvoluntary; for example, one's extended family of origin is given or ascribed, and the relationships found as one grows. Sociological research has shown that urban dwellers tend to form their social networks, their communities, out of people who are brought together for reasons other than geographical proximity. Voluntary associations, such as political action groups, support groups, and so on, are a common part of modern urban life, with its large population centers and the greater availability of critical masses of people with special interests or needs. Communities of place, centered around family-neighborhood-church-school are more likely, for urban dwellers, to be supplanted by other sorts of communities, resulting in what the sociologist Melvin Webber has called "community without propinquity."[39] As the sociologist, Claude

---

[34] Claude Fischer, *To Dwell among Friends* (Chicago: University of Chicago Press, 1982), p. 1.

[35] Cf. Richard Sennett, "An Introduction," in Sennett, ed., *Classic Essays on the Culture of Cities* (New York: Appleton-Century-Crofts, 1969), pp. 3–22.

[36] Cf. Stanley Milgram, "The Experience of Living in Cities," *Science* 167 (1970): 1461–68.

[37] Fischer, *To Dwell among Friends*, pp. 97–103.

[38] Ibid., pp. 193–232.

[39] "Order in Diversity: Community without Propinquity," in Robert Gutman and David Popenoe, eds., *Neighborhood, City and Metropolis* (New York: Random House, 1970), pp. 792–811.

Fischer, has stated it, in urban areas "population concentration stimu-
lates allegiances to subcultures based on more significant social traits"
than common locality or neighborhood.[40] But most important for our
purposes, these are still often genuine communities, and not the cess-
pools of "Rum, Romanism, and Rebellion" sometimes depicted by anti-
urbanists.

Literature reveals that women writers have been both repelled and
inspired by urban communities. The city, as a concentrated center of
male political and economic power, seems to exclude women altogether.[41] However, as literary critic Susan Merrill Squier points out, the
city can provide women with jobs, education, and the cultural tools
with which to escape imposed gender roles, familial demands, and
domestic servitude. The city can also bring women together, in work or
in leisure, and lay the basis for bonds of sisterhood.[42] The quests of
women who journey to cities, leaving behind men, home, and family,
are subversive, writes literary critic Blanche Gelfant, and may well be
perceived by others "as assaults upon society."[43] Cities open up for
women possibilities of supplanting communities of place with relationships and communities of choice. Thus, urban communities of choice
can provide the resources for women to surmount the moral particularities of family and place which define and limit their moral starting
points.

Social theorists have long decried the interpersonal estrangement of
urban life, an observation which seems predominantly inspired by the
public world of conflict between various subcultural groups. Urbanism
does not create interpersonal estrangement *within* subcultures but,
rather, tends to promote social involvement.[44] This is especially true
for people with special backgrounds and interests, members of small
minorities, and ethnic groups. Fischer has found that social relationships in urban centers are more "culturally specialized: urbanites [are]
relatively involved with associates in the social world they [consider]
most important and relatively uninvolved with associates, if any, in
other worlds."[45] As Fischer summarizes, "Urbanism . . . fosters social
involvement in the subculture(s) of *choice,* rather than the subculture(s)

[40] Fischer, *To Dwell among Friends,* p. 273.
[41] Cf. the essays in Catherine Stimpson et al., eds., *Women and the American City* (Chicago: University of Chicago Press, 1980, 1981); and the special issue on "Women in the
City," *Urban Resources* 3 (Winter 1986).
[42] "Introduction" to Susan Merrill Squier, ed., *Women Writers and the City* (Knoxville:
University of Tennessee Press, 1984), pp. 3–10.
[43] Blanche Gelfant, "Sister to Faust: The City's 'Hungry' Woman as Heroine," in
Squier, ed., *Women Writers and the City,* p. 267.
[44] Fischer, *To Dwell among Friends,* pp. 247–48.
[45] Ibid., p. 230.

of circumstances."[46] This is doubtless reinforced by the historically recent, and sometimes militant, expression of group values and group demands for rights and respect on the parts of urban subcultural minorities.

We might describe urban relationships as being characteristically "modern" to signal their relatively greater voluntary basis. We find, in these relationships and the social networks formed of them, not a loss of community, but an increase in importance of community of a different sort from those of the family-neighborhood-church-school complexes. Yet these more voluntary communities may be as deeply constitutive of the identities and particulars of the individuals who participate in them as are the communities of place so warmly invoked by communitarians.

Perhaps it is more illuminating to say that communities of choice foster not so much the constitution of subjects as their reconstitution. We seek out such communities as contexts in which to relocate and renegotiate the various constituents of our identities, as Adrienne Rich sought out Jewish community in her college years. While people in a community of choice may not share a common history, their shared values or interests are likely to manifest backgrounds of similar experiences, as, for example, among the members of a lesbian community. The modern self may seek new communities whose norms and relationships stimulate and develop her identity and self understanding more adequately than her unchosen community of origin, her original community of place.

In case it is chosen communities which help us to define ourselves, the project of self-definition would not be arising from communities in which we merely found or discovered our immersion. It is likely that chosen communities—lesbian communities, for example—attract us in the first place because they appeal to features of ourselves which, though perhaps merely found or discovered, were inadequately or ambivalently sustained by our *un*chosen families, neighborhoods, schools, or churches. Thus, unchosen communities are sometimes communities which we can, and should, leave, searching elsewhere for the resources to help us discern who we really are.

A community of choice might be a community of people who share a common oppression. This is particularly critical in those instances in which the shared oppression is not concentrated within certain communities of place—as it might be, for example, in the case of ethnic minorities—but, rather, is focused on people who are distributed throughout social and ethnic groupings and who do not themselves

[46] Ibid.

comprise a traditional community of place. Unlike the communities of ethnic minorities, women are a paradigm example of such a distributed group and do not comprise a traditional community of place. Women's communities are seldom the original, nonvoluntary, found communities of their members.

To be sure, nonvoluntary communities of place are not without value. Most lives contain mixtures of relationships and communities, some given/found/discovered, and some chosen/created. Most people probably are, to some extent, ineradicably constituted by their communities of place, their original families, neighborhoods, schools, churches, or nations. It is noteworthy that dependent children, elderly persons, and all other individuals whose lives and well-being are at great risk, need the support of communities whose other members do not or cannot choose arbitrarily to leave. Recent philosophical reflection on communities and relationships not founded or sustained by choice has brought out the importance of these social networks for the constitution of social life.[47] But these insights should not obscure the additional need for communities of choice to counter oppressive and abusive relational structures in these nonvoluntary communities by providing models of alternative social relationships and standpoints for critical reflection on self and community.

Having attained a critically reflective stance toward one's communities of origin, one's community of place, toward family, neighborhood, church, school, and nation, one has probably at the same time already begun to question and distance oneself from aspects of one's "identity" in those communities, and, therefore, to embark on the path of personal redefinition. From such a perspective, the communities of place uncritically invoked by the communitarians appear deeply problematic. We can concede the influence of those communities without having to endorse it unreflectively. We must develop communitarian thought beyond its complacent regard for the communities in which we once found ourselves, toward (and beyond) an awareness of the crucial importance of "dislocated" communities, communities of choice.

[47] Cf. Baier, "Trust and Antitrust"; Held, "Non-Contractual Society"; and Pateman, *The Problem of Political Obligation.*

[15]

Political Animals and Civic Friendship

John M. Cooper

One of the most fundamental propositions of both Aristotle's ethical and his political theory is his claim that by its *nature* the human being is a πολιτικὸν ζῷον—to use the conventional translation, a "political animal," or, perhaps a bit less misleadingly, an animal that lives in cities. This proposition plays an important role in the argument of *EN A*. It is cited at *A* 7, 1097b 11 as the ground for holding that whatever a human being's happiness or flourishing ultimately turns out to consist in, it must be something that suffices not just for his own individual good but also somehow includes the good of his family, his friends and his fellow-citizens.[1] In the second chapter of the *Politica* Aristotle cites it again (at *A* 2, 1253a 2–3), this time as a conclusion drawn from his quasi-genetic account of the constitution of city-states from the union of households into villages and villages into the larger social units

This essay was originally published in *Aristoteles' "Politik": Akten des XI. Symposium Aristotelicum* (Proceedings of the XIth Symposium Aristotelicum), ed. Gunther Patzig (Friedrichshafen/Bodensee: Vandenhoeck & Ruprecht, 1990):220–41. Reprinted by permission of Vandenhoeck & Ruprecht. A list of abbreviations used for the works of Aristotle in in-text citations appears at the end of the essay.

[1]Construed literally, what Aristotle says is that the final good (τὸ τέλειον ἀγαθόν) for any individual must be *sufficient* both for his own and for his family's, friends' and fellow-citizens' good. I take it, however, that the weaker connection to these others' goods indicated in my summary is what he intends; the datives in γενεῦσι etc. 1097b 9–10 are to be taken only loosely with αὐταρχες (or ἀρχοῦν, understood from αὐταρχες). Significantly, these same key expressions (τέλειον and αὐταρχεϛ) figure prominently in Aristotle's argument for the naturalness of the *polis* in *Pol. A* 2; at 1252b 28–29 he says the *polis* is the κοινωνία τέλειος, . . . πάσης ἔχουσα πέρας τῆς αὐταρκείας. The two applications of these key-words are connected: the normal human being's final, and in itself sufficient, good depends essentially upon his willing and active participation in a common life together with others in a city, i.e., in a fully-realized, complete human community, which is by itself sufficient to support the *whole* of what human life at its best requires. How this can be so is the main subject of this paper.

called πόλεις.[2] Because households and villages, his argument goes, are indisputably natural forms of organized life for human beings— they make it possible for creatures with the natural limitations of human beings to survive relatively easily and comfortably in their natural environment—so also must cities be, since (whatever else cities do) they certainly make more secure and comfortable the means of livelihood already, but less securely, provided by households and villages. Aristotle recognizes that this does not show that everything that civilization in cities brings can be justified as answering to needs of human beings that result from natural and unavoidable facts about their physical make-up and the natural circumstances of human life. But, if true, it does show that the sort of life characteristic of human beings in cities is not governed *simply* by arbitrary and optional conventions originating from nothing more than historical happenstance. To this extent cities can demand the abiding respect of independent-minded persons, as they might not be able to do if they were (and were known to be) merely conventional and not in any way natural habitats for human beings. For, on this view, *some* form of city life is something human beings need if they are to live secure and comfortable lives.

Aristotle goes further, however. In reaching his view that city-life is natural for human beings he says, in a famous phrase (1252b 29–30), that though cities come *into* being for the sake of life (i.e. in order to make possible the secure and comfortable life I just referred to)—τοῦ ζῆν ἕνεκεν—they *are* (they exist) for the sake of "living well," of a good life (τοῦ εὖ ζῆν ἕνεκεν). Whatever exactly Aristotle means by a *good life*, it is clear that he thinks it is not normally available at all, not even in a less secure or less complete form, to human beings except in cities. Later on I will say something further about this good life and about how Aristotle intends to link the need for that sort of life to fundamentals of human nature and the natural circumstance of human life. For the moment I simply note that when at the beginning of the *Politica* Aristotle concludes that the city is a natural thing and that the human being is by its *nature* a political animal (1253a 1–3), he is thinking not just of the ways in which city-life secures the means of livelihood already provided to a human population by household and village life, but of further supposed goods (whichever ones are included in "living well") that (normally) only life in a city makes possible. That the human being is by nature a political animal means that these further goods as well are ones whose status as goods is supposed to be grounded in human nature.

---

[2] I translate πόλις throughout by "city." But it is important to bear in mind that by πόλεις a Greek intended not merely what we call cities, but these taken together with their agricultural hinterland.

Now in these two passages of *EN A* and *Pol. A* the context makes quite clear what Aristotle means by "political," when he says that human beings are political animals. With one significant exception the same holds good with all the other passages in the ethical and political treatises where Aristotle mentions the political nature of human beings (*Pol. A* 2, 1253a 7–18; *Γ* 6, 1278b 15–30; *EE H* 10, 1242a 19–28; *EN Θ* 12, 1162a 16–19; *I* 9, 1169b 16–22). He means that human nature demands that, in general and as a normal thing, human beings live in *cities* of some sort: cities (πόλεις) themselves or citizens (πολῖται) are explicitly mentioned in both of our passages and in all but one of the others,[3] and the etymological connection between πολιτικόν and πόλις is plainly in the forefront of Aristotle's mind in all of them. To be a πολιτικόν animal is, he plainly means, to be one suited to live in πόλεις. So Ross's rather picturesque overtranslation of φύσει πολιτικὸν ὁ ἄν-θρωπος at *EN A* 7, 1097b 11 as "man is born for citizenship" does not seriously distort Aristotle's meaning.

But cities are many-faceted social phenomena; moreover, as Aristotle was acutely aware, they can exhibit a variety of social structures and political organizations. Given this complexity and these variations, one wants to know as exactly as possible what it is in and about cities and life in them that Aristotle thinks human beings because of their natures need. What, so to speak, does Aristotle think is essential to city-life as such, that all cities, perhaps with differing degrees of success, give their human inhabitants and that family-life and village-life necessarily do not suffice for? Nothing in the two passages discussed so far addresses this question, particularly when one takes into account "living well," as well as mere "living," as something the city is for. But there are two further passages (one in the *Politica,* the other, perhaps surprisingly, in the *Historia Animalium*) where Aristotle talks about the political nature of human beings that do offer the beginnings of an answer to our question.

Significantly, in these passages, unlike those from which we began, Aristotle introduces a biological perspective. Speaking from the biological point of view he is able to say something appropriately concrete about human nature and so to suggest what it is about city-life that humans most fundamentally need. The two passages in question are, first, *Pol. A* 2, 1253a 7–18 (the continuation of the passage from *Pol. A* 2 I summarized above). Here Aristotle compares human beings with other (as he calls them) "herding" animals (ἀγελαῖα), such as bees (this is *his* example). Secondly, there is a surprisingly neglected passage near

---

[3]*EN I* 9, 1169b 16–22; but even here ὀθνεῖοι may be foreigners and not just strangers, so that the connection with cities and fellow-citizens will be clear enough by implication.

the beginning of the *Historia Animalium* (*A* 1) which makes it possible to interpret this *Politica* passage correctly.[4] The *Historia Animalium* passage runs as follows.[5]

[4]If this *Historia Animalium* passage is less neglected than it formerly was that is no doubt due to two good recent articles that devote special attention to it: R. G. Mulgan, 'Aristotle's Doctrine that Man is a Political Animal,' in: *Hermes* 102 (1974), 438–45; and W. Kullmann, 'Der Mensch als Politisches Lebewesen bei Aristoteles,' in: *Hermes* 108 (1980), 419–43. I have profited from both these discussions, especially Kullmann's. Richard Bodéüs has drawn my attention to his article 'L'Animal politique et l'animal économique,' published in *Aristotelica: Mélanges offerts à Marcel De Corte (Cahiers de philosophie ancienne* 3, Liège 1985, 65–81) after I had finished this part of my paper.

[5]At *A* 1, 488a 2 there seems no doubt that one must bracket καὶ τῶν μοναδικῶν, with Schneider and Peck (I translate Peck's text). If one keeps the manuscript reading then Aristotle will be saying that some animals that live in large groups *and some animals that live alone* are political, while others in each classification are scattered or dispersed. One might, of course, attempt on Aristotle's behalf to make sense of the idea that some of the μοναδικά animals are nonetheless political. Perhaps some of them live apart most of the year but come together briefly to do some common work; perhaps although the adults of some species live separately from one another the young continue to live with a parent even after they have become able to feed and defend themselves, so that these species satisfy the condition for living "more politically" that Aristotle refers to at *Θ* 1, 589a 1 ff.; and other ways of achieving the same result might also occur to one. Aristotle himself, however, offers no encouragement for such speculation. Aside from this passage (i.e., *A* 1, 488a 1–14) the term μοναδικόν apparently occurs only once in the biological works. That is in *I* 40, 623b 10, where Aristotle introduces a long discussion (chs. 40–43) of bees and other (as he says, 623b 7) insects that make a honeycomb. He distinguishes nine γένη of such creatures, six of them ἀγελαῖα and three μοναδικά. The three μοναδικά are two types of σειρήν (not subsequently, nor apparently elsewhere, further described by him) and the βομβύλιος or bumble-bee. To the bumble-bee he devotes a total of one sentence, in ch. 43 (629a 30ff.): the bumble-bee gives birth under rocks, right on the ground (i.e., without having a hive the way the other wax-producers he has described do), and makes an inferior kind of honey. The bumble-bee is manifestly not by Aristotle's criteria a political animal, and there seems no reason to suspect the σειρῆνες differed in this respect. So far, therefore, as anything Aristotle actually says about any particular ones of the μοναδικά animals goes, we have no basis for thinking that *Aristotle* recognized any μοναδικά political species at all.

It seems better, therefore, to suppose that at *A* 1, 488a 2, having distinguished the ἀγελαῖα (the ones that live in large groups, the "herding" ones) from the μοναδικά (those that live alone, the "solitary" ones), Aristotle in fact went on to subdivide the ἀγελαῖα into political and scattered: what he wrote was καὶ τῶν ἀγελαίων τὰ μὲν πολιτικὰ τὰ δὲ σποραδικά ἐστιν. This is confirmed below, 488a 8–9, where Aristotle gives his criterion for being political and adds, appropriately if the political are intended as a subgroup of the ἀγελαῖα, that not all ἀγελαῖα satisfy it. Moreover, all the examples he gives of πολιτικά animals are also ἀγελαῖα.

But if this is right, what explains the manuscript corruption? Aristotle has just mentioned that some animals of each of the largest classes he recognizes (the footed, the winged and the swimming animals) live together in large groups (τὰ μὲν ἀγελαῖα) while others live alone (τὰ δὲ μοναδικά), while yet others "dualize," i.e., (I take it) are sometimes found in herds and sometimes found living alone. After introducing the subdivision here between the political and the scattered or dispersed animals (τὰ μὲν πολιτικὰ τὰ δὲ σποραδικά ἐστιν) he returns to the first division, giving examples of both winged and swimming animals that live in herds (he omits to give examples of footed animals, such as sheep and cattle, presumably because herding footed animals are well known to everyone), and having done that mentions that human beings dualize (488a 7). In context, coming immediately after these lists of ἀγελαῖα, it seems most natural to take

There are also the following differences among animals, that depend upon their ways of life and their actions. Of both footed, winged and swimming animals, some herd together and others live solitarily, while others 'dualize.' And some of the herding ones are political while others live scattered. Now herding animals are for instance (among the winged animals) the pigeon family, the crane and the swan (no crook-taloned bird

---

this as saying that human beings dualize between living in large groups and living alone, i.e. dualize between belonging alongside these others among the herding animals, and not doing so but instead being solitary in life-style. (The alternative is to understand humans as dualizing between being political and being scattered or dispersed, but the intervention of ἀγελαῖα μὲν οὖν . . . ἁμίαι makes this difficult, if not quite impossible. Kullmann's suggestion, *op. cit.* 432, that humans dualize between being herding and being *scattered* animals can't be right, since it draws one term of the opposition from the pair herding-solitary and the other from the pair political-scattered: it was perhaps awareness of this anomaly that led him to put it forward only with a query.) So Aristotle belatedly gives humankind as an instance of the dualizers mentioned at 488a 1–2, the ones that cannot neatly be classed as either herding or solitary animals. Yet in the next sentence but one he classifies human beings as political animals: for animals to be political is, he says, to have as their function (ἔργον) some single common work, which not all herding animals, but only some—human beings, bees, wasps, ants and cranes—do. Here human beings are counted among the herding animals. And that might seem to contradict their classification as dualizers. In fact, as I will argue below, there is no contradiction. But if one thought there was, it is easy to see how the text must be corrected to get rid of it: at 488a 2 read καὶ τῶν ἀγελαίων καὶ τῶν μοναδικῶν, thus making the division between political and scattered animals cut through the prior division between herding and solitary animals, so that human beings, all of whom Aristotle implies (488a 7) either live in herds or solitarily, are after all included as a group in the larger class (which now becomes the union of the herding and the solitary animals) being divided into the two sub-groups, the political and the scattered. In that case, when human beings are classified as political just below no contradiction results. The human beings, though as a group political in character, can nonetheless dualize between being herding and being solitary animals, because as Aristotle will now have said, some of each of these larger groups are political in character.

But to make this "correction" betrays a misunderstanding of the way Aristotle employs the notion of "dualizing." He can say that an animal dualizes in some respect (as he says the seal does between being a land-animal and a water-animal because though it has a lung and breeds on land it feeds in the sea and spends most of its time there) while nonetheless classifying it as *basically* belonging on one side or the other of the fence in question (as he classifies the seal as basically a water-animal, Z 12, 566b 31). A revealing passage for our purposes is *GA Δ* 4, 772b 1–6, where Aristotle says both that human beings dualize between having a single offspring and having several or many and that it is most natural for them to have one only; multiple births, being rare, are caused by excess fluidity and heat in the parents' bodies. So in our passage of *HA A* 1, human beings dualize between living in large groups and solitarily, but the latter arrangement is exceptional and a departure from the norm, so that basically the human being can be classed, as by implication Aristotle goes on to class it, when at 488a 10 he says it is a political animal, among the ἀγελαῖα.

Our manuscripts thus result from a misunderstanding of the implications of Aristotle's saying at 488a 7 that human beings dualize (between living in herds and living solitarily). That does not in fact count against their being classified as *basically* herding animals, and so does not conflict with the apparent implication of 488a 9–10 that, being political animals, human beings live in herds. Hence there was no good reason to alter the text at 488a 2, as someone apparently did, to make the political animals something other than a sub-group of the herding ones.

is a herder), and among the swimmers many kinds of fish, for instance those called migrants, the tunny, the pelamys and the bonito. The human being 'dualizes.' Political animals are those that have as their function (ἔργον) some single thing that they all do together, and not all the herding animals have that. The human being, the bee, the wasp, the ant and the crane are political animals. Some of these are under leaders and others are rulerless, for instance the crane and the bee family are under leaders while ants and thousands of others are rulerless. And some of both the herding and the solitary animals have a fixed home while others move from place to place. (A 1 487b 33–488a 14)

The gist of the *Politica* passage is that human beings are political animals in a higher degree (μᾶλλον) than e.g., bees or cranes or other similarly herding animals because they possess language.[6] Human beings alone have the capacity to conceive of their own and others' long-term and short-term advantage or good, and so to conceive of justice and injustice as well, since (though Aristotle does not say this explicitly here)[7] in general what is just is what is to the *common* advantage or good of some relevant group. Accordingly, they also have language, which is necessary in order for them to communicate these conceptions to one another: nature gives other animals, which are aware only of what is more or less immediately pleasant and painful, as refined a means of communication as they can use, by giving them the ability to call out to one another by barking, chirping, mooing, etc. As a consequence of having language the kind of work that human beings can do together, in which their being political animals will show itself, is of a much higher order of complexity than that which bees or cranes can manage.

---

[6] I disagree with Bodéüs (*op cit.*), who insists that by calling the human being μᾶλλον πολιτικόν at A 2, 1253a 7–8 Aristotle means that human beings have a better claim to the description πολιτικόν than other animals do (so that by implication he would be counting only the human being and not the bee, etc., as a πολιτικὸν ζῷον at all), and not that human beings are more πολιτικόν, πολιτικόν in a higher degree. On Bodéüs' interpretation Aristotle would be taking away from the non-human "political" animals this description that he had given them in the *Historia Animalium*, in order to avoid the supposed untoward consequences of "masking" under that generic description what is specific to human beings among animals. But the linkage between this *Politica* passage and that from *HA A* 1 is not just close but positive: here again it is with other ἀγελαῖα, including bees, that Aristotle compares human beings, precisely the ones he counted as πολιτικά in *Historia Animalium*—not with all other animals in general, as would suit Bodéüs' interpretation better. So one cannot reasonably avoid taking Aristotle here to assert that some other herding animals are indeed πολιτικά, but that human beings are πολιτικά in a special and distinctive, more complete way. Given the implicit reference to the classification in *HA A* 1, therefore, μᾶλλον πολιτικόν must be comparative. Compare Θ 1, 589a 1. Had Aristotle wanted here to correct what he says in the *Historia Animalium*, he could easily have written: διότι δὲ πολιτικὸν ὁ ἄνθρωπος μόνον τῶν ἀγελαίων ζῴων, δῆλον.

[7] But see EN Θ 9, 1160a 13–14; Pol Γ 6, 1279a 17–19; Γ 12, 1282b 16–18; Γ 13 1283b 35–42.

Because they can conceive of and communicate their thoughts about their own and others' long-term and future good, and the common good which constitutes justice, human beings can form and maintain households and cities, whereas bees can only have hives and cranes only form elaborate and differentiated migration-schemes.[8] Human beings, then, like bees or cranes, are political animals in what is from the point of view of zoology (though not of course etymology) the fundamental sense of having a work or function that the members of a human group all do together; but because in this case the common work involves maintaining the structure and organization of a *city*, they are political in the further, more literal, sense of being naturally suited to life in cities, to the life of citizens.[9]

---

[8]On bees, see *HA E* 21–22 and *I* 40. Aristotle does not repeat his classification of bees as political, and does not make a point of mentioning any single special work that bees undertake in common. (They cooperate in many different tasks in the hive and outside it that Aristotle does mention, e.g., at *I* 40, 627a 20ff.) But presumably it is the hive and the differentiated life in it that he has in mind. For cranes see *HA I* 10 (again no repetition of the classification as political, and no focus on a single activity undertaken by all in common).

Aristotle's distinction towards the end of the *Historia Animalium* passage quoted in the text between political animals that are "under leaders" and those that are "rulerless" makes it clear that in speaking of "some single thing" the members of a species do together he does not mean something *all* the members of a species cooperate together in doing. He means rather that the political species are naturally found in groups that are defined by the fact that all the members of each group (those, say, which are all under a given "leader") cooperate together in such an activity.

[9]*HA Θ* 1, 588b 30–589a 4 (which should be read together with *GA Γ* 2, 753a 7–17) links the "political" character of a species with its members' intelligence (φρόνησις), on the one hand, and, on the other hand, their tendency to live with and see to the upbringing of their offspring. The *De Generatione Animalium* passage, while not referring explicitly to any kind of animal as political in nature, does say that the more intelligent animals, which also have better memories, and which concern themselves for a longer period with their offspring's upbringing, come to have συνήθεια καὶ φιλία ("intimacy and attachment," tr. Peck) for them even when fully grown. The suggestion is that greater intelligence in animals naturally shows itself in a more intensive and prolonged relationship between parents (or at least mothers) and offspring; this in turn generates ties of affection and friendship (in effect, what in the human case Aristotle calls family friendship, συγγενικὴ φιλία, *EN Θ* 12, 1161 b 16ff.); and "political" ties, both for human beings and for other animals are in some way natural extensions of these family ties. (On the connection between family friendship and political friendship, see n. 15)

Although in these passages he makes no mention of a single common work that members of political species, as such, engage in, I assume Aristotle is presupposing, as he says explicitly in *HA A* 1, that such a common work is the essential mark of a political species. Certainly the emphasis on intelligence fits in very well with this assumption, since the cooperation and differentiation of function involved in such a single work evidently requires a relatively high degree of intelligence. And while rearing broods of offspring to maturity need not involve any work engaged in within a community wider than an immediate family, Aristotle's point seems to be that that kind of cooperative concern is the natural training ground for some more extensive cooperation in which an animal's political nature is more properly exhibited. (This explains why in both passages he seems to take it for granted that the more intelligent, more family-oriented species are all of

There is much of interest in these passages. First of all, as just noted, and surprisingly, when in the *Historia Animalium* Aristotle classifies the human being together with the bee and the crane, etc., as political animals he does not mean, despite the literal meaning of the word, that all these kinds of animals live in cities (πόλεις). There is no reference anywhere in the passage to cities or to citizenship, as there is in all the other passages from the *Politica* and *Ethica* where the political nature of human beings is alluded to. On the contrary, as he himself explains, the criterion being invoked is whether or not an animal species (only herding animals are in question, naturally) is such that it has an essential work that its members all engage in together (with the differentiation of function that goes along with that). If it does, it counts as "political," if not not, and in that case it gets classified as "scattered." (So by this classification oxen, sheep and cattle are not political but scattered animals: obviously, being scattered is not a matter of how close to or far apart animals of a species typically stand from one another as they go about their daily business of feeding and so on, but whether what they spend their time doing is something that they have to be together to do, because it is something they do in common, as a community.)

So the fundamental point about the nature of human beings that grounds the biological classification is that humans have the capacity for, and are regularly found, taking part in cooperative activities involving differentiation of function. This important point is something that the passages of the ethical treatises and the *Politica* that I first cited, where the political nature of human beings is linked simply to their fitness for life in cities, do not bring clearly to light. What we learn from the *Historia Animalium* theory and its extension in *Pol. A* 2, 1253a 7–18 is that active participation in a city's life is that single function (ἔργον) which all the human beings belonging to that city perform together, and in the performance of which their character as political animals consists. This counts as a *single* function because, as Aristotle's

---

them herding animals, and not solitary ones: only such could be political in any active sense.)

It is true that Aristotle says at *GA Γ* 2, 753a 14–15 that birds are less family-oriented than "human beings and certain quadrupeds," and that they don't develop "intimacy and attachment" toward their offspring when grown up. Birds are, accordingly, "less political"—because, I take it, the common work they nonetheless do engage in together, not being grounded in a communal family work, is less extensive. There is no reason to interpret Aristotle in either the *HA Θ* 1, or the *GA Γ* 2 passage as implying that animals like the crane, which engage in a common work but do not show the extended family concern of such *more* political animals as human beings are not political at all. (In thinking about the implications of these passages about animal intelligence for Aristotle's classification of some animals as political in nature I have profitted from discussions with Jean-Louis Labarrière and from reading his unpublished paper on 'La phronesis animale.')

account of the structure and constitution of a city makes clear, a city is a complex entity having as its ultimate elements not individual human beings as such, but human beings *in* families, households, villages, and other associations, κοινωνίαι: the part of a person's active life that is carried out as a family-member or as a farmer in a particular locality, say, is seen as part of the large complex of activities making up the life of the city of which this family and this locality are parts.[10] Once one brings the biological perspective provided by our *Historia Animalium* passage to bear on the interpretation of the proposition that human beings are political animals, one can see that the fundamental aspect of city life that in Aristotle's eyes marks it as natural for human beings is its involving the cooperative working together of all those who take part in it in an interlocking, differentiated, mutually supporting, single set of activities. What's essential to cities, however they may vary in other respects, is that they involve their citizens in this kind of common activity. In effect, it is by doing that that cities can provide a more secure and comfortable life than households and villages not integrated into a city can do (as we saw earlier Aristotle claims), and we may begin to anticipate that whatever exactly Aristotle means by saying that cities exist for the sake of a good life, and not just for the sake of life, this will turn out to be a life led in some more or less specific version of this kind of cooperative activity.

So far I have left Aristotle's notion of the political activity as an essentially cooperative one rather abstract. In order to begin to flesh it out somewhat, it will be useful to turn to Aristotle's distinction (drawn first in *Pol. Γ* 6, 1279a 17–21) between the "correct" (ὀρθαί) constitutions and the "erroneous" (ἡμαρτημέναι) ones or deviation-forms (παρεκβάσεις). Since Aristotle says the deviation-forms are contrary to nature (Γ 17, 1287b 41), we can examine life in the correct kinds of city to discover what he expects city life to be like if things do go according to nature. That should show us what he includes among the cooperative activities in which the human being's political nature shows itself.

Aristotle's criterion for a "correct" constitution is deceptively simple. A "correct" constitution is one in which the government aims at the common advantage (τὸ κοινῇ συμφέρον, Γ 6, 1279a 17; τὸ κοινόν συμφέρον, Γ 7, 1279a 28–29); in the deviation-forms the government aims instead at the advantage of the office-holders themselves (and their families) as a group. But to whom is the advantage sought in correct constitutions common, and in what sense is it common?

To the first question the natural answer would seem to be: common

[10]Cf. Γ 9, 1280b 40–41: πόλις δὲ ἡ γενῶν καὶ κωμῶν κοινωνία ζωῆς τελείας καὶ αὐτάρκους.

to all the citizens, i.e. all the free, native-born residents. In fact, I think this is what Aristotle does intend: it is at least suggested by Γ 13, 1283b 40–41, where Aristotle speaks of "correct" rules as being "for the advantage of the whole city and for the common advantage of the citizens." But if we put Aristotle's view in this way we must recognize that we are using the word "citizen" in a way that departs from his own explicit theory in Γ 1–2 of who the citizens of a city are. According to this theory, the citizens of a city are just those who have the right to take part in the judicial and/or the deliberative functions.[11] But if we were to use the term "citizen" in Aristotle's official, narrow sense in saying that correct forms of political organization aim at the citizens' common advantage, the result would be that certain correct forms would collapse into their corresponding deviation-forms. Thus, under the rule of a king, one of the types of constitution Aristotle counts as "correct," the monarch reserves to himself and his personal appointees both the deliberative and the judicial function—so that, if the aim of a king was the common advantage of what Aristotle *officially* counts as citizens, there would in fact be no distinction between rule by a king and a tyranny, its deviation-form. For in such a monarchy the unique ruler would also be the sole citizen, and so he would rule simultaneously in the sole interest of himself (as ruler) and in that of the citizen body (himself as citizen). Hence such a monarchy would also be a tyranny; rule by the ruler solely in his personal interest. Likewise there would be no distinction between aristocracy and oligarchy, either. (Aristotle's criterion would still separate "polity" from democracy.) So the citizens, whose common advantage is consulted in the correct constitutions, must include the office-holders, jurymen and assembly-members, but at least in aristocracy and monarchy others besides. How is this larger class of citizens to be determined? Aristotle speaks in this context (at Γ 7, 1279a 35–36) of those whose common possession and common activity the city is (οἱ κοινωνοῦντες αὐτῆς) as the ones whose advantage the correct governments seek, and by implication he describes a city when correctly constituted as an association in common of its *free* inhabitants (κοινωνία τῶν ἐλευθέρων, Γ 6, 1279a 21). This suggests that

[11]As Newman notes, *The Politics of Aristotle*, vol. I, Oxford 1887, 229 (and cf. 324 and 569–70), Aristotle himself occasionally uses the word πολίτης more widely than his official account permits. Newman refers to *H* 13, 1332a 32–35, and he might have added Γ 7, 1279a 31–32 and Γ 14, 1285a 25–29. These passages make it clear enough that Aristotle occasionally employs the word πολίτης in very much the same broad sense that, as I argue in what follows, he needs in order to make clear what he means by aiming "at the common advantage of the citizens." I would maintain, therefore, that even though the interpretation I offer of what this means employs the word "citizen" in a sense different from Aristotle's official one, it is a sense that Aristotle himself not only needs but actually employs on occasion, as well.

the citizens in the broad sense include all the free-born native residents, with the presumed exclusion of the non-slave laborers, both urban and agricultural (cf. Γ 5, 1278a 6–13). These it is, whether the form of government is a kingdom, an aristocracy or the government in which all the (male) free-born natives participate that Aristotle calls a "polity," whose common advantage is sought in correctly organized cities.

But now we must ask, in what sense is the advantage sought an advantage that belongs to the citizens (i.e., the free-born native residents) *in common?* One way in which this might be conceived is on the model of a joint-stock company. If I own 10% of a company's stock and you own 20%, then anything that improves the competitiveness of the company or increases its earnings or profits, and so on, is for our common advantage. Here the common advantage can be broken down into the sum of the individual advantages of each of us, and these individual advantages are themselves definable and measurable independently of reference to our jointly-owned company and its advantage. If, for example, the company's profits increase a certain amount because of some change in tax rate or tax policy, and my dividend goes from $100 to $200 and yours from $200 to $400, then this act of the government has been to my and your advantage by those amounts, and this advantage, being measurable in such financial terms, is definable without reference to the company and its advantage. The company's advantage is only the causal condition of my and your separate advantages. In a case like this if you and I combine to work for our common advantage we can, and presumably will, each be working for his own single advantage, aiming at this by means of the advantage of the company, which includes our separate advantages as constituent parts. Likewise, if some third party should take an interest in the success of our company this person would be taking an interest in our and the other stockholders' common advantage in this purely additive sense.

In an interesting chapter of *Politica* book Γ Aristotle clearly and explicitly rejects this commercial model for the kind of community a city constitutes, and implies a different account of what the common advantage of its participants consists in. Partisans of an oligarchic constitution, he says (Γ 9, 1280a 25–31), think that a city is an association (or common enterprise—$\varkappa o\iota\nu\omega\nu\iota\alpha$) that came into and continues in existence merely for the sake of possessions ($\varkappa\tau\eta\mu\alpha\tau\alpha$), i.e., for the sake of preserving, exchanging and increasing possessions for their economic value. And their standard of political justice, which specifies unequal shares in political power, corresponding to the unequal quantity of possessions brought into the common stock by the participating citizens, would be perfectly reasonable if their conception of what a

city essentially is were correct. However, on the oligarchic conception a
constitution is like a commercial treaty between two separate countries,
establishing an agreement as to how trade and other business is to be
conducted between their respective citizens, with guarantees for the
citizens of each against various forms of cheating by the citizens of the
other. And it is plain, Aristotle says, that the kind of common enterprise a city is is badly misrepresented by any such conception of a civic
constitution. For, surely, a single city with commercial relations carried
on inside it is quite a different thing from two separate cities bound by
commercial treaties and carrying on a similarly active and varied trade
with one another. One difference Aristotle mentions is important but
relatively superficial—the absence in the two-city case of a single, common system of courts and magistracies governing the commercial relations in question (1280a 40–b 1). But a second difference goes deeper:
the people in the two cities carrying on mutual trade and commerce
"do not concern themselves about what kind of persons the ones in the
other city ought to be, nor are they concerned that no one covered by
the agreements *be* unjust (or be vicious in any way at all). They are only
concerned that they *do* nothing unjust to one another" (1280b 1–5). By
contrast, within a single city, people do have this further concern; of
course they want not to be cheated or otherwise treated unjustly, in
business or anywhere else, but they also care what kind of people their
fellow-citizens are. They want them to be decent, fair-minded, respectable, moral people (anyhow, by their own lights).

One should note carefully just how strong a claim Aristotle is making
here. He says those in one city who exercise their rights under treaties
for mutual commerce have no general concern about the moral characters of those in another city with whom they do business: they do not
concern themselves that "no one covered by the agreements *be* unjust
(or be vicious in any way at all)." And he implies that civic relations
among citizens of a single city, since they are not merely commercial,
do involve just these concerns. That is, he holds that in cities we find a
general concern on the part of those living under the constitution of a
city and participating in its civic life for the moral characters of all
those similarly engaged—a concern that *no one* taking part in civic life
be unjust or indeed vicious in any way. This is a concern of each citizen
for each other citizen, whether or not they know each other personally,
and indeed whether or not they have had any direct and personal
dealings with one another whatsoever. The open-ended scope here
envisaged for this mutual concern of fellow-citizens for one another's
good character is, as we shall see more fully below, a crucially important
feature of common life in a city as Aristotle conceives it.

But is it really true that fellow-citizens do have such a concern for one another's good character? No doubt they would in any of the types of state Aristotle himself most favors, since such cities would be governed under a constitution, fully accepted by the citizens themselves, taking as its first aim to make the citizens good.[12] But would they, for example, under the very oligarchic constitution that Aristotle in this passage is trying to show is misguided? Why think that where the constitution was just an elaborate commercial treaty, eschewing all reference to people's characters and any concern for what they are *like* personally, people would differ in this aspect from the citizens of two distinct cities linked by extensive trade relations? On reflection, it turns out to be very plausible that they would, and that Aristotle is right to make this fact a central objection against the oligarchic and in general commercial view of the kind of community a city is.

Even in twentieth-century liberal states, some of which (anyhow in their official ideology) fit the commercial conception rather well, Aristotle's observation seems to hold good (and in Greek city-states the features that make it do so were even more pronounced). There seems no denying that ordinary Americans, for example, are characteristically quite a bit concerned about the moral standards of people prominent in government, business and industry, and concerned in quite a different way from the concern they presumably also feel about the morality of people in similar positions in foreign countries, even ones with which the United States has extensive trading and business relationships. The typical American when she hears, say, about the attitudes Wall-Street brokers and commercial bankers have apparently quite routinely been holding about privileged information that comes their way in their professional work, or about sleaziness in government circles, feels injured in ways she certainly does not feel in hearing similar things said about people in high places abroad. Independently of any way one may expect to suffer financial losses or other direct injuries to one's interests from these people's behavior, one feels injured and diminished simply by there being such people in positions like that. Something is wrong with *us*, one feels, that among us that sort of person is found in that sort of place. That the same and worse happens in some other country may be reason to introduce special safeguards to protect our financial interests there, or, out of sympathy for the people of that country, to express our moral condemnation of

---

[12]And it is noteworthy (see Newman *ad loc*) that Aristotle goes on only to say that (not people in general, but only) those who care about εὐνομία do think about how to make people politically good, and that *cities that deserve the name* have to concern themselves about virtue (Γ 9, 1280b 5–12). He does not go on to say explicitly, what 1280b 1–5 implies, that the citizens in general, under whatever constitution, do (normally) concern themselves about what their fellow-citizens are like as persons.

that behavior, or even to join organizations directed toward removing those evils by concerted international financial pressure, etc. But it's nothing to us *personally*. Apart from a legitimate general concern we may feel about immorality wherever it occurs, it's nothing to us *Americans* what, say, French or German or Italian businessmen are like: that's the exclusive concern of the French or the Germans or the Italians, in the sense that *they* are the ones personally injured and diminished by it.

These effects of national feeling are felt more widely, too. Americans take pride in the self-discipline and hard work of the American working force, the inventiveness, entrepreneurial spirit, and skill of American industrialists, the imaginativeness and vigor of American writers, and so on.[13] (That these characteristics may largely be mythical does not matter for the point I am making.) This is pride not just in accomplishments, but even more in the qualities of mind and character that (are presumed to have) made them possible. Furthermore, it seems that, typically, citizens even of a modern mass democracy feel tied to one another in such a way and to such an extent that they can and do take an interest in what their fellow-citizens quite generally are like as persons; they want to think of them as good, upstanding people, and definitely do not want them to be small-minded, self-absorbed, sleazy. What their fellow-citizens are like matters to them personally, it seems, in ways that the personal qualities of the citizens of a foreign country do not, because they feel some connection to, some involvement with— almost some responsibility for—the former that they do not have for the latter, and this makes them feel that what their fellow-citizens are like, for better or for worse, somehow reflects on themselves.[14]

In this chapter of *Pol. Γ*, then, Aristotle decisively rejects the commercial model for the kind of community a city is. What kind of community is a city, then, if it is not to be conceived on the commercial model? Aristotle indicates his own view a little later in the same chapter, when he goes on (*Γ* 9, 1280b 23–1281a 2) to explain the nature and source of the special bond between fellow-citizens that grounds their concern for one another's personal qualities. Aristotle says quite explic-

---

[13]Leaving aside, of course, those who may for one reason or another feel excluded from full participation in American life, or, again, those who may think the potential good effects of these qualities are seriously compromised by injustices in the social and economic setting in which they operate, or by other contextual factors. On the importance of considerations of justice in this connection, see below.

[14]Aristotle's point, then, against oligarchic constitutions is that the official view taken in oligarchic cities of the nature of the civic bond—that it is, or is essentially like, a contract or treaty or other agreement voluntarily entered into for mutual gain— misrepresents the *actual* nature of the citizenly ties that the citizens of the oligarchic city, like all other cities, evince. The constitutions that Aristotle ranks more highly simply take explicit notice of this fact about all cities, the oligarchic ones among the others, and give it the weight in the constitution itself that it deserves to have.

itly that it is friendship (φιλία, 1280b 38) that does this. Friendship, he says, being the deliberate decision to share one's life with another (ἡ γὰρ τοῦ συζῆν προαίρεσις φιλία, 1280b 38–39), is responsible for such practices in cities as "connections by marriage, brotherhoods, religious festivals, and the pursuits in which people share their lives" (1280b 36–38). And these, in turn, he evidently means to say, provide the specific sort of connectedness that, in Greek cities, grounds the interest in and concern by each citizen for the qualities of mind and character of his fellow-citizens generally that he has been insisting distinguishes citizenly ties from those provided by contractual agreements for mutual economic advantage.[15] For his purpose in mentioning these more limited contexts for common activity and the role they play in the city is to explain how it comes about that cities differ from commercial partnerships in the way he said earlier in the chapter that they do. Since that involved a concern of each citizen for each other citizen's character, he must mean that these less extensive types of common undertaking give rise to and reinforce the common activity of civic life itself, and the friendship that is specific to that life. In general, even in a Greek city-state, no citizen is bound to each of his fellow-citizens through mar-

---

[15]One should recall here Aristotle's criticisms (*Pol. B* 2–4) of the plan proposed in Plato's *Respublica* (V 457 C–464 B) for unifying the ideal city by making each of the rulers speak, think and feel about each other ruler in the way in which members of a close-knit, harmonious family speak, think and feel about one another. In effect, Socrates in the *Respublica* proposes doing away with separate families and separate family ties (among the rulers), replacing them with ties of exactly the same kind and strength linking each ruler to each other. He thinks of the civic friendship needed in order to unify and stabilize the city as impossible so long as loyalty to the city can come into conflict with loyalty to one's family. The only effective civic friendship, he thinks, will be one resulting from the extension to the whole ruling group of just those family ties which in other, historical, cities serve to compromise it. This kind of all-inclusive family relationship is impossible in principle, Aristotle thinks (*Pol. B* 4, 1262a 31)—when you call all of the children of a certain age "my son" or "my daughter," knowing that a large group of your fellow-rulers do the same, you don't and can't think and feel about them in the ways a true parent does. The misguided attempt to achieve this *both* does away with true family ties *and* makes impossible true civic friendship. All you get is a watered-down family friendship. This means that people will neither concern themselves about selected others as their sons, daughters, husbands, cousins, nor about their fellow-citizens in general. Once the family is gone, the use of the words that originally connoted family-relationships to refer instead to fellow-citizens generally, will not carry with it the thoughts and feelings that bind family members to one another (*B* 4, 1262b 15–24), and nothing will have been done to encourage the different thoughts and feelings appropriate to fellow-citizens. On Aristotle's view civic friendship must rest upon an understanding of the *special* ways that fellow-citizens are related to one another in a common work, and these do not necessarily compete with, but supplement, the links between family-members. Civic friendship, Aristotle insists, is a specific type of friendship, distinct (e.g.) from family friendship; furthermore, it does not exist at all except where there also exist families, brotherhoods, etc., with their own specific forms of friendship, to which it is added as a natural completion: see *EN Θ* 9, 1160a 9–10; 1160a 21–30; *EE H* 9, 1241b 24–26.

riage, or membership of some brotherhood, or one or another other
personal relationship of friendship. Hence whatever special concern
the members of these associations may come to have for one another's
characters will obviously be inadequate for Aristotle's purpose here.
So, although Aristotle does not say it here explicitly, the kind of friendship he has in mind is what in the *Ethica Eudemia* he discusses at some
length under the name "civic friendship," ἡ πολιτικὴ φιλία, and refers
to as such four times in the *Ethica Nicomachea*.[16] According to Aristotle,
then, a city is a kind of community that depends upon the friendly
interest that the citizens take in one another's qualities of mind and
character, as well, of course, as upon their common economic interests.
In such a community the way or ways in which the government seeks to
promote the citizens' good as a *common* good will depend upon the
specific character of the friendship that forms the political bond within
it, and the ways in which "civic friends" have and do things in common.

[16]Oddly, this expression, or a close relative, seems to occur at most only once in the
Politica. (The φιλία τῇ πολιτείᾳ referred to at *E* 9, 1309b 9 (cf. 1309a 34) and *B* 8, 1268a
24 is a different thing.) This is at *Δ* 11, 1295b 23–24, where the run of the argument
seems to go best if πολιτικῆς is taken with both φιλίας and κοινωνίας. Aristotle's point is
that it is important to avoid the enmity that exists when a contemptuous rich class rule
over an envious mass of poor people. Aristotle is clearly conceiving of this contempt and
envy as being felt by the individual rich and poor persons for the members of the other
group *en masse:* he has in mind a class phenomenon. So, therefore, the φιλία that
Aristotle says such feelings preclude, but implies would be achievable if the middle class
had power (see 1295b 29–32), can only be πολιτικὴ φιλία—a friendship felt by each
citizen for the other citizens *en masse*, and the only kind of friendship Aristotle recognizes
that can be felt quasi-anonymously for a whole group of people. Newman (*ad loc*) says,
but without explanation, that "πολιτικῆς goes only with κοινωνίας, not with φιλίας."
That, however, is quite unsatisfactory: it is true enough that people who respectively
have contempt and envy for one another are not good candidates for friendship of
whatever sort, but Aristotle is not talking about contempt and envy in general, but about
these feelings as experienced by whole classes for one another, and what that undermines is not friendship in general but civic friendship in particular. So it does seem
greatly preferable to take πολιτικῆς here with φιλίας as well as with κοινωνίας.
    "Civic friendship" is discussed at length in *EE H* 9–10 (see also *H* 7, 1241a 32), where
it is classified as a special form of "advantage friendship," friendship κατὰ τὸ χρήσιμον
(*H* 10, 1242b 22–23; 1243b 4). The references in *EN* are at *Θ* 12, 1161b 13; *I* 1, 1163b
34; *I* 6, 1167b 2 and *I* 10, 1171a 17. *I* 6, 1167b 2–4 makes it clear that in the *EN* too
Aristotle classifies πολιτικὴ φιλία as an advantage friendship, although he nowhere does
so explicitly. The same thing is implied by *Θ* 9, where in discussing civic friendship,
though not under that name, he emphasizes that the *civic* community, the kind of
community to which this kind of friendship is proper, is formed and survives for the sake
of the common advantage of those belonging to it. Aristotle's very lengthy discussions of
civic friendship in *EN Θ* 9–12 and *EE H* 9–10 show clearly that he regarded this kind of
friendship, though it is only a form of advantage friendship, as a very important one; he
by no means treats it as a minor variation of no fundamental, independent interest. The
prominence of civic friendship in the *Ethica Nicomachea* and the importance Aristotle
attributes to it there is specially significant, since it seems clear that *EN Θ* 9–12 is
intended as summarizing central aspects of the political theory developed in the *Politica.*
Accordingly, we can claim Aristotle's own testimony that in the *Politica*, too, civic friendship plays a crucial, though as I have noted a somewhat inexplicit, role.

In order to see what this is, we must first be clear about the fact that, although Aristotle in the two *Ethics* treats civic friendship as a form of advantage-friendship, a friendship based upon the experience or expectation of mutual benefit from the activities in which it is expressed, civic friendship, like other forms of advantage-friendship, is really a *friendship*. Aristotle emphasizes in *Pol. Γ* 9 that whereas mere mutual commerce does not involve any interest in one another as persons, any concern for what kind of people these are that one is dealing with, in civic friendship, even though it is based upon the expectation of mutual benefit just as much as such commercial relationships are, this additional interest is present. That is easy enough to understand if, like all relationships deserving the name "friendship", civic friendship involves mutual good will, trust and well-wishing, and the mutual interest that fellow-citizens have in one another's characters is part of that good will and well-wishing. Thus what Aristotle says in *Pol. Γ* 9 confirms what I have argued elsewhere about civic friendship in the *Ethica Nicomachea:*[17] where civic friendship characterizes a population there exists, as a recognized and accepted norm, a certain measure of mutual goodwill, and also mutual trust, among the people making up the population. Each expects his fellow-citizens in their dealings with him (political, economic, and social) to be motivated not merely by self-interest (or other private particular interests) but also by concern for his good for his own sake (for his qualities of mind and character, as Aristotle emphasizes in *Pol. Γ* 9, but also for other elements in his good). And in return each is ready to be so motivated in his dealings with them. This means that in a city animated by civic friendship each citizen has a certain measure of interest in and concern for the well-being of each other citizen just because the other *is* a fellow-citizen. Civic friendship makes fellow-citizens' well-being matter to one another, simply as such.[18]

[17]See J. M. Cooper, 'Aristotle on the Forms of Friendship,' in *Review of Metaphysics* 30 (1977), 619–48, especially 642–48 on civic friendship.

[18]Civic friendship is therefore a very special kind of friendship, different in important ways from personal friendships (whether of pleasure or advantage, or ones based on character). At *EE H* 9, 1241b 13–17, Aristotle introduces his account of civic friendship by speaking explicitly of kinds (εἴδη) of φιλία, differing among themselves in accordance with the differences in the κοινωνία (common enterprises) regulating the specific activities of which the φιλία in question consists: πολιτικὴ φιλία is one of these εἴδη, the one that regulates precisely those activities of which the πολιτικὴ κοινωνία itself consists, making them be carried out in the spirit of friendship appropriate to them. In the *Ethica Nicomachea* Aristotle does not use the terminology of εἴδη φιλίας in this connection, but his doctrine is exactly the same: see Θ 9, 1159b 26–31. There is no cause for surprise that this friendship, unlike the personal friendships from which Aristotle naturally begins his consideration of φιλία, does not require any degree of intimacy nor even any personal knowledge of one another on the part of the "friends." Since the κοινωνία in question does not require intimacy and personal knowledge, neither, obviously, could

Here, and not coincidentally, the comparison with a family is instructive. In a family (perhaps a somewhat idealized one—but this idealiza-
tion is obviously important to Aristotle), the good fortune or success or
good character of one member is *experienced* by the others as somehow
part of their good as well, and in fact we do think it constitutes a
contribution to the good of the other family-members. Think of how
parents respond to their children's successes, and of how we refer to
the character of the children's lives when we intend to be saying how
things are for the parents. The members of my family are *my* people,
and any good enjoyed by any of them is shared in also by me, because
as members of a family what affects them affects the family, and I too
am a member of that. Civic friendship is just an extension to a whole
city of the kinds of psychological bonds that tie together a family and
make possible this immediate participation by each family-member in
the good of the others. Civic friendship makes the citizens in some
important respects like a large extended family (though they are also,
obviously, quite unlike a family in other respects).

Plainly, the common advantage of a civic community conceived as
Aristotle conceives it, like that of a family, does not consist wholly
(though of course it might well consist partly) of something that can be
broken down into a sum of separate advantages belonging individually
to the citizens one by one. To the extent that each citizen participates in
the good of the others, a good that may belong in the first instance to a
single individual (whether a material possession or a good quality of
mind or character) becomes a communal good shared in by all who are

---

the φιλία specific to it. One should bear in mind that in describing in very general terms
the conditions that hold good for friendships, of whatever type, in Θ 2 Aristotle says only
(1155b 34–1156a 5) that friends must both wish their friends well for the friends' own
sake, and know this fact about one another—not that they must be intimate with one
another, or even know each other in person. Intimacy and personal knowledge are not
the only ways of knowing (or anyhow reasonably coming to believe) that such mutual
good will exists, and they are not even the normal way such mutual good will gets
communicated in every context where it exists. In the political context, knowledge of the
nature of the constitution, of the general level of support for it among the different
elements of the population, and of what's generally expected of people in that society is
the normal way of knowing about these things, and it is sufficient, sometimes, to establish
a reasonable presumption of good will on the part of one's fellow-citizens generally.

Taken together, these considerations show, I think, that Julia Annas was wrong in
'Plato and Aristotle on Friendship and Altruism,' in *Mind* 86 (1977), 532–54 to think that
in seeking to accommodate such "objective" kinds of φιλία as civic friendship, into a
common framework with the personal ones Aristotle grossly failed to square his views on
the objective with his account of the personal friendships. Annas' bias in favor of the
personal friendships (understandable given *our* concept of friendship) prevents her
from seeing that Aristotle from the outset of his discussion holds together in his mind—
as the Greek concept of φιλία itself did—the phenomena of both the personal and the
objective types of φιλία, and sets out to give a comprehensive, systematic account of
them all.

members in good standing of the community. Insofar as part of the common good of the citizens is thus a set of communal goods, it is not divisible into separate shares at all, but remains indissolubly an "advantage" of the common enterprise itself in which the members of the community are associated. The citizens share equally in the whole of this part of their common good, just because they are associated in the civic enterprise and care about it.

At the beginning of *EN Θ* Aristotle says, obviously approvingly, that "friendship seems to hold cities together, and lawgivers seem to be more concerned about it than about justice. For . . . when people are friends they have no need of justice, but those who are just [to one another] need friendship in addition, and the strictest form of justice is found in friendship" (*Θ* 1, 1155a 22–28). Indeed, Aristotle says that every community (and he explicitly includes here the family as well as the city) carries with it both a specific kind of friendship and a specific set of standards of justice (*Θ* 9, 1159b 26–27; 1159b 35–1160a 3). But justice plays a distinctive role in the constitution of civic friendship that so far as I can see it does not play in families.[19] Even if the specific standards of justice appropriate to a family are seriously violated in various ways—if, say, the children are cold and neglectful of the parents, perhaps because earlier on the parents themselves were arbitrary, dictatorial and selfish—the bonds which tie family members together and make each participate in the good of the others are not entirely destroyed. The parents, however neglected and wronged they may feel and be, are nonetheless affected for better or worse by the successes and good fortune and the good characters of the children (and vice versa). Injustice seems not, of itself, to destroy the relationship (the "friendship") and so it does not do away with the participation by each in the others' good. But this is not so for civic friendship.

Consider, for example, an aristocracy, one conceived according to Aristotle's lights as governed by the morally best people among the citizens. If the virtue of the rulers and their opportunity to exercise it in those most favorable of conditions for the exercise of virtue, the public affairs of a city, is bought at the price of limiting the moral development of the other citizens, or denying them appropriate opportunities to give effective exercise to good moral qualities they possess, then this would not only be an injustice (one recognized even by the aristocratic conception of justice officially countenanced under

---

[19]I do not say that Aristotle was aware of this difference. At *Θ* 11, 1161a 30–32 he takes note of the fact that in the deviant forms of constitution there is necessarily less civic friendship between rulers and ruled, because of the injustice of the constitutions. Tyranny, being the most unjust constitution, is also the least characterized by civic friendship.

that form of constitution),[20] it would for that very reason also destroy the friendship existing among the citizens. If those excluded from active participation in the political life of the city recognized their exclusion as an injustice, they would see themselves as being exploited by the rulers for the rulers' own benefit. Their trust would thus have been violated, and a natural consequence of an uncorrected violation of trust is its destruction. Since civic friendship consists in part of the mutual trust of the citizens that they are all effectively concerned for one another's good, the destruction of this trust destroys the friendship too.

Civic friendship, then, requires that those bound together by it (seem to one another to) be behaving justly in their mutual relations (anyhow basically so). Being clear about the role of justice in making civic friendship possible is especially important because it helps one to understand just what it means to say a city is a community (a κοινωνία) and what would be involved in the "common advantage" of the citizens who make up such a community. In a city animated by civic friendship the citizens are engaged in a common enterprise, an enterprise aimed at a common good, in two different senses. First of all, each regards the others as wishing for and implementing through their actions his individual good (as he also intends in his actions their individual good), as and to the extent justice requires. The good in question certainly includes material interests, but is not limited to that: moral and intellectual good, regarded as individual accomplishments, are included as well. So the common good of the community will consist first of the ways in which, by the organization of civic life, the individuals making it up each severally benefit from it, that is, benefit in ways that are assignable to them each separately *as* individuals. In an Aristotelian aristocracy, for example, the well-born "better" people benefit by the education they receive that helps them to develop good moral and intellectual qualities, and by the opportunity they later enjoy to exercise these qualities in the direction of the community's affairs. The common people benefit, too, because such a group of aristocrats are actively concerned for the good of their fellow-citizens, as justice demands, and make a principle of seeing to the economic well-being of their less well-endowed fellow-citizens and to such moral and intellectual development as they are capable of, so far as providing for that does not unfairly limit the full development of the excellences of the better-endowed.

---

[20]See *Pol. Γ* 17, 1287b 37–39 for a clear recognition by Aristotle of the ways in which conceptions of justice vary with political constitutions. See also *EN Θ* 11, where Aristotle again marks off the conceptions of justice at work in different kinds of constitution, but this time links these differences to differences in the bases of the respective civic friendships.

To this extent, the common advantage of a city is the sum of the advantages of its citizens, separately considered. But where, as in this kind of aristocracy (but also in monarchies and under the more popular governments Aristotle calls "polities"), civic life involves civic friendship, it includes more than this. For where each aims in her cooperative activity at the good of the others, and not just at her own good, the good attained in the first instance by the others becomes, and is conceived of by herself as being, also a part of her own good. In this way the aristocrat participates in the good that comes to the ordinary citizens in their common life, because that is a conscious objective of many of those morally fine activities in which his principal citizenly function is carried out, and of course the attainment of one's conscious objectives (if, anyhow, one is right, as ex hypothesi this man is, to adopt them in the first place) makes a direct contribution to one's own good. And the ordinary citizen likewise participates in the moral and intellectual goods achieved directly by the aristocrat. That is because these are good things achieved in the course of a common life the organizing principles of which he endorses and to which he willingly contributes his part. These are, so to speak, *his* aristocrats, so that their intrinsically good qualities and intrinsically good activities are part of the enlarged good that he comes to experience by not just living in this city but being a willing, active part of it.

This account of the common good or common advantage aimed at by the government of a "correctly" constituted city brings into view something important that is easily missed. When Aristotle says that cities exist for the sake of τὸ εὖ ζῆν (living well)—not just for living, or even for living together, the sharing of life (τό συζῆν)—his official view is that the "living well" in question is that of the households and village-communities that logically pre-exist the city and from which it is constituted. Sometimes, as in a remarkable passage of *Pol. Γ* 9, Aristotle is explicit about this: a city is "the common participation in living well by households and families, for the sake of a complete and self-sufficient life" (ἡ τοῦ εὖ ζῆν κοινωνία καὶ ταῖς οἰκίαις καὶ τοῖς γένεσι, ζωῆς τελείας χάριν καὶ αὐτάρκους, 1280b 33–34). The "living well" aimed at in cities is not, anyhow not immediately, the "living well" of the individual citizens residing in it. What is aimed at is rather the living well of the constituent households and village-communities. Individual citizens' lives are affected just insofar as, in one way or another, the good living of the communities to which they individually belong carries with it the individual citizens' living well too.

But to what extent does the living well of a community imply the living well of its individual members? Plainly, in well-constituted cities of all types, and especially in monarchies and aristocracies as Aristotle conceives them, the city aims through its political and social institutions at providing both for the material well-being and for the fullest possible development and exercise of the highest and best qualities of mind and character of the citizens.[21] The city and its constituent sub-communities cannot live well otherwise than on this condition. But of course in any city, however successful, many, perhaps most, of the citizens will not attain the highest degree of civilized perfection, because of congenital limitations in their natural capacities (if not for other reasons as well). The city itself, however, will live well if those who are naturally capable of a very high degree of mental and moral perfection attain and sustain it through life in the city, and the others attain as high a degree of perfection as they are naturally capable of. So, at a minimum, one could say that in the best, most successful cities an excellent life is provided for those individuals (presumably a small number) capable of leading it, while the others get as nearly excellent a life as they are severally able to manage, given their natural limitations.

But relying on the preceding analysis, we can go further. For according to Aristotle, when civic friendship animates the life of a community, as of course one would expect it to do in any correctly constituted city, each citizen participates in *all* aspects of the good achieved through the common activity that constitutes civic life. This means that even those who are less well endowed for the excellences of mind and character share in the exercise of the excellences of the better-endowed citizens. In this way all the citizens of a successful city achieve, either directly through their own individual activities, or at second remove through participation in the city's good of which these activities are a prime element, an active, perfected, self-sufficient life.[22]

---

[21]Aristotle does not say much in detail, either in the *Politica* or in the *Ethics*, about how life in a well run, well constituted city does encourage the moral improvement of the citizens. One may, perhaps, think first of laws explicitly framed so as to require of the citizens the doing of certain actions (and omission of others) that, if engaged in regularly and in the right spirit, will, Aristotle thinks, lead eventually to the acquisition of the moral virtues. (In *EN E,* as is well known, Aristotle emphasizes that "the law" requires the citizens to do acts of courage, temperance, good temper and all the other moral virtues: see 1, 1129b 19-25.) Equally important, however, is the fact that in such a city, animated by civic friendship, the mature citizens care very much about one another's characters and encourage one another and the young in the virtues by showing what the proper spirit is in which the acts of the virtues are to be done, and by making it clear that in their view acting in that spirit is the central and indispensable part of any human being's own personal good. Life in such a city is a moral education, quite apart from what the laws do or do not *require* the citizens to *do* (or refrain from doing).

[22]Aristotle's introduction in *Pol. H* 1–3 to his discussion, beginning in ch. 4, of the ideal best city—i.e., the best constitution for a city that enjoys ideal conditions with respect to size and character of population, natural resources, etc.—gives evidence that the analysis just presented spells out implications of Aristotle's theory of friendship that he himself accepted. He begins (*H* 1, 1323a 17–19) by saying that in general one should expect a constitution which is best (for any population) to be such that those living under it lead the best life available to them in the given external circumstances. Later, again, he says (*H* 2, 1324a 23–25) that, necessarily, the best constitution will be that arrangement under

With this account of civic friendship before us we can now see the full implications of Aristotle's thesis that the human being is by nature a political animal. This means, first, that like certain other herding animals, human beings have a natural capacity and tendency tó live together in cooperative communities in which each benefits from the work of the others as well as from his own. But secondly, because human beings can develop conceptions of, and communicate to one another their ideas about, the long-term good both of themselves and others and the common good of a whole group of people living and working together, human beings have the natural capacity and tendency to form communities (and, in particular, cities)[23] in which the life of

---

which anyone (of the relevant group, i.e., of those having a part in the political life of the city) could act in the best way and live happily—the best constitution must not discriminate against any group among the citizens, but must provide the conditions under which (*modulo* the natural wealth of the land, native talents of the population, etc.—the ὑπάρ-χοντα of *H* 1, 1323a 18) this life is available to them, if only they do their part. When, accordingly, he raises the question (*H* 2, 1324a 5–7) whether happiness is the same for each individual person and for a city, he is not concerned merely for the question of meaning—whether what it is for a city, as such, to be happy and successful is the same, *mutatis mutandis*, as what is for a single person. (Indeed he settles this question of meaning almost immediately, by *H* 2, 1324a 13.) A major concern in the subsequent discussion is to see that there really is the coincidence he has declared there must be between happiness for the city and happiness for the participant citizens. (Another major concern is to deal with the threat that cities in pursuit of their own happiness will always seek hegemony or even despotic power over neighboring cities: on this see Carnes Lord, *Education and Culture in the Political Thought of Aristotle,* Ithaca, N.Y., 1982, ch. 5.) Against this background I think it is right to attach significance to some of Aristotle's language as he formulates and discusses the relationship between happiness for the city and happiness for the individual. When he first raises this question he asks whether the same life is the most worth choosing for everyone taken in common and taken separately (κοινῇ καὶ χωρίς, *H* 1, 1323a 21). In answering that it is the same (1323b 40–41; *H* 2, 1324a 5–8; *H* 3, 1325b 30–32), viz. the life devoted to the exercise of the virtues both moral and intellectual, he glosses the judgment that it is "best for everyone taken in common" with its being "best for a city" (*H* 2, 1324a 6) or "best for cities taken in common" (*H* 1, 1323b 41) or again "best for cities and human beings taken in common" (*H* 3, 1325b 32). The emphasis in these glosses on the happiness of a city being the common happiness of its people suggests strongly that the virtuous life that a city leads when it is organized into and governed as a true aristocracy is being thought of as a life led *by its citizens* in the broad sense of "citizens" that I have distinguished—the (free) ἄνθρωποι (1325b 32) whose common possession or activity it is. If under such a constitution "everyone in common" leads the best life, then even someone who is not himself a virtuous person and so not constantly exercising virtues in his daily life is nonetheless in a secondary way leading a virtuous life, by having his live merged in the life of the whole city which itself *is* a virtuous one, by reason (primarily) of the virtues possessed, and exercised in its political and otherwise communal life, by its ruling class.

[23]The reason why Aristotle thinks cities in particular, and not merely various more limited associations for a common life, are needed and naturally pursued by human beings, is that only cities are complete and self-sufficient associations, associations capable of developing to their fullest extent, and giving appropriate scope for the exercise of, the virtues of mind and character which are the core of the natural good for a human being. See above nn. 1, 15, and T. H. Irwin's contribution to *Aristoteles' "Politik,"* esp. 74ff., 84ff.

all is organized in pursuit of a *common good*—a good that is common not just in the sense that each severally gets some part of a sum-total of distributable benefit, but in the strong sense that it is achieved in or belongs to the common activity that is the single life they all jointly live by merging their lives with one another's. But this common good is not available to them except on the basis of their all being, and feeling themselves to be, bound together by the bonds of civic friendship. And in the most successful cities, thanks to civic friendship, there is an important sense in which *all* the citizens, even those who individually lack the highest attainments of mind and character, can be said to be living a good and excellent life.[24]

Abbreviations

EE	*Ethica Eudemia*
EN	*Ethica Nicomachea*
GA	*De Generatione Animalium*
HA	*Historia Animalium*
Pol.	*Politica*

The letters of the Greek Alphabet represent the book numbers within each work.

A	α	I	*N*	ν	XIII
B	β	II	*Ξ*	ξ	XIV
Γ	γ	III	*O*	ο	XV
Δ	δ	IV	*Π*	π	XVI
E	ε	V	*P*	ϱ	XVII
Z	ζ	VI	*Σ*	σ	XVIII
H	η	VII	*T*	τ	XIX
Θ	θ	VIII	*Y*	υ	XX
I	ι	IX	*Φ*	φ	XXI
K	ϰ	X	*X*	χ	XXII
Λ	λ	XI	*Ψ*	ψ	XXIII
M	μ	XII	*Ω*	ω	XXIV

Please note that the Bekker pages, e.g., "1213a17-19," provide precise references to the text even without book numbers.

[24]I made extensive revisions to this paper after the symposium, in response to the criticisms contained in Julia Annas' excellent official commentary (especially excellent where she was more firmly in disagreement with my own views), and to written and oral comments of several of the other symposiasts. I made especially substantial additions and changes in reply to questions and criticisms of D. J. Furley and T. H. Irwin. I am indebted also to M. M. Mackenzie for perceptive and, for me, fruitful comments on the original embryo of the paper, presented to a Princeton Classical Philosophy Conference in December 1983; to John R. Wallach, and to Richard Kraut for discussion and written comments on an intermediate version of the paper.

INDEX

Library of Congress Cataloging-in-Publication Data

Friendship : a philosophical reader / [edited] Neera Kapur Badhwar.
    p.   cm.
Includes index.
ISBN 0-8014-2854-8. — ISBN 0-8014-8097-3 (pbk.)
1. Friendship.   I. Badhwar, Neera Kapur.
BJ1533.F8F84   1993
177′.6—dc20   92-56786